EYEWITNESS **COMPANIONS**

Beer

MICHAEL JACKSON

EDITOR-IN-CHIEF

"LIKE WINE, BEER IS GROWN—IT IS AN AGRICULTURAL PRODUCT, PERHAPS THE FIRST KNOWN TO CIVILIZATION."

Michael Jackson

LONDON, NEW YORK, MUNICH,
MELBOURNE, AND DELHI

Project Art Editor Caroline de Souza
Senior Art Editor Susan Downing
Managing Editor Dawn Henderson
Editorial Assistant Ariane Durkin
Production Editor Ben Marcus
US Editor Jenny Siklós

Additional text contributions by Lorenzo Dabove,
Alastair Gilmour, Geoff Griggs, Tim Hampson,
Bryan Harrell, Stan Hieronymus, Conrad Seidl,
Willie Simpson, and Derek Walsh

Produced for Dorling Kindersley by

cobaltid

The Stables, Wood Farm, Deopham Road,
Attleborough, Norfolk NR17 1AJ, UK
www.cobaltid.co.uk

Editors
Marek Walisiewicz, Kati Dye, Louise Abbott,
Jamie Dickson, Maddy King, Steve Setford

Art Editors
Paul Reid, Lloyd Tilbury, Darren Bland,
Claire Oldman, Annika Skoog, Shane Whiting

First American Edition, 2007

Published in the United States by
DK Publishing
375 Hudson Street
New York, New York 10014

08 09 10 11 10 9 8 7 6 5 4 3 2

ED469 Nov-07

Published in Great Britain by Dorling Kindersley Ltd.

A catalog record for this book is available
from the Library of Congress.

ISBN 978-0-7566-3155-0

DK books are available at special discounts when purchased in bulk for sales
promotions, premiums, fund-raising, or educational use. For details contact:
DK Publishing Special Markets, 375 Hudson Street, New York,
New York 10014 or SpecialSales@dk.com

Color reproduction by Colourscan, Singapore
Printed by LRex, China

Discover more at

www.dk.com

Introduction by
Michael Jackson 10

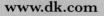

CONTENTS

WITHIN THE WORLD OF FOOD AND DRINK, THERE LIVES A FAMILY BLESSED WITH ETERNAL LIFE—THE FAMILY OF THE FERMENTED. THERE IS AN ELEMENTAL APPEAL TO THOSE FOODS AND DRINKS THAT ARE FATHERED BY FERMENTATION. THERE IS WITHIN THEM A SENSE OF THE WILD.

Fermentation is the action of yeast propagating itself. The strain of yeast may be cultured, but its forebears came from the wild. Yeasts are living organisms. They descend from Heaven even more gently than the rain. We cannot feel them. If we could see them, our naked eye would embarrass them. They multiply by the million. They are a prolific, potent, powerful, and yet furtive life-force. Their dusty caress inspires bread dough to rise, conjures sensuous odors from cheese, imparts piquancy to pickles and vinegar, and adds the alluring tang of temptation to both wine and beer.

HITTING THE SPOT

There are moments when a glass of wine or a pint of beer comes to mind, and nothing else will suffice. This is not a question of thirst or a requirement for alcohol. Beer can be a very enjoyable thirst-quencher, but water is more effective. If alcohol is required, beer is the weakest choice, trailing in third place behind wines and spirits. When one thirsts for a glass of wine or a pint of beer, the brain gradually perceives the desire as a half-heard whisper. The volume is slowly turned up, creating a gentle, purring reverberation throughout the nervous system. It seems a pleasurable massage at first, then becomes tenacious. You are in the hands of higher authority that brooks no argument. It is desire, and the streetcar cannot leave its lines. Your destination is a rendezvous with a drink.

Characterful ales, such as Black Sheep, can evoke a powerful longing for a pint.

Edward FitzGerald's translation of the *Rubáiyát of Omar Khayyám* set a seductive standard of simplicity for enjoyment of food and drink. I, too, would relish "a jug of wine, a loaf of bread and thou," but on occasion might prefer stout, soda bread, and Saint Brigid – the patron saint of brewing in Ireland, who could miraculously turn bathwater into beer.

Wine and food have always been soulmates. So have beer and food, long before it was fashionable. Wine also enjoys its own company, as does beer. These are open marriages, but wine and beer are both part of the food-and-drink patrimony of their regions. The wine lands have olives, tomatoes, aubergines, and bell peppers, shamelessly flaunting their colors and squishy juiciness above ground. The beer countries are more devoted to meat and potatoes, and to root vegetables of less vivid colors—but they have a sensuality of their own.

THE CLASS DIVIDE

Wine and beer are companions of honor: the world's two great fermented drinks, derived from grape and grain respectively. Thus conjoined by the force of language, they are too often rent asunder by social snobbery.

Cantillon's "wild" beers are produced by spontaneous fermentation, and rank among the most elegant and refined drinks in the world.

Perhaps snobbery explains why, for decades, wine was explored and celebrated (perhaps excessively?), and beer ignored (or taken for granted?).

Wine was the drink of the early empires: Constantinople, Athens, and Rome. It was also embraced by the ruling elite of Napoleonic France and by the Spanish Hapsburgs. But while the ruling classes enjoyed the finest vintages, peasants and the burgeoning middle classes also drank wine. In Austro-Hungary, Germany, the Low Countries, and the British Isles, the lord of the manor cellared fine wines, but also brewed beer for himself and his serfs. These regions were the first to industrialize. The agricultural roots of beer became less obvious as production geared up. Beer, being a long drink, could rehydrate a steelworker or remove eight hours of coal-dust from a miner's throat. Its malt sugars could restore his energy, and beer soothed his tired frame, too. It worked as hard as he did. He was too tired to analyze or describe its aromas and flavors; nor was anyone else available to provide such a service for him.

A GENEROUS GRAIN

The grape is not the only fruit to yield wine, but it is the most commonly used. Its fragility means that it grows in a narrower terroir (range of conditions) than grain, and that its fruit is best vinified where it is grown. These factors restrict the cultivation of grapes, making wine more expensive to produce —a fact that inspires respect

Barley and grapes are simple ingredients, but the drinks that are made from them—beer and wine—help to define the meaning of civilization.

among those who have no other criteria for excellence. Grain for beermaking (usually barley) is robust, grows in a much wider terroir, and is imported by countries throughout the world so that they can brew their own "local" beers. As an immigrant worker, John Barleycorn (the noble hero of Robert Burns's ballad) compounds the awkwardness of looking frighteningly strong with Rasputin-like resilience. Surely John Barleycorn's blood was beer, and its quintessence whisky?

THE BREWING REVOLUTION

One revolution follows another: first there was wine, then came beer. Neither the great European winemakers nor even the American consumer understood the potential of California and the western US—or of the New World in general. A tasting that became famously known as "The Judgment of Paris" changed all that. Now the words "New World" and "wines" fit like a silk stocking on a shapely leg.

Alaskan Smoked Porter is a robust product of the US brewing renaissance.

Today, neither European brewers nor most drinkers on either side of the Atlantic have yet grasped that tomorrow's most exciting styles of beers will be American in conception. At first glance, this seems unlikely. The great Czech brewing cities of Plzeň and Budweis may wonder just how thinly their names can be stretched in the US. When will the "line extensions" reach breaking point? Light

Beer; Dry Beer; Ice Beer; Clear Beer; Low-carb Beer. Each of these contrivances is an apology that says: "Our beer is too heavy, too sweet, too dark…." Each was launched onto the market with a marketing budget of millions, making them all costly contrivances indeed. But children weaned on cola may, as adults, prefer a penitent poser to a proper pint.

Beer lore is overgrown with myths. One of the most stubborn asserts that the darker the beer, the stronger it is. There is literally not a grain of truth in this. The color in beer is created by the the way grains are dried. This cannot increase the alcohol in the finished beer, although the opposite can be true. If the grain is highly roasted, as for a stout, it will be less fermentable and therefore yield less alcohol than a paler malt. This truth, however often it is repeated, seems less potent than the myth. As long as

consumers insist that a beer that is light in color, body, and taste must therefore be weak in alcohol, brews of this type remain open to the accusation of affecting innocence while recruiting young slaves to the Demon Drink.

The nation that makes the world's lightest-tasting beers also produces the most assertive brews. Tomorrow's classics will evolve from a new breed of American brews that are categorized by their admirers as "Extreme Beers." These are the most intense-tasting beers ever produced anywhere in the world. They include classic European-style stouts that are richer, toastier, and roastier than anything yet produced in Ireland; ales massively more bitterly appetizing than any in Britain; "wild" beers (*see pp.40–1*) more sharply, quenchingly sour than their Belgian counterparts; wheat beers so spicily phenolic as to make a Bavarian choke on

Café Centro is the ultimate "high end" beer bar, and is located in one of New York's most expensive districts. Beer is now a prestige product.

his mid-morning weisswurst; and pilsners so aromatic as to tempt the Good Soldier Schweik—the eponymous hero of Jaroslav Hašek's comic novel.

Sometimes the new US beers combine elements from more than one style, but with a view to achieving greater distinctiveness rather than to merge into blandness. The best example I ever experienced was the Smoked Porter of the Alaskan Brewing Company (*see p.239*). Porter is an old British style, but drying malt over a smoky wood fire is a technique from Franconia. The Germans use beechwood from nearby forests; the Americans employ alder, which grows in Alaska and is used to smoke local salmon. When I suggested that this beer would make a good accompaniment to bagels and lox, the brewery's owners put my theory to the test. We flew a helicopter up into an ice field and enjoyed a classic East Coast breakfast in a definitively Western outdoors setting.

The Alaskan Brewing Company has an impressive record of both creative and commercial success. Like

San Francisco's Anchor Brewing produces a number of traditional ales, including a porter. This marginalized British style is now thriving in the US.

many such enterprises, it is owned by former homebrewers. Their governing body, the Brewers Association, has its roots in a similar organization for amateur beermakers. The founder of the American Homebrewers Association, Charlie Papazian, was himself inspired by the work of an early beer writer in Britain, and by that country's Campaign for Real Ale (*see p.153*).

THE MIRACLE OF BEER

How was beer born? Early hunter-gatherers, frustrated by the limited seasonal availability of berries and fruits, tried to store them. Wild yeasts turned them into wine, but it lacked nutritional value. Civilized behavior arrived with the first beers; communities were established specifically to grow grain—but for what purpose? When people first mixed cereal grains with water, what did they expect the result would be? Did they imagine something like porridge, polenta, or bread would be produced? Again, wild yeasts came into play, and created beer. This made people feel "blissful," and beer was deemed a suitable drink for use in sacred rituals.

The Aramaic scrolls that were the foundation of the Bible have Jesus miraculously turning water into "strong drink." The Greeks translated this as "wine," but the Saxon version of the Gospels refers instead to "beer." The periods spent in the wilderness by Christ and St. John inspired hermitages, and later monasteries, that played a central role in the development of both wine and beer. They did so as centers of community, farming, and study. Some still make wine or beer (not to mention bread, cheese, brandies, and nougats). Monks and nuns are still working conscientiously to improve the quality of our lives, tending not only to our spiritual welfare but also to our social, and even sensual, needs.

THE BEER OF KINGS

The most sacred site in the world of beer is at Freising, a short ride from Munich by suburban train. Founded on a hilltop, the Benedictine monastery of Weihenstephan ("Sacred Stephen") was licensed to make beer in 1040. The site was later acquired by the Bavarian royal family, and is now owned by the state. Weihenstephan claims to be the world's oldest brewery and is home to the brewing faculty of the Technical University of Munich, the world's most famous brewing college. The brewery produces about 10 different styles of beer, half of which are wheat brews.

The history of the nearby Hofbräuhaus Freising rivals that of Weihenstephan. Brewing has taken place there since at least 1160 and may have had fewer interruptions. The name Hofbräuhaus

A biochemist analyzes hop residues at the Technical University of Munich's brewing faculty at Weihenstephan in Germany.

means Royal Court Brewery. This designation crops up several times in different German states. The Hofbräuhaus Freising was the brewery of the bishop's household and court for 400 years. It then passed into royal hands and, through marriage, to the Count of Moy (the title derives from a site near St. Quentin in Picardy, France), whose family had fled France at the time of the Revolution. Like Weihenstephan, the Hofbräuhaus Freising also produces wheat beers.

The Bavarian royal family exercised a monopoly on the brewing of wheat beers from the 1400s to the late 1800s, ostensibly to protect supplies of grain earmarked for the production of bread. The last brewer they

Bavaria is the home of classic wheat beers, such as Schneider Weisse.

employed, Georg Schneider, went on to establish his own business. The Schneider family still owns a restaurant not far from the Munich Hofbräuhaus, and now has its own brewery near Kelheim on the Danube River.

Today, these three historic breweries—Weihenstephan, Hofbräuhaus Freising, and Schneider—all continue to produce characterful wheat beers in the Bavarian style. The examples made by Weihenstephan are distinctly fruity; to my taste they have notes of apple and perhaps blackcurrant. The examples from the Hofbräuhaus Freising seem to me to have a more bananalike character, while those from Schneider possess a clovey spiciness more typical of the style.

The brewing industry of the Czech town of Plzeň, birthplace of pilsner, has monastic roots.

Another monastery that later passed into the hands of Bavarian royalty was at Kaltenberg, to the west of Munich. Various castles were built on this site, the last of which was constructed partly to plans drawn up by the architect of Neuschwanstein Castle, which later provided the inspiration for Walt Disney's iconic Sleeping Beauty Castle. The present Prince Luitpold of Bavaria continues to operate a brewery at the castle. It produces a range of delicate-tasting wheat beers and dark lagers.

CELTIC INFLUENCES

The name Kaltenberg probably derives from references to the Celts, a race that is believed to have originated somewhere east of Bavaria, possibly in Turkey. There are also brewing sites close to former Celtic settlements in Plzeň in Bohemia and Lembeek in Belgium. This suggests that the Celts may have brought brewing from the ancient world to Europe. The last stop on their route would have been Ireland. Another possibility is that beer traveled with seafarers from the ancient world, journeying through the Straits of Gibraltar to finish up, again, in Ireland. Although there is no specific evidence of his being a brewer, the Irish missionary-monk St. Columba said in his Rule (a list of dictums for monks, defining virtuous conduct) that communities should grow barley. Another of the Irish missionary monks, St. Gall, founded a brewing abbey in Switzerland. There were three brewhouses at this abbey during the ninth century, according to floor plans still kept in St. Gallen town library. The abbey has since been rebuilt without the benefit of such facilities.

BEER IN HOLY ORDERS

There are said to have been more than 500 monastic breweries throughout Europe before those in England were sacked by Henry VIII, and those on the Continent by Napoleon. Germany has many former abbey breweries, whose names usually begin with the word *Kloster* (cloister) or *Stift* (seminary). The name Munich itself derives from the German word for monks (*München*). The city still possesses breweries whose names bear witness to monastic origins: Augustiner,

Monasteries, such as Ettal in Bavaria, were the cradle of many European brewing traditions and shaped the development of modern beermaking.

Franziskaner, and Paulaner. Two active monastery breweries that lie a short bus ride from the city are Andechs and Ettal—both of which are Benedictine institutions. Their beer gardens are popular weekend destinations for locals and tourists alike.

God wants us to be happy, suggests the wordless smile of this Trappist monk, while Orval's beer speaks for itself. Their brewhouse is beautiful, too.

CHURCH AND STATE

As elsewhere in Europe, both church and state played a part in the brewing history of Bohemia, which is now part of the Czech Republic. While Plzeň became a brewing town as a result of monastic activities in the 13th century, the town of Budweis (*see p. 75*) to the south—Plzeň's main rival in brewing terms—made beer for the royal family. Its brews were proudly known as the "beers of kings" several hundred years before a certain brand produced in St. Louis, Missouri, was marketed as the "the king of beers."

Today, the second-largest brewery in Plzeň is called Gambrinus. This is a corruption of the name of Jan Primus (1371–1419), the first Duke of Flanders.

Scholar, scientist, composer, poet, and brewer, Hildegard of Bingen was a prescient priestess.

Legends of formidable beer-drinking have grown up around his memory, and he is widely celebrated as the immortal King of Beer. I have seen references to him in many parts of the brewing world, as far apart as Helsinki in Finland and Columbus, Ohio.

HILDEGARD AND HOPS

A wide variety of herbs, berries, and spices were once used in beermaking. Records dating from the end of the first millennium make frequent mention of *gruit* (a blend of herbs) as a common brewing ingredient in Europe. It typically included marsh plants like bog myrtle and wild rosemary, but there were local variations. On the island of Gotland, between Sweden and Latvia, I have seen farmhouse brewers make a hop-based tea, which they use to sterilize equipment before starting work. This seems to support the view that the original role of the hop was to prevent infections (which would have made the beer sour or acrid). Records dating from the 8th century show that hops were commonly grown at abbeys, but not specifically for use in beer.

The first unequivocal mention of hops being used in brewing is in the writings of St. Hildegard (1098–1179), abbess of the Benedictine abbey of Rupertsberg near Bingen, not far from the German city of Mainz. Abbess Hildegard did not mention that the hop plant is a member of the cannabis family. She did, however, recommend the use of cannabis and also provided the first written account of the female orgasm. Hildegard of Bingen is something of a New Age heroine.

THE LADY OF THE LAKE

Italy to Belgium seems a mighty leap, especially given that it was probably made on horseback. In the 9th century, Countess Mathilde from Tuscany was wandering by a lake near Florenville in the Belgian province of Luxembourg. While gazing into the still waters, she lost a golden ring. Distraught, she prayed to God that it might be returned to her. If it were, she pledged, she would establish an abbey by the lake. When a trout rose from the lake with the ring in its mouth, the countess made good on her promise. The Abbey of Orval ("Valley of Gold") was founded in 1070 by Benedictines from Calabria. After being sacked several times, it was rebuilt between 1929 and 1936 as a Trappist abbey. Many Belgians saw this as the crowning act of the centenary year of their modern kingdom. The brewery at Orval produces a very dry ale (*see p.144*), which I regard as a world classic.

HOPPING ACROSS THE WATER

There is still a hop garden outside the Benedictine abbey of Affligem in Belgium. The abbey, established in 1074, brewed until the outbreak of World War II. It now lends its name to a brewery nearby, which is owned by Heineken. Among such collaborations between God and Mammon, this one produces particularly characterful brews. There is a theory that Affligem introduced

The redbrick facade of the Shepherd Neame brewery in Faversham, England, is incongruously reminiscent of a Baptist chapel.

The abbey brewers of Yorkshire were followed by secular beer-makers, such as Theakston.

on to make porter and stout. No single product, beer or otherwise, is so closely associated with a country as Guinness with Ireland. Despite the best efforts of its marketing team to destroy its singularity, it remains a hoppy brew.

THE TWO MOLLIES

If Abbess Hildegard were to visit Dublin, she could discuss sensuous pleasures over a pint with Molly Bloom, the lusty heroine of James Joyce's *Ulysses*. When they were ready for another round, they could meet the other Molly (of Dublin folklore and song). I would suggest that they take Miss Malone to the Porterhouse brewpub (*see p.172*), where an oyster stout might be in order. Perhaps, like oysters themselves, this beer is one of those pleasures that some people adore and others cannot abide. No beer can please everyone, and any brewer who embraces that objective is on a fool's mission. The enjoyment of a particular beer is one of the most personal of passions. A neighbor of mine who had just returned from his first trip overseas rushed into our local pub, ordered a pint of his favorite beer, placed it on the bar, and gazed lovingly at it in anticipation of its "welcome home" kiss. "I promise", he sighed, "that I will never leave you again."

"And which beer is your favorite, Mr. Jackson?" I am often asked. "Depends where I am, my mood, and the moment," I reply. It might be an oyster stout, a Belgian wheat beer, or a Vienna lager. *Vive la différence! Viva la revolución.*

hopped beer to England, on the other side of the North Sea. Abbeys are said to have given rise to brewing in Faversham (home of Shepherd Neame, England's oldest brewery) and Burton, the somewhat attenuated brewing capital of the country. The Yorkshire Dales, a part of England once famous for its abbeys, also has two breweries that can indirectly trace their lineage to such an institution: Theakston and Black Sheep. Across the border in Scotland, the Belhaven brewing company (*see p.169*) claims its origins can be traced to a monastery on a nearby island.

THE LUCK OF THE IRISH

In Ireland, the Smithwicks Brewery in Kilkenny is built around the ruins of an abbey, and the brewery of George Killian Lett is believed to have had its origins in a friary. The two stout-producing breweries in the city of Cork also have strong religious connections: Murphy's originally took its water from a well consecrated to Our Lady, and in 1985 I was invited to the blessing of a new brewhouse, which was carried out by the Bishop of Cork. Historically, Murphy's was known as the city's Roman Catholic brewery, while at the other end of town, Beamish and Crawford was Cork's Protestant brewery.

Richard Guinness, born around 1690, managed the household and estate for the rector of Cellbridge in County Kildare. One of his tasks was to brew beers for the dinner table. He probably made an ale, but his descendants moved

Michael Jackson

The iconic branding of Guinness dry stout instantly evokes the distinctive, peat-like aroma that characterizes a glass of the Black Stuff.

From grain
to glass

AS THE WORLD'S TWO GREAT FERMENTED DRINKS, WINE AND BEER CAN HELP EXPLAIN EACH OTHER. EVEN PEOPLE WHO NEVER DRINK WINE KNOW THAT IT IS MADE FROM GRAPES. BUT WHAT IS THE COUNTERPART IN BEER? EVEN SOME PEOPLE WHO DRINK A GLASS EVERY DAY ARE UNSURE…

In the making of wine, the grape is crushed to provide a juice that is full of sugars. The grape itself provides aroma and flavor; the sugars are fermented to create alcohol. The equivalent in beer is often described rather pedantically as cereal grain. It is most often barley, but wheat, rye, oats, and several other grains may also be used.

In essence, beer is a drink made from grain (usually barley) and flavored with aromatic hops.

However, when harvested, grain is usually too hard to be fermented. It must be first steeped in water, allowed partially to germinate, then dried, in order to render its sugars soluble. This is the process of malting.

Just as some grapes are reserved to be eaten, so a substantial part of the world's grain crop is used to make bread, cookies, and cake. Or, for that matter, our breakfast cereals. If your breakfast emerges from a box promising health and goodness, your bowl may contain grapes that have been dried to become raisins, along with the seeds or grains of various cereal crops. At beer festivals, playful young Americans like to wear T-shirts showing a glass of beer and the legend "breakfast of champions," a slogan borrowed from a breakfast cereal.

A rather sophisticated homebrew club in Chicago once held a competition in which entrants were required to make a beer from a recipe that included a box of breakfast cereal. The winner used a seven-grain cereal to produce an appetizingly nutty, credible beer. In Belgium, when the Bosteels brewery launched its Karmeliet beer, much emphasis was laid on its containing six different grains. The brewery said that the beer had been inspired by the fashion for multigrain breads.

The Spanish word for beer, *cerveza*, and the Old French *cervoise*, are a further reminder of the drink's cereal origins. The Germanic variations—beer, *bier*, *bière*, *birra*—share their etymology with the word barley.

Skilled brewers create beers that excite all the senses. Color, head texture, and aroma set the scene for that first sip.

Grain

Most people know that bread is made from grain, but not every regular beer drinker realizes that the starting point for every glass of beer is a field of cereal—usually barley, but possibly other grains, such as wheat, rye, oats, rice, spelt, millet, or even sorghum.

Beer is a drink made from fermented cereals. Natural sugars are extracted from the cereal grains using hot water; hops are added, and the liquid is boiled, clarified, and fermented. End of story? Well, not quite. At every stage, the brewer has close control over the ingredients, the techniques used to extract and enhance flavor, and the conditions under which the beer is brewed.

Barley grains contain starch in their floury kernels. This starch is the basis for the brewing process.

To begin, the brewer has a wide range of grains from which to choose. Traditionally, barley is used because its sugars are relatively easy to release from the grain and it makes a beer with soft, clean flavors. However, many brewers mix barley with smaller proportions of other grains to modify the flavor of the resulting beer. Adding small quantities of wheat can enhance the roundness of the flavor and improve the stability of the head when the beer is poured. Oats impart a silky smoothness, rye provides a hint of spiciness, while corn can lighten body and make the beer appear clearer. Some beers—notably wheat beer—are made with little or no barley content.

Not surprisingly, brewers tend to favor the grains that grow best locally—hence the prevalence of corn and rice-based beers in the US. In Europe, barley remains king, although this was not always so: until the 18th century, Bohemian beer was brewed mainly from wheat, a little from barley, and in bad years even from oats. The future may see barley supplanted as the brewer's grain of choice—our warming climate may affect barley harvests in beer's northern European heartlands and force brewers to seek alternatives.

VARIETIES OF BARLEY

Different varieties of grape usually produce very different wines; and few of us would mistake a white wine made from Chardonnay grapes for a red made from Shiraz.

Distinctions between varieties of barley also exist, but are less clearly expressed in the resulting brew. German and Czech brewers favor spring-sown barley, for example, saying that this produces a cleaner, sweeter flavor. The Belgians and British favor winter-sown crops, because they are robust and provide more firmness of flavor.

There are three main types of barley, which are distinguished from one another by the number of seeds at the top of the stem. Barley seeds grow in either two, four, or six rows along the central stem. European brewers traditionally use two-row barley, because it has a higher starch-to-husk ratio than four- or six-row barley. In the US, six-row barley is more commonly used, because it is more economical to grow in warmer climes and has a higher concentration of enzymes needed to convert the starch in the grain into sugar. It is said to produce a huskier, sharper flavor. In the UK, the classic ale barley is Maris Otter, although it is gradually being pushed aside by strains that yield more fermentable sugar per ton.

USING DIFFERENT GRAINS

Many craft brewers are now experimenting with using different blends of grain, and organic ingredients. Leading the way in the UK is the Prince of Wales's Charitable Foundation and Duchy Originals range of beers. Duchy Original Winter Ale uses a variety of organic cereals. The recipe includes the historic Plumage Archer barley malt, along with Prince Charles's Home Farm's organic rye and oats, added to give complexity and fullness of flavor to the beer.

Prince Charles samples a pint of beer. His Duchy Original range of beers is brewed at Wychwood in Oxfordshire, England.

WHERE BARLEY IS GROWN

Wine and beer might compete for attention in the bar, but grape and grain rarely vie for the same space on the farm. Wine grapes mostly grow between 30° and 50° latitude, in both the northern and southern hemispheres, often on slopes that give an advantageous aspect to the sun. In contrast, fine barley is cultivated mainly in the northern hemisphere between latitudes of 45° and 55°. Barley likes temperate to cool weather, gentle sun, rich but well-drained soil, and reasonably flat land. Some brewers believe that inland continental barleys produce better malt than those grown in maritime climates, but others would disagree.

Grapes have delicate skins that make them poor travelers, so wineries are typically close to their vineyards. Barley grains are far more robust, and do not start to give up their sugars until they start to germinate. This means that grains can be transported over long distances to start the first part of their processing into beer—malting. Here, the grains are made to germinate and then quickly dried before the plant develops. The sugars contained in the processed barley—or malt—can then be extracted, ready for fermentation.

The quality of barley is determined by its aroma, and the size and shape of the grains, as well as the quality of the "beard."

GRAIN TO MALT

Wine-making is relatively straightforward because grapes give up their sugar-rich juice easily when crushed, and fermentation can begin without further treatment. By contrast, the sugar in a barley grain is locked up in the form of starch, which does not readily dissolve in water, and so is harder to extract. To release the starch, grain requires soaking (steeping) in water for a couple of days, followed by gentle warmth for about a week. This triggers the start of germination, mimicking the growth of a seed in the ground. As the seed germinates, the complex molecules of starch, protein, and cellulose inside the husk start to break down into smaller chemical units.

Traditionally, this germination stage is carried out on the stone floor of a long building called a maltings or malthouse; moist grains (known at this stage as green malt) are spread out on the gently sloping floor to a depth of around 4 in (10 cm) and are turned and raked to

Germinating barley grains are known as green barley, and smell strongly of pumpkins.

aerate them and to stop the grains from sticking together. Floor maltings like these need intensive labor and are costly to operate; some still exist, and many brewers maintain that they produce premium beers. However, it is far more common today for malting to be carried out in modern vessels—rotating drums in which air is blown through a bed of grain for a period of four to six days.

Often the supply of air is humidified, to make sure that the grain does not dry out, and the grain is turned mechanically.

INTO THE KILN

After a few days, germination is stopped by heating the green malt in a kiln. It is first dried and then "cured" at a higher temperature to stop all changes within the grain. Kilning is a complex process, in which combinations of air-flow and heat are tightly controlled to make a specific product—kilning conditions are very different, for example, for a lager malt compared to an ale malt. The kilned product—now called malt—has a moisture content of between three and six percent and looks very similar to unmalted grain. However, that which

At Paulaner, barley grains are spread in long ventilated boxes, and turned by a machine that runs above on fixed tracks. These are called malting "streets," and Paulaner has 10 of them. The grains spend a week here, beginning to germinate.

The color of a beer is strongly linked to the color of the malt from which it is made. Throughout Europe, this color is measured on the European Brewers' Convention (EBC) scale.

was once hard and unchewable can now be crunched like a firm cookie, releasing wonderful tastes of sweet, malty sugars in the mouth.

COLOR AND FLAVOR

The color and flavor of wine is influenced by the length of time it is in contact with grapes' skins. By analogy, beer gains much of its color and flavor from the malt used in its production.

Malting, whether carried out by kilning (as described above) or by heating the grain on a mesh floor over an open fire, doesn't just stop the germination; it gives color to the malt. The more intense the kilning, the stronger the color of the malt and the more likely it is to contain caramelized sugars. Careful selection of the right malt is, therefore, an important part of the brewer's art. A gently kilned malt will be light in color, and impart soft, delicate flavors and golden hues to the beer; a more intensely kilned malt will be darker in color and the resulting brew will have sweeter, more biscuity toffee flavors. The very darkest malts are full of dark chocolate and roasted coffee notes. In Bavaria, Germany, and in some US microbreweries, malt is dried over alder or beechwood, where it takes on smoky flavors that are transferred to the beer.

Some malts, such as Pilsener, Pale Ale, Vienna, and Munich, are named after the beers they will produce, while others are named for their characteristics—such as aromatic, biscuit, or chocolate. Many beers are made with a blend of malts, each giving different colors and flavors to the beer, to make drinks of complexity.

Finally, malt from the kiln is put through a machine known as a deculmer, to remove the "culm"—the small rootlets that have emerged from each seed. The culm is a valuable by-product of the malting process, and is sold as a high-protein animal feed.

IN THE BREWERY

After a period of storage, the malt is carried to the brewery, where it is cracked in a mill and turned into a "grist," which looks like a very coarse, crunchy flour. The grist is soaked in hot water (around 150°F/65°C) in a vessel often called the mash tun; the water selected by the brewer adds its own character to the beer (*see p.30*). Typically, mashes have about three parts water to one part malt, and are allowed to stand for about one hour. Mashing converts the starches that were released during the malting stage into sugars that can be fermented.

Mashing the grist can be a simple one-stage infusion process—like making a pot of tea—or it can involve a series of infusions in different vessels at different temperatures; the time taken to complete the mashing process, and the temperatures used, will vary from brewery to brewery and beer to beer.

Once the sugars have been released the sweet liquid is known as wort (from the Germanic word meaning "root:" the sweet liquid being the root of the beer). The wort is separated from the now-spent grains and then transferred into a kettle, also known as a brewing copper, ready for the next stage— flavoring with hops (*see p.31*).

The mash tun contains a porridgelike mix of grist and hot water. The starch in the grist is released to provide fermentable brewing sugars.

Water

More than 90 percent of a glass of beer is water. The beer's taste and texture is in part shaped by the quality of the water—and more specifically the trace minerals it contains. These minerals can influence the biochemistry of the living process of brewing.

Good water makes good beer, and for this reason, brewing regions blessed with high-quality water are the traditional homes of the world's best-loved brews.

The most prized water contains happy balances of certain minerals, particularly calcium and magnesium. These are the minerals that put the hardness into hard water—the ones that cause your electric kettle to "fur up"—and affect the water's mouthfeel. For example, the best pilsners owe part of their mild character to the soft water around the Czech town of Plzeň, whereas Munich lagers gain their tougher taste from the hard water used by their brewmeisters. At one time, Burton upon Trent in England was home to more than 200 breweries, largely because the high gypsum (calcium sulfate) content of the water made it ideal for the production of robust English ales.

Calcium and magnesium also play important roles in the biochemistry of brewing: calcium, for example, helps to buffer the alkalinity of most malts and so maintains optimum conditions for the enzymes (biological catalysts) that drive the brewing process. Other mineral elements present in water will also shape the process: trace levels of zinc and copper are desirable because they are needed by the yeast cells that carry out fermentation; but too much of either, and the resulting beer may become cloudy. Similarly, traces of sulfate can give beer a lively sharpness, but too much and the beer becomes bitter.

Today, with all the tools of modern chemistry at their disposal, brewers can adjust almost any water supply to produce just the right balance of minerals for the beer they intend to make. The brewing of good beer is no longer dependent on chance and the quality of the local water supply.

Donnington Brewery in Gloucestershire, England, has been producing traditional beers since 1865. Water is key to the quality of its products.

Hops, herbs, and spices

Throughout the history of beermaking, brewers have added all manner of herbs and spices to their beers. But head and shoulders—quite literally—above all these ingredients is the hop, the towering "bine" that produces the small flowers so prized by brewers.

Fruit, herbs, spices, flowers, tree bark, and sap have all in their time been used as additives in beer. Their purpose was to add fermentable sugars, to alter the flavor of the beer (or to cover its imperfections), and to prolong its life, allowing the beer to be stored and transported before drinking.

Hops are particularly valued as an additive because they impart complex flavors, aromas, and bitterness to the beer; they have antiseptic qualities; and they help to clarify the brew. The hop plant carries the botanical name *Humulus lupulus*, which roughly translates as "the wolf of the soil," from the tendency of its roots to spread widely. Hop plants are dioecious, meaning that male and female flowers occur on separate plants; only the female flowers—which resemble small, green pine cones—produce the aromatic oils and resins used in brewing.

HOP HISTORY

The hop plant is native to Europe and Asia—texts from ancient Babylon record the growing of hops, and the Romans are known to have harvested and eaten the shoots. Hops have been used for centuries in folk remedies—as a herbal antibiotic and anti-inflammatory, and as a cure for insomnia. However, the first confirmed use of hops specifically for beermaking comes from the writing of a polymath nun, Abbess Hildegard of

The traditional hop bine stands more than 16 ft (5 m) tall. Modern "hedgerow" varieties grow to a more modest 7 ft (2 m) in height.

Bingen (*see pp.18–19*). In 1067, she wrote: "If one intends to make beer from oats, it is prepared with hops." By 1300, hops were being used by brewers throughout France, Holland, and the Netherlands, but they came to England only in the 1400s. According to one writer, not only were the British slow to appreciate the attributes of the hop, but people believed they would be poisoned by the new-fangled drink, which bore no resemblance to the unhopped ales that were more customary in Britain.

By the 1700s, hops had crossed the Atlantic, where they prospered in the US states of Oregon and Washington and

Hop "cones" are the female flowers of the hop, a climbing plant that bears its pendantlike flowers in late June in the northern hemisphere.

over the border in British Columbia. Today, hops are grown as far afield as New Zealand, Japan, and China.

A WORLD OF HOPS

Modern brewers have scores of varieties, or cultivars, of hops from which to choose, each with its own unique characteristics. Varieties popular in England, such as Fuggles and Goldings, have a fine aroma and are low in acid— ideal for making English ales. The Northdown hop, which is higher in acid and so brings more bitterness to the beer, is grown and valued in Belgium and Bavaria for its bittering qualities. From Bohemia in the Czech Republic around the town of Žatec come Saaz hops, renowned for their delicate, flowery bouquet; these are classically used in pilsner beers. In Germany, the Hallertau and Tettnang hops, named after areas near Munich and Lake Constance, are revered for their aromatic qualities, while in North America the Cascade hop, with its wonderful citrus aromas, is grown in the Yakima Valley of Washington State.

AT THE BREWERY

Hops may arrive at the brewery in one of a number of forms: whole cones, pellets, powder, or extracts.

Full-flower hops at Victory Brewing, Pennsylvania. Hops are dried as soon as possible after they are harvested, to retain their fresh, green color.

The hops are added to the sweet wort (*see p.29*), then boiled in a sealed vessel called a copper or kettle.

Traditionally, the copper was made— as the name suggests—from copper, but modern versions are made of stainless steel and heated with internal or external steam coils. This treatment releases two vital components from the hops—resins and oils. During boiling, the hop resins link together to form long chemical chains, and it is these that give the beer its bitterness. The oils, in turn, give the beer its "hoppy" aroma, which can be wonderfully complex, with notes of pine, flowers, citrus, and other fruits.

Hop oils are volatile chemicals, evaporating readily. If all the hops are added at the beginning of the boil, much of their aroma may be lost. So when brewing traditional lagers, a fraction of the hops is held back and added later in the boil so that more of the oils remain in the wort—a process called late-hopping. By comparison, brewers of ale may add a handful of hops to the cask right at the end of the process (a process called dry-hopping), to retain a complex mixture of oils, and therefore aromas, in the beer.

Many brewers will use a cocktail of hops, with each variety contributing its own aromas and levels of bitterness; some use just one variety, and this tends to produce beers with very assertive but singular characteristics.

Heather Ale Fraoch, made in Scotland, is based on an ancient Pict recipe that uses heather rather than hops to flavor the beer.

EXOTIC ADDITIVES

Hops are by far the most common, but not the only, additives used to enhance beer. Specialty beers around the world include other spices and herbs, such as orange, ginseng, ginger, saffron, elderberry, juniper, and even chili peppers. Belgium has a long tradition of adding spices to beers—its witbiers are flavored with coriander, Curaçao, and lemon zest, with hops playing almost no role in driving the aroma or flavor—but there is a more widespread revival in the use of herbs and spices, led by the new microbrewers and brewpubs experimenting with ingredients.

Hops are added to the brewkettle. Here, pressed hop flowers are being used, but sometimes the brewer will add hop pellets or a jamlike extract.

OFF THE BOIL

After boiling, which typically lasts for one to two hours, the brew is strained. The residues of hops or other additives are removed, either by use of a centrifuge or a strainer known as a hop back. Some brewers first put more hops into the hop back so that the brew is strained through this, to add still more flavor.

The wort is now quickly cooled by passing it over a heat-exchange device—basically a coiled copper tube through which cold water is run. Further cold treatment may be needed to clarify the wort—this is particularly important for lagers and pale ales. If necessary, the cooling process is continued until proteins dissolved in the wort precipitate and fall out; the resulting beer is certainly clearer, but at the cost of some flavor.

At this point, the natural sugars in the wort, which first formed in the growing grain warmed by the spring and summer sun, are ready for their ultimate transformation. This is the magical process of fermentation (*see overleaf*).

MEASURING BITTERNESS

One of the hop's major contributions to beer is bitterness. This is measured using the International Bitterness Units scale—or IBU for short. A beer's IBU is set by the amount of hops used and their acid content—the higher the IBU, the more bitter the beer. A light American lager may have an IBU as low as 5; a Belgian lambic, between 10 and 25; an assertive English ale, such as Timothy Taylor's Landlord, could range from 25 to 50; and a robust Imperial stout could have an IBU of more than 50.

TIMOTHY TAYLOR'S LANDLORD

Yeast

Beer, like wine, cheese, and bread, owes its special character to yeast—a microscopic fungus. It is yeast that transforms sugar in the wort into alcohol, giving the beer its power to inebriate, but also adding new dimensions to its texture and spectrum of flavors.

Yeast is all around us. Its spores are carried in the air, and it grows wherever it settles on a suitable "soup" of organic compounds. It digests these foods to fuel its growth and reproduction, meanwhile transforming them into its waste products—carbon dioxide and alcohol. This is fermentation.

Ancient brewers must have stumbled across fermentation by happy accident. A store of grain, allowed to become wet, would have produced a primitive "wort." Transformed by the unseen, unknown agent of yeast, this would have produced a liquid that had distinct life-enhancing qualities. Across Asia, Africa, and Latin America, porridgelike brews made with locally grown cereals, roots, and saps were transformed into "beer" drinks by spontaneous fermentation.

THE WILD ONES

The biology of fermentation remained a mystery until the mid-19th century, when yeast was identified as the agent of

Lambic beers are thirst-quenching brews, first produced five centuries ago. They take time to mature properly, but have great character.

transformation. Despite subsequent advances in brewing science and biotechnology, some beers are still made the old way, harnessing wild airborne yeasts. This type of fermentation—called spontaneous fermentation—is famously used by the commercial brewers of the Zenne Valley in Belgium to make lambic beers, which have a very distinctive dry, vinous flavor with a sour aftertaste. The windows of the brewery are left open to allow wild airborne yeasts to settle onto the wort. However, in a modern brewery, the introduction of yeast is a more controlled process.

Digestion of the wort by the yeast is startlingly visible in this traditional open fermentation tank as the liquid bubbles and foams.

Large steel fermentation tanks are easy to maintain and clean; they have largely supplanted traditional open, wooden tanks.

In today's breweries, fermentation starts when yeast is added to the cooled wort, held in a large conical-cylindrical stainless-steel vessel. The yeast is commonly transferred from the last batch of fermentation, in a process called pitching, but specialist yeasts may be bought in from yeast banks maintained by the brewing industry.

A bung seals the vessel, allowing controlled amounts of carbon dioxide gas to escape: the gas retained in the vessel gives the beer its natural carbonation, or fizz. After the sugars have been digested by the yeast, fermentation slows down. The beer is cooled to promote the settling of the yeast and other proteins in the liquid, which clarifies the beer. Pressure is maintained inside the tanks to keep the beer carbonated. Finally, the beer is filtered to remove residual yeast and is ready for bottling.

Fuller's Vintage Ale is a bottle-conditioned beer. Its flavors develop over time.

YEAST VARIETIES

The type of beer produced depends on various aspects of the fermentation process, starting with the type of yeast used. There are two principal varieties— top-fermenting and bottom-fermenting yeasts. Top-fermenting yeasts (Latin name *Saccharomyces cerevisiae*) form a foam on the surface of the fermenting liquid. They are active at relatively warm temperatures of 59–68°F (15–20°C) and are commonly used in the production of English and Belgian ales. The ale spends at least seven days in fermentation, after which the yeast head is taken off, and the beer undergoes a secondary, slower fermentation at a lower temperature to release its complex fruity flavors and soften its harsh tones.

Bottom-fermenting yeasts (*Saccharomyces carlsbergensis*), which are used to make lager, collect at the bottom of the tank and are active at lower temperatures of around 50°F (10°C). The beer is stored (lagered) for 30 days or longer at low temperatures, during which time the beer mellows and becomes smoother.

BOTTLE-CONDITIONING

Some beers are bottled without having been filtered, or with extra yeast added to the bottle. Here, the final fermentation takes place in the bottle, so these beers— such as Belgian wits and British bottle-conditioned beers—may be cloudy when poured. Some brewers have developed a sticky yeast that stays stuck to the side of the bottle when the beer is poured out.

STRENGTH AND QUALITY

As with wine, the alcoholic strength of a beer is no indication of its quality. Most beer drunk in the world is under 5% ABV, and many of the most flavorsome English ales weigh in at less than 4% ABV. Strength provides a beer's body, and should be matched to the occasion: on a summer's day something light in body, like Pilsner Urquell, is a joyous refreshment. With dinner, a fuller-bodied beer is ideal, maybe a Sierra Nevada India Pale Ale or a Wells & Young's London Ale. But for a nightcap, a malty, strong Thomas Hardy's Ale or a Samichlaus fits the bill.

Beer styles

IN A RESTAURANT, NO ONE ORDERS: "A PLATE OF FOOD, PLEASE," SO WHY DO PEOPLE ASK FOR "A BEER?" THIS REQUEST USUALLY BRINGS FORTH A BLAND INTERNATIONAL BREW PURPORTING TO BE A PILSNER. BETTER TO ASK: "WHAT'S LOCAL?" OR CHOOSE THE STYLE THAT SUITS THE MOMENT.

Some beers just look stylish; others are classics of their style. However famous their brand-names, almost all internationally known golden lager beers were distantly inspired by the Czech classic, Pilsner Urquell. But there are at least 50 other major styles of beer, all quite different. There is a moment for each.

Her name suggests another style, but Pennsylvania microbrewster Carol Stoudt's Pils is hoppy and fragrant.

To quench a thirst, nothing beats a tart, slightly sharp brew. The outstanding styles in this respect are the oak-aged Flemish red ales, and Berliner weisse ("Berlin white"), a threatened species. Or, try the revived Leipziger gose, rediscovered since the Berlin Wall came down.

A really cold day provides a rare excuse for a really strong beer: a Baltic porter or Russian Imperial stout, perhaps. Inclement weather is a wonderfully versatile justification for a beer. Foggy days in London are long gone, but misty evenings prevail in San Francisco: Anchor's Old Foghorn Barley Wine is hoppy enough to be an aperitif, too, in that gastronomic city. Thomas Hardy's Ale goes well with a book at bedtime. So does another malty brew, darker but less strong, Köstritzer Schwarzbier ("Black Beer"). It, too, reappeared from behind the Wall, but in earlier times, was Goethe's favorite, especially when he was not feeling well. Perhaps he found its sweet maltiness restorative. The West German brewer who bought Köstritzer told me: "This is the first beer I ever drank." How was that possible? I reckoned he had been born only just before Germany was divided. "Yes," he said, "but I was breastfed, and my mother drank Köstritzer Schwarzbier as a tonic."

Michael Jackson

Belgium has a brew for every occasion. Some are deeply traditional, but new styles—like the Champagne-method Brut beers—keep on coming.

Belgian wild beers

Wild yeasts gave humankind its first beers, and ever since, brewing
science has dedicated itself to taming the erratic behavior of these living
organisms. Except, that is, in one small European valley, where old-style
trial-and-error brewing produces the wild beers of Belgium.

Why persist with a difficult, slow,
unpredictable method of production,
when brewers and scientists have spent
a couple of centuries conquering all of
those difficulties? Because beers made
with wild yeasts have a spontaneity that
cannot be matched by cultured yeasts.
The comparison might be live music
versus an impeccably engineered
recording: Django Reinhardt versus
Yehudi Menuhin; bebop versus Baroque.
As might be expected, wild beers have
wild flavors: woody, winey, acidic, fruity,
spicy, faintly smoky, food-friendly—
anyone with the slightest interest in food
and drink, aromas and flavors, should
aim at least to taste this style of brew.

The wild beers of Belgium are known
as lambics, a name most commonly
thought to derive from the town of
Lembeek, in Flemish Brabant. Before
the World Wars, these were the local beers
of Brussels. There were lambic breweries
to either side of the city, along the Zenne
River. Today's half-dozen survivors,
a couple of new breweries, and two or
three blenders (a unique feature in this
style of beermaking) are all on the west
side, fanning out from the river into a
rustic district called Payottenland.

Payottenland is Breugel country. The people, their
roistering, their pitchers dispensing beer with an
onion-skin hue, are still much as the artist promised.

HOW LAMBICS ARE MADE

Lambic is brewed from a grist of at least
a third raw wheat, the remainder being
malted barley. Hops are used, but not so
much for flavor as for their original
antiseptic and preservative purpose;
hop-bitterness would not sit well in these
tart brews. For this reason, most lambic
brewers follow a course that confounds
brewing dogma. While other brewers
want their hops to be mint-fresh, any
surpluses left hanging around can always
be sold to the lambic-makers. If that goes
against modern brewing practice, so does
the whole basis of lambic production.

Conventional brewers go to
extraordinary lengths to keep wild yeasts
out of their premises, insisting on tiled or
stainless steel surfaces that can be kept
hospital-clean. Lambic breweries are
more like farmhouses. They leave

KRIEK AND FRAMBOISE

Cherries (*krieken* in Flemish) from the suburb
of Schaarbeek gave rise to the use of the fruit
in the local beer style, lambic. The use of
raspberries seems to have come later.
Traditionally, whole cherries were added to
the maturing beer, the stones adding an
almondy dryness to the beer's tart acidity. By
no means all lambic becomes fruit beer, nor
is all lambic fruit beer made in the traditional
way. Some brewers produce a small quantity
of "old"-style kriek and framboise, and a far
larger volume of fruit beers that are made
with lesser fruits and heavily sweetened.

windows and vents open to tempt wild yeasts to have their way with the brew in the bathlike wort-cooling vessels. In some breweries, wild yeasts live in molds on the wooden walls, or in the barrels used for both fermentation and maturation; for while beer can be fermented and matured in a matter of days, and few take more than three weeks, lambics require one to three summers.

WHY HERE?

Several factors conspire to make this the natural home of lambics. This region is known for its Brabant red wheat. Water is rarely in short supply where western Europe's greatest rivers head for the sea. There are plenty of bigger breweries to provide aged hops. The Belgian love of gastronomy has caused millions of wine barriques, port pipes, sherry casks, and Madeira drums to be imported over the centuries. Once drained of wine, much of this cooperage has settled down to life in lambic breweries. The valley accommodates more than 200 wild or semi-wild yeasts, including specifically local examples such as *Brettanomyces lambicus* and *B. bruxelliensis*, and in this still, cool, and misty climate, they flourish without becoming overexcited.

Frank Boon brews gueuze in Lembeek itself, possibly the source of the term "lambic."

SPECIAL LAMBICS

Gueuze, often spelled geuze, is by far the most common member of the lambic family. Young and old lambics are blended and bottled to create a Champagnelike sparkle. The young, perhaps one summer old, still contains fermentable sugars. The old has developed a complex yeast structure to continue the fermentation in the bottle. Most lambic brewers produce both a sweetened, toned-down style and an authentic interpretation produced according to the "old" method. According to the grammar and language of the label, the classic version will be identified as Oud/Oude or Vieux/Vieille.

The Belgian fruit beers kriek (fermented with sour cherries) and framboise (with strawberries) may be based on a lambic beer (*see box, facing page*). More rarely seen today is faro, once a popular everyday version of lambic sweetened with dark candy sugar to balance the acidity. The name may date from the Hapsburg era when Spain ruled Belgium. Some breweries make modern-day versions of this workers' restorative.

The Cantillon brewery in Anderlecht, Brussels, prides itself on being a "living museum" to gueuze, but is also a fine place to sample lambics.

Beers made with wheat

In recent years, wheat beers have become fashionable all around the world. This family of styles includes the most refreshing and summery of beers: easy to drink, but with plenty of flavor, unlike the neutral-tasting lagers commonly consumed in summer.

If wheat beers are so refreshing, why aren't all beers made from wheat? One reason is that not all beers are meant to refresh. Another is that wheat is tricky for the brewer. Because it does not have a fully developed husk, it can clog the brewing vessels. It does not act as its own filter, as the huskier barley does. This was originally the reason for wheat beer being hazy. With today's techniques, it is easy to produce a bright wheat beer, but many consumers prefer the "natural" hazy look. The cloudiness is also why wheat beers are often called "white."

BELGIAN WHEAT BEERS

The town of Hoegaarden, in the heart of Brabant wheat country, was famous for this style until its wheat beers were swept away by golden lagers in the 1950s. A decade later, Pierre Celis (*see also p.230*) revived the style. As a young man, he had worked in the last of the town's breweries, and felt that there was still a demand for the local brew. He built a new wheat-beer brewery, and discovered a completely new, younger, market. Today, almost every brewery in Belgium makes wheat beer, modeled to varying degrees on Celis' original. This is a hazy beer, made from equal parts raw wheat and malted barley, and spiced with coriander seeds and Curaçao orange peel.

Spicy, full-flavored Schneider Weisse, from Kelheim on the Danube River, is a classic south German wheat beer with a distinct yeast character.

Easy-drinking and refreshing, its citrussy fruitiness is balanced by a restrained fruity dryness. There are also many Belgian-style wheat beers elsewhere in the world. The Flemish and French words for white are *wit* and *blanche*; wheat is *tarwe* or *froment*.

LEIPZIGER GOSE

When the Berlin Wall came down and Germany was reunified, Leipziger gose was a salty, spicy surprise from the East. Salt and coriander are added to the beer, which also has a lemony acidity. It was originally a low-strength refresher like its Berlin brother, but the grain mix in the grist, the fermentation method, and the strength it is brewed to are now similar to a South German wheat beer. Gose is said to have taken its name from the Saxon town of Goslar, where it was first brewed, and to have subsequently been produced in Halle and Döllnitz for the nearby city of Leipzig.

Often served with local cheese, gose is sometimes offered with the almondy liqueur Allasch, caraway Kümmel, or cherry "brandy."

GERMAN WHEAT BEERS

In northern Germany, the wheat beer tradition is very local, and vestigial. Leipzig's gose style is experiencing a revival (*see box above*), but Berliner weisse, the only really tart wheat beer produced in Germany, is increasingly hard to find; where it is served, it may be offered "dosed" with sweetening syrups (*see pp.107, 108*). But in the south, wheat beer, always much more widespread, has been booming in recent decades. Most of Bavaria's 600 or so breweries produce at least one example, and the state's blue-and-white colors often feature on the label. This popularity extends into the neighboring province of Baden-Württemberg. But the style's heartland is undoubtedly in the villages surrounding Munich, whose university has the world's most famous brewing faculty and collection of brewing yeasts, at Weihenstephan (*see also p.15*). Early work here doubtless led to the selection of ideal local strains for wheat beers, and these impart a very distinctive clovelike aroma, which, combined with a soft fruitiness (often reminiscent of plums, dessert apples, and even blackcurrants), typifies a south German "weiss" or "weizen" beer.

WEISS OR WEIZEN?

Wheat beers in Germany may be called weissbier or weizenbeer. Weiss ("white") might seem more appropriate to a hazy, unfiltered beer, leaving weizenbier ("wheat beer") for the clear type, but there seems to be no such rule. Brewers claim geographical preferences in terminology between Franconia, the Palatinate, Swabia, and other parts of the South, but the evidence is inconclusive.

Filtered versions often have such brightness and clarity that they deserve the epithet "crystal," and are called kristallweizen. Some drinkers find the taste and mouthfeel brighter and cleaner, too. It may be heresy to say so, but some of the fruity notes emerge with more elegance when they are not shrouded by the dustiness of even the finest sediment and the lingering suspicion of dead yeast cells.

HEFEWEIZEN/HEFETRUB/MIT HEFE

Terms like those above are used to indicate a sedimented wheat beer: "mit hefe" simply means "with yeast." "Trub"

A traditional Berlin custom is to sweeten the tart weisse beer with syrups, usually of either raspberry (red) or, more rarely today, sweet woodruff (green).

has the same etymology as the English words trouble and turbulence. In this instance, it refers to the turbidity created by the sediment. Young eco-aware Germans see hazy wheat beer as the "wholefood" of the drinks world.

DUNKELWEIZEN

Although the summery image of wheat beers is well served by the pale types, the dark style need not be held back for fall. The cool of late afternoon is excuse enough. The dark malts taste like hard toffee, coating the fresh-apple flavors spun by the yeast. There is not only toffee apple, but sometimes banana, too. Could this be the dessert beer to go with a Chinese meal?

WEIZENBOCK

The crisp fruitiness of wheat becomes richer and firmer in the bock versions of weizen beer, higher in strength at around 6.5–8.5% ABV. Dark versions of these beers are doubly delicious. To the toffee-apple and banana flavors suggested in the dunkelweizen is added the greater intensity of flavor and the warming influence of alcohol. It is as though the dessertlike characteristics were being enhanced by a dab of cream and a splash of Sambuca or even absinthe. The classic example in this style is Aventinus, from the respected Schneider Brewery at Kelheim, on the Danube.

In southern Bavaria, traditionalists prefer their wheat beer gently warmed to release more aromas and flavors. The little buckets contain warm water.

STEINWEIZEN

The word stein here indicates not the typical stoneware drinking vessels of Bavaria, but a very old method of brewing. Before the engineering skills existed to make large copper brew-kettles, wooden vessels were used. It was not feasible to boil the brew by setting a fire underneath a wooden structure. An alternative was to heat stones ("Steine") and then shovel them into the vessel. This method sounds unlikely, but was well documented. In 1982, the technique was revived by a brewery in Coburg, Bavaria, to produce a wheat-based "steinbier." The company later moved to the Augsburg area and has since ceased production. Variants on the theme have been produced by one or two American breweries, notably Bosco's in Tennessee. The hot stones not only bring the brew to the boil but also acquire a patina of caramelized barley malt. The stones are later placed in the lagering vesels, in which the sugar stimulates a further fermentation. The end result is to impart a smoky, molasseslike toffee flavor to a brew that nonetheless contrives to be light in body, clean in palate, and still a refreshing wheat beer.

SCHNEIDER AVENTINUS

Some Belgian classics

The most individualistic brewers in the world are those of Belgium. Some beers from this small country are so distinctive as not to fit any style. Among them are several classics that have spawned so many imitators that they have become styles in themselves.

FLEMISH REDS

The most refreshingly tart of all beers are some of the reddish-brown brews produced in about 10 towns in Flanders. Their sharpness is daring to the point of being vinegary. If that sounds an unlikely word of praise for a beer, it may be understood by people who enjoy the balsamic condiments of Italy or even Greek retsina. These beers usually gain their color from Vienna malts. Their tartness achieves its thirst-attacking potency during long periods of maturation (sometimes more than two years) in fixed wooden tuns, in which acid-producing bacteria are likely to be resident. The most famous brewery in this style, Rodenbach, has about 200 of these tuns, some containing more than 13,000 gallons (500 hectoliters) in 10 halls—it is perhaps the most unusual brewery in the world. A more recent producer in the New World is New Belgium Brewing in Colorado. In the absence of wooden tuns, this brewery uses wine barriques from the Napa Valley.

FLEMISH BROWNS

There is no longer a clear dividing line between Flemish reds and the milder, darker specialties made in and around the town of Oudenaarde and points east. The classic Oudenaarde Brown, Leifmans Goudenband, has in recent years been reformulated as a stronger, sweeter beer and is best known as the base for a kriek and a framboise. It remains a very characterful beer, and broadly similar products with varying degrees of tartness or sweetness still characterize the brewing scene in the Flemish-speaking parts of Belgium. Some are spiced, and outstanding examples are the Gouden Carolus variations made in Mechelen, in the province of Antwerp.

SAISONS

These summer seasonal beers were originally refreshers and restoratives for the farming folk of Hainaut in French-speaking Belgium. After almost vanishing two or three decades ago, they have now become fashionable, and are also being made in other French-speaking provinces and in Flanders.

Red beer from Rodenbach is aged in massive oak casks resembling those of a winery until it is ready to bear the label "Grand Cru."

There are about 10 Belgian brewers producing saison, and many more have in recent years taken up the style in the US. Saisons usually have a distinctively bronze color; a huge, herbal, fruity bouquet; and a firm, crisp, cleansing palate, the last attribute probably due to hard water. While they share these characteristics, they are achieved by a variety of different methods. It is hard to pin down the secret of saison, but most admirers believe that it is in that enigmatic life-force, the yeast. The classic example is Saison Dupont, made in what is the definitive Belgian farmhouse brewery.

BELGIAN ALES

While almost all Belgian specialties could be called "ale," there are Belgian products that closely resemble British ales. Some are conscious copies; others are produced under license from British brewers; but some are examples of a native Belgian style. They may bear the word "ale" on the label, or may be identified as Spéciales Belges. Although this style is in decline, there are still many examples, the best known being Palm and De Koninck. The latter, the pride of Antwerp, has a distinctively soft, clean, maltiness, which is balanced by a wonderfully fresh Saaz hop character. Like many beers around the world, it expresses itself far better on draft than in the bottle.

WICKED BEERS

Foreigners often mispronounce Belgium's most famous strong golden ale as "DuVell." This beer is not produced in the French-speaking part of the country; it comes from the heart of Flanders. When it was first produced, one brewery worker is said to have commented: "that's the devil of a beer." Hence the name, a corruption of the Flemish word for His Satanic Majesty. The beer is indeed capable of leading one into

The devil is in the detail: Duvel's glasses are engraved inside, which releases more bubbles into the traditional billowing head.

temptation. First, people who insist on the myth that dark beers are strong and pale ones harmless find that they have made a Faustian bargain when they order a "Doov'l" (the correct pronunciation). Nor does the extremely floral aroma and relatively light body offer any warning that this is a beer of 8.5% ABV. A lot of sugar is used, but without the unpleasantly candyish results that might have ensued. The devil's secrets are in the choice of an unusually pale malt; wonderfully fragrant Saaz and Styrian hops; and a very clean production process, with long periods of warm- and cold-conditioning. The result is a beer of extraordinary individuality, widely copied but without much success. Almost all of its imitators use names that imply at the very least mischief if not pure evil intent.

The Abbaye de Nôtre Dame de Scourmont is home to Belgium's famous Chimay Trappist brewery.

ABBEY BEERS

While Austria and Germany have beers produced in half a dozen active abbeys and a couple of convents, and many more brews that assume the names of long-vanished cloisters, these no doubt Godly brews do not have a single unifying style. Most are simply good examples of whatever is the local style.

However, in Belgium, six Trappist abbeys own breweries, and the products of these establishments do have a family relationship. In their early days, they would have each produced dark ales at three different strengths. This approach derived from the understanding that one batch of grain could be mashed three times (*see box, right*), producing a strong ale, an everyday brew, and a small beer. (This custom is reflected in the English pub name "The Three Tuns".) This typical range has been refined over the years, and is now likely to include both pale and dark beers. Often the pale brews are identified as "blonde," and the dark brews will be of middling strength,

at perhaps 6.5% ABV. The strongest brew, the triple (*see box, below*), will usually be bottle-conditioned, and also by far the most characterful. Many of these beers are made with pale or dark candy sugars that often impart a rummy character, and almost all are top-fermenting.

BIÈRE BRUT

This is a new style, introduced in the early 2000s by rival brewers in the small town of Buggenhout, to the northwest of Brussels. The old-established château brewery of the family Bosteels has a bière brut called Deus. The revivalist brewery of the family De Landtsheer has several variations on the theme in its Malheur range. These beers are top-fermented, then bottle-conditioned with Champagne yeast cultures. They are matured in the bottle, after which the yeast sediment is removed by the Champenois method of turning, freezing, and *dégorgement*. Many beer-lovers feel that, in their interplay of delicacy and gently fruity, spicy complexity, these brews have more character than most Champagnes. They also look more elegant, as they hold their head extremely well, flaunting their "Brussels lace" in a way that the wines of Epernay and Rheims cannot.

DOUBLES AND TRIPLES

In Belgium, running water through the mash-tun three times produces the strongest beer in the first run—around three times as strong as that from the third run, hence the term "triple". Midway comes the "double", from the second run. Before widespread literacy, beer casks were branded with an iron to indicate the potency of the contents. The most common motif was a Christian cross—single, double, or triplicate.

WESTMALLE TRAPPIST TRIPLE

Porters and stouts

Dark, smooth, and mysterious, porter seems almost to have vanished into the long shadows of history, although sightings are still reported in unlikely countries, such as Lithuania and China. Meanwhile, younger brother stout is enjoying a spectacular revival in the US.

In the earliest days of the industrial era, "plain porter" was the restorative drink of the British working man, and the least demanding on his pocket. As the author Flann O'Brien noted: "When life looks black as the hour of the night, a pint of plain is your only man." Porter was made in assorted strengths, and "plain" was the weakest and cheapest. The most potent porters were produced for export by steamship, especially to the cold lands around the North Sea and the Baltic.

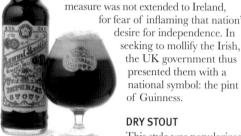

Imperial stout was big and bold enough to survive export to the chilly climes of the Baltic.

Gradually, these stronger porters assumed names of their own: double stout and foreign export stout, for example—although some beer historians think that the emergence of "stout" as a distinct style primarily reflected a change in technology. Porters were made with highly kilned brown malts that imparted a taste sometimes described as "peaty." The term stout seems to have become much more common after the introduction of a roasting technique that employed a rotating drum similar to that

used for roasting coffee. Porter-brewing in mainland Britain dwindled with the approach of World War I, when the government placed restrictions on malt roasting in order to conserve fuel. This measure was not extended to Ireland, for fear of inflaming that nation's desire for independence. In seeking to mollify the Irish, the UK government thus presented them with a national symbol: the pint of Guinness.

DRY STOUT

This style was popularized by Guinness, the most famous producer of dry stout. Although there are only about 10 breweries in the whole of Ireland, the volumes produced by Guinness are considerable, and its two local rivals in the production of dry stout, Murphy and Beamish, are both members of international groups. Guinness is still the driest of the Irish stouts, by virtue of its hoppiness and some *Brettonamyces* yeast influence. Murphy's stout has a maltier character, and Beamish is more chocolatey. The medal-winning Porterhouse Brewery in Dublin produces the most assertive porters and stouts.

SWEET STOUT

Porters and stouts were originally made by a process of blending long-matured beers (stock ales) with younger brews in order to achieve an equilibrium of flavor and microbiological stability. As this created a tartness, sugar was sometimes added when the beer was served. This later gave rise to sweet stout, stabilized by pasteurization. An English classic is Mackeson, which has a milk churn on its label. This refers to the use of milk sugars (lactose), which adds

The success of Guinness has made the dry stout style famous all over the world. Ireland's smaller breweries offer variations on the theme.

sweetness and smoothness and increases the calorie count. In the hungry years after World War II, "milk stouts" like Mackeson were regarded as a tonic, especially by nursing mothers and the elderly. Although Mackeson survives, the style has almost vanished in Britain —but at the most recent Great American Beer Festival no fewer than 18 examples were judged.

IMPERIAL STOUT

Why were only the strongest porters exported to northern Europe? One reason was that, being bottle-conditioned, they could continue to ferment during transit, thus preventing spoilage. Also, the alcohol was itself a protection against wild yeast infections. A third reason was that these powerful brews seemed an enjoyable protection against the cold. Catherine the Great, a woman of considerable appetites, even commanded the local St. Petersburg breweries to produce beers in this style, which they still do today. The influence of Catherine and the Tsarist rulers of Russia accounts for the "Imperial" designation. The key characteristic of an Imperial stout, aside from its strength, is a "burned fruit" flavor similar to that found in Christmas and fruit cake, produced when the roasted malts are fermented to high levels of alcohol. Thus, in addition to being a fine winter warmer, Imperial stout makes a wonderful dessert beer.

OTHER VARIATIONS

Given that oysters and stout are such a happy marriage, several brewers have combined the two, the oysters adding an appetizingly savory tinge for the robust drinker.

The term milk stout can no longer be used in Britain, because it implies a health benefit.

Another hugely successful variant is the Smoked Porter (surely a world classic) devised by Alaskan Breweries of Juneau (*see p.239*). Other US brewers have used honey in stout to great effect. Coffee and chocolate have also been happily employed. (Brooklyn Black Chocolate Stout, another world classic, uses no chocolate, but achieves with malt a flavor as rich and distinctive as a Sacher torte.) And oatmeal stout, invented as a creamy, "nutritious" pick-me-up in post-World-War-II Britain, is undergoing a revival in the US. Because oatmeal gelatinizes, it can easily block the mash tun, making production difficult. Despite this, there were 37 examples of the style at the Great American Beer Festival (*see p.236*) in 2006.

In the time of Dickens, oysters were a very inexpensive food offered as a bar snack, and they remain an excellent partner to stout.

Ales of the UK and US

When the British colonized America, they brought their beer with them. Over time, the brewing traditions of the two countries diverged, and GIs stationed in England during World War II were appalled by the warm beer. In recent decades, the two have grown closer again.

In the days of the Founding Fathers, the first New England beers had names like Tadcaster Ale and Worcester Ale. But gradually the British tradition lost ground to the Czech and German styles of later settlers. Ales and porters continued to be made in the east, but gradually surrendered character to compete with nationally marketed lagers.

But in 1977, President Carter signed a bill legalizing homebrewing, and craft brewers began to fight a rearguard action. Among the well-traveled post-Woodstock generation, British ales became cult brews. Styles such as pale ale and barley wine were embraced by US homebrewers, and the example of breweries such as Anchor (*see p.244*) encouraged amateurs to turn pro.

The Czech and German traditions and, excitingly, those of Belgium, also influenced new US brewers, but British ale culture was central. Today, it is hard to disentangle British and US styles of ale, except to say that the originals are frequently outstripped in character by their North American "offspring."

GOLDEN ALES

The complex flavors offered by ale yeast do not have to be accompanied by the nutty textures of the darker malts. Brewers in the northeastern US often made "golden ales" that paired ale yeast with lager malts. But their anaemic appearance presaged a gradual decline in character: American ales such as Genesee 12 Horse and Little Kings Cream Ale eventually became only marginally distinguishable from lagers. It is to be hoped that this fate should not befall characterful English golden ales such as Hopback's Summer Lightning—delicate but full of the sweetness of Maris Otter barley malt;

Fuller's brewery in London is noted for its robust English ales. Its ESB beer is so widely emulated in the US that it has become a style.

Rotating rakes keep the barley "juice" flowing in this traditional English mash tun at ale-brewers Hall and Woodhouse, of Dorset.

the fragrance of East Kent Goldings hops; and the bananalike fragrance of the house yeast. Another microbrewed golden ale, Crouch Vale Brewers Gold, was overall champion at the Great British Beer Festival twice in the mid-2000s.

MILD

One of the attractions of golden ales for novice drinkers is that their pale color suggests a light body and low alcohol content. By the same token (as valid as a wooden nickel) darker beers are believed to be heavier and stronger. Mild ales may be bronze, but are more usually darkish brown. These are light but malt-accented, sweetish beers that once quenched the thirst of Britain's manual workers: a coal-miner might drink 10 or 20 pints to get the dust out of his throat. For drinkers who are nervous of bitter flavors and alcohol, then mild, at only 4% ABV and with only the gentlest hop character, is the perfect solution. Sadly, this is now a rare style.

BITTER

The principal style of ale in Britain today, bitter ale is usually amber in color and hop-accented. Most drinkers know it simply as "bitter" and are confused about the category "ale." The other types of ale would include pale, brown, and so on. Bitter defines this style only as compared to mild. Drinkers who grew up with bitter may well regard the epithet as indicating an adult taste, but many younger drinkers think it sounds negative. Many breweries avoid the term, preferring just a brand name.

BROWN ALES

These ales were once produced all over Britain, and really were brown. In that incarnation they were also very sweet.

With the trend to paler colors, the dark brown style of ale has almost vanished and been replaced in part by the amber-brown, nuttier, drier style typically produced in Newcastle and the northeast of England. Taking much of their aroma and flavor from crystal malt, these have a more savory, grainy character. The Brooklyn Brewery in New York produces excellent beers in this style.

SCOTTISH STYLES

As in England, breweries in Scotland traditionally had a typical range of three draft ales, commonly known as light, heavy, and wee heavy (*see p.170*). Scottish ales were generally less bitter than their English counterparts: possibly because the Scots used fewer hops, being so far from the growing regions; or perhaps because Scottish brewers wanted a "warming," toasty, maltier character. Wee heavy is the style that personifies Scottish ale in the eyes of the world, and many US brewers now make similar beers, in some cases using small amounts of peated malt.

HOPBACK
SUMMER
LIGHTNING

OLD ALE

The original meaning of this designation is probably to suggest an old method or style rather than a long period of ageing. Most beers described as old ales have a color somewhere between ruby and dark brown. Some, like Old Hooky, from a charming steam-powered brewery in Banbury in Oxfordshire, are little more than stronger versions of a mild ale. Others, like Theakston's Old Peculier from Yorkshire, are medium-strong beers, with a slightly syrupy mouthfeel and complex sugary notes and fruitiness. The classic, strong Gales Prize Old Ale always had a component of wood-ageing when it was brewed in Hampshire. The beer is now being produced by Fullers in London, where serious efforts are being made to maintain its distinctively Calvadoslike aroma and flavor.

BARLEY WINE

If an ale brewery has an especially strong product, it will typically be called a barley wine. The name implies that it is as strong, and perhaps as noble, as a wine. US brewer Garrett Oliver, whose barley wine is called Monster, has suggested that the grapey designation was adopted when the Napoleonic Wars threatened a supply of Bordeaux wine to Britain. The style has been in severe decline in its native country of late, but some wonderful barley wines are being produced in the US, especially on the West Coast. While the original British barley wines were very malty, the US style is much hoppier.

GOOSE ISLAND
INDIA PALE ALE

INDIA PALE ALE

The British Raj in India needed a steady supply of beer. How else could you run the world's biggest empire? The problem was that beer exported from England degraded during its long, hot sea journey around the Cape. The solution was to brew beer to a slightly higher density than a normal pale ale and hop it much more heavily. The hops really came into their own in this style as an anti-infectant. British brewers have never stopped producing IPAs, but most of their current efforts are barely distinguishable from an ordinary pale ale or bitter. The Meantime Brewery of Greenwich is a rare exception. Another is Fuller's IPA, now hard to find.

The "steam" beer of San Francisco was once in danger of extinction, but it was revived by the Anchor Brewing Company in the 1970s.

German ales

The overwhelming majority of German beers are what English drinkers would call lagers, although Germans themselves rarely use the term. But there are exceptions, notably the sour beers of Berlin and Leipzig (*see p.107*) and the "ales" of Düsseldorf and Cologne.

When the lagering technique of bottom-fermentation spread westward from Bavaria (*see p.54*), some individual breweries and brewing cities held out for their own traditions. The most notable refuseniks were the brewers of Cologne and Düsseldorf. Both these cities retain top-fermenting beers that might broadly be categorized as ales, although that term is also not in common use in Germany.

KÖLSCH FROM COLOGNE

Kölsch is simply an adjective formed from Cologne—Köln, as it is correctly named. Kölschbier is its local specialty. Cologne is a city of neighborhoods, each of which had its own brewpubs until the depredations of two world wars. After World War II, big breweries entered the market, and the brewpubs gradually began to cooperate to defend their territory. In competing with pilsner they have come close to a policy of: if you can't beat them, join them.

To the outsider, kölsch looks and tastes very similar to a pils—perhaps a little softer, with a very faint (raspberrylike?) esteriness and a less assertive dryness. The key difference is that it is produced with a top-fermenting yeast, similar to that used in English ales. The combination of very pale malts, German hop varieties, a local variation of ale yeast, and a period of cold maturation produces a style that is delicate and therefore regarded by some as a little bland. It has, nonetheless, proven almost impossible to copy by even the most knowledgeable and talented of US microbrewers. It also has an extraordinary versatility: both a stealthy aperitif and a remarkably stomach-settling digestif. Several famous brewpubs remain, with their own rituals:

A traditional sign guides drinkers to the door of the Zum Uerige brewery and pub in Düsseldorf. The city's signature brew is an altbier.

a distinctive style of small cylindrical glass; uniformed waiters (*see p.100*); and typical local snacks. There are a dozen or so breweries in Cologne and a number of surrounding small towns, protected by a wine-style *appellation contrôlée*.

DÜSSELDORF ALTBIER

In Germany, "alt" means old—unless you are brewing in Düsseldorf, where it refers to the use of the "old" method of top-fermentation. The Düsseldorf brewers generally use a significant proportion of malt that is similar in character to a British crystal or Vienna type. This results in a deep bronze to full copper color, with a pronounced edge of dry maltiness. This is then balanced with a firm punch of hops, usually of the Spalt variety. Producers of altbier are fewer in number and less restricted geographically than those of kölsch, but the outstanding examples are still made in the very heart of the city, in the brewpubs of the old town.

FRÜH KÖLSCH

Lager beers

Contrary to popular belief, lager is not in itself a beer style. Rather, it designates bottom-fermented beers (*see p.35*) that, like wines, are "laid down" to age (the word "lager" can mean both "bed" and "cellar"). Within this group are many distinct styles to discover.

The Germans invented lagering, and Germany has one of the richest geographical portfolios of lagers. The Germans themselves, however, rarely describe a beer as a "lager," even when it fits the image the word conjures up elsewhere in the world. A German brewery's basic, everyday golden lager beer is more likely to be called a "hell," or "helles" (a word related to the English word "yellow.") It is likely to have an alcohol content of 4.25–4.5% ABV. Bright and clear, its aroma and palate will be very gently malt-accented, with a restrained hop bitterness. "Kellerbier" usually indicates a golden lager that has been more heavily hopped so that it can be dispensed unfiltered, with a low carbonation. Consumed fresh, it can be astonishingly appetizing. In the variant called krausenbier, a small dose of unfermented beer is added to the lagering tank to initiate secondary fermentation. Another variation is zwickelbier—this is a standard beer served directly from the lagering tank with no special treatment.

UNSER BÜRGERBRÄU
SUFFIKATOR

BOCK AND ITS VARIANTS

"Bock" simply indicates a strong or extra-potent lagered beer. The name probably derives from the name of the town Einbeck, which specialized in beers brewed to a high strength in order to survive shipping. When these beers reached Munich, the southern accent turned "beck" into "bock;" as bock is the name for a billy goat (like "buck,") this animal became a visual symbol of the style. In Einbeck, citizens had brewing rights. They did their own malting, spreading the grain in lofts and drying it by natural ventilation. With malt made in this way, the beer was probably a hazy yellow or pale tan color. The descendant of this style is the pale Maibock—a crisp, refreshing beer produced for early summer. Recent years have also seen an increase in pale, crisp versions called heller-bocks.

Traditionally, bock beers are malty, full-bodied, and smoothly warming. In the past they were invariably deep copper to garnet in color. Their typical strength is 6.5% ABV. They are usually

Bamberg is one of Germany's regional brewing capitals; its specialty is a smoked bottom-fermented beer known as "Rauchbier."

seasonal, made variously for winter or spring, not only in Germany, but also in the Netherlands, the USA, and even such outposts of Germanic influence as Namibia. An all-malt grist and long lagering times (three months is now more common than the original nine) give authentic bock beers a clean palate and excellent length.

Extra-strong bocks are called doppelbocks ("double-bocks"), and beer names ending in "–ator" typically indicate a rich, dark, malty lager of this style. German examples include Löwenbräu Triumphator, Augustiner Maximator, and Ayinger Celebrator. The style has been taken up by US microbreweries with names such as Procrastinator (a witty epithet for a beer that has a very long lagering time) and Terminator.

Eisbock is beer's answer to ice wine. Because water freezes before alcohol, ice wine gains in strength and sweetness from the concentration of sugars in the grape during freezing weather. "Ice bock" undergoes a similar transformation during lagering. Beer lore has it that this style came into being through the laziness or fecklessness of an apprentice, who left casks of beer outdoors during a cold snap. Much of the water froze out, leaving a stronger beer, with the result that some brewers deliberately froze their casks to achieve the same effect.

Tanks dominate the exterior of the Budvar brewery at České Budějovice in the Czech Republic. The town has long been a brewing rival to Plzeň.

DORTMUNDER EXPORT

Given the increasing uniformity of golden lagers around the world, it might have seemed a good idea for cities with their own styles to maintain the difference. Dortmund's export style was not hugely distinctive, but did have its own raison d'être. These beers were somewhere between gold and bronze in color; sometimes slightly stronger than an everyday beer at 5–5.25% ABV, with a distinctively mineral dryness from the local water. This slightly more robust style was intended to satisfy the population of Europe's biggest coal and steel region. There are now only one or two breweries in Dortmund, and although the style still exists it has become somewhat vestigial, usurped by the pilsner style (*see pp.56–7*).

ROSTOCKER
BOCK HELL

DUNKEL, DUNKLES

When one of these words is the only designation on a beer label in Germany, the contents will normally be a dark lager. This was the original style of lager in Germany, and it is still made in many parts of the world, although not heavily promoted. It is sometimes identified in other countries as being a Munich-style (Münchner) or Bavarian-type lager. At its best, it has a medium-dry, toasty, coffeeish aroma and palate with a very lightly spicy hoppy dryness in the finish. This style was becoming less distinctive in palate and paler in color and was generally in decline when black beers (*see below*) began to enjoy their revival. In some cases, breweries had only just dropped their dunkel, on the principle that dark beers were out of fashion, when they found themselves replacing it with something much darker.

SCHWARZBIER

"Black beers" are, unsurprisingly, the darkest of German beers (except perhaps for the odd porter). The style is especially associated with Bad Köstritz, a spa town on the Elster River in Thuringia, in the former East Germany. Its mineral-rich sand baths are said to cure rheumatism, and the local beer is reputed to have restored the health and appetite of Germany's greatest writer,

VIENNA LAGER

In the early 1800s, the Munich brewers Gabriel Sedlmayer and Anton Dreher (*see p.182*) traveled in Europe, especially England, studying new techniques of malting and brewing. On their return, Dreher made a clear beer with a distinctively copper color. This "Vienna style" of lager was introduced by Sedlmayer's brother, Josef, as a seasonal special for the Munich Oktoberfest. Sadly, neither Vienna nor Munich today pursue the rich, nutty Vienna style, but it can be enjoyed in the Oktoberfest-beers of US microbrewers and in Christmas and Easter seasonal beers in Scandinavian countries.

Oktoberfest celebrations in various parts of the world typically feature clear beers that are a little darker and stronger than a standard lager.

Johann Wolfgang von Goethe. The beer was probably top-fermented then, but is today a very dark lager with an aroma and palate reminiscent of bittersweet black chocolate. After reunification, the success of Köstritzer Schwarzbier inspired many other breweries; now, schwarzbier has become a style distinctly more robust than dunkel. German schwarzbiers are quite close in flavor and body to some Czech *tmave* ("dark") and *granat* ("garnet") beers. They may also have been the inspiration for the long-established Japanese black beers, and they have certainly spawned a new generation in the USA.

PILSENER, PILSNER, PILS

The name of the world's most famous and ubiquitous lager style quite simply means a product or style from the city of Plzeň, which is in Bohemia. The adjective attached itself to a particular beer in 1842, when a new brewery in the city made the world's first bright, golden beer. Bohemia was a province of the Austrian Empire at that time; now, with Moravia, it forms the Czech Republic. The golden beer was

KÖSTRITZER
SCHWARZBIER

made possible by a refinement in malting, in which direct heat was replaced by warm air. Its brightness captured the imagination of drinkers at a time when mass-produced glass was replacing stoneware and metal drinking vessels—part of an industrial revolution that was also bringing steam-power to the production and distribution of beer. At the same time, a new market was created in a union between three powerful German-speaking entities: the Austrian Empire, Bavaria, and Prussia. Emigrants from all three countries spread the word about bright beer to the US.

The pilsner brew was not only bright; it was also delicious, thanks to the quality of barley malt from the Hana region of Moravia and hops from Bohemia's Žatec, or Saaz region. The Saaz hops imparted an especially fresh, herbal aroma and a firm but elegant finish that defined the style. Today, the brewery also places emphasis on its triple-decoction mashing methods, which are considerably more elaborate than the techniques used by most other breweries.

PROTECTING THE NAME

When the brewery in Plzeň made its first golden beer, the protection of trademarks did not exist. Allusions to "pilsner-style" beers had spread throughout Europe by the time legislation existed to prevent the term being misused. In Germany, a compromise solution insisted that the words pilsener, pilsner, or pils should be preceded by the actual town of production—as in Bitburger Premium Pils, Jever Pilsener, and Radeberger Pilsner. German pilsner brewers generally try hard to reproduce the trademark elegant hop aroma, bitterness, and good malt character. But even here, the personality of these beers is diminishing toward a more international denominator. This erosion has created more "international" manifestations in Belgium, the Netherlands, and Denmark respectively. In the US, the pilsner style gave rise to bland mass-market lagers, lightened in body and flavor by being made with corn or rice. It is a piquant fact that the original brewery in Plzeň is now owned by the same company as Miller, the latter known for its "lite" beer, allegedly "a fine pilsner."

PILSNER TODAY

Today, the Czechs insist that the term pilsner should be used only on a beer made in that city, although they have injured their case in recent years by allowing their beer to be made under license in other cities and countries. The original brewery is identified on Czech labels as Plzeňský Prazdroj, and elsewhere by the German Pilsner Urquell. A sister brewery, Gambrinus, makes a similar beer that is a little lighter in body and palate.

The typical color of the malts used in Plzeň is slightly higher than those employed by imitators elsewhere in the world. The level and the quality of hops is also, in general, higher in Plzeň, but many breweries follow the preference for the Saaz variety if they are producing what they care to term a pils.

Directly descended from the original clear, golden beer, Pilsner Urquell is among the best beers of its type on the market.

Enjoying beer

BEER IS THE WORLD'S MOST POPULAR ALCOHOLIC DRINK, AND YET IT IS OFTEN TAKEN FOR GRANTED. IT CAN HAVE AS MANY NUANCES OF COLOR, AROMA, AND TASTE AS A FINE WINE, AND IT IS A DRINK OF WONDERFUL, LIFE-ENHANCING COMPLEXITY. THE BETTER YOU UNDERSTAND BEER, THE MORE YOU WILL ENJOY IT.

Many people enjoy a glass of beer without knowing anything about its rich heritage, natural ingredients, or life-enhancing properties. It is so much more than a thirst-quenching drink —it is a beverage that has helped to shape cultures, from the southern tip of Latin America to the Arctic Circle, and it still brings people together in celebration today.

Hops can bring a huge variety of aromas and flavors to a beer, and also have preservative qualities.

The ingredients of most beers (grain, hops, yeast, and water) are deceptively simple. Although basic, these elements can be made to yield a symphony of colors and aromas, and a chorus of tastes. The art, craft, and skill of brewers across the world help to make beer into the world's most refreshing alcoholic drink. Beer is a wonderful, vibrant product, that deserves to be respected and looked after properly, so that it can be enjoyed at its best.

Some people believe that wine is the only drink that goes with food, or that it is the only drink that is compatible with a healthy lifestyle. Still others associate greatness with names such as Cabernet, Chardonnay, Chablis, or Champagne, but not with the names of the world's finest beer styles. However, when people lay aside their preconceptions and take time to appreciate drinks with their eyes and nose as well as with their palate, they start to discover how rich and satisfying beer is, with a whole spectrum of colors, tastes, and aromas to savor.

Finally, you will get the most out of beer by being adventurous. The lagers of the big international brewers may be reassuringly familiar, but they are standardized, industrial products. The joy of trying a locally made craft brew is that every sip will tell you something about the region's history and traditions, and its taste will remind you that it has been made with care.

Beer is the best long drink in the world, and it is drunk in nearly every corner of the globe. It brings people together like no other form of refreshment.

Beer-hunting

There has never been a more tantalizing time to be a beer-hunter. Cheap travel, the global movement of goods, and the Internet all make it easier to track down the world's classic brews. Whether drinking at home or in a bar, there is no need to settle for bland, mediocre beers.

Walk into a bar, even in one of the great brewing regions, and ask for a beer, and the chances are you will get an insipid brew—the type that could be served to you in thousands of similar bars the world over. The most interesting beers are minority tastes, so bartenders often assume that you want a mass-market brand. The truth is, the best beers—those with the greatest range of aromas, colors, and flavors—must be hunted down.

Fortunately, beer culture is becoming more recognized worldwide, and most cities now have at least one good beer bar, staffed by people with expertise and a real enthusiasm for beer. Having a large selection of beers doesn't necessarily mean that a bar is a great place to drink—sheer numbers are no guarantee of interest or quality. A better guide is whether the staff are well informed. The Netherlands and Belgium have the best-run specialty beer bars with the most knowledgeable staff, and in Britain it is now relatively easy to find good cask-conditioned ale.

The world of beer is rich and varied, contrary to the impression given by most mass-market bars. Many superb beers are out there; it just sometimes takes a little time and effort to get hold of them.

No visit to Japan is complete without sampling Sapporo beer at the original brewery and museum in Sapporo, Hokkaido.

TOURISM AND TOURS

Beer tourism is a growing industry, and various companies offer trips to the great brewing regions —be it to the heart of Payottenland and the Senne River valley in Belgium (the home of lambic) or Bamberg in Germany, or to Canada and the craft brewers of British Columbia and Quebec. These are trips for true beer connoisseurs and beer gourmands.

Beer tourism need not be limited to organized trips. Any independent traveler can take time to check out the local beers at source. Many breweries have visitor centers where you can buy and sample beer after touring the brewery. For beer-hunters visiting England, Oxfordshire's Hook Norton Brewery is a must. The brewery tour takes in an 1890 steam engine, which still powers this Victorian brewery, and ends at the taproom in the old maltings. Likewise, a trip to the Czech Republic should include the city of Plzeň. At the grandiose Pilsner Urquell museum and visitor center, drinkers can sample a genuine pilsner, brewed in the city that created this world-famous style. These are just two examples—every country has its own highlights. Happy hunting!

But finding places to drink or buy the world's best brews is not always simple. Thankfully, many countries now have beer consumer organizations that publish and support guides to good bars and specialty beer stockists. They often also organize beer tastings and festivals.

Another invaluable resource for the beer hunter is the Internet. There are plenty of good websites that provide excellent guides to world beers and beer styles. Sites worth looking at include www.beerhunter.com, www.ratebeer.com, and www.beeradvocate.com.

Beer can also be purchased online, not only from the breweries and micros themselves, but also from specialist beer retailers. For example, Beers of Europe (www.beersofeurope.co.uk) allows people in the UK to order beers from more than 75 different countries and have them delivered direct to their home.

Today, news of a good brew travels fast in the beer world, and geography is no longer an obstacle to supply. Beers produced by a small craft brewer in one country can often be found on sale many thousands of miles away. In fact, the lambic beers of the Brasserie Cantillon in Brussels, Belgium, are now on sale in more bars in North America than in the city in which they are brewed.

Having obtained your beer, make sure that you drink it while it is still fresh. Pasteurized bottled beer will keep for a year before it slowly starts to deteriorate. Even beers that are alive in the bottle should be bought young and drunk sooner rather than later. Some beers, however, will mature over time, but only if stored correctly (*see box, right*).

HOW TO STORE BEER

Beers that mature over time need to be stored in cool conditions (at serving temperature), and also in the dark, as light can cause components in the hop residue to react and produce unpleasant, skunky flavors. Unless it is sealed with a cork, beer should be kept upright, rather than on its side.

Stored correctly, such beers develop handsome, often winey flavors. Thomas Hardy's Ale can be stored for 25 years, gradually releasing wonderful Madeira notes and complex, warming spices.

THOMAS HARDY'S ALE

Know your beer

Beer, like wine, can be drunk purely for pleasure, but a little knowledge can enhance the experience. What style is the beer? Should it be cloudy? Is it at the right temperature? Why does it taste of oranges and coffee? Getting the details right adds an extra dimension to your enjoyment.

The rituals of wine-drinking add to its enjoyment, and so it is with beer. The Belgians probably have the most seductive beer-drinking rituals. Beers are lovingly stored in cool cellars before being delivered to the table for serving, often in individualistic glasses.

As drinking beer with meals has become more acceptable, the look of the beer on the table has also grown in importance. The Champagne-style packaging of a DeuS Brut des Flandres, from the Bosteels brewery in Belgium, suggests a world of aristocratic sophistication, an impression that is strengthened as the cork is popped and the foaming beer is poured into a winsome flute. The best beer bottles are not

Stylish beer bottles and eye-catching labels, which are increasingly part of beer culture, can tell you much about the character of a beer.

only attractive, but also manage to communicate the character of their contents. For example, the strength and idiosyncratic character of the Rogue Imperial Stout bottle from the US is an excellent match for the forceful intensity and personality of the beer inside. The label on a bottle is the key to a world of sensory experience. It should describe the beer's style,

Pouring beer can dictate not only whether the head is modest, creamy, blossomy, or towering, but also how the beer releases its aromas and flavors.

ingredients, and strength. From these, the drinker can intimate the color, aroma, taste, and appearance of the beer.

SERVING BEER

Beer should always be served at the correct temperature—check the bottle for details. A pilsner like Jever should be chilled to 41–45°F (5–7°C) to bring out its light, clean malt taste and dry bitterness. An artisanal bière de garde, on the other hand, is best served warmer, at 52–55°F (11–13°C), to enhance its luscious fruity overtones.

Pouring the perfect beer starts with a clean glass free from grease and finger-marks. It must not be too warm; a hot glass straight from a dishwasher will do nothing for the beer. Open the bottle, taking care (if it is a bottle-conditioned beer) not to disturb the yeast. Then tilt the glass to about 45° and carefully pour the beer down the side of the glass. As you continue pouring, slowly straighten the glass to vertical, and watch the white foaming head miraculously appear. If the beer has some sediment, most people will stop pouring before the yeast drains into the glass. Some people do

Which glass? Snifter glasses are best for strong ales (*left*), nonic glasses for porters (*center*), and tall flutes for pilsners (*right*).

like to drink the sediment, and will swirl the residue into the glass, giving the beer a distinctly hazy hue.

Beer is the only alcoholic drink to have a foaming head. It is created as the carbon dioxide rises up through the beer and adheres to proteins created by the malted cereal. Although how fast you pour can vary the size of the head, different beer styles typically have different heads. Kölsch and weissbiers are deservedly crowned with a flamboyant, billowing head. American pale ales are more restrained, but there will still be a bold collar of foam atop the beer. On many English pale ales, the head is understated, and in some cases non-existent.

GREAT GLASSES

Great beers demand great glasses. If you order a hazy, spiced Hoegaarden it will typically be served in a chunky tumbler, while with a flourish a waiter will pour a Leffe into an audacious goblet. A kölsch is best suited to a tall, narrow, straight glass. Barley wines call out for a snifter or oversized wine glass, from which to sip the rich, warming beer. A stout—its gorgeous, white head contrasting starkly with its jet-black body—looks perfect in a nonic glass, and a bière de garde looks equally entrancing in a tulip-style glass, with its head embraced by the incurving rim.

With the beer at the right temperature and poured with expert skill into the appropriate style of glass, all that's left to do is to sit back, drink, and enjoy.

Beer and food

The marriage between food and wine has long been acknowledged as made in heaven. But beer, as an aperitif, as an accompaniment to fine food, or at the end of a dinner instead of a brandy—or even used as a cooking ingredient—is, like Caesar's wife, beyond reproach.

Beer is a wonderful companion to food. Like wine, the attributes of a beer can be used to complement or contrast with the flavors and textures of a dish. Today, there are many chefs across the world who are challenging the assumption that only wine is fit for the finest menus. A carefully chosen beer is as good, indeed often better, a companion to food as a fine wine. Anyone who has ever tasted fresh oysters with stout, for example, knows that while Champagne and Chablis have their merits, there are occasions when beer really is best.

Brewery restaurants and brewpubs are often the best places to receive an education in beer and food pairing. At the Redoak Brewpub in Sydney, Australia, for example, the signature tasting board (below) is designed to take the diner through a progression of partnerships. Japanese-style beef tataki on sesame bean shoots is matched with a pilsner; a dark English-style ale complements a duck and pistachio cappelletti on white bean purée; smoked venison sausage with apple sauerkraut is enhanced by a glass of smoked "rauch" beer; and braised pork belly and apple on coriander salad is paired with an oatmeal stout. The diners' palates become increasingly attuned to the tastes and flavors of the dishes and beers as they move across the board.

BEER AND FOOD IN BELGIUM

With no indigenous wine culture, the Belgians have developed a highly sophisticated beer cuisine. The "wild beers" of Belgium—lambics, gueuze—

The Redoak Brewpub's "tasting board" features a quartet of quite complex dishes with beers to complement them.

Waterzooi, the classic rich and creamy Belgian fish stew, is partnered well by a lively Belgian triple such as this Karmeliet brew.

not only stimulate the appetite themselves, they also make perfect partners for hors d'oeuvres such as sharp Belgian cheeses and sausage, and white wheat beer is the classic accompaniment for steamed mussels and piping-hot frites. But beer plays an integral role in fine dining, too. At Jan Buytaert's Michelin-starred restaurant De Bellefleur, in Kapellen near Antwerp, beer and food pairing rises to illustrious heights. A Brut Reserve, bottle-fermented in the Champagne style, is suggested to accompany a tartare of tuna garnished with caviar. A heavenly St. Feuillien Abbey Triple is served with breast of guinea fowl, morel mushrooms, and truffles, and in a double finishing flourish, a cheese marinated in De Koninck ale is served with a special edition ale from the St. Bernardus brewery, as potent as many wines.

THE BEST OF BRITISH

In England, the British Guild of Beer Writers has been pairing beer and food at its sumptuous annual dinners for 20 years. At the most recent, celebrity chef Brian Turner created a Cornish

crab and bacon cake to be served alongside Shepherd Neame's Whitstable Bay Organic Ale. The main course was roasted Irish venison, accompanied by Cains 2008 Cultured Beer; and the meal finished with chocolate fondant and Wells & Young's Double Chocolate Stout. Only British ales feature on these occasions, but Michelin-starred British restaurants such as Le Manoir aux Quat'Saisons and Aubergine have inspirational, international beer lists. At Le Gavroche in London, chef Michel Roux Jnr serves Liefmans Kriek cherry beer with his spicy seared tuna dish. It has proved so successful that he now offers a beer list that is as distinguished as any menu of vintage wines.

A pint of British bitter with roast beef or a hunk of bread and good English Cheddar is hard to beat. But British beer styles can also provide solutions for some foods that are notoriously difficult to pair with wine. A golden ale goes well with asparagus, a powerful flavor that can ruin many a wine; a nutty brown ale in the Newcastle style is excellent with a Caesar salad (although one might hesitate to suggest such a combination to Tyneside's shipyard workers); and a strong "old ale" is a match even for pickled herring. And in England, of course, beer has long been recognized as the ideal accompaniment for Indian food, something of an anathema to wine. Recently at London's eminent Bombay Brasserie, head chef Sriram Aylur

Smoked beer (this is a German Rauchbier) and smoked foods are a marriage of equal partners.

comprehensively explored matching Indian dishes with beers. Worthington's bottle-conditioned White Shield attracted much praise for its versatility across the menu, a fitting tribute for a historic India pale ale. The dry and alluring spiciness of Czech Žatec pilsner merged seamlessly with nearly every dish. Belgium's Palm Speciale ale had a love affair with lamb rogan josh, while Grolsch Weizen wheat beer developed a sympathetic relationship with shrimp and fish curries, balancing their savoriness with attractive, almost tropical fruits.

STATESIDE PAIRINGS

In the US, many chefs both cook with beer and match it to foods. The Higgins restaurant in Portland, Oregon, carries a beer list that would be the envy of many a bar. Higgins' cooking focuses on Pacific Northwest ingredients and traditional French techniques, incorporating an eclectic range of influences from around the world. Germanic and Belgian traditions in US craft brewing come to the fore in pairings of local beers with meat, smoked

seafood, and cheese platters. At the upscale Gramercy Tavern in New York, diners can pair Lindemans Pêche Lambic from Belgium with toasted vanilla bean marshmallows. However, there is a homegrown ale for every traditional US dish. Try a Munich-style dark lager with sausage or pastrami; a US Oktoberfestbier

Rochefort 10 has a wonderful, lingering chocolate aftertaste, made infinitely more intense when paired with Belgian chocolate.

BEER AND CHOCOLATE

Beer has a wonderful affinity with chocolate. This is because they share the same basic taste, which is a balance of bitterness—derived from the cocoa beans in chocolate and the hops in beer—and sweetness—from the chocolate's sugar and beer's malted barley. They also deliver a similar mouthfeel: chocolate melts in the mouth, while the alcohol in beer creates a warming sensation. Try dark chocolate truffles with Coopers Sparkling Ale or a lambic fruit beer; a chili truffle with Sierra Nevada IPA; or a coffee chocolate bar with Hook Norton's opulent Double Stout.

A BEER-WITH-FOOD HERO

Garrett Oliver, brewmaster at the Brooklyn Brewery, New York, says that beer can be paired with any food. It is his ambition for every good restaurant to carry a beer list as well as one for wine, so that people can discover for themselves that beer is a deserving companion to the finest food. His writings are inspirational, and show that the pairing of good beer—which he calls an "affordable luxury"—with serious food is a truly creative, life-enhancing experience.

Garrett Oliver is the author of the acclaimed *The Brewmaster's Table: Discovering the Pleasures of Real Beer with Real Food.*

with fried chicken; pilsner with tacos; a new-generation, fruity US pale ale with steak; or a Vienna lager—a style that is almost extinct in Europe itself—such as Great Lakes' fine Eliot Ness with Chicago-style pizza.

BEER IN COOKING

Beer has a long and glorious history as a culinary ingredient. Sublime dishes, such as Welsh rarebit, carbonnades, and fondues, all owe their character to beer. Throughout culinary history, chefs have understood that beers have a unique potential to excite the taste buds.

Beer as a marinade or braising agent is less abrasive than wine and does not mask the flavor of the main ingredients in the way that a rich, robust Burgundy dominates a boeuf bourguignon. Once the alcohol in beer has evaporated in the cooking, it leaves behind an alluring hint of barley and hops that is certainly in tune with modern chefs' search for marriages of simple, natural flavors.

The other great attribute of beer is its natural carbonation. When used in food, those bubbles that dance vivaciously across the tongue can raise even the most stolid recipe, which is why beer is included in Christmas and winter puddings, batters, breads, cakes, and even ice creams and sorbets.

But beer has a third, underestimated but entrancing value to chefs— its versatility and range of tastes, aromas, colors, and textures. From the understated lightness of a pale ale or lager through the more robust Belgian ales to the profound sumptuousness of a stout, beer lends itself well to almost any culinary dish. It can be used to tenderize raw fish or braised meat. Bolder beers add color to a sauce or intensity to a soup. Beer can be used in a dressing, poured over fruit, or added to the cooking liquor when boiling a ham. Indeed, sometimes it is the simplest artisanal combinations that allow great beers to shine. Basting Bavarian smoked pork or ham with dark lager adds a comforting sweetness to the meat, which is wonderfully enhanced by a glass of the lager with the meal – a perfect example of beer's ability to both inspire and satisfy.

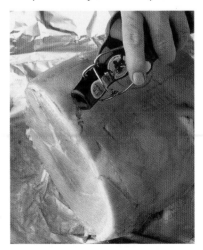

A baked ham basted with dark Munich-style lager is a Bavarian favorite, but a sweet and malty Irish red ale would make a fine substitute.

Great brewing nations

THERE ARE FEW COUNTRIES IN THE WORLD IN WHICH BEER HAS NOT BEEN BREWED—IF NOT TODAY, THEN IN THEIR FAR-DISTANT PAST. BUT IN SOME—THE GREAT BREWING NATIONS FOUND IN THE FOLLOWING PAGES—WHAT MAY HAVE STARTED AS A HAPPY ACCIDENT HAS BEEN ELEVATED OVER THE CENTURIES INTO AN ART.

The first known recipe for the brewing of beer is from one of the world's greatest and most ancient civilizations, that of Mesopotamia, in what is today the arid heart of the Middle East. But in general, beer-brewing is a craft native to cooler climates, where wine-making grapes do not grow but hops and grains (principally barley) thrive. While modern transportation has made it possible to brew beer virtually anywhere, the "beer band," where most of the world's greatest beers are produced, stretches across northern Europe and into the Ukraine, then re-emerges in northern outposts of China and in Japan; then skips over the Pacific to North America, where the Northwest and Northeast US, not to mention Canada, have some of the oldest and richest of brewing traditions. In the southern hemisphere, this productive zone is paralleled by brewing enclaves in a narrow band crossing South America, southern Africa, southern Australia, and of course New Zealand and Tasmania.

Beers served on draft, tap, or cask are a special pleasure for the well-traveled beer-hunter.

While few subjects arouse deep-seated patriotism in quite the way beer does in those that love it, this book is for the explorer that exists within us all. With it, you can discover your inner beer-hunter, for on the pages that follow are cataloged the creators of some of the world's greatest beers— and some of the places where these beers can be enjoyed. For each nation, we have chosen a representative selection of that country's finest brewers, whether long-established traditionalists or modern-day innovators. For each, space permits only a taster of the range of beers they offer, with information on the style, alcohol content, appearance, and, most importantly, the aromas and flavors. The aim of this book is not only to direct you to the best beers, but also to inspire you to seek out more. It is a companion to a wonderful world, in which you will discover that a beer is very much more than "just a beer."

Mass production and the bottling line have enabled beers to travel long distances to the beer-lover: the choice has never been greater.

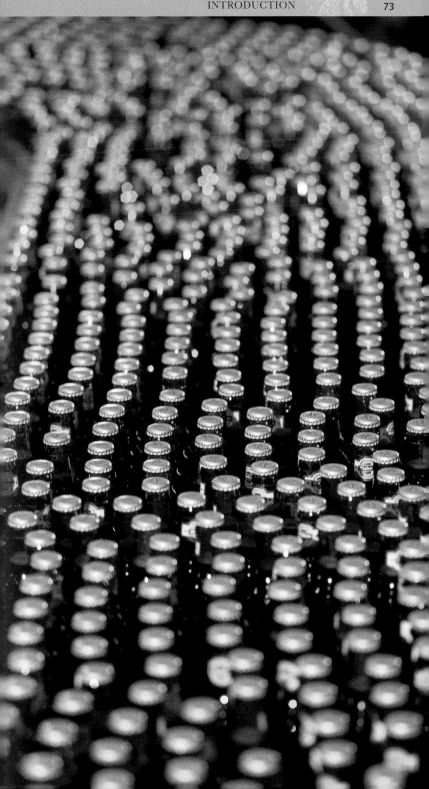

CZECH REPUBLIC

Some people regard the Czech Republic as the greatest beermaking nation, and the country takes great pride in its brewing heritage. Czech breweries may have been the first to use hops, more than 1,000 years ago, and later invented the world's most popular beer style, pilsner.

B eing first in all fields of beer-related endeavor is almost a national obsession. Czechs claim the first beer museum in the world; the first brewing textbook, published in 1585 by Tadeáš Hájek; the first pilsner, and the first Budweiser.

The first Czech brewery was built in Cerhenice in 1118, and fine spicy hops from Žatec (known as Saaz in German) and Ustek were shipped along the Elbe to markets in Hamburg after 1101. Many towns and cities were given charters to develop cooperative "citizens' breweries" from the 13th century onward. Bohemian hops were so prized that King Wenceslas IV decreed that anyone caught exporting cuttings from which new plants could be grown would be put to death.

Czech beers were brown in color until 1842, when Josef Grolle from Bavaria was contracted—by the whole town of Plzeň, to all intents and purposes—to develop a new beer for the Plzeňský Prazdroj brewery, to rival a new style emerging from Vienna. Great technical progress was driving industry at that time, with advances particularly in the mass production of glassware. Examined through the new-style tumblers, Grolle's clear, golden, cold-fermented beer was visually attractive, and its spicy hop and sweet Moravian malt flavors were sensational. It was given the name Pilsner Urquell (from Plzeň, the "original source") and the style, now known as pilsner, sent shockwaves across Europe. The Plzeňský Prazdroj company now produces one fifth of the Czech Republic's beer and is its biggest exporter.

Another notable brewing town is České Budějovice. It was once called Budweis—which explains the name of its main product, Budweiser Budvar—and a century-old trademark dispute still rumbles on between Budvar and the US Anheuser-Busch company over the name.

Czech industry was nationalized when the country became a Communist state after World War II. Ironically, a lack of investment in new equipment and technology meant that traditional brewing methods were still in daily use when the system collapsed in 1989. Another interesting feature of the Czech brewing industry is the fact that beers are rated in degrees, according to a method devised in the 17th century by Professor Balling of Prague. Confusingly, degrees refer not to alcoholic strength but malt extraction rates. For example, a 12° beer has around 5% alcohol by volume.

A band entertains diners at the historic U Fleků brewpub in Prague (*see p.79*). It was founded in the 15th century, and is a haven for beer-lovers.

BERNARD

✉ 5 Května 1, 396 01 Humpolec
🖳 www.bernard.cz

A family brewery in Humpolec dating from the 16th century was revived as the Bernard brand in 1991, quickly gaining a reputation for producing distinctive, full-bodied, unpasteurized beers. Bernard has its own malting house and draws water from the Bohemia-Moravia highlands. In 2000, Duvel Moortgat (*see p.126*) of Belgium acquired a 50 percent share of the business.

▮ CELEBRATION LAGER 5.0% ABV ●
Pale lager ● A golden, Champagne-style beer that undergoes final fermentation in the bottle. Delicate herb-like hop and yeast aromas overlay a peppery bitterness that slips into a grassy finish.

▮ AMBER LAGER 4.5% ABV ● Pale lager ● Brewed using a caramalt (a light-colored, sweet malt variety) to create bitterness balanced by a fine toffee aroma that is retained on the palate.

BUDWEISER BUDVAR

✉ Karolíny Světlé 4, 370 21 České Budějovice
🖳 www.original-budweiser.cz

King Otakar II of Bohemia granted the city of České Budějovice (Budweis in German) the right to brew beer in 1265. In the 15th century, it had some 44 breweries and was home to the Royal Court Brewery, which was permitted to call its products the "Beer of Kings." The Budějovický Pivovar company was founded in 1895 by astute local businessmen who were custodians of the town's brewing permits, and its name has since become synonymous with

When Budweiser Budvar arrived on the US market, disputes followed.

Czech enterprise and tenacity. The brewery has undergone almost continuous modernization since its inception and was nationalized in 1945. The current management took over in 1989, and since then output has nearly tripled, although a long-running trademark dispute with American giant Anheuser-Busch over the Budweiser name has been a constant distraction.

Budweiser Budvar enjoys Protected Geographic Indication (PGI) status, meaning it can be brewed only in České Budějovice.

▮ PREMIUM LAGER 5.0% ABV ●
Pale lager ● Light golden and inviting with an attractive head, some floral and grapefruit traces on the nose, and a dry, biscuit-malt palate, with an oily mouthfeel rounding off to a bitter-sweet malt finish.

▮ DARK LAGER 4.7% ABV ● Dark lager ● Coffee liqueur on the nose with a bitter hop palate and a malt edge. Licorice and cinnamon in the finish.

▮ BUD SUPER STRONG 7.6% ABV ●
Premium pale lager ● A 200-day maturation period takes this beer to a superior level. Dark golden, malty, and rich, with infusions of honey and fig.

BUDWEISER BURGERBRAU

✉ Lidická 51, 370 54 České Budějovice
🖳 www.budweiser-burgerbrau.cz

The oldest firm brewing today in this southern Bohemian city was granted its license in 1795 and exported its first small batch of Budweiser Bier to the US in 1875.

BUDWEISER BUDVAR PREMIUM

Budweiser Burgerbrau became Court Supplier to the Württemberg king Wilhelm II in 1895, a title it has used ever since. Major modernization took place in the 1990s, and most of the 5.8m gallons (220,000 hectoliters) produced annually is now sold under the Samson Budweiser Bier brand.

▮ PREMIUM LAGER 4.7% ABV ●
Pale lager ● Some butterscotch and citrus fruit on the nose and a creamy, malty palate with a honeyed sweetness and well-balanced, peppery, dry hop finish.

▮ ORIGINAL LAGER 5.0% ABV ●
Pale lager ● Hop, vanilla, and herb aromas; a bitter-sweet mouthfeel with a veil of malt in the flavor and a trace of tobacco to the finish.

EGGENBERG

✉ Latrán 27, 38115 Český Krumlov
🖳 www.eggenberg.cz

Brewing tradition in the historic town of Krumlov dates back to 1336. The Eggenberg family took power there in 1622 and the brewery moved to its present site in 1625. During this period, it is estimated that one local house in eight was a tavern. High-quality beer was produced for the nobility, while servants and farmers had to make do with a thin, watery product.

The manor passed to the House of Schwarzenberg in 1719, who developed the brewery extensively. A period of state control after World War II was followed by privatization, and in 1991 Dionex Inc. took control and remains in charge today.

PREMIUM LAGER 5.0% ABV • Pale lager • A powerfully floral aroma with sweet butterscotch notes. Clean, firm, and balanced, lightly sweet and zesty; bitter finish.

DARK LAGER 4.6% ABV • Dark lager • Deep brown in color, with a malty, sweet toffee mantle wrung from its astute blend of malts.

GAMBRINUS

✉ U Prazdroje 7, 304 97 Plzeň
🖰 www.gambrinus.cz

Gambrinus, or Jan Primus, is the secular patron saint of beer. The brewery that takes his name shares a malthouse, filtration facilities, and some filling lines with Pilsner Urquell (*see p.78*), although the two brewhouses are detached, so it could be argued that they are separate breweries. Gambrinus is a subsidiary of Plzeňský Prazdroj, which is owned by global giant SABMiller.

PREMIUM 5.0% ABV • Pale lager Sweetly malty with a fresh grass aroma, lemon; touches of butteriness with moderate bitterness emerging from its full flavor and a minty hop aftertaste.

SVĚTLÝ 4.7% ABV • Pale lager • Has a honeyish, grassy aroma with a malt and vanilla palate and a bitter conclusion.

HEROLD

✉ 262 72 Březnice
🖰 www.heroldbeer.com

Beer has been brewed in Březnice since the 15th century, and the Baroque castle that the Herold brewery occupies is fully restored in a program that began in 1720. After modernization in 1906, the brewery was even able to generate its own electricity. Herold was nationalized in 1945, and assigned to the

Municipality of Březnice, after which ownership passed between large brewing groups. In 1998, American investment revitalized its fortunes and product quality increased immensely.

TRADITIONAL CZECH LAGER 4.1% ABV • Pale lager Known as "the working person's workhorse beer." Has a light herbal hop aroma and light malt background that progresses via dryness and smoothness to a spritzy hop finish.

BOHEMIAN BLACK LAGER 5.3% ABV • Dark lager Some vanilla creaminess in the distinct four-malt character and an oily richness, with bitter chocolate flavors and a cedary, dry finish.

BOHEMIAN WHEAT BEER 5.1% ABV • Wheat beer • A clever twist on the classic Bavarian style. Perfumed hop flavor with apple notes and an unusually full body advancing to a dry finish.

KOZEL

✉ Ringhofferova 1, 251 69 Velké Popovice
🖰 www.beer-kozel.cz

GAMBRINUS
PREMIUM

The history of Velkopopovický Kozel can be traced back to the 15th century, but it did not really grow commercially until purchased by the Ringhoffer family, who installed new equipment in 1874. Modernization and expansion followed, along with exports to Germany. By 1934, Kozel was the third-largest brewer in the country but was nationalized in 1945. Following Czech independence, Kozel merged with Plzeňský Prazdroj in 1999 and shortly afterward became part of SABMiller.

KOZEL
PREMIUM

PREMIUM 4.8% ABV • Pale lager Intensely hoppy and sparkling with a fine balance of malt and a pleasant bitterness.

DARK BEER 3.8% ABV • Dark lager • Ruby-colored with an unusual dark head. Aromatic hops dominate the fragrance and dark malt influences its bitterness and caramel-tinged flavor.

KRUŠOVICE

✉ 270 53 Krušovice 1
🖰 www.pivo-krusovice.cz

Founded in 1517 and purchased by Emperor Rudolf II in 1581 for the Czech crown, Krušovice is now owned by a corporation whose major shareholder, Binding Brauerei (now Radeberger) of Frankfurt, invested capital that allowed a tripling of output. Much prestige was attached to the brewery's regular delivery of beer to the office of Václav Havel, president of the Czech Republic until 2003.

IMPERIAL 5.5% ABV • Pale lager Light golden in color with a dry straw aroma. Its deliciously bitter and sharp palate is balanced by a floral hop and malt finish.

DARK BEER 3.8% ABV • Dark lager • Has a light hop aroma that continues into the flavor, where roast malt and caramel meet earthy and nut nuances before fading into a citrus-hoppy finale.

OSTRAVAR

✉ Hornopolní 57, 728 25 Ostrava 1
🖰 www.ostravar.cz

The Czech Joint Stock Brewery was founded in 1896 and financed by local capital. Its brewing recipes are still closely guarded secrets handed down through several generations of brewmasters. A complete overhaul was undertaken in

1968 and a new high-capacity brewhouse came onstream in 1987. In 1997 Ostravar became part of the Pražské Pivovary company and, later, global giant InBev.

PREMIUM 5.1% ABV • **Pale lager** • A rich head; malt and leafy hop aroma; full-bodied, with a robust bitter bite that eases off on the aftertaste.

KELT 4.8% ABV • **Stout** • A dark Irish-style stout with pronounced hop and roasted barley aromas that continue on the palate, joined by hints of chocolate and licorice and a bitter and exceptionally dry aftertaste.

PILSNER URQUELL

✉ U Prazdroje 7, 304 97 Plzeň
🖰 www.pilsner-urquell.com

October 5, 1842 is etched in beer-lovers' minds as the day that the original pilsner was first produced. At that time lagers were brown in color, but a Bavarian brewer, Josef Grolle, who was hired to run a new "citizen's brewery" in Plzeň, created a fresh, golden brew that was a sensation.

The Plzeňský Prazdroj company now produces one-fifth of the country's beer and is its biggest exporter. The triumphal stone arch above the brewery entrance is just about the only historic part of the brewery to remain; its massive, iconic, wooden brewing vessels have been replaced by stainless steel versions, which some believe has affected flavor, although Urquell remains one of the world's great beers. The company is now owned by SABMiller, an international group that also controls Radegast, Kozel, and Gambrinus.

PILSNER URQUELL 4.4% ABV • **Pale lager** • An elegant, full-flavored, and clean lager with ripe bitterness and a herbal hop dryness. Its flowery, spicy aroma is well balanced by a delicious flavor of soft barley malt.

PILSNER URQUELL

PLATAN

✉ Pivovarská 1, 398 12 Protivín
🖰 www.pivo-platan.cz

Owing its name to an avenue of plane trees that leads to the brewery, Platan is based in South Bohemia on a site where brewing has been practiced since 1598. The Schwarzenberg family bought it in 1711 and built a new plant in 1876. By 2006, output had reached 10.5m gallons (400,000 hectoliters). Platan produces the strongest Czech beer, Schwarzenberské Knížecí 21° (10.5% ABV).

JUBILEJNÍ 5.0% ABV • **Pale lager** Subtle malt and distinct hop aromas with fruit and grain influencing the flavor, touched off by toasted nuts and a vanilla and honey sweetness.

JEDENÁCT 4.9% ABV • **Pale lager** • A lightness of aroma and cornlike delicacy on the palate; finishes sharp and clean.

RADEGAST

✉ 739 51 Nošovice
🖰 www.radegast.cz

The most modern brewery in the Czech Republic, Radegast was founded by the state, producing its first brew in 1970. Ecological awareness is high in this protected area of Beskydy, and Radegast—named after a folkloric god of hospitality and fertility—is a conscientious producer; it was the first Czech brewery to receive an ISO9002 certificate—a demanding industrial quality standard. The company has been part of the Plzeňský Prazdroj conglomerate since 2001.

ORIGINAL 4.0% ABV • **Pale lager** A light malt and spice hop nose with a crisp, grainy bitterness and long hop finish.

PREMIUM 5.0% ABV • **Pale lager** Pale gold in color; a characteristic herbal hoppy aroma, good bitterness, and medium malt intensity straying into caramel notes.

REGENT

✉ Trocnovské 124, 379 01 Třeboň
🖰 www.pivovar-regent.cz

Founded in 1379, Regent is one of the world's oldest breweries. It received its current name from Jakub Krčín, 16th-century regent of Rosenberg. By the 18th century, the original old castle brewery was struggling to cope with demand and a new brewery was created in 1712, with a further rebuild in the late 19th century.

Regent was nationalized in 1945 and became a cooperative before being privatized in 1992. It has been owned by brothers Ferdinand and Václav Stasek since 2000.

BOHEMIA REGENT LAGER PALE 5.0% ABV • **Pale lager** A floral aroma with a hint of cinnamon spice and a sparkling, rich barley malt and toffee palate with hints of honey slipping into a gentle and dry hop finish.

BOHEMIA REGENT LAGER PALE

STAROPRAMEN

✉ Nádražní 84, 150 54 Prague 5
🖰 www.staropramen.com

Staropramen began brewing on the banks of the Vltava River in 1871, in what was Prague's industrial quarter—where demand was assured. From the start, it was perceived as a Czech brewery producing Czech beer, giving it an advantage with nationalist consumers. This image was enhanced in 1880, when Emperor Franz Joseph praised Staropramen beer and signed the brewery's visitor book in Czech rather than German.

Much reconstruction took place in the 1930s, including the building of a four-vessel brewhouse, and the company was nationalized in 1945. From 1994, the British company Bass made significant updates, and the business is now controlled by global giant InBev, producing an annual 37m gallons (1.4m hectoliters.)

STAROPRAMEN PREMIUM LAGER

🍺 **PREMIUM LAGER 5.9% ABV •**
Pale lager • Deep golden in color, its rich hoppy aroma and bite unveils a full-bodied, smooth thirst-quencher with a finish known as "*riz*" (just right).

🍺 **DARK 4.4% ABV • Dark lager**
Deep in color but light in body, soft and smooth, with sweetish caramel notes and some malty licorice and aniseed; an underlying floral hop flavor to the finish.

U FLEKŮ

✉ **Křemencova 11, 110 01 Prague 1**
🖰 **www.ufleku.cz**

Without doubt the most famous brewpub in the country, U Fleků was founded in 1499. A dining hall, stylish furnishings, traditional decoration, and a picturesque courtyard make it a point of pilgrimage. Many of the brewery's unusual features, such as stacked cooling vats and oak fermenters, were modernized in a 1986 refurbishment. A small museum displays beer artefacts and traces the history of brewing.

🍺 **FLEKOVSKY TMAVY LEZÁK**
5.5% ABV • Dark lager • A classic Czech dark lager. Unfiltered and complex, its roasted coffee and cream aromas blend into a bitter palate with spicy hop, raisin, and licorice flavors.

ŽATEC

✉ **Žižkovo 81, 438 01 Žatec**
🖰 **www.zateckypivovar.cz**

Žatec (Saaz in German) is famed worldwide for the quality of its hops, which have been produced locally since the 10th century, according to documentary evidence. The Society of Privileged Brewers was established in Žatec in 1261, and its beers were in demand by the nobility, being praised for their "essence, strengths, and virtues" in a tract that dates from 1585.

By the 18th century, there were 30 malt houses and four breweries in Žatec. A new brewery began production in the town's ruined castle in 1800, and was gradually modernized. Significant investment under entrepreneurial ownership has allowed this brewery's ancient open fermentation vessels to be refurbished, funded a brewhouse update, and built a high-tech bottling and kegging plant.

🍺 **BLUE LABEL 4.6% ABV • Pale lager •** Light golden, with a sweet malt aroma and a hint of grassy hops. A complex flavor with some banana fruit emerging from a biscuit malt base on to an understated hop finish.

🍺 **EXPORT 4.6% ABV • Pale lager**
Bready aroma and herbal nuances, with some malt on the flavor and an apple sourness with bitter honey piquancy steering toward an all-too-delicate spicy hop bitterness.

SOMETHING FOR THE LADIES?

Not all Czech beers are pilsner-style. Dark beers (*černé*) and light ones (*světlé*) are very popular, with some of the best examples coming from Kozel, Herold, and Krušovice. Because of their relatively low alcohol content, dark beers are often referred to as "ladies' beers." According to the experts, the best temperature to drink them is between 45 and 50°F (7 and 10°C). The 1987, Oscar-nominated Czech film, *My Sweet Little Village*—also voted the country's favorite comedy movie ever—reveals the best way to ensure the beer's correct temperature: by storing it on the seventh step down to the cellar.

This dark beer from the Kozel brewery in Velké Popovice, near Prague, may look as if it packs a punch, but in fact is just 3.8% ABV.

GERMANY

Germany has more breweries than any other country in the world, with around 1,300 in active production. Born of a rich beermaking heritage, the country's 15–20 classic styles range from the smoked rauchbier of Franconia to the acidic weissbier of Berlin.

Beer has played a key role in German life for centuries. It once formed part of mystic rituals, such as drinking to the ancient gods, in which the firmament was interpreted as a large brewing kettle presided over by Thor, the head brewer of Valhalla. Thunder was thought to be the sound of the kettle being cleaned.

A little mysticism lingers to this day, especially concerning the right way to dispense beers. Many German beer aficionados maintain that a pilsner takes seven minutes to pour properly. There is no evidence that this practice improves the quality of the beer (on the contrary, the beer gets stale if you pour it too slowly), nor do any records exist of the "seven-minute rule" being mentioned anywhere before 1970. Nevertheless, this belief is widespread and firmly linked to the more conventional idea that a beer should look great. In Germany, beers are expected to have a big, stable head that leaves traces of lace in the glass.

Pilsner is the most popular beer style in Germany, accounting for about two-thirds of the country's total output. Almost all large breweries—with the notable exception of the wheat-beer specialists of Bavaria—brew one or more pilsners. So do most brewpubs, known in Germany as *Gasthausbrauerei*, although unlike their counterparts in other countries their output is styled after the standard products of industrial breweries. Almost every *Gasthausbrauerei* brews a more or less hoppy pilsner and a dunkel (dark lager), and many also produce a hefeweizen.

Lesser-known beer styles tend to be confined to specific regions: Cologne's kölsch (*see p.53*), the altbiers of the towns along the Rhine River, and the Berliner weisse style (*see p.43*) are the last remnants of a tradition of diversity that dates from the time when every town in Germany had its own unique beer style. In 1614, Heinrich Knaust wrote one of the earliest books on German beer, in which he listed more than 120 distinct German beer styles. Virtually all of them are now extinct: there is no "benichen" beer in Lüneburg any more, no "schluntz" in Erfurt, and no trace of a beer named "Israel" in Lübeck. Knaust was not only a seasoned traveler who made pilgrimages to a great number of breweries, but also a philosopher. He described the "Israel" style as a wheat beer so strong that the drinker's body had to wrestle with it as the biblical patriarch Jacob did with an angel.

Beer gardens are a common sight all across Germany. The brewer's coat of arms, flags, and a brewery logo point the way.

Munich and the south

Augsburg • Erding • Regensburg • Rosenheim • Traunstein

Think of Germany, and it is hard not to think of the beer culture of Bavaria. Brimming liter steins, oompah bands, exuberant festivals, and the Alps as a towering backdrop all contribute to its massive proportions —which to the locals are as natural as going to church on Sundays.

To tell the truth, it is not only foreigners who believe that all German beer culture has its roots here. Many Germans living north of the rivers Main and Danube consider Bavaria and Swabia, to the south of the rivers, to be beer paradise. This corner of Germany – Bavaria in its pre-1806 boundaries – is the region where weissbier was invented; where the climate makes beer gardens more attractive than in the cooler provinces in the north; and where every village has its Volksfest, or people's festival.

A Volksfest thanks God for his expansive generosity, and embraces it. Hundreds, often thousands of villagers link arms, sway, and offer up toasts, and with each "ein Prosit!" comes another Alpine spectacle – teams of rosy-cheeked barmaids bearing huge, frothing beer steins. The village brewery will have made a Festbier for the occasion. It may be a little stronger than the usual brew, or have been matured for a little longer— possibly without a commensurate increase in price, if the brewer wishes to thank customers for their loyalty through the year. Germans love their local beers, which in other countries are so often stupidly overlooked in favor of heavily advertised national brands. A local beer is likely to be more individualistic, with fewer concessions to scale, and surely will be fresher. Even the biggest festival of them all, Munich's huge Oktoberfest, offers only one style of beer, strictly from the city's own half-dozen or so big breweries, to its six million visitors.

The parade of decorated brewers' drays marks the start of Munich's Oktoberfest, and the tapping of the first barrels of Oktoberfestbiers.

ALTENMÜNSTER

✉ Allgäuer Bräuhaus, Schwendener Straße 18, 87616 Marktoberdorf

🖰 www.allgaeuer-brauhaus.de

Allgäuer, formerly in Kempten, moved production to the former Sailerbräu of Marktobersdorf in 2003—a modern brewing plant with historic roots. Founded in 1453, Sailerbräu specialized in the production of more or less historic beers; for some time they even produced a stone beer. The brewery now produces the Altenmünster range of beers, sold nationwide in flip-top bottles by the Radeberger group.

🍺 **BRAUER BIER URIG WÜRZIG** 4.9% ABV • Bavarian helles Golden lager; malty, somewhat fruitcake-like nose; mild taste with medium body; a hint of bitterness in the aftertaste.

🍺 **JUBELBIER** 5.5% ABV • Fest-märzen • Dark reddish-brown; a hint of coffee in the nose; medium body, rich in toasty flavors without apparent sweetness; mild bitterness in a very dry aftertaste, with no taste or aroma of hops.

ALTENMÜNSTER JUBELBIER

ANDECHSER

✉ Klosterbrauerei Andechs, Bergstraße 2, 82346 Andechs

🖰 www.andechs.de/brauerei/

The Benedictine abbey of Andechs is a prominent landmark on Bavaria's "sacred hilltop" south of Munich—its Baroque church attracts as many pilgrims as the nearby brewery tap, the Bräustübl. Brewing in the cloister dates back to 1455 but only in the last 25 years have Andechser beers become widely available. The bock beers have made the brewery famous—but they are not available on tap on weekends.

🍺 **BERGBOCK HELL** 6.9% ABV • Bock • Intense gold; a hint of orange peel in the nose; full-bodied, well balanced; some fruity (dried apricot?) aromas to finish.

🍺 **DOPPELBOCK DUNKEL** 7.1% ABV • Doppelbock • Reddish-brown; English Christmas-cakelike aroma; roasted malts and a subtle fruity sweetness, then a cocoalike bitterness and a dry aftertaste.

APOSTELBRÄU

✉ Eben 11–13, 94051 Hauzenberg

🖰 www.apostelbraeu.de/

A small family brewery north of Passau in easternmost Bavaria, Apostelbräu focuses on beers brewed from spelt. Spelt was called "the best and warmest of all cereals" by the saint and visionary Hildegard of Bingen—who has many followers in Germany—inspiring the Hirz family to start developing brewing recipes for these specialty beers in 1990. Although many experts told them that spelt was not suitable for brewing, Rudolf Hirz has proved them wrong and made the beer a huge success.

🍺 **DINKEL NATURTRÜB** 4.8% ABV • Unfiltered ale • Reddish-golden; fruitcake and lemon zest aromas; medium body, very soft mouthfeel, and a hint of pineapple; no apparent bitterness.

AUERBRÄU

✉ Münchener Straße 80, 83022 Rosenheim

🖰 www.auerbraeu.de

Founded in 1887, Auer was taken over by Paulaner (*see p.90*) in 1984, but still has a remarkably independent brand and product portfolio. It also sponsors many local festivals, including the Rosenheimer Herbstfest, Rosenheim's much smaller version of the Oktoberfest, usually held in early September. Auer is also involved in a conservation project to protect the wood grouse that has been pictured on its logo ever since Johann Auer founded the brewery.

🍺 **ROSENHEIMER PILS** 5.0% ABV • Pilsner • Golden, with a very stable head; intense, fruity hop aroma; dry, finishing with a noble yet quite intense bitterness.

🍺 **HERBSTFEST MÄRZEN** 5.5% ABV • Fest-märzen • Pale amber; malty nose; full-bodied and not too bitter.

🍺 **ROSENHEIMER WEIZENBOCK** 7.0% ABV • Weizenbock Reddish-brown; very intense banana and grape aromas; sweet on the palate, yet enough carbonation and hops to balance; very fruity.

AUGUSTINER

✉ Landsberger Straße 31–35, 80339 Munich

🖰 www.augustiner-braeu.de

Munich's oldest brewery was founded in 1328 by Augustine monks who ran a popular tavern in the city center. Although the brewery was taken away from the church more than 200 years ago, the owners are still proud of its monastic roots—including the fact that Martin Luther himself paid a visit to the cloister in 1511 on his travels to Rome. As Luther loved beer, he very probably sampled his fellow monks' brew.

The brewery has moved twice, first to Neuhauser Straße, in what is now the city's pedestrian zone (it still maintains a popular brewery tap here), and in 1885 to its present location. Augustiner has traditionally never advertised, a practice that has earned the brewery a lot of local respect.
It produces eight different beers (including two

bock-strength brews), but its fame is based chiefly on its Edelstoff, which is more or less style-defining for Oktoberfest Spezial beers.

🍺 **EDELSTOFF** 5.6% ABV ●
Oktoberfest-märzen ● Golden, with a firm white head; fruity, citrussy hop aroma; medium body; a long-lasting malty aftertaste.

🍺 **WEISSBIER** 5.4% ABV ●
Hefeweizen ● Golden to orange, not too hazy; cloves and mint in the nose; full-bodied yet refreshing; banana and lemon in the aftertaste.

AYINGER

✉ Münchner Straße 21, 85653 Aying
🖥 www.ayinger.de

The small village of Aying, just southeast of Munich (easily reached by S-Bahn), owes its fame to this brewery and the Inselkammer family, who run not only the brewing company but also two taps with beautiful beer gardens and a folk museum. The company was founded in 1878 by Johann Liebhard; one beer garden still bears his name. The brewery was moved away from the picturesque church depicted on the label a decade ago—it is now in a modern building that also houses a company museum. The beer range has changed a lot recently, now

AYINGER CELEBRATOR

focusing on wheat beers and on the doppelbock exported as Celebrator to the USA.

🍺 **KIRTA-HALBE** 5.5% ABV ●
Unfiltered märzen ● Ayinger's Oktoberfestbier: dark amber in color, with a fruity nose reminiscent of pears. Full-bodied, with a nutty aftertaste.

🍺 **UR-WEISSE DUNKEL** 5.8% ABV ● Hefeweizen
Amber to brown, hazy. Fruity aromas, cloves and bananas; medium to full body, lots of malt aromas, yet a dry and slightly bitter aftertaste.

🍺 **WEIZENBOCK** 7.1% ABV ● Weizenbock ● Golden to orange, with lots of yeast sediment; ripe banana aroma; sweet, banana milkshake-like on the palate, then a spicy (cloves, pepper, cinnamon?) bitterness.

🍺 **CELEBRATOR** 6.7% ABV ●
Doppelbock ● Very dark brown; complex roasty notes; very full-bodied and almost sweet; toasty aromas, a hint of lard.

BÜRGERBRÄU BAD REICHENHALL

✉ Waaggasse 1–3, 83435 Bad Reichenhall
🖥 www.buergerbraeu.com

This impressive historic brewery building, dating back to 1633, sits in the town center of Bad Reichenhall in the southeasternmost corner of Germany. Murals ornament the exterior of the brewery as well as the walls of the newly renovated tap. There is a modern, easy-drinking lager under the brand name of Alpenstoff, but their more traditional beers are all called "Unser Bürgerbräu." Head-brewer Werner Kunert seems to enjoy brewing bock beers.

🍺 **ALPENSTOFF** 5.3% ABV ●
International lager ● Light copper; red apple aromas; refreshing and slightly sweet, hardly bitter.

🍺 **RUPERTUS WEIZENBOCK** 7.0% ABV ● Weizenbock
Coppery, lots of yeast deposit; lends itself to decanting. Light banana in the nose; very sweet on the palate; spicy (nutmeg?) and fruity (apricot, strawberries); a cocoalike bitter finish.

🍺 **HALLGRAFEN BOCK** 7.2% ABV ● Bock ● Deep golden; sweet and fruity aroma; full-bodied, with hints of apple strudel and almonds; very well balanced with an aromatic bitterness.

🍺 **SUFFIKATOR** 7.3% ABV ● Doppelbock
Intense copper-red; aromas of sandalwood and a hint of burned rubber; full-bodied, with warming alcohol rather than sweetness; dry bitterness and nutty flavors in the aftertaste.

BÜRGERBRÄU BAD REICHENHALL SUFFIKATOR

DEIL

✉ Babenhauser Straße 2, 89296 Osterberg
🖥 www.deil.de

This country brewery lies on the eastern (Bavarian) banks of the Iller River, which divides the states of Bavaria and Baden-Württemberg. Here, Georg Deil brews organic beers with water that is "activated" by the so-called Grander process. He claims that this gives his brewing water higher energy levels and thus gives more intensity to the taste.

🍺 **ÖKO-PILS** 4.8% ABV ● Pilsner
Dark golden; very aromatic, herbal (wormwood?) and citric nose; full-bodied and soft mouthfeel, yet bitter.

🍺 **FESTTAGSWEIZEN** 5.5% ABV ● Hefeweizen ● Dark golden, only slightly hazy; quite full-bodied but still refreshing, with a hint of citrus zest in the aftertaste. There are bananalike aromas, but not too overwhelming, and the full body maintains a perfect

WEISSBIER AND THE REINHEITSGEBOT

Even though wheat beer, or weissbier, is the regional specialty of Bavaria, it does not feature at Munich's Oktoberfest. The reasons for this can be traced back some 500 years, to the passing of Germany's most famous brewing law, the "purity requirement" or Reinheitsgebot.

Five hundred years ago, brewing beer from wheat was such a common practice in Germany that it actually led to food shortages, as brewers competed with bakers to secure supplies of the grain. To restore order, on April 23, 1516 Duke Wilhelm IV of Bavaria enforced the so-called "Reinheitsgebot," which made it illegal for brewers to use any other cereal than barley—which is not suitable for baking bread—for their beers. (Such is the nature of privilege, however, that the Duke exempted himself from his own law, granting himself, and the subsequently built Hofbräuhaus, or court brewery, the exclusive right to brew wheat beer in Bavaria.) However, the Reinheitsgebot also forbade the use of any other ingredients but water, malted barley, and hops in bottom-fermented beers, thus excluding not only fruits and spices, but also all manner of more dubious ingredients commonly added to beer, such as nettles and mushrooms. This gave Bavarian beers a guarantee of purity that was a distinct commercial advantage, and so the law was soon adopted throughout Germany.

Brewing with wheat was legalized again in the early 19th century, and the Reinheitsgebot is no longer enforced—allowing specialties such as fruit beers to be "legal" once more—but its legacy nevertheless is German beer's proud reputation for purity and quality.

Munich's Hofbräuhaus, a lively tavern, was once Bavaria's state brewery, and the only one in the region licensed to brew wheat beer.

balance between malty sweetness and acidity.

WEIHNACHTSBIER 5.8% ABV • Fest-märzen • Light amber, with aromas of frankincense and banana peel, this lager is surprisingly dry and spicy without apparent sweetness and just a hint of bitterness in the aftertaste.

ERDINGER WEISSBRÄU

✉ Lange Zeile 1 + 3, 85435 Erding
🖱 www.erdinger.com

The world's largest wheat-beer brewery was founded in 1886 when wheat beer—freed from the prohibition of the Reinheitsgebot (*see p.85*) but still out of style—became popular again. Although Erdinger was well established in its local market, by the 1960s all its wheat-beer business was still more or less local—and it was declining, too. Undeterred, owner Werner Brombach ran national advertising campaigns in the early 1970s promoting wheat beer as the typical style for Bavarian beer. At that time few breweries spent much on marketing, and Brombach's campaigns made a big impact. Erdinger is ubiquitous now—although the flagship product has lost some of its character on the way to becoming an international brand.

WEISSBIER MIT FEINER HEFE 5.3% ABV • Hefeweizen
Opaque straw color; just a hint of banana and cloves; highly carbonated; medium body with very little aroma; low bitterness in the aftertaste.

PIKANTUS 7.3% ABV • Weizenbock • Dark brown; very low banana aroma, a hint of roasted nuts; refreshing and still sweet, chocolatey and slightly alcoholic. Peppery, spicy aftertaste with a lingering malty sweetness.

ERDINGER WEISSBRÄU WEISSBIER MIT FEINER HEFE

FÜRST WALLERSTEIN

✉ Berg 78, 86757 Wallerstein
🖱 www.fuerst-wallerstein.de

The brewery of the Duke of Oettingen-Wallerstein has a history of more than 400 years. It is situated in a castle complex near the small medieval town of Nördlingen. Duke Wallerstein has built a modern visitor center into his 17th-century castle, which also has a riding hall and, of course, a restaurant.

FÜRSTEN PILS 4.9% ABV • Pilsner • Very pale golden; a hint of resin in the nose; herbal notes, refreshing and not too much body at first impression, and an intense, almost metallic bitterness in the aftertaste.

WEISSER BOCK 6.8% ABV • Weizenbock • Dark amber and very cloudy with a stinging, orchidlike smell that almost hides the banana that dominates the first sip. Very rich and sweet with hints of tropical fruits, such as pineapple and mango.

WEISSBIERPILS 5.1% ABV • Pils/weizen hybrid • Golden with an intense haze; yeasty and orange-peel aroma; highly carbonated, medium body but a dry, bitter, almost metallic aftertaste.

GRIESBRÄU ZU MURNAU

✉ Obermarkt 37, 82418 Murnau am Staffelsee
🖱 www.griesbraeu.de

Halfway between Munich and the Alps, this charming brewpub occupies the site of a brewery that operated between 1676 and 1917. The present buildings date from 1836 and contain an up-to-date hotel, a restaurant, and a beer garden.

The brewpub was opened in 2000 in the part of the complex that was formerly used as stables for cattle—some of the historic vaults can still be seen, and the brewhouse and bar fit in perfectly. Owner Michael Gilg regularly holds beer seminars and invites jazz musicians to perform in the beer garden or brewhouse.

HELLES 5.0% ABV • Bavarian helles • Golden and slightly hazy; yeast very present in the nose; light to medium body; very low bitterness.

WEISSE 5.6% ABV • Hefeweizen Amber to orange and very cloudy; clove and banana aromas; fruity sweetness, high carbonation, and some bitterness in the aftertaste.

HOFBRÄUHAUS MÜNCHEN

✉ Staatliches Hofbräuhaus, Hofbräualle 1, 81829 Munich
🖱 www.hofbraeu-muenchen.de

The Hofbräuhaus am Platzl in downtown Munich prides itself on being the best-known tavern in Europe, and is visited by thousands of tourists every day. The present building was constructed in 1897 on the site of the old brewery, while brewing operations were relocated to the suburb of Riem. The Hofbräuhaus München is still owned by the Bavarian state. Its history dates back to 1589 when Duke Wilhelm V built a brewery to supply his household and court servants. From 1602 to 1806 this brewery held a state monopoly for brewing wheat beer (which it then licensed to other court breweries). Head-brewer Elias Pichler was the first to brew Bavarian bock beer, in 1614.

ORIGINAL 5.1% ABV • Bavarian helles • Golden; malty nose; very mild

FÜRST WALLERSTEIN FÜRSTEN PILS

on the palate, medium body, creamy mouthfeel, and just a hint of hops.

SCHWARZE WEISSE 5.1% ABV • Hefeweizen • Dark brown and very hazy; cloves, banana, caramel in the nose; full-bodied with roasty notes but still refreshing owing to the high carbonation.

HOFBRÄUHAUS TRAUNSTEIN

✉ Hofgasse 6–11, 83278 Traunstein

🖰 www.hb-ts.de

Traunstein's former state brewery, founded in 1612 to brew wheat beer, was at one time extremely profitable for the Bavarian court, as it supplied the workers of the local salt refinery—which the court also owned. The staff of the salt works numbered nearly 200—and one can imagine that it must have been thirsty work! In 1806 this brewery was one of the first of several dozen Bavarian Hofbräus to be privatized when the state monopoly on wheat-beer-brewing ended. In 1896 the brewery was bought by the Sailer family, which still runs it today. They have not only been extremely successful with exports but have also founded several brewpubs, including Lindenbräu in Berlin's Sony Center.

WEISSBIER LEICHT 3.3% ABV • Hefeweizen • Pale golden with a lot of yeast deposit; fruity, orchidlike nose; refreshing, dry and spicy, clove aromas coming through in the finish. No apparent bitterness.

DUNKEL 5.3% ABV • Dark lager Dark copper; chocolate aromas; refreshing, fruity (a hint of apricot) and a smooth mouthfeel that smacks of milk chocolate.

EXPORT-HELLES 5.3% ABV • Bavarian helles • Golden; aromas of summer flowers

and herbs; medium to dry body; hint of apple to finish.

FÜRSTENTRUNK 5.7% ABV • Fest-märzen • Golden; a fruity hop aroma and distinctive bitterness balances the almost sweet overall impression.

KALTENBERG

✉ Schlossstraße 8, 82269 Geltendorf-Kaltenberg

🖰 www.kaltenberg.de

Part of this brewery is situated in the castle of Prince Luitpold von Bayern in Kaltenberg (the other part, including production of the wheat beers, is in Fürstenfeldbruck).

HOFBRÄUHAUS MÜNCHEN SCHWARZE WEISSE

Every summer the castle grounds are the stage for one of the largest re-enactments of a medieval tournament, with thousands of guests dressed in historic costumes—and of course large quantities of beer drunk to hail the host. Until fairly recently the royal brewery produced three brands—Kaltenberg, Prinzregent Luitpold, and König Ludwig. The last name was originally applied only to their dark beer, but it has now been selected as brand name for a premium range.

KÖNIG LUDWIG DUNKEL 5.1% ABV • Dark lager Mahogany laced with light brown; roasty malt aroma, with faint cocoa and toffee. Medium body and lots of roastiness; dry finish with very little hop character.

KÖNIG LUDWIG WEISSBIER HELL 5.5% ABV • Hefeweizen • Golden with intense haze; clove and banana aromas; smooth and full body; finishes with a hint of hoppy bitterness.

RITTERBOCK 9.0% ABV • Doppelbock • Dark reddish-brown, no head; intense

chocolate aroma; medium bitterness without sweetness; warming alcohol, yet roasty and dry in the aftertaste.

LÖWENBRÄU

✉ Nymphenburger Straße 7, 80335 Munich

🖰 www.loewenbraeu.de

After several mergers (with Spaten-Franziskaner and Interbrew), Löwenbräu has become part of the InBev group. The brewery claims to date back to 1383, although the name Löwenbräu was not registered in brewing records until 1746–7. Löwenbräu's real success story began with Georg Brey, who bought the company in 1818 and made it the first and largest industrial-scale brewery in Munich. Löwenbräu was the first privately owned brewery in town to brew bock beer (in 1848); a marketing pioneer, it registered the lion trademark in 1886; and it was the first to brew more than 26m gallons (1m hectolitres) a year, in 1928. It was also quick off the mark in licensing production to the USA – the license to Miller in 1974 marked a turning point in the company's history. In recent years, Löwenbräu has tried to find its way back to its roots – back to being as "original" as one of its beer names suggests.

ORIGINAL 5.2% ABV • Bavarian helles • Pale golden; a hint of pear in the nose; medium to full body; an underlying bitterness with herbal aromas in the aftertaste.

URTYP 5.4% ABV • Märzen • Golden; aromas of young wine; full-bodied and rich in herbal aromas.

KALTENBERG KÖNIG LUDWIG DUNKEL

TRIUMPHATOR 7.6% ABV • Doppelbock • Dark brown; intensely sweet malt aroma; burned malt; sweet and tasty malt flavor, little toastiness and a very alcoholic finish.

Bavarian hefeweizen, once a regional beer style from Munich and eastern Bavaria, has now become a world standard. Because of its relatively low bitterness, it is popular with younger drinkers who dislike the astringent character of highly hopped pilsners.

PAULANER

✉ Hochstraße 75, 81541 Munich
🖰 www.paulaner.de

In 1627 the Brothers of St. Francis of Paola established a monastery in Au, a suburb of Munich, and in 1634 they began to brew beer. It became a local custom for the Duke of Bavaria to drop by once a year and be handed a mug of the extremely strong "Sankt Vater Bier," or "Salvator"— and while he was drinking it, Brother Barnabas would tell him what the people of Bavaria really thought about his reign. This tradition is recalled today at the tapping of Salvator in the middle of the Lent season, and on the beer's label *(see right)*. Both cloister and brewery were secularized in 1799. There were spectacular mergers in the 20th century, first with Thomasbräu (1928), then Hacker-Pschorr (1979), and Auerbräu, Reichelbräu, and Mönchshof (1986). Today Paulaner is part of Brau Holding International, which is itself partly owned by Heineken.

🍺 **HEFEWEISSBIER NATURTRÜB**
5.5% ABV • Hefeweizen • Orange in color, extremely hazy; intensely sweet nose with

banana and spice; very full body and a finish with a hint of citrus aromas.

🍺 **SALVATOR** 7.9% ABV • Doppelbock • Reddish-brown; fig and molasses aromas; full-bodied and creamy, not too sweet; fruity aromas in the relatively dry finish. Ages very well.

PRÖSSLBRÄU

✉ Dominikanerinnenstraße 2–3, 93186 Pettendorf-Adlersberg
🖰 www.braugasthoefe.com/gasthof/proesslbraeu

This former cloister dating to 1275, on the top of the Adlersberg, just northwest of Regensburg, was acquired by the Prössl family in 1838. They now run it as a brewery with restaurant and beer garden. It is one of the few breweries that brew a doppelbock all year round —although there is a special tapping on the Sunday before Easter each year.

🍺 **PALMATOR** 6.5% ABV • Doppelbock • Dark nut-brown; sweet nutty cake, plums, and dried dates in the nose; very full-bodied with roasted malt bitterness, some coffee, and a

creamy mouthfeel; fruity and even refreshing aftertaste. Ages extremely well for many years.

PAULANER SALVATOR

RIEDENBURGER

✉ Hammerweg 5, D-93339 Riedenburg
🖰 www.riedenburger.de

Michael and Martha Krieger's small country brewery makes only organic beers with unique ingredients, some not used in Bavarian brewing for centuries. These include the lesser-known grain spelt, and also emmer and einkorn, which are ancestral varieties of wheat.

🍺 **HISTORISCHES EMMER BIER**
5.5% ABV • Strong ale • Nut-brown and very hazy; hints of plum and vanilla; very full-bodied, yet surprisingly dry aftertaste.

🍺 **EINKORN EDELBIER** 5.0% ABV • Blond ale • Golden and hazy with a sweet nose; extremely soft mouthfeel, and a touch of nutmeg and vanilla in the aftertaste.

🍺 **5-KORN-UR-BIER** 5.0% ABV • Dark ale • Dark brown; caramel and nuts in the nose; rather sweet and creamy mouthfeel; just a hint of bitterness in the aftertaste.

A SPECIALTY FOR EXPORT

A former fermentation cellar outside the city of Kelheim holds a special secret: Georg Schneider keeps hundreds of crates of his famous Aventinus there, maturing slowly before being shipped to the USA. This is the result of an initiative by German-born Matthias Neidhard, who imports specialty beers into the USA for B. United International. Some of them— vintage Aventinus and Wiesen Edel-Weisse, as well as Uerige Doppelsticke and Berliner Style Weisse—are only available outside Germany, because a matured weizenbock or an intensely hopped hefeweizen are much more intense than the average German palate would tolerate.

Specialist importers B. United International bring distinctive beers to the USA, such as bottle-aged Aventinus from Schneider Weisse *(facing page)*.

RIEGELE

✉ Frölichstraße 26, 86150 Augsburg
🖰 www.riegele.de

This brewery, close to Augsburg's main train station, was founded in 1386 as "Zum Goldenen Roß" ("The Golden Horse"). It was bought by the Riegele family in 1884, who built the Art Deco brewhouse in 1911. Riegele brews a relatively broad spectrum of beers and aims to educate its customers about different beer styles.

🍺 **RIEGELE LEICHTE WEISSE** 2.9% ABV • Hefeweizen
Opaque straw color; intense clove aroma; surprisingly full-bodied; dry aftertaste.

🍺 **COMMERZIENRAT RIEGELE'S WEISSE** 5.0% ABV • Hefeweizen
Pale and hazy; banana and other tropical fruit (mango? pineapple?) in the nose; refreshing, some bitterness in the aftertaste.

🍺 **RIEGELE ALTE WEISSE** 5.0% ABV • Hefeweizen • Nut-brown; strong banana-peel aroma; spicy and refreshing while still full-bodied and even sweet in the aftertaste.

🍺 **RIEGELE FEINES URHELL** 4.7% ABV • Bavarian helles
Straw-colored; fruity (honeydew melon) aromas; full-bodied yet refreshing; fruity aftertaste.

🍺 **AUGSBURGER HERREN PILS** 4.7% ABV • Pilsner • Golden in color, with a big head; pineapple-like hop aromas; soft and mild mouthfeel. Quite full-bodied, with a refreshing bitterness in the aftertaste.

🍺 **RIEGELE SPEZIATOR DOPPELBOCK** 7.5% ABV • Doppelbock • Dark brown; earthy malt aromas in the nose; sweet and fruity aromas (dried cherries, fresh figs) in the balanced mouthfeel; a spicy, hoppy aftertaste.

SCHLOSSBRAUEREI HERRNGIERSDORF

✉ Schlossallee 5, 84097 Herrngiersdorf
🖰 www.schlossbrauerei-herrngiersdorf.de

With a founding date of 1131, this small family business is considered to be the oldest surviving privately owned brewery in the world. Paul Pausinger and his wife Petra maintain the old traditions, including open fermentation—but they also try new marketing strategies. Their black lager beer, "Publiner," is aimed at a young clientele that would normally drink stouts in the (admittedly scarce) Irish pubs in the

SCHLOSSBRAUEREI HERRNGIERSDORF TRAUSNITZ PILS

Hallertau area, Bavaria's hop-growing region. This and the Sündenbock are also used in liqueurs. The brewery regularly participates in festivals that have to do with hops.

🍺 **TRAUSNITZ PILS** 5.2% ABV • Pilsner • Named after a castle in the nearby town of Landshut, this pils has an intense hoppy nose, a medium body, and a herbal, spinach- and romaine lettucelike bitterness.

🍺 **HURAXDAX** 5.3% ABV • Hefeweizen • The name of this wheat beer in a local dialect means "brisk" or "verve;" it shows a lot of haze, an intense clove and some banana aroma, very mild carbonation, and a lingering hop-bitterness.

🍺 **SÜNDENBOCK** 7.3% ABV • Bock • The Publiner's stronger version: reddish-black, with a very stable head; some roasted malts in the nose; roasty bitterness, but just a hint of sweetness on the palate. Dry and toasty aftertaste.

SCHLOSSBRAUEREI UNTERBAAR

✉ Hauptstraße 18, 86674 Baar
🖰 www.schlossbrauerei-unterbaar.de

This brewery has 1608 as its official founding date, but it may actually be 100 years older: the oldest brewing privilege for Unterbaar dates from November 24, 1508. The castle seems to have brewed ever since. In 1962 Otto Philipp Freiherr Groß von Trockau bought the brewery and modernized it—also constructing a new production line for wheat beers in 1969.

🍺 **DUNKLES WEIZEN** 5.5% ABV • Hefeweizen • Copper-red; a hint of peach and gooseberry in the nose; very refreshing and surprisingly hoppy.

🍺 **ALTBAYERISCHES NATURTRÜBES HEFEWEIZEN** 5.7% ABV • Hefeweizen • Pale amber; very intense aromas (ripe banana, jellybeans, cloves); full-bodied and sweet on the palate, but still refreshing; dry aftertaste.

🍺 **ANNO 2000** 5.7% ABV • Fest-märzen • Golden, very stable head; caramel in the nose; full-bodied with an almost creamy texture; nutty, but not too intense bitterness in the aftertaste.

🍺 **MÄRZEN** 5.7% ABV • Märzen • Pale amber, stable head; leather and pears in the nose; full-bodied, slightly sweet, with just a little bitterness to balance.

SCHNEIDER WEISSE

✉ Emil-Ott-Straße 1–5, 93309 Kelheim
🖰 www.schneider-weisse.de

The history of Schneider Weisse begins at the Hofbräuhaus in Munich (see p.86) where Georg Schneider I was head-brewer in 1855. This was a time when wheat beer was not too

SCHNEIDER WEISSE ORIGINAL

AVENTINUS 8.2% ABV • Weizen/doppelbock • Dark chestnut color; banana and cocoa aromas; spicy fruitiness, almost refreshing owing to high carbonation, though the warmth in the mouthfeel is a reminder of its alcoholic strength. No apparent bitterness.

SPATEN-FRANZISKANER

✉ Marsstraße 46–48, 80335 Munich

🖰 www.spatenbraeu.de; www.franziskaner-weissbier.de

Spaten-Franziskaner, now part of the global brewing group InBev (along with former local rival Löwenbräu), started as a brewery close to (but not owned by) the Franciscan cloister in Munich in 1361. In 1927 it merged with the Spaten Brewery, one of the big 19th-century success stories in Munich brewing. Spaten's owner Gabriel Sedlmayr Jr. traveled to the leading breweries in Bohemia and Great Britain, along with Anton Dreher of Schwechater in Vienna and Georg Lederer of Nürnberg. The three then modernized their breweries—embracing industrial-scale production, they installed modern maltings, and pioneered cold cellars for long maturation periods (and later, ice machines). While Franziskaner is one of the best-established wheat-beer brands, the once prominent Spaten brand seems to have disappeared in recent years.

At the Oktoberfest, liters of festbier are traditionally accompanied by a snack of Brezn, or pretzels—baked dough twists that may be salted or sugared.

popular, but Schneider believed in the product, acquired his own brewery (the former Maderbräu im Tal) in 1872, and started production under his own name, but to the historic recipe. In 1927 the Schneider family acquired the Weisses Bräuhaus in Kelheim, a former Hofbräuhaus with a 300-year history of producing wheat beer. In World War II, their brewery in Munich was heavily damaged, and all production was moved to Kelheim. In recent years the range has broadened considerably; three beers (Vintage Aventinus, Aventinus Eisbock, and the organic Wiesen Edel Weisse) are made primarily for export.

ORIGINAL 5.4% ABV • Hefeweizen • Light brown and yeasty; intense clove and banana-peel aromas in the nose; spicy fruitiness on the palate; light and refreshing, with very mild bitterness.

WEIZEN HELL 5.2% ABV • Hefeweizen • Pale and intensely hazy; intense spicy aromas; full-bodied and almost sweet, with banana aromas and just a hint of bitterness.

WIESEN EDEL WEISSE 6.2% ABV • Hefeweizen • Golden-orange, cloudy; very fruity (banana, grapefruit) in the nose. Highly carbonated, smooth on the palate, relatively bitter.

SPATEN OKTOBERFESTBIER

SPATEN OKTOBERFESTBIER 5.9% ABV • Fest-märzen • Pale amber; slightly sweet malt aromas in the nose; full-bodied and slightly sweet, mild bitterness.

FRANZISKANER HEFE WEISSBIER HELL 5.0% ABV • Hefeweizen Golden to copper; intense banana aroma; medium body with a subtle sweetness, balanced by a citrussy and dry aftertaste.

THORBRÄU

✉ Max Kuhnle GmbH & Co. KG, Wertachbrucker-Tor-Straße 9, 86152 Augsburg

🖰 www.thorbraeu.de

The name of this 425-year-old brewery has little to do with the ancient German god Thor (responsible for thunder and brewing), although the label of its "Celtic" beer seems to suggest otherwise. "Thor" stands for the old town gate near the brewery. Its owner and head-brewer Maximilian Kuhnle is reaching out to a younger clientele with a broad range of beers including the organic Celtic.

🍺 **CELTIC** 5.0% ABV • Vienna lager Rich golden color; hops and some citrus and apple in the nose; full-bodied, yet bitter in the aftertaste.

🍺 **MAXIMILIAN'S KELLERBIER** 5.5% ABV • Unfiltered lager • Hazy golden color; aromas of yeast, summer flowers, and pears; medium body, spicy bitterness in the aftertaste.

THURN UND TAXIS

✉ Am Kreuzhof 5, 93055 Regensburg

🖰 www.thurnundtaxisbiere.de

The dukes of Thurn und Taxis pioneered postal services in Europe, and when these were nationalized in the 19th century, the family bought vast quantities of land along with the industries on it. At one time at the beginning of the 20th century, they owned 120 (albeit rather small) breweries. For some time beer production was concentrated in Schierling near Kelheim, where Thurn und Taxis was the first in modern German brewing history to brew a rye beer, which changed names three times: born as Schierlinger Roggen, it was renamed Thurn und Taxis Roggen,

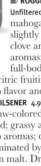

THURN UND TAXIS PILSENER

then in 2000 Paulaner Roggen. In 1996 Thurn und Taxis merged with Paulaner and most of its production was transferred to Munich and Rosenheim—yet a large brewpub remains on the site of the castle in Regensburg. In 2005 the rye beer regained the Thurn und Taxis brand name.

🍺 **ROGGEN** 5.3% ABV • Unfiltered ale • Dark mahogany, only slightly hazy; spicy, clove and ginger aromas; medium- to full-bodied, balanced by citric fruitiness and some hop flavor and bitterness.

🍺 **PILSENER** 4.9% ABV • Pilsner Straw-colored with a stable head; grassy and citruslike hop aromas; dry and dominated by hops rather than malt. Dry finish.

UNERTL MÜHLDORF

✉ Weißgerberstraße 7–15, 84453 Mühldorf am Inn

🖰 www.brauerei-unertl.de

One of two breweries with the same brand name—the Unertl family in Mühldorf is related to the one in nearby Haag. Both were founded in the late 1920s. This is the smaller concern, with a capacity of 396,000 gallons (15,000 hectolitres) compared to 660,000 (25,000), and is more adventurous —it converted over to totally organic production in 2001.

🍺 **DINKEL WEISSE** 5.2% ABV • Unfiltered ale • Hazy orange; lemon, clove, and banana aromas; light to medium body; no apparent bitterness.

🍺 **MÜHLDORFER GOURMET WEISSE** 5.5% ABV • Hefeweizen Cloudy copper color; intense banana aroma; sweet and full-bodied, creamy mouthfeel with more banana; some bitterness to balance.

WELTENBURGER KLOSTER

✉ Benediktinerabtei Weltenburg, Asamstraße 32, 3309 Kelheim/Donau

🖰 www.weltenburger.de

A small brewery in a beautifully decorated baroque Benedictine abbey on the banks of the Danube River, Weltenburg was founded by two monks, Eustasius and Agilus, followers of St. Columban—one of the patron saints of brewing. The oldest records of brewing at the cloister date back to 1050. This makes Weltenburg the oldest abbey brewery in the world. However, not all beers of the Weltenburger brand are brewed here: those labeled "Marke Weltenburger" come from the Bischofshof brewery in nearby Regensburg; those labeled "Weltenburger Kloster" are brewed here.

🍺 **URTYP HELL** 4.9% ABV • Bavarian helles • Straw-colored; creamy and malty with a medium body and a long-lasting aftertaste of caramel and hops.

🍺 **BAROCK DUNKEL** 4.7% ABV • Dark lager • Dark reddish-brown; chocolate aromas; very full body, and a toasty bitterness with little hop character.

🍺 **WINTER-TRAUM** 5.7% ABV • Fest-märzen • Light copper; vanilla and hop aromas; very full-bodied, fruity (dates and lychees) with toasted malt notes and a distinct hoppiness. Dry finish.

🍺 **ASAM BOCK** 6.9% ABV • Bock • Chestnut-brown in colour, with a chocolatey nose; intense sweetness, and a dry, cocoalike aftertaste.

WELTENBURGER KLOSTER WINTER-TRAUM

🍺 **WELTENBURGER PILS** 4.7% ABV • Pilsner Very pale straw color; perfumed, floral hop aroma; medium body, very intense hoppiness, and a dry and spicy aftertaste.

Karlsruhe and the southwest

Bitburg • Darmstadt • Frankfurt • Hornberg • Offenburg

No other region of Germany has such a great reputation for gourmet dining as the southern part of the Rhine. Here, influences from nearby Alsace and Switzerland have inspired chefs in some of Germany's most famous restaurants, and the brewers have risen to the challenge.

In the beer world, Germany's southwest has long been known for the fact that it resisted the trend toward the now all-too-common pilsners. In Baden-Württemberg the "export" style that originated in Dortmund is still more popular than pilsner, and the range of beers on offer has been broadened further still by various brands of wheat beer. This has prompted the pils-brewers here to turn to more interesting beer recipes, in order to ensure that their pilsners can be clearly differentiated from the much milder Export. As a result, the pilsners of this region tend to be hoppier and more aromatic than elsewhere in Germany.

Tettnang, the hop-growing area just north of Lake Constance, is a major supplier of hops to southwest brewers.

The aroma profile of Tettnanger hops is quite similar to that of Bohemia's famous variety, the Saaz, and this small hop-growing region has gained an international reputation in recent years, even though it is much smaller in terms of acreage, yield, and variety than the more prominent Hallertau region in Bavaria.

While no town in the region has gained as great an international reputation in the brewing world as Munich has in neighboring Bavaria, the university towns of Karlsruhe, Freiburg, Heidelberg, Tübingen, and Trier are renowned for their beer traditions. And Stuttgart plays host to Cannstadter Wasen, the local version of the Oktoberfest, which is held on a former parade ground in Stuttgart's suburb of Bad Cannstadt.

The town of Heidelberg was the setting for the 1920s operetta *The Student Prince*, with its famous beer-quaffing anthem, "The Drinking Song."

BADISCHE STAATSBRAUEREI ROTHAUS

✉ Rothaus 1, 79865 Grafenhausen
🖰 www.rothaus.de

Founded by the Benedictine monastery of St. Blasien in 1791, this brewery was nationalized only 15 years later by the then newly formed state of Baden. Built on a 3,000 ft (1,000 m) mountain in the Black Forest, it is the highest brewery in Germany. In recent years it has expanded considerably, and now has an output of 24.2m gallons (915,000 hecto-liters)—and is proud to have no advertising budget: they have a loyal clientele, especially among students.

🍺 **TANNENZÄPFLE PILS**
5.1% ABV • Pilsner • Rothaus likes to add "Zäpfle" ("cone") to the name of their beers when they come in small, 330 ml bottles. Tannezäpfle ("fir-cone") is their regular pils. Very pale straw; intense, resiny (hence the name) hop aroma; light to medium body, and noble, yet intense bitterness in the aftertaste.

🍺 **EISZÄPFLE MÄRZEN EXPORT**
5.1% ABV • Märzen • The "icicle": a creamy lager with a hint of caramel and hay in the nose; full-bodied, well balanced by hops that give a spicy, almost celerylike note.

BERGBRAUEREI ULRICH ZIMMERMANN

✉ Brauhausstraße 2, 89584 Ehingen-Berg
🖰 www.bergbier.de

The Zimmermann family took over this brewery in 1757, when it had already been in existence for 313 years. They say they take time with their beers—and they prove it when they take

maturation to an extreme: on German Beer Day, April 23—the day on which reputedly the Reinheitsgebot (beer purity law) of 1516 was announced (*see p.85*)—they brew a batch that stays in the cellar for 120 days.

🍺 **BERG ORIGINAL** 5.0% ABV •
Bavarian helles • Golden; apple strudel in the nose; full-bodied to sweet on the palate, very smooth mouthfeel, just enough hops (Hallertau Tradition) to balance.

🍺 **23.04 DAS JAHRGANGSBIER**
5.7% ABV • Fest-märzen
A strong lager, with 15.16 degrees Plato (that and the name reflect the date of the Reinheitsgebot). Golden in color, with a sweetish malt aroma. Full-bodied yet very hoppy, with herbal notes and bitterness in the aftertaste, with some nutty and citrussy aromas.

🍺 **ULRICHSBIER** 5.3% ABV •
Vienna lager • Amber to copper; malty nose; full-bodied to sweet, with a nutty bitterness in the aftertaste.

🍺 **SCHÄFLESHIMMEL** 5.6% ABV •
Unfiltered lager • A unique bottle-conditioned lager, pale golden and only slightly hazy (at least when carefully decanted); vanilla aromas in the nose; a very smooth texture with soft maltiness and a spicy, bitter aftertaste.

BERGBRAUEREI ULRICH ZIMMERMANN ULRICHSBIER

BINDING

✉ Darmstädter Landstraße 185, 60599 Frankfurt
🖰 www.binding-lager.de

Conrad Binding, a cooper and brewer, acquired a brewpub in downtown Frankfurt in 1870, increased its production, and moved it to the present site in Frankfurt's southern suburb Sachsenhausen

in 1881. It functions both as a large regional brewery (which also produces Germany's best-selling non-alcoholic beer, Clausthaler) and as headquarters for the brewing arm of the Oetker group, which carries the name Radeberger Gruppe. The eagle displayed on the Binding label has the same shape as the one on a fountain near the "Römer," Frankfurt's city hall. Binding acquired the Schöfferhofer brewery of Mainz in 1921.

🍺 **RÖMER PILSENER** 4.9% ABV •
Pilsner • Golden, with a malty, vanillalike aroma; well-balanced bitterness and a spicy, slightly herbal hoppy aftertaste.

🍺 **SCHÖFFERHOFER DUNKLES HEFEWEIZEN** 5.0% ABV •
Hefeweizen • Copper-colored with some haze; banana and pear aromas; medium body, with a nutty aftertaste.

BISCHOFF

✉ An den Hopfengärten 6, 67722 Winnweiler
🖰 www.bischoff-bier.de

Christian Bischoff started his brewery in a small barn in Winnweiler in 1866—at a time when a large part of what is now the state of Rhineland-Palatinate still belonged to Bavaria. The address, "An den Hopfengärten," suggests that he had a local hop supply when he moved the brewery to the present location in 1884. The brewery, still family-owned, has been modernized; some parts of the former installation are preserved in a small museum on site. The Bischoff family also owns a brewpub in downtown Kaiserslautern, which is used as a pilot brewery for specialty brews such as their Rauchbier.

🍺 **PREMIUM PILSENER**
4.7% ABV • Pilsner
Golden, with a floral

BINDING RÖMER PILSENER

aroma; medium body with very distinctive floral hop taste, but comparably little hop bitterness.

FALKENSTEINER UR-WEISSE
5.2% ABV • Hefeweizen • Amber with a lot of haze; tangerine aromas; sweet yet refreshing and fruity on the palate; no apparent bitterness.

DOPPELBOCK 7.5% ABV • Doppelbock • Dark brown; chocolate aromas; medium-bodied, intensely hoppy, with a long, lingering bitterness.

BITBURGER

✉ Bitburger Brauerei Th. Simon, Brauereistraße, 54634 Bitburg
🖰 www.bitburger.de

A single-product brewery with an output of 110m gallons (4.19m hectoliters)—and flagship of Germany's third-largest brewing empire, which also encompasses König Pilsner, Köstritzer, Licher, and Wernesgrüner. Bitburger Pils is the best-selling kegged beer in Germany; the brewery claims to have 42,000 accounts for tap beer. In spite of its size, Bitburger has been a family business ever since it was founded in 1817—the Simon family has been running the brewery since 1842, when Ludwig Bertrand Simon married the daughter of

Bitburger is bottled in sloping, long-necked, and stubby bottles to suit different markets.

brewery founder Johann Peter Wallenborn. Bitburger was early in introducing a strictly focused brand personality: their well-known slogan "Bitte ein Bit" ("A Bit[burger], please") dates back to 1951; products like "Schwarzer Hahn" and Bockbier were axed in the early 1960s in favor of the Pils; and in 1964, Bitburger introduced their exclusively designed pils glass—at a time when they brewed far less than 13 million gallons (500,000 hectoliters).

PREMIUM PILS
4.8% ABV • Pilsner
Golden, with some citrus in the nose; medium body, modest bitterness, with a long-lasting grassy hop aroma.

BITBURGER
PREMIUM PILS

ENGEL BRÄU

✉ Crailsheimer Engel-Bräu, Haller Straße 29, 74564 Crailsheim
🖰 www.prostmeinengel.de

Crailsheim once had 14 breweries; this is the only survivor. Set up as a

brewpub in 1877, Engel today is modern and efficient, brewing 1.4 million gallons (55,000 hectoliters) a year. Managed by the Fach family, it is successfully handling tough competition —but still brews 20-plus beers each year (although many of these are seasonals).

WINTER BOCK 7.2% ABV • Bock
Red-brown, sweet, fruity (mango?) nose, full-bodied; chocolatelike bitterness.

FÜRSTENBERG

✉ Fürstlich Fürstenbergische Brauerei, Postplatz 1–4, 78166 Donaueschingen
🖰 www.fuerstenberg.de

This was once the private brewery of the Dukes of Fürstenberg, who ruled the area between 1283 and 1806. The family still resides in the charming little town of Donaueschingen and their brewery was only recently taken over by Brau Holding International (BHI). The bottom-fermented beers share a soft mouthfeel combined with estery notes—effects of the local Black Forest water as well as the yeast strain that is cultivated in Donaueschingen.

PREMIUM PILSENER 4.8% ABV • Pilsner • Very pale golden; grainy notes and hop flowers in the nose, estery fruitiness on the palate and a medium body; intense bitterness dominates the finish.

RIEGELER LANDBIER 5.2% ABV • Helles • Pale amber; sweet nose with hints of resin and freshly chopped wood; full-bodied, with a soft, hazelnutlike bitterness in the aftertaste.

WEIZEN HEFE HELL 5.3% ABV • Hefeweizen Golden, hazy; banana aromas; full-bodied, muffin-like sweetness with vanilla undertones; surprisingly bitter and dry finish.

GROHE

✉ Nieder-Ramstädter Straße 3, 64283 Darmstadt
🖥 www.grohe-gastro.de

This brewery in the southern part of Darmstadt was heavily damaged during World War II. Although the interior of the brewery and the brewery tap have been renovated several times since, the facade is preserved in the same rough style in which it was rebuilt in 1945, reputedly with help from guests eager to drink again the beer they had loved so much before the destruction.

PILS 4.8% ABV • Pilsner Golden-colored; a hint of butterscotch aroma and ripe pears, balanced with a robust, lingering bitterness.

HESSISCHE LÖWENBIER-BRAUEREI

✉ Brauereistraße 5, 34323 Malsfeld
🖥 www.hessisches-loewenbier.de

This impressive red-brick brewery was built in 1870. There are plans to convert part into a museum and

tourist attraction (a landing stage for rafts on the Fulda River is already operational), while beer production is still ongoing under the ownership of Frank Bettenhäuser, who rescued the brewery after it went bankrupt in 2003.

PILSNER 5.0% ABV • Pilsner Deep golden; intense, fruity hop-nose and some orange-peel aroma; medium body with plenty of hoppiness and surprisingly little bitterness.

EXPORT 5.6% ABV • Dortmunder export Golden, with a sweet, red-applelike aroma; full-bodied, with just a hint of bitterness in the aftertaste.

HEFE-WEIZEN 5.2% ABV • Hefeweizen • Golden to orange in color, quite hazy; fruity aromas (pears, morello cherries?); highly carbonated; tart and spicy in the aftertaste.

FÜRSTENBERG PREMIUM PILSENER

HIRSCH BRAUEREI HONER

✉ Friedrichstraße 34, 78573 Wurmlingen
🖥 www.hirschbrauerei.de

Several German breweries have a stag in their name and logo. This one is located east of the Black Forest in Baden-Württemberg, and is owned by the Honer family. Brewing began in 1782 and the brewery has been modernized several times, with a total reconstruction of the copper-lined brewhouse in 2006. They brew a wide range of beers, including two different, albeit not very hoppy, pilsners and an unfiltered zwicklbier.

HIRSCH HEFE WEISSE 5.2% ABV • Hefeweizen • Dark golden with some haze; banana-peel aroma in the nose; some sweetness on the palate, clove and cinnamon aromas, and a decent bitterness.

WEIHNACHTSBIER 5.2% ABV • Fest-märzen • Red-amber;

sweet, caramel-like nose; full-bodied but still balanced; has no apparent hop aroma.

HIRSCH PILS 5.0% ABV • Pilsner Golden, with caramel aromas, yet surprisingly dry and refreshing with a nutty, lingering bitterness.

HONER PILS 5.0% ABV • Pilsner Straw-colored, with a haylike aroma and a subtle bitterness that gives the beer an almost nutty character.

ZWICKL 5.2% ABV • Unfiltered lager • Opaque-golden; perfumed (nutmeg?) and flowerlike aromas; medium body; a bitterness that comes out only in the dry finish.

HOEPFNER

✉ Haid-und-Neustraße 18, 76131 Karlsruhe
🖥 www.hoepfner.de

Castlelike brewery buildings of red sandstone, dating from 1898, open their gates for a festival every spring. Hoepfner is one of the few German specialty breweries that produces its own malt and cultivates its own strains of yeast. The Hoepfner family (whose name suggests that their ancestors were hop merchants) sold the brewery to brewing conglomerate BHI in 2004—Friedrich Georg Hoepfner was

GERMAN PORTER

In the 18th and 19th centuries, English ales— and especially porters— were as popular in southern Germany as they were in the Baltic region. Porter was soon to become a premium beer style. German porter was stronger, more chocolatey, and less tart than that brewed in England. However, its popularity slumped at the outbreak of World War I, when patriotic brewers dropped "the beer with the English name" from their portfolios.

In its castellated brewery, Hoepfner calls itself "a stronghold of the art of brewing."

promoted to the BHI board. The brewery still acts independently; its culinary ventures include a porter-bread, porter-pretzels, and even a porter-cake, sold by local bakery-chain Visel.

▮ PORTER 5.8% ABV ● German porter ● Mahogany to black in color thanks to Munich, crystal, and black malts that give a smoothness wrapping the burned notes. Tettnang and Saaz hops provide noble bitterness and a lingering hop aroma.

▮ GOLDKÖPFLE 5.5% ABV ● Dortmunder export ● Pale amber; intense hops (Hallertau) in the nose; estery and fruity (apples, grapes); surprisingly low perceived bitterness.

▮ PILSNER 4.7% ABV ● Pilsner ● Straw-colored, very intense hop aroma in the nose (Tettnang); medium to full body, balanced by plenty of bitterness.

KETTERER

✉ Frombachstraße 27, 78132 Hornberg

🖥 www.kettererbier.de

This small family brewery lies in a narrow valley in the northwestern Black Forest. Michael Ketterer has recently explored a new wellspring near the small town of Hornberg and introduced a new brewhouse —both seem to have made his beer even smoother. Most Ketterer beers are available in 330 ml flip-top bottles, nicknamed "Fläschle."

▮ PILS 5.0% ABV ● Pilsner ● Straw-colored; a hint of yeast in the nose. Malty flavor, medium body; very intense bitterness and noble hop aromas (Tettnang) in the finish.

▮ SCHÜTZEN-BOCK 7.5% ABV ● Foreign extra stout ● Mahogany to black, slightly hazy. Very chocolatey aromas in the nose; sweet and full body, but still well balanced, with a bitterness reminiscent of red wine from an oak cask. One of the few German beers that age extremely well.

HOEPFNER PILSNER

SCHNITZER BRÄU

✉ Marlener Straße 9, 77656 Offenburg

🖥 www.schnitzerbraeu.de

Bettina Wohlschelgel founded this small brewery close to the French border near Strasbourg in 2006 to specialize in brewing gluten-free beers from millet. Schnitzer is a wholesale company for organic food.

▮ GERMAN HIRSE PREMIUM 5.0% ABV ● Specialty lager Dark golden, almost no lace; sweet nose with a hint of apricot and cashew nuts. Full-bodied, like fried polenta, yet refreshing on the palate with nutty and herbal aromas; not too much apparent bitterness.

WALDHAUS

✉ Waldhaus 1, 79809 Weilheim-Waldhaus

🖥 www.waldhaus.de

This brewery takes hopping to an extreme. Founded by a retired civil servant in a former forester's lodge back in 1833, it has been run by the Schmidt family since 1894. Owner Dieter Schmidt believes in very slow fermentation (in open fermenters) and maturation (in horizontal storage tanks), which generally results in more estery, full-bodied beers.

▮ DIPLOM PILS 4.9% ABV ● Pilsner Very pale straw color; intense, haylike fresh hop aroma and some sweetness in the nose; surprisingly full-bodied yet well-balanced and dry finish.

▮ SPEZIAL 5.6% ABV ● Dortmunder export ● Pale golden; malt and walnuts in the nose; full, almost sweet body, spicy and refreshing palate; roasted nuts but little hops in the aftertaste.

▮ OHNE FILTER 5.6% ABV ● Unfiltered lager ● Pale golden and very hazy; yeast and a hint of vinegar in the nose; spicy and refreshing on the palate; medium-bodied with an underlying sweetness, vanilla aromas, and low bitterness.

▮ HEFE FUN 5.7% ABV ● Hefeweizen ● Opaque straw color; little in the nose but a lot of flavor; full-bodied, spicy (a hint of vanilla, ginger, and nutmeg), and refreshing, with a lingering sweetness.

Cologne and the northwest

Dortmund • Düsseldorf • Issum • Mönchengladbach • Münster

Germany's most densely populated state, Nordrhein Westphalia has three native beer styles—Düsseldorf's altbier being the broadest category. "Export" was first brewed by Heinrich Wenker in what was then the Krone brewpub in Dortmund, while Cologne has kölsch.

Cologne is a world capital of carnival celebrations—and in the days of carnival, the city is bursting with people enjoying themselves and their kölsch beer. Served always in small, 200 ml glasses, it is unique: kölsch is an appellation that is protected just as wine is in other parts of Germany by European Union common law. Technically speaking, kölsch is defined simply as a pale, top-fermented bitter beer, but the so-called "Kölsch Konvention" restricts its production to Cologne itself and to a few villages in the vicinity.

In rival Düsseldorf the drink of choice is alt, a dark top-fermented beer. "Alt" literally means "old," and it is a common belief that the term altbier refers to the age of the beer—but altbier, like most German beers, is drunk very fresh. In the towns along the Rhine, "alt" simply identifies beers made with the "old" top-fermentation method in contrast to the "new" bottom-fermenting technology.

Until fairly recently kölsch was unavailable in Düsseldorf, while alt is extremely rare in Cologne. Düsseldorf and Cologne are the only cities on the Rhine that have their own "proprietary" beer styles—and the people in these towns are very proud of them. In contrast, Dortmund's Export style, the classic "worker's" beer from the middle of the 19th to the mid-to-late 20th century, has lost most of its popularity in its city of origin. In fact, it is now much easier to find export beers in the southwest than the northwest region.

Cologne's Gaffel brand harks back to the "Gaffeln" or guilds of medieval times; the brewers' guild was a political force.

THE KÖBES OF COLOGNE

In the taverns of Cologne, the waiters in their blue aprons are invariably called Köbes—an expression derived from the name Jacobus. This is due to the fact that Cologne is a Catholic stronghold, and in former centuries, pilgrims on their long journey to the alleged grave of St. Jacobus (James) in Santiago de Compostela in Spain would stop in Cologne for a few days to pray—and meanwhile make a living as waiters. A shell on their hat would identify them as pilgrims to St. Jacobus—hence the shortened and misspelled "Köbes."

Uniformed waiters in Cologne wear a white shirt, black pants, and a blue apron and tie, the latter tucked away from brimming kölsch glasses.

DIEBELS

✉ Brauerei-Diebels-Straße 1, 47661 Issum
🔗 www.diebels.de

Founded by Josef Diebels in 1878, this was a family business until taken over by InBev in 2001. Although starting out with a range of beer styles, Diebels became successful by reducing that to just one beer—Diebels Alt—in the early 1970s. Diebels managed to double its output every six years to over 26m gallons (1m hectoliters) and to make the local altbier style a nationally available specialty. But in recent years altbier has lost ground and Diebels has diversified, introducing a Pils in 2005.

🍺 **ALT** 4.9% ABV • Alt
Copper to mahogany; neutral nose with faint caramel malts. Medium to sweet body with roasted malt aromas and a mild bitterness in the finish. No apparent hop aroma.

🍺 **PILS** 4.9% ABV • Pilsner
Deep golden with very little head. Malty nose with just hints of herbal hop aroma; quite full-bodied; a medium to low bitterness level.

DORTMUNDER ACTIEN BRAUEREI

✉ Steigerstraße 20, 44145 Dortmund
🔗 www.dab.de

The last surviving large brewery in Dortmund, now owned by the Radeberger group, today produces all the Exports that put Dortmund on the brewing map. Kronen was the Wenker family brewery that reputedly invented the Export style, while Dortmunder Union (DUB) had the greatest influence in making Export popular. It was Fritz Brinkhoff, head brewer of DUB from 1870 to 1923, who systematically shipped pale lager instead of the then-popular dark "Bavarian" (Munich-style) beer to distant markets, and promoted it as a new style. Although Brinkhoff preferred to remain a simple employee, he became one of the richest men in Germany of his time. His contract granted him a basic wage and free lodging in the brewery, plus a small fee called "Kaßmännchen" of about 20 pfennigs per hectoliter. But of course, as production

DORTMUNDER ACTIEN KRONEN EXPORT

soared so did his income; indeed Bismarck once commented in one of his speeches that he earned less than a brewer in Dortmund.

🍺 **KRONEN EXPORT** 5.1% ABV •
Dortmunder export • Claims to follow Heinrich Wenker's original recipe of 1843. Golden in color, almost pils-like foam; intense malty sweetness in the nose. Very full-bodied but with an underlying delicate hoppiness with noble hop aromas.

🍺 **DAB EXPORT** 5.0% ABV •
Dortmunder export • Straw-gold color; a nutty, malty aroma and very low bitterness make it clearly different from the other Export beers from the same brewhouse.

🍺 **UNION EXPORT** 5.3% ABV •
Dortmunder export • Lighter in color and body but stronger in alcohol and even more pilslike than the two beers above. The hoppiness, however, appeals only to the nose, while the bitterness seems to be harsher than in the Kronen Export.

🍺 **DAB PILSNER** 4.8% ABV • Pilsner
Very pale blond; yeasty and herbal notes in the nose; relatively full.

🍺 **UNION SIEGEL PILS** 4.8% ABV •
Pilsner • Extremely pale blond; predominantly bitter, with very fine carbonation; strong herbal, pepper- and citrus-like notes in the aroma; extremely dry finish.

DAB DIÄT PILS 4.8% ABV • Dry beer • Diät Pils is the German version of dry beer and this is a particularly hoppy example. Very pale; a hint of almonds in the aroma; the bitterness is dry as can be.

FRÜH

✉ Cölner Hofbräu P. Josef Früh KG, Am Hof 12–18, 50667 Cologne
🖰 www.frueh.de

Früh's brewery tap is almost as famous as the cathedral across the square. Founded in 1904, the brewery has become famous for its restaurant as well as for the mild version of kölsch that it serves. The location of the tap and offices (the brewhouse has been moved to the outskirts of Cologne) is the former residence of the Duke of Brabant—possibly the same Jan Primus whose name became known as Gambrinus.

FRÜH
KÖLSCH

KÖLSCH 4.8% ABV • Kölsch • Light golden color; little-to-no hop aroma; medium body with just a hint of bitterness; clean and crisp aftertaste.

FÜCHSCHEN

✉ Brauerei im Füchschen, Ratinger Straße 28, 40213 Düsseldorf
🖰 www.fuechschen.de

Beer has been made at this unpretentious brewpub in downtown Düsseldorf, just outside the pedestrian area, since 1640, and since 1848 has been sold under the sign of the fox (Füchschen means "foxkin" or "little fox"). You can also eat well here.

ALT 4.5% ABV • Alt • Reddish-brown; toasted malt aroma with some fruitiness (plums? dates?) and haylike hops; medium body with almost cocoalike malt on the palate, quickly overtaken by the intense bitterness and noble aromas of Saaz hops.

GAFFEL

✉ Privatbrauerei Gaffel Becker & Co., Eigelstein 41, 50668 Cologne
🖰 www.gaffel.de

"Gaffeln" is an old word for the guilds that once played a key role in Cologne's social and economic life. The Gaffel brewery sits on the site of an earlier brewhouse founded in 1302. It is owned by the Becker family, who promoted the kölsch style by establishing a chain of pubs across Germany called "Ständige Vertretung" (also the name of West Germany's diplomatic mission in the East until 1989). The beer, however, has lost some of its distinct hoppy character in recent years.

KÖLSCH 4.8% ABV • Kölsch • Light straw in color; little aroma but extremely refreshing. Light body and some peachlike aromas in the finish.

HÖVELS

✉ Hoher Wall 5–7, 44137 Dortmund
🖰 www.hoevels-hausbrauerei.de

This brewpub in downtown Dortmund offers seminars, tastings, and hands-on brewing experience for its consumers. The pub was renovated in 2006 and has won awards for its cuisine; on the menu are hearty dishes, such as suckling pig in a beer sauce, that actually use the beer in their recipes. A bottled version of Original is sold in local supermarkets.

ORIGINAL BITTERBIER 5.5% ABV • Amber ale • Reddish-dark amber in color with a firm, creamy head. Some caramel-like sweetness in the nose

HÖVELS
ORIGINAL
BITTERBIER

and a robust bitterness with a refreshing pepper-like aftertaste.

KÖLNER VERBUND BRAUEREIEN

✉ Bergisch Gladbacher Straße 116–134, 51065 Cologne
🖰 www.sion.de

The Radeberger group's brewery in Cologne brews several of the famous kölsch brands (and some less famous for the off-trade, too) on the location of the former Bergische Löwenbrauerei, once a lager brewery with a broad range from pilsner to doppelbock under the Höhenhaus brand. They specialized in kölsch after World War II and now brew this style in different, quite distinctive versions.

KURFÜRSTEN KÖLSCH 4.8% ABV • Kölsch • Golden, with a quickly fading head. Sweet, cornlike aroma, a hint of pears; full-bodied and almost sweet; but well balanced with a medium bitterness.

SION KÖLSCH 4.8% ABV • Kölsch • Very pale golden, with a relatively robust head; less body (but also less malt aroma) than other beers of the same style; refreshing and dry with herbal hop notes to finish.

KÜPPERS KÖLSCH 4.8% ABV • Kölsch • Intense gold, stable white head; grassy and floral (violets?) hop aroma; very dry and intensely bitter, with a lot of herbal hop aromas.

PINKUS MÜLLER

✉ Kreuzstraße 4–10, 48143 Münster
🖰 www.pinkus-mueller.de

Münster once had 150 top-fermenting breweries. Pinkus Müller is the only one that survives, along with its brewery tap— a key attraction in the town. Altbier in this area is much paler in color; and while "alt" in this context does not mean "old" (*see p.99*), Pinkus Müller really does have some "old" altbier in its cellars. About 10 percent of production is left to mature for over a year in a conditioning tank, where it is deliberately laced with lactic bacteria to give it extra tartness. This old beer is then blended with fresh altbier to make it more refreshing.

MÜNSTERSCH ALT 5.1% ABV • Alt • Golden, with little head. Grainy aroma in the nose and a hint of lactic acid; light to medium body, little carbonation, yet very refreshing with medium bitterness in the finish.

CLASSIC 4.2% ABV • Sour ale • An unfiltered altbier available only on tap. It has a generous dose of aged altbier in the blend. Orange peel aromas in the nose; a very tart overall impression.

PILS 5.2% ABV • Pilsner Pale straw color; haylike aromas; medium body and a quite estery overall impression with herbal Tettnang hop aromas in the finish.

PINKUS MÜLLER MÜNSTERSCH ALT

SCHLÖSSER

✉ Münsterstraße 156, 40476 Düsseldorf
🐾 www.schloesser.de

This brewery was founded in downtown Düsseldorf in 1873 to brew altbier, or *obergäriges Düsseldorfer Lagerbier* ("top-fermenting Düsseldorfer lager") as it was known until World War II. It moved to its present location in 2004.

SCHLÖSSER ALT 4.8% ABV • Alt • Reddish-brown; slight toastiness in the nose; distinctive, slightly sulfury taste with underlying caramel-sweetness and a long-lasting, but not too intense bitterness. One of the more flavorful commercial altbiers.

STEFANUS

✉ Mennrath 59, 41179 Mönchengladbach
🐾 www.zum-stefanus.de

Michael Kolonko, who studied brewing in Franconia, took over the family's tavern on the southern outskirts of Mönchengladbach in 1999 and installed a small brewhouse. He introduced Bavarian brewing recipes which he reinterprets in a northern style.

HELL NATURTRÜB 5.0% ABV • Unfiltered lager • Pale golden and slightly hazy; some hops in the nose (Hallertauer Perle); a medium to full body balancing the bitterness.

DUNKEL NATURTRÜB 5.4% ABV • Unfiltered lager • This bottom-fermented beer could easily be mistaken for an altbier. Very intense toastiness and a balance of hop- and roasted malt aromas both in the nose and on the palate. Hops (Target, Magnum, and Perle) dominate the aftertaste.

UERIGE

✉ Berger Straße 1, 40213 Düsseldorf
🐾 www.uerige.de

This lively corner brewpub in downtown Düsseldorf is very popular with locals and tourists alike. Beers on tap come from wooden barrels rolled out from the narrow cellars below. All the bottled beer, notably the so-called Sticke (*stickum* means "secretly" in the local dialect), comes in flip-top bottles. The brewery has an output of 500,000 gallons (19,000 hectoliters) per year—all brewed in the relatively small copper brewhouse located between the bars. While the kettles are state-of-the-art inside, the Schnitzler family

loves to use traditional methods both in packaging and brewing: they only use whole hops and cool their wort in a traditional coolship (an open, shallow tank) and a copper Baudelot cooler.

ALT 4.7% ABV • Alt • Dark copper; intense, resiny, and citric hop nose; dry with just enough body; a touch nutty, fruity (apples, pears); intense bitterness from aromatic hops along with chocolatey toastiness.

WEIZEN 5.0% ABV • American-style hefeweizen • Golden with not too much haze; wheat aromas, a little fruit (pears? lemon zest?); medium body; refreshing and somewhat bitter in the aftertaste.

STICKE 6.5% ABV • Strong ale The "bock" version of the alt, available only on the third Tuesdays of January and October. Dark copper; an extremely citric, peppery hop nose with some caramel; very full-bodied but no apparent sweetness; powerful hoppy bitterness with a hint of roasted walnut.

DOPPEL STICKE 8.5% ABV • Barley wine • The export version of Sticke: deep dark brown; pungent alcoholic smell, intense maltiness both in the nose and on the palate; very full body and a lot of sweetness, very well balanced by the intense bitterness. At 75+ IBUs it claims to have the highest bitterness level in Germany.

UERIGE WEIZEN

Hamburg and the north

Bremen • Einbeck • Flensburg • Kassel • Rostock • Stralsund

The further north you go, the bitterer the beer gets—this is common wisdom in Germany, and many of the biggest pilsner breweries in the country can indeed be found in the northernmost provinces. But these breweries have also developed some interesting strong beers.

Hamburg was called the "brewhouse of the Hanseatic League" in medieval times; large quantities of beer were shipped by the members of the league, a powerful trading alliance of northern European states, to places as distant as London and Novgorod. The most expensive (and reputedly strongest) beer of the time came from the small town of Einbeck. This town made the head-brewer a public servant, who would visit each citizen's home with a brewkettle to ensure the high quality and strength of homebrewed beer. Most of this beer was put up for sale afterward as "Einbeckisch Bier," which sounds very similar to a request for "ein bock beer" ("one bock beer")—at least it seems to have done in Bavaria, where

Einbecker-style beer was brewed and sold in Munich's state Hofbräuhaus from 1621 onwards as "bock."

Although bock plays only a minor role in Germany's brewing statistics— 0.7 percent of the country's total output in 2006 was bock, compared with 60.3 percent pilsner—many breweries have taken up the production of bock-strength beers in recent years, albeit as seasonal products. Many famous pilsners, on the other hand, have been "dumbed-down," losing a lot of their once style-defining noble hop aroma and characteristic bitterness.

Veltins, in the hiking country of the Sauerland, was one of the pioneers of the "premium pilsner" trend, but also makes light and alcohol-free beers.

ASGAARD

✉ Brauerei Schleswig
Königstraße 27, 24837 Schleswig
🖥 www.asgaard.de

This brewery and restaurant lies in the small town of Schleswig that gave its name to Germany's northernmost state. Schleswig is an ancient Viking settlement (they called it Sliesthorp), and the Asgaard brewery has a definite Viking theme. It brews some seasonal beers, including a Maibock.

📧 NORDISCHES WEIZEN 5.0% ABV ● Hefeweizen ● For a long time (until Flensburger started to brew its Weizen) this was the most northerly example of Bavarian-style wheat beer. Dark gold and intensely hazy; fruity (pineapple? citrus zest?) and caramel-like aromas; medium body with relatively little carbonation and almost no perceiveable bitterness.

📧 DAS GÖTTLICHE PREMIUM BIER 4.8% ABV ● Amber lager ● Dark amber color and an estery nose give the impression that this is stronger than it actually is. Full-bodied, but in no way sweet, with a robust, long-lasting bitterness and Hersbruck hop aromas.

ASTRA

✉ Holsten Brauerei AG,
Holstenstraße 224, 22765 Hamburg
🖥 www.krombacher.de

This down-to-earth brand is firmly rooted in Hamburg's lively St. Pauli quarter, although it seemed doomed several times in the 1990s. Originally a brand of the Bavaria St. Pauli brewery, just off the Reeperbahn (a building that was demolished in 2005), Astra gained its popularity not only with local folk and tourists who visit the brewery tap on the Reeperbahn itself,

but also in music clubs in other big cities. It is now brewed in Hamburg's twin city Altona by Holsten (a subsidiary of Carlsberg).

📧 URTYP 4.95% ABV ● Dortmunder export ● Pale golden, with a stable head; very little hop aroma in the nose. Medium to full body, and just enough hop bitterness to balance and some herbal notes in the finish.

BECK'S

✉ Am Deich 18/19, 28199 Bremen
🖥 www.becksbeer.com

Since 2002 Beck's has been the flagship brand of InBev Germany, and also its largest beer export. Heinrich Beck, Lüder Rutenberg, and Thomas May founded the brewery in 1873 with the international market firmly in mind, and began exporting almost immediately. Beck's Pilsner was a hit in foreign markets even before it was first sold in Germany, in 1949. The domestic market had been provided for by Haake Beck since 1921, and the two breweries merged in 1981.

📧 PILSNER 4.8% ABV ● Pilsner ● Very pale straw; just a hint of haylike hop aroma. Light to medium body and a mild bitterness in the finish.

BECK'S
PILSNER

Brewed in Bremen, Beck's pilsner is the biggest-selling German beer in the US.

📧 HAAKE BECK KRÄUSEN 4.9% ABV ● Unfiltered lager ● Dark golden, hazy Zwicklbier with herbal and yeasty aromas. Medium body; a distinctive, long-lasting bitterness with some citrus notes.

EINBECKER BRAUHAUS

✉ Papenstrasse 4–7, 7574 Einbeck
🖥 www.einbecker.com

Einbeck, the town that gave bockbier its name, once had 742 small breweries: in 1794 they founded a common brewery to brew bockbier. The Einbecker Brauhaus is today a 22m-gallon (850,000-hectoliter) brewery in the center of the town. First records of shipping Einbecker beer date back to April 28, 1378, and the beer was even promoted by Martin Luther, who drank it publically at the Reichtag in Worms.

📧 UR-BOCK 6.5% ABV ● Bock Deep golden in color; intense malty nose, full-bodied and almost sweet, balanced well by a high level of hop bitterness; almondlike and herbal bitterness in the aftertaste.

📧 UR-BOCK DUNKEL 6.5% ABV ● Bock ● Dark copper; very fruity (mango, papaya, pineapple) aromas; initial roasted malt bitterness, almost lardlike aromas, hint of rye bread;

surprisingly dry and long-lasting finish dominated by roasted malts and hops.

FLENSBURGER

✉ Flensburger Brauerei Emil Petersen, Munketoft 12, 24937 Flensburg

🖑 www.flensburger.de

For several years in the 1970s, Flensburg's brewery was the only one in Germany to use flip-top bottles—so unique and popular that they were prominently featured in the then-famous Werner comic-strip series. Until that time Flensburger, founded in 1888, had been perceived as a fairly traditional pilsner, but its new success with younger drinkers encouraged the brewery to retrench and launch new products, including, in 2007, an organic Kellerbier.

🍺 **PILSENER** 4.8% ABV • Pilsner Golden, with a firm head; a herbal nose. Medium body and a distinct bitterness; dry aftertaste.

🍺 **KELLERBIER** 4.8% ABV • Unfiltered lager • Amber-colored and (unlike most kellerbiers) obviously filtered. Some malty aromas and sweetness; hints of nuts, a relatively dry hoppy finish.

HÜTT

✉ Brauerei Bettenhäuser, Knallhütte, 34225 Baunatal

🖑 www.huett.de

The Knallhütte is a former coaching inn just outside Kassel. They started brewing in 1752 and while they have grown substantially in recent decades, they are still firmly rooted in gastronomy. Frank Bettenhäuser likes to link his brewery to the fairy tales popular in the region.

🍺 **LUXUS-PILS** 4.9% ABV • Pilsner Pale golden with a stable head; grassy aromas, very dry, with a noble bitterness in the aftertaste.

🍺 **SCHWARZES GOLD** 4.9% ABV • Dark lager • Very dark red; delicate, flowery hop aroma;

medium body with some caramel, distinctive bitterness to balance.

🍺 **HEFEWEIZEN DUNKEL** 5.2% ABV • Hefeweizen • Reddish-brown with a strong haze; banana and chocolate in the nose; refreshing and spicy (nutmeg?); dry finish without any apparent bitterness.

JEVER

✉ Friesisches Brauhaus zu Jever, Elisabethufer 18, 26441 Jever

🖑 www.jever.de

This brewery, set up in 1848, literally put the small coastal town of Jever in the Friesland region on the map when, in the 1930s, it was acquired by the Bavaria St. Pauli brewery of Hamburg, which then distributed its beer nationwide. Although its bitterness levels have fallen significantly, Jever Pilsener is still regarded as the reference for a dry German pilsner—even by competing brewers. Like many other pils breweries, they have introduced new products—Jever Fun is the hoppiest non-alcoholic beer in Germany.

🍺 **PILSENER** 5.0% ABV • Pilsner Pale golden; haylike herbal aromas; very dry with a hint of summer flowers and an intense bitterness.

JEVER PILSENER

LÜBZER

✉ Mecklenburgische Brauerei Lübz, Eisenbeissstraße 1, Lübz

🖑 www.luebzer.de

The Lübzer brewery, set up in 1877, was one of the important pils breweries of the German Democratic Republic—some of its pils was even exported to the West in the 1980s. It may have been considered the "eastern" version of Jever at the time, and some of the typical symbols of the Jever brand (most prominently the lighthouse) are also used by Lübzer. After the collapse of the Communist regime, the brewery was modernized and expanded, and it changed hands several times to be finally taken over by Carlsberg. It was one of the first large breweries to reintroduce stronger beers.

🍺 **PILS** 4.9% ABV • Pilsner Pale golden color; a faint hop aroma; relatively high carbonation that masks the malty body; dry aftertaste with some grassy and hay-like hop aromas at the finish.

🍺 **URKRAFT** 6.0% ABV • Strong lager • Amber, with less of a head than the pils. Some malt and honey in the nose; full-bodied and well balanced with a refreshing, spicy, peppery bitterness. Some alcoholic warmth in the aftertaste.

PRIVATBRAUEREI ISERLOHN

✉ Grüner Talstraße 40–50, 58644 Iserlohn

🖑 www.iserlohner.de

Once one of the smaller pils breweries in the Sauerland, Iserlohner, founded in 1899, grew to its present size when bigger breweries in the neighborhood became all-pils-producers. At first it followed suit, but realized sooner than the rest that there was still demand for different beers. It now brews a range of eight.

■ **PILSNER** 4.8% ABV •
Pilsner • Golden with
a stable head; medium
body; noble but not
very intense bitterness.
■ **1899** 4.9% ABV • Amber
lager • Dark copper;
roasted malt, marzipan
and chocolate aromas;
medium body with
more notes of marzipan
and chocolate.
■ **WEIZEN** 5.2% ABV •
Hefeweizen • Amber and
cloudy; banana and
citrus aromas; sweet
and fruity; dry finish.

ROSTOCKER

✉ Hanseatische Brauerei
Rostock, Doberaner Straße 27,
18057 Rostock

⌂ www.rostocker.de

Rostock has a rich brewing
tradition from the time of
the Hanseatic League. Many
of the cobbles on the streets
arrived in medieval times as
ballast on empty inbound
sailing ships that were to carry
away barrels of beer. Earliest
brewing documents date
back to 1258, but the present
brewery is a 19th-century
brick building with an

PRIVATBRAUEREI
ISERLOHN
WEIZEN

impressive cellar as
brewery tap. The
brewery was
nationalized in 1947
then re-privatized in
1991 when it became
part of the Beck's
group. Beck's sold
Rostocker to Brau
und Brunnen in 2002
—a firm taken over by
the Radeberger group
two years later.
■ **PILSNER** 4.9% ABV •
Pilsner • Straw color
and little hop aroma;
quite harsh bitterness,
just enough
body. Surprising
sweetness in
the aftertaste.
■ **BOCK HELL** 6.9% ABV • Bock
Amber-colored; sweet, fruity
nose with hints of plums and
figs. Very full-bodied,
caramel taste but not too
sweet, balanced by an
intense bitterness but no
apparent hop aromas.
■ **FREIBEUTER** 9.0% ABV •
Doppelbock • Copper-red with
little lace. Very sweet nose,
with raisins and dried
pineapple. Sweet on the
palate, some roastiness, giving
way to a robust, almost
refreshingly spicy bitterness.

A true-to-type German
pilsner prides itself on
a firm, stable head.

STRALSUNDER BRAUEREI

✉ Greifswalder Chaussee 84–85,
18439 Stralsund

⌂ www.stralsunder.de

Stralsund's brewery was
founded in 1827 to supply
seaside resorts on the Baltic
coast with local beer. It was
nationalized as "Volkseigener
Betrieb" (VEB) after World
War II and bought by a large
wholesaler, Hans Nordmann,
in the 1990s. Realizing the
opportunities of brewpubs,
he founded a chain of
them under the name "Zum
Alten Fritz;" many of these
do not now brew their own
beer but get it from
Stralsunder. The premium
brand is named Störtebeker
after the pirate Nicolas
"Klaas" Störtebeker who
sailed the Baltic Sea in the
late 13th century.
■ **STÖRTEBEKER BERNSTEIN**
WEIZEN 5.3% ABV • Hefeweizen
Amber, little haze, intense
lacing; banana, pineapple,
and mango aromas; medium
body and dry aftertaste with
lingering banana aroma.
■ **STÖRTEBEKER HANSE PORTER**
4.0% ABV • Dark lager • Dark
mahogany; sweetness in the
nose and palate; almost
syrupy, with coffeelike malt
bitterness to balance.

VELTINS

✉ An der Streue, 59872 Meschede

⌂ www.veltins.de

This large brewery began life
as a brewpub that was taken
over by Clemens Veltins in
1852. It is firmly independent,
although there are takeover
rumors every other year.
Veltins focuses on its Pilsener
in its customized bottles and
has grown sales to 70m
gallons (2.6m hectoliters)—yet
like others, it has introduced
beer-mixes that boost sales
without helping the quality
image of the beer.
■ **PILSENER** 4.8% ABV • Pilsner
Pale golden, with a grassy
hop aroma. Medium body;
an intense bitterness.

Berlin and the east

Dresden • Erfurt • Jena • Leipzig • Meissen • Potsdam

The reunification of Germany has changed the country's beer scene completely. Not only have some companies from the former West Germany taken over former DDR breweries, but characterful beers from the East have also conquered western markets.

Berliner weisse, the light, refreshing, and aromatic beer with its high lactic acidity, has long been regarded as Germany's only sour beer. It is not. Several sour beer styles have survived in the former German Democratic Republic, albeit on a very small scale. Gose, once the local beer of the town of Goslar, is now held in high esteem as the specialty beer of Leipzig—thanks to Hartmut Hennebach, who continued to run the traditional gose tavern "Ohne Bedenken" even under Communist rule. Leipzig's gose is a wheat beer with lactic fermentation that gets its dry aftertaste from salt added to the brew—so it actually makes you thirsty as you drink it. There are two commercial examples: Döllnitzer Ritterguts-Gose, and the one from Bayerischer Bahnhof (*see below and p.108*). Another historic beer that undergoes lactic fermentation is Jenaer weisse. Threatened with extinction when Jena's Stadtbrauerei closed, it survives today as "Wöllnitzer Weisse" in one small brewpub.

Berliner weisse, however, remains the best-known sour wheat beer. In the early 19th century, practically all beer brewed in Berlin was Berliner weisse, and in the 1890s, it still accounted for one-third of production. But today, if one discounts a version made for export in Leipzig, there is only one commercial example—Kindl Weisse—left.

Leipzig's imposing Bayerischer train station buildings have been converted into a brewpub.

WEISSE "MIT SCHUSS"?

Berliner weisse is hard to find even in Berlin's beer bars—and if it is on the menu, it will generally be offered "mit Schuss," meaning with a "red" shot of raspberry syrup or a "green" shot of syrup made from woodruff (*Galium odoratum*). This habit destroys the beer's delicate aromas—and it has become widespread only in recent decades. In the first half of the 20th century, other mixtures were popular that have since gone out of style: "Stangenbier" was a mix of Berliner weisse with unfiltered pilsner, while "Weise mit Strippe" meant weisse with a shot of caraway liqueur.

Startlingly colored sugar syrups are used to make the sour beer Berliner weisse more palatable for less robust palates.

APOLDAER

✉ Vereinsbrauerei Apolda, Topfmarkt 14, 99510 Apolda
🖥 www.vereinsbrauerei-apolda.de

The brewing tradition in this Thuringian town north of Weimar dates back to 1440, when the first documents for the town's common brewers as well as the castle brewery were issued. The Vereinsbrauerei united its two remaining breweries in 1887 (hence the name "Verein," meaning "union"). It now brews 3m gallons (118,000 hectoliters) per annum and has widened its product portfolio significantly. It now brews four (at least slightly) different pilsners.

🍺 **APOLDAER 1806** 5.0% ABV • Helles • Amber; malt and toffee in the nose; full body and a nutty bitterness. Some butterscotch and a faint hop bitterness in the finish.

🍺 **APOLDAER GLOCKENPILS** 4.8% ABV • Pilsner • Straw-colored; freshly cut grass and marshmallows in the nose; dry overall impression; intense, somewhat harsh and long-lasting bitterness.

🍺 **APOLDAER EXPORT** 5.2% ABV • Dortmunder export • Pale golden; aromas of roasted nuts, medium body and bitterness, and hazelnuts in the aftertaste.

BAYERISCHER BAHNHOF

✉ Brau & Gaststättenbetrieb GmbH & Co. KG, Bayrischer Platz 1, 04103 Leipzig
🖥 www.bayerischer-bahnhof.de

Thomas Schneider installed this very large brewpub in Germany's oldest surviving train station, a listed building dating back to 1842. It focuses on the production of Leipzig's traditional very tart gose style, although it also offers a schwarzbier, a pilsner, and a Bavarian-style weissbier. Recently Schneider has ventured into the production of other sour beers; it makes a version of Berliner Weisse for export to the USA.

🍺 **ORIGINAL LEIPZIGER GOSE** 4.6% ABV • Sour ale • Very hazy, orange-colored wheat beer (60% malted wheat in the grain bill), which can also be bought in a traditionally long-necked flip-top bottle. Lactic aroma mixes with the typical clove aromas of wheat beers, plus some coriander. Medium body and a distinct tartness in the dry finish.

🍺 **BERLINER STYLE WEISSE INTERPRETATION** 3.1% ABV • Sour ale • Very pale and hazy; sourdough and cherry-yogurtlike aromas; refreshing, with surprisingly little sourness and just a hint of bitterness (almonds?) in the aftertaste.

BERLINER BÜRGERBRÄU

✉ Müggelseedamm 164–166, 12587 Berlin
🖥 www.berlinerbuergerbraeu.de

This mid-sized brewery on the Müggelsee, a lake on the eastern outskirts of Berlin, was nationalized after World War II. During Communist rule Bürgerbräu upped its reputation by exporting large quantities of relatively cheap but good beer to western countries. In 1992 the Häring family, which also owns the Hofmark brewery in the Bavarian town of Cham, took over, making this Berlin's largest family-owned brewery. Distribution today is more or less limited to eastern Berlin.

🍺 **ROTKEHLCHEN EXPORT** 5.3% ABV • Dortmunder export • Amber; medium body, crisp yet malty, with some roasted malt and a dry aftertaste with very little hop aroma.

🍺 **HELLER BOCK** 6.8% ABV • Bock Dark amber in color; strong caramel aroma; medium body with spicy, alcoholic undertones; very low perceived bitterness.

🍺 **BERNAUER SCHWARZBIER** 5.2% ABV • Dark lager • Dark brown; caramelly nose; slightly sweet and chocolatey; surprisingly dry aftertaste.

🍺 **GERMAN DRY** 5.0% ABV • Haposhu Bürgerbräu's version of a

BERLINER BÜRGERBRÄU ROTKEHLCHEN EXPORT

Japanese Haposhu—a beer in which less than 25 percent of the grain is malted (the rest is unmalted barley). Paul Häring prides himself in using only grain in the beer instead of adding sugar, the usual practice in Japan. The brew (which cannot be labeled "beer" in Germany as it does not comply with German purity laws) is gold in color, lightly carbonated, with a firm head and a dry bitterness.

BERLINER-KINDL-SCHULTHEISS-BRAUEREI

✉ Indira-Ghandi-Straße 66–69, 13053 Berlin
🕆 www.berliner-kindl.de

Many of the most famous Berlin breweries closed in the period when the city was divided, between 1945 and 1989—and the situation got even worse after reunification. The Radeberger group has consolidated the market and concentrated the production of Berliner Kindl, Schultheiss, Potsdamer Rex, and Berliner Pilsner in one mega-brewery in the eastern part of town. Schultheiss's intensely aromatic Berliner Weisse, which could take 20 years of bottle-ageing, was axed in 2006—but the precious *Lactobacillus* cultures seem to have found their way into the somewhat improved recipe for Kindl Weisse.

📖 **KINDL WEISSE** 3.0% ABV ● Sour ale ● Extremely pale and opaque, with a fruity, citric smell that has an underlying earthy or tarlike note. The intense sensation of the sourness is complemented by a dryness and fruitiness in the aftertaste. The high lactic acid content will keep this beer reasonably fresh for at least three years.

📖 **BERLINER PILSNER** 5.0% ABV ● Pilsner ● A brand originating in Berlin's east, and probably

BERLINER-KINDL-SCHULTHEISS-BRAUEREI
BERLINER PILSNER

the best-selling beer in Germany's capital—golden in color, with a herbal, marshmallowlike aroma and a rather full-bodied overall impression.

📖 **KINDL JUBILÄUMS PILSENER** 5.1% ABV ● Pilsner ● Golden color; grassy aroma; sharp, intense bitterness but balanced with a hint of residual sweetness.

BRAUGOLD

✉ Schillerstraße 7, 99096 Erfurt
🕆 www.braugold.de

Thuringia's capital Erfurt has a rich brewing history. Every inner-city building with a hole at the side of its main entrance is likely to be an early brewhouse. Whenever beer was ready, the owners would simply stick a broom into the hole to announce that fact to the public. A more formal approach prevailed in 1888, when this brewery was built at its present location. The Braugold brand was introduced in 1956, under Communist rule. Forty years later, in 1996, the 6.6m-gallon (250,000-hectoliter) brewery returned to the Riebeck group, which had owned it prior to 1945.

📖 **BOCK** 6.5% ABV ● Bock Amber; caramel aroma; full-bodied, slightly sweet; a robust bitterness, hints of walnut.

BÜRGERLICHES BRAUHAUS SAALFELD

✉ Pößnecker Straße 55, 07318 Saalfeld
🕆 www.brauhaus-saalfeld.de

Founded in 1892, this small brewery emerged from Communist rule in rather bad shape but then saw

massive private investment. It is now one of the small private breweries along the "Bier- und Burgenstraße," a tourist route that takes in a number of local towns with appeal for the beer-lover. Its Ur-Saalfelder won the märzen category of European Beer Star in 2006.

📖 **UR-SAALFELDER** 5.6% ABV ● Fest-märzen ● Amber-colored with a malty, slightly sweetish nose; full-bodied and well balanced with toasty aromas as well as hoppiness.

FELDSCHLÖSSCHEN

✉ Cunnersdorfer Straße 25, 01189 Dresden
🕆 www.feldschloesschen.de

This was founded as a "Bavarian-style" brewery by a manor house (the so-called Feldschlösschen) in 1838. Most of the production was moved in 1981 to a new brewery, a landmark on the southern bank of the Elbe River in the suburb of Coschütz. The historic brewery buildings on the more centrally located Budapester Straße, which survived the bombings in 1945, have been splendidly refurbished as a brewery tap. The company was taken over by Holsten (since 2004 a subsidiary of Carlsberg), which has owned another Feldschlösschen brewery, in Braunschweig, since 1992.

📖 **PILSNER** 4.9% ABV ● Pilsner Pale golden, with a good head; a hint of butterscotch aroma; medium to full body and a restrained bitterness reminiscent of Bohemian lagers.

📖 **ZWICKEL** 5.0% ABV ● Unfiltered lager ● Golden with a faint haze; a hint of pears and apples in the nose; very soft, almost creamy mouthfeel and very mild bitterness.

📖 **SCHWARZER STEIGER** 4.8% ABV ● Dark lager Reddish-black;

FELDSCHLÖSSCHEN
SCHWARZER STEIGER

WHO OWNS GERMAN BEER?

Up until the middle of the 1990s, Germany was the only country in Europe whose breweries had not been the subject of any big takeovers by international brewing groups—but in the 21st century, this situation has changed dramatically.

With some 1,300 breweries—most of them far from profitable—the German beer market did not seem attractive to international investors in the 1990s. And the large German brewers who had built 40-percent over capacity believed that beer business in Germany worked differently from abroad.

In 2002, Belgium's Interbrew (now InBev) proved them wrong. It now sells 330m gallons (12.5m hectoliters) of beer on the German market. First it acquired Diebels and Beck's in the north, then, in 2003, Hasseröder in Thüringen and Munich's Spaten-Löwenbräu. The other big breweries in Munich, Paulaner and Hacker-Pschorr, had already become part of the BHI conglomerate, a joint venture with Dutch giant Heineken. Carlsberg, too, is trying to make its brands (Holsten, Lübzer, Duckstein, Feldschlösschen) national household

Paulaner in Munich is part of BHI, now Germany's fourth-largest brewer, producing 180m gallons (6.8m hectoliters) per annum.

Schlösser is one of a number of breweries across Germany (plus one in the Czech Republic) that belong to Radeberger.

names—even though their success (137m gallons/5.2m hectoliters) is so far limited to the north.

The Radeberger group, the brewing branch of food giant Dr. Oetker, is the largest all-German brewing empire (343m gallons/13m hectoliters)—but aside from Allgäuer Brauhaus, it has not found a foothold in the south yet. Nor has its rival Bitburger, despite having made Köstritzer as successful a brand as "Bit;" it claimed a market share of 8.5 percent in 2006 (203m gallons/7.7m hectoliters). Meanwhile, Germany's best-selling beer brand—147m gallons (5.6m hectoliters) —is hardly to be found in any beer statistics because many of its competitors do not even recognize it as a brand at all: Oettinger, owned by the Kollmar family, focuses on discount beers for the off-trade made by a handful of breweries across the country.

toasty and fruity notes (blueberry, wild strawberry) in the nose; dry overall impression, somewhat reminiscent of wine; roasted notes dominating the aftertaste.

FORSTHAUS TEMPLIN

✉ Braumanufaktur Forsthaus Templin, Templiner Straße 102, 14473 Potsdam

🖰 www.braumanufaktur.de

Jörg Kirchhoff and Thomas Köhler bought this historic tavern and installed a small brewery in 2002. The buildings just south of Potsdam date back to 1756 and have been used as a tavern since they were sold by the Bismarck family in 1834. The present building not only features a decorative brewhouse, but also a long bar and a large beer garden—everything decorated with antlers to emphasize a forest ("Forst") theme. Most of the beer produced here is made with organically grown ingredients.

🍺 **POTSDAMER STANGE** 4.8% ABV • Amber lager • Dark amber; a faint apple aroma; soft mouthfeel, surprisingly not as much sourness as one

would expect from historic descriptions of the style; some hop aroma in the aftertaste.

🍺 **WEIHNACHTSBOCK** 7.0% ABV • Bock • Almost black; a lot of caramel in the nose; very full-bodied and sweet with an intense taste of licorice that gives way to hoppy bitterness and aroma in the aftertaste.

HALLESCHES BRAUHAUS

✉ Hallesche Spezialitätenbrauerei Kühler Brunnen, Große Nikolaistraße 2, 06108 Halle/Saale

🖰 www.hallesches-brauhaus.de

This multistory brewpub just off the market square in Halle was founded in 2005. However, the modern interior is built into a Renaissance-era building that was founded in 1521 as a meeting place for the citizens. Its main product is a kölsch-style beer that for legal reasons cannot be called kölsch. The dark Albrecht beer is named after Cardinal Albrecht von Brandenburg, who ruled in the town when Hallesche's Kühler Brunnen building was built.

🍺 **HALLSCH** 4.8% ABV • Kölsch • Pale golden; a hint of fruit in the aroma; medium body

Halle has one of the few brewpubs that are modern in design; the beers remain traditional.

and a faint hop bitterness in the aftertaste.

🍺 **ALBRECHT DUNKEL** 4.5% ABV • Dark lager • Dark copper; very little toasty aroma; full-bodied without sweetness, with a refreshing tartness in the finish.

HAMMER BRÄU

✉ Bahnhofstraße 42, 01587 Riesa

🖰 www.hammerbraeu.de

A modern brewpub, with a large central bar built into a somewhat futuristic artificial hill. Unlike most brewpubs in Germany, this one is very open in giving details about its brewing recipes and discussing the beer with its customers.

🍺 **GOLD** 4.8% ABV • Dortmunder export • Pale golden and bright; very full-bodied but well balanced with nutty notes and a relatively dry hop finish.

🍺 **RIESENBRÄU** 4.9% ABV • Amber lager • Copper-colored, with an intense roasty aroma. The overall impression is nevertheless dry and more hoppy than chocolatey and malty.

HASSERÖDER

✉ Auerhahnring 1, 38855 Wernigerode

⌂ www.hasseroeder.de

Germany's fourth largest brewery started out in 1872 as "Zum Auerhahn"—the "wood grouse" that still features in the logo. The real success story began in 1990 after the German Democratic Republic collapsed, and Hasseröder Pils became the best-selling pilsner in eastern Germany. Hasseröder, now owned by InBev, is positioned as a very masculine product, and is heavily advertised at soccer and boxing events.

▥ **PREMIUM PILS** 4.8% ABV ● Pilsner ● Pale golden; flowery, faintly camomilelike nose; light to medium body and a harsh, long-lasting, somehow nutty bitterness.

▥ **PREMIUM EXPORT** 5.5% ABV ● Dortmunder export ● Deep golden in color; malty nose; full-bodied with a robust bitterness to balance.

KNEIPEPUR

✉ Lewaldstraße 23A, 14774 Plaue bei Brandenburg an der Havel

⌂ www.kneipepur.de

This brewpub in Plaue (west of Brandenburg city) can produce a batch size of a mere 130 gallons (5 hectoliters)—yet they may be

the most unusual 130-gallon batches brewed in all Germany. Gernot Brätz prides himself on brewing at least 20 different beers every year, including beers flavored with raspberries and cherries (these recipes call for 200 lbs/90 kg of fruit for every 130 gallons/500 liters of beer), juniper, rye, or extreme levels of hops. Many of his creations brewed since 1997 are one-offs never repeated; others reappear more or less regularly on the beer menu. While Gernot Brätz brews, his wife Karola prepares buffet dinners— Kneipepur has won fame for its beer-oriented cuisine.

▥ **GERMAN STOUT** 5.2% ABV ● Oatmeal stout ● This dark reddish-brown stout includes oats and roasted rye, wheat, and spelt malts. Toasty nose; just enough body; nutty, toffee, and cocoa flavors; persistent bitterness.

KÖSTRITZER SCHWARZBIERBRAUEREI

✉ Heinrich Schütz Straße 16, 07586 Bad Köstritz

⌂ www.koestritzer.de

Köstritzer's influence on the change in taste of the German beer-drinker can hardly be overestimated. Similar to Guinness, the black Köstritzer Schwarzbier was regarded as a health food for many centuries (the brewery itself was founded in 1543) and even recommended by doctors. This helped the brewery survive Communist rule—until 1991 it made special "nourishing" versions (sweetened with grape-sugar) and a bock-style version of the schwarzbier. On the other hand, Köstritzer started to brew a pils for the regional market. Before the Bitburger group took over Köstritzer in 1991, there were fears that, with just 820,000 gallons (31,000 hectoliters) produced each year, the schwarzbier would disappear because pils was so

KÖSTRITZER SCHWARZBIER

much more popular. But Bitburger aimed to establish schwarzbier as a national style and quickly succeeded in doing so. While schwarzbier was virtually unknown in West Germany until 1989, the traditional style from Thuringia has now gained a strong foothold in the whole country, with 1.3 percent of the beer market, and 11m gallons (430,000 hectoliters) of Köstritzer Schwarzbier accounts for more than half of all schwarzbier production in Germany. The brewery is close to Weimar, the city where national poet Goethe used to live. There is proof that he was an early consumer of Köstritzer Schwarzbier, which is why he appears in many Köstritzer ads.

▥ **SCHWARZBIER** 4.8% ABV ● Dark lager ● Almost black, brown head; chocolate aromas; medium body, and a complex bitterness in the aftertaste, where toasty and hoppy aromas are in balance.

MEISSNER SCHWERTER

✉ Schwerter Brauerei Wohlers, Ziegelstraße 6, 01662 Meissen

⌂ www.schwerter-brauerei.de

This modern brewery and restaurant was built in 1997 in an industrial area just outside Meissen—but it can trace its roots back to a downtown brewhouse built in 1430. Under the crossed-swords logo (also used by the famous Meissen porcelain industry) head-brewer Bernd Heitmann brews his well-established German porter (which has significantly increased in strength in recent years) and some experimental brews alongside the usual pils and dark lager.

▯ RED LAGER 4.9% ABV • Amber lager • Reddish-copper; vanilla aromas in the nose; malty but not too full-bodied. Some sweetness balanced with noble hops.

▯ PORTER 6.5% ABV • German porter • Reddish-brown to black; intense coffee aromas; bittersweet chocolate on the palate; warming alcohol and surprisingly dry bitterness.

PAPIERMÜHLE

✉ Erfurter Straße 102, 07743 Jena
🖰 www.papiermuehle-jena.de

This regional brewery started out as a brewpub in 1996 and was vastly enlarged 10 years later. The spacious brewpub, including an elegant restaurant, still exists in the old part of the buildings. The location is an old mill on the western outskirts of Jena that has been there at least since 1298. It was converted to

paper production in 1657, and a tavern was added in 1737. After enlarging the brewhouse, Papiermühle revived some old brands formerly produced by Jena's own Stadtbrauerei, which closed in the late 1990s, including Burschen-Pils and Schellenbier.

▯ BURSCHEN-PILS
4.5% ABV • Pilsner
Dark golden to light amber; medium-bodied; relatively little bitterness in the dry aftertaste.

▯ DEUTSCHES PILSENER
4.5% ABV • Pilsner
This beer comes in a filtered version in bottles and unfiltered on tap. Full-bodied and a little grainy, but well balanced with a hearty bitterness.

▯ SCHELLENBIER
5.8% ABV • Bock
Although a bock by its original gravity (16.8%), this almost black beer is relatively light in alcohol, with lots of residual sugar. Aromas of licorice, roasted malt; pleasant herbal bitterness in the finish.

Jena's Papiermühle has been a paper mill, a tavern (where, in the early 19th century, Napoleon once stayed), and a brewery.

RADEBERGER
PILSNER

RADEBERGER

✉ Dresdner Straße 2, 01454 Radeberg
🖰 www.radeberger.de

This brewery just outside Dresden was the first in Germany to be founded as a pilsner-only brewery, in 1872. Up until World War II Radeberger tried to be as similar to Pilsner Urquell as possible. Under Communist rule, Radeberger became rare in its country of origin but proved to be a very successful export. The company was taken over by the Oetker group in the early 1990s, when the brewery was completely rebuilt; the brand proved to be so valuable that Oetker named its whole brewing arm after Radeberger. The beer itself, once the most hoppy and aromatic beer in the East, has lost some of its character.

▯ PILSNER 4.8% ABV • Pilsner
Golden with a stable head; nutty nose, very little hop aroma although the palate is dominated by a crisp bitterness; dry aftertaste.

REUDNITZER

✉ Leipziger Brauhaus zu Reudnitz, Mühlstraße 13, 04317 Leipzig
🖰 www.reudnitzer.de

Since other breweries in the vicinity closed, Reudnitzer, a large brewery in the industrial area of Saxony's largest town, has become home to traditional brands. Sternburg, for example, was one of the few nationally renowned brands in the 1900s (as "Sternburg'sche Dampfbrauerei" from Lützschena), but while it survived both wars and Communist rule it found itself repositioned in the 1990s as a discounted brand that changed hands several

times, finally ending up in the Radeberger group.

STERNBURG EXPORT 5.2% ABV ● Helles ● Golden, with a slightly grapelike aroma; very mild with medium body and just a hint of bitterness.

REUDNITZER PILSNER 5.0% ABV ● Pilsner ● Pale golden; haylike hop aromas, light to medium body and a distinctive bitterness.

REUDNITZER FESTBIER 5.6% ABV ● Fest-märzen ● Deep golden; full-bodied with a marzipan-like palate ending in an intense, lingering bitterness.

RHÖN-BRAUEREI DITTMAR

✉ Fuldaer Straße 6, 36452 Kaltennordheim
🖳 www.rhoenbrauerei.de

This was Kaltennordheim's communal brewhouse, where the citizens brewed their own beer until 1875, when the brewhouse and brewing privileges were sold to Friedrich Christian Dittmar and Margarete Marschall. The brewery was run by their family until it was nationalized in 1972 by the Communist regime. It was returned to the Dittmar family in 1990 and they carefully rebuilt it not only as a working brewery but also as a tourist attraction in the Rhön natural reserve.

DUNKLER DOPPELBOCK 7.4% ABV ● Doppelbock ● Very dark brownish-red, almost like a tawny port. Sweet plum-puddinglike nose, some walnut; very full-bodied and sweet; again plums on the palate and a hint of cocoa.

ROSENBRAUEREI

✉ Dr.-Wilhelm-Külz-Straße 41, 07381 Pößneck
🖳 www.rosenbrauerei.de

Pößneck is a town with a rich brewing tradition. In the 16th century, the local beer was exported to towns such as Weimar, which took several days of transportation. The

brewery "bei der Rosen-mühle" ("near the rose-mill") was built between 1863 and 1866. The Wagner family ran the brewery until 1950 when it was nationalized, and then regained it in 1991.

ROSEN DUNKLER BOCK 6.5% ABV ● Bock ● Reddish-brown, with little foam. Sweetish toffeelike aroma; delicate, somewhat herbal overall impression. Fruity, plum-puddinglike aftertaste.

TALSCHÄNKE

✉ Pennickental 44, 07749 Jena-Wöllnitz

The village of Wöllnitz once had at least two breweries of which the ruins can still be seen. But this small and unpretentious brewpub was newly founded in 1997 long after the other breweries were closed down. Owner Kai Hoppe claims that he got his weissbier recipe from one of them (Brauerei Barfuss, which closed in 1983 owing to a lack of spare parts). His Weisse, made from barley malt, undergoes some lactic fermentation.

WÖLLNITZER WEISSBIER 2.5% ABV ● Sour ale ● Very pale amber, with intense haziness; intense refreshing lactic acidity; still full-bodied and just a hint of bitterness in the aftertaste.

UR-KROSTITZER

✉ Brauereistraße 12, 04509 Krostitz bei Leipzig.
🖳 www.ur-krostitzer.de

Krostitz manor gained its brewing privilege on May 11, 1534, and has been brewing ever since. Nearby Leipzig was a boomtown in the late 19th century and Krostitzer (from 1904, "Ur-Krostitzer") beer grew with it. The Ur-Krostitzer brewery was nationalized by the Communists in 1949 and

reprivatized in 1990. The impressive drum-maltings went out of operation at that time, while modern fermentation and lager-tanks were installed, giving the beer a more "western" quality. Ur-Krostitzer now belongs to the Radeberger group.

FEINHERBES PILSNER 5.0% ABV ● Pilsner ● Golden, with some lace; malty, lilaclike nose; some sweetness and a nutty bitterness.

SCHWARZES 4.9% ABV ● Dark lager ● Dark brown with a white head; cocoalike nose; dry and chocolatelike without sweetness.

WERNESGRÜNER

✉ Bergstraße 4, 08237 Steinberg-Wernesgrün
🖳 www.wernesgruener.de

The historic buildings in front of the modern brewhouse and lager cellars are proof of the long brewing tradition in this small Saxony town. Beer was first made here by Schorersches Gut ("Schorer's Manor") in 1436 and the nearby Gläsersche Anwesen ("Glaser's Estate") in 1589. These two breweries put the name Wernesgrün on the beer trade map, remaining independent as Grenzquell and Erste Wernesgrüner Aktienbrauerei until after World War II. In 1974 the Communist regime merged the two to create just one premium pilsner brand from Wernesgrün. At this time the pilsner was noticeably somewhat harsher than it is today. Nowadays annual production is roughly 15 million gallons (560,000 hectoliters) and is distributed by Bitburger throughout eastern Germany.

PILS LEGENDE 4.9% ABV ● Pilsner ● Deep golden colored; very dry and crisp; medium bitterness and little hop aroma.

WERNESGRÜNER PILS LEGENDE

Nürnberg and Franconia

Bad Staffelstein • Bamberg • Bayreuth • Kulmbach • Tauberbischofsheim

Bavaria's north has the region's greatest density of breweries and has developed its own beer culture. Most breweries are extremely small—in some cases these are brewpubs that have been in existence for centuries. And they brew unique beers, too.

The medieval city of Nürnberg and the Baroque town of Bamberg are the centers of Franconian beer culture—but this culture can hardly be explored without taking a trip to the smaller villages in the surrounding countryside. Although many small breweries have disappeared in recent decades, there are some breweries that still apply the old technology of maturing their beer in lagering tanks that are unsealed—which results in very mild lagers with extremely low carbonation. These beers are called *ungespundetes* ("nonbunged") or, often, "kellerbier" (cellar beer) and tend to be intensely hopped, too.

These traditional brewing methods can be studied in a handful of brewery-related museums—most notably the Fränkisches Freilandmuseum in Bad Windsheim. In this museum, there are public brewing sessions from time to time in one of the three historic brewhouses. The common brewer's product is "zoigl," a simple, unfiltered lager that was the farmer's beer in former centuries. "Zoigl" also denotes the brewer's star, the hexagram that is the symbol of the mystique behind the brewer's art. A popular interpretation of the magic symbol (*shown on p.80*) is that the three sides of one of the triangles represent the elements earth, fire, and air (for which read yeast) needed in brewing, while the other triangle represents the ingredients water, grains, and hops.

Franconian brewers Fässla, Spezial, and smoked-beer specialist Schenkerla are all based in the pretty Baroque town of Bamberg.

BRAUEREI MICHAEL

✉ Kirchenlamitzer Straße 64–66, 95163 Weißenstadt
🖳 www.brauerei-michael.de

This small family brewery, founded in 1906, decided in its 98th year to focus on organic beers. Owner Hermann Michael contacted wholefood stores as far afield as Berlin and created the Luchs ("lynx") line of beers (the animal is native to the Fichtelgebirge mountains around Weißenstadt). At a time when most other German brewers were axing light beers, Michael proceeded to introduce a new one: "Das Schlanke Bier" ("the slim beer") made its debut on the brewery's 100th birthday.

🍺 **DAS SCHLANKE BIER** 2.9% ABV •
Pilsner • Organic lager marketed under the Ökowellness label. Light golden; intense herbal aroma joined by some grainy notes. Surprisingly full-bodied owing to the dominant Tettnang hop aromas and the underlying bitterness.

🍺 **LUCHS BIER DINKEL** 5.6% ABV •
Dark ale • Brewed with more than 50 percent malted spelt; dark amber, with a hint of banana and blueberries in the nose. Refreshing fruitiness on the palate, very little bitterness.

🍺 **LUCHS BIER WEISSBIER**
5.6% ABV • Hefeweizen • Very pale golden, slightly hazy; little aroma but a surprising spiciness on the palate reminiscent of cinnamon and coriander.

DISTELHÄUSER

✉ Grünsfelder Straße 3, 97941 Tauberbischofsheim-Distelhausen
🖳 www.distelhaeuser-brauerei.de

The Bauer family has run this mid-sized brewery since 1876 and the present owner, Stefan Bauer, has established strong links with the Slow Food movement, which regularly holds presentations at the brewery. Distelhäuser has also pioneered beer tastings for visitors, and while other German breweries stay on the safe side by only entering national competitions, Distelhäuser keeps winning medals at international events, such as the World Beer Cup.

🍺 **PREMIUM PILS** 4.9% ABV
• Pilsner • Pale golden; a slightly fruity (apricotlike) malt aroma and an intense herbal hoppiness in the nose; light to medium body; crisp carbonation. Well-balanced malt and hops; dry, bitter, hoppy finish.

🍺 **HEFEWEIZEN HELL**
5.4% ABV • Hefeweizen Gold to orange, with very intense haze; pineapple, peach, and banana in the nose but no sweetness; finish is extremely dry.

DREI KRONEN MEMMELSDORF

✉ Hauptstraße 19, 96117 Memmelsdorf
🖳 www.braugasthoefe.biz/dreikronen/cms/core/

The name "Drei Kronen," which probably refers to the crowns of the three Magi, is a common one for pubs and even breweries in this region, so to tell one from another, they often append its village name. This one is a massive old inn in a small town east of Bamberg. As with most other small Franconian breweries, owner Hans-Ludwig Straub focusses on on-premise sales of his beers (although there is some bottling). He is also chairman of the "Private Brauerei-gasthöfe," an initiative of small breweries that run their brewery taps themselves and aim to educate their customers about fresh beer.

DREI KRONEN MEMMELSDORF STÖFFLA

🍺 **STÖFFLA** 4.5% ABV •
Smoked lager • Copper-colored and slightly hazy, very stable head; smoky and fruity (plums, pears) aromas. Full-bodied with medium bitterness and a lingering smokiness.

🍺 **LAGER** 4.5% ABV • Unfiltered lager • Amber, slightly hazy; very sweet malty nose, but less sweet on the palate. Long, lingering maltiness with just a hint of hops in the finish.

The charming Drei Kronen Hotel is a flagship of Private Brauerei-gasthöfe—brewery-owned taverns, restaurants, and hotels.

FÄSSLA

✉ Obere Königstraße 19–21, 96052 Bamberg

🏠 www.faessla.de

Roland Kalb runs a cosy tavern that looks as if it has remained unchanged for 100 years. The beers taste very authentic, too—but they come from a state-of-the-art brewery in a rear building. The front building with the brewery tap dates back to 1649. On the inside it is decorated with mural paintings of dwarves engaged in brewing the beer and rolling the barrels out to the tap. A barrel-rolling dwarf also forms part of the brewery's logo.

🍺 **LAGERBIER** 5.5% ABV • Märzen
Deep golden with a creamy head; slightly nutty malt nose with a hint of grassy hops; full-bodied, even sweet on the palate but drier and hoppier in the finish.

🍺 **GOLD-PILS** 5.5% ABV • Pilsner
Golden, with a big, stable white head; herbal, peppery nose; hops dominate the palate and contribute to the full-bodied impression. Finishes dry and hoppy, with haylike aromas.

🍺 **ZWERGLA** 6.0% ABV • Dark lager
Mahogany; sweet, malty, molasseslike aroma; sweet on the palate with some burned malt and herbal hoppy notes in the finish to balance.

HUPPENDORFER BIER

✉ Brauerei, Brennerei und Gasthaus Grasser, Huppendorf 25, 96167 Königsfeld

🏠 www.huppendorfer -bier.de

This small brewery and tavern was founded by the Grasser family in 1750 —but brewing seems to have taken place in this remote village at least since the late 15th century. The brewery tap is very basic, but they are

KULMBACHER
AG EKU 28

enthusiastic about their beer and the spirits they distill.

🍺 **VOLLBIER** 5.0% ABV • Dark lager
A dark amber-colored beer also available as "Zwergla" if bottled in 330 ml bottles. Very full-bodied; aromas of nuts and raisins; mild carbonation, finishing with hoppy aromas.

🍺 **KATHREINBOCK** 7.5% ABV • Bock
Golden, with a very stable head; in strength almost a doppelbock, but very easy to drink owing to the high bitterness level that balances the sweetness. Long-lasting floral hop aromas.

KNOBLACH

✉ Kremmeldorfer Straße 1, 96123 Litzendorf-Schammelsdorf

🏠 http://mon.de/ofr/ knoblach.123275

A large country tavern with a beer garden and a 53,000-gallon (2,000-hectoliter) brewery— all run by Michael Knoblach, a real "hop-head." His family started the business in 1880. Most of their beers also come in bottles, but they do not seem to travel too well. Several breweries in this area are a comfortable walking distance apart; Drei Kronen in Memmelsdorf is less than an hour's hike away.

🍺 **KELLERBIER** 5.0% ABV •
Unfiltered amber lager • Dark amber, slightly hazy; very low carbonation, lots of hop bitterness from the start overlaying a malty body. Intense grassy aromas; a dry, lingering aftertaste.

KULMBACHER AG

✉ Lichtenfelser Straße 9, 95326 Kulmbach

🏠 www.kulmbacher.de

Kulmbach's last remaining large brewery took over

the business of rivals Erste Kulmbacher, Mönchshof, Reichelbräu, and Sandlerbräu in 1996. There is one small brewpub in town, Kulmbacher Kommunbräu, founded in the early 1990s to act as a counterbalance to the local brewing giant. Since 1994 Lichtenfelser Straße has also been the home of the Bavarian Brewery Museum.

🍺 **EKU 28** 11.0% ABV •
Doppelbock • Arguably the most prominent beer from Kulmbach. Amber-colored; malty, sweetish nose with a hint of apples and vanilla. A stinging alcoholic character mingles with the maltiness; very full body and a long-lasting sweetness.

MAISEL
WEISSE
ORIGINAL

🍺 **KAPUZINER WEISSBIER** 5.4% ABV • Hefeweizen
Pale golden with some haze; bananas and yeast in the nose. Medium-bodied and refreshing, with some citrus and pear flavors, and a hint of hops in the aftertaste.

MAISEL

✉ Gebr. Maisel KG, Hindenburg-straße 9, 95445 Bayreuth

🏠 www.maisel.com

This brewery started in 1887 as a family-owned large operation— a history well documented in Maisel's brewing museum, which claims to be the largest of its kind in the world. Maisel started as a bottom-fermenting brewery and the first wheat beer was introduced only in 1955— a pale, filtered "Champagner-weizen," which at that time denoted a kristallweizen. Wheat beers laid the foundation for Maisel's success in later years.

🍺 **WEISSE ORIGINAL** 5.4% ABV •
Hefeweizen • Orange to amber, very little haze; citrus and banana aromas; light to medium body; a little hay-like bitterness in the finish.

WEISSE KRISTALL 5.2% ABV • Kristallweizen • Dark golden, but bright, with a lot of visible carbonation. Citrussy nose with a hint of banana. Some sweetness and more banana to finish.

EDELHOPFEN 4.9% ABV • Dry beer • A "Diät-Pilsener"— the German category of low-carb beers. Darker (dark golden) and definitely hoppier than international examples. Extremely dry in the aftertaste.

SCHLENKERLA

✉ Brauerei Heller, Dominikaner Straße 6, 96049 Bamberg
🖰 www.schlenkerla.de

A name almost synonymous with smoked beer. The building of the brewery tap was first mentioned in 1405, but there is no evidence of brewing from that time— apparently it was a cooper's (barrelmaker's) shop that was later acquired by a nearby cloister. The first barrel of smoked beer was rolled out in 1678. Legend has it that the malt had picked up the smoky taste from a nearby fire; although the monks considered the beer spoiled, they decided to use it anyway. It turned out to be a big success. Today Brauerei Heller uses selected beechwood logs, aged for three years before they provide the smoke to kiln Schlenkerla's

SCHLENKERLA
MÄRZEN

malts. The beers go well with smoked meats and dark breads; the Urbock is seen as the ideal accompaniment to a good cigar.

MÄRZEN 5.1% ABV • Smoked märzen • Copper to mahogany in color; smoky nose; dry mouthfeel with an almost pilslike hop aroma that comes in before the smoke takes over again.

RAUCHWEIZEN 5.2% ABV • Smoked hefeweizen • Dark brown, hazy; smokiness along with chocolate and banana in the nose; full-bodied, almost sweet; very low carbonation but still refreshing. Surprisingly dry aftertaste, again dominated by smoke.

URBOCK 6.5% ABV • Smoked bock • Brown to copper; very intense smoky nose with hints of sweetness. Intensely full-bodied and slightly sweet, flavors of smoked plums and dates, more smoke than hops at the finish.

SCHNEIDER—ZUR KANNE

✉ Bachgasse 15, 91781 Weissenburg
🖰 www.schneider-bier.de

The town of Weissenburg in southern Franconia claims to have invented the bratwurst. This sausage is prominently featured (braised and served with a black beer gravy) in the small brewery and restaurant that is the home of Thomas Schneider. Schneider also owns the Bayerischer Bahnhof in Leipzig (see p.108).

SCHNEIDER BRÄU WEIZEN NATURTRÜB 5.0% ABV • Hefeweizen • Peachlike aroma in a honey-colored beer; very refreshing and light-bodied, with almost no bitterness.

EDLES MÄRZEN ALTFRÄNKISCH 5.6% ABV • Fest-märzen • Amber; some roasted malts and a definite sweetness in

KELLERBIER

Usually an unfiltered, heavily hopped lager with low CO₂ levels, Kellerbier is a drink to be consumed "on top of the cellar," which is a Franconian expression for a beer garden. The term can be traced back to the primitive cooling systems of former centuries: brewers used to plant horse-chestnut trees on top of their beer cellars, to provide leafy shade and thus keep the beer stored below cool. Drinkers soon discovered that this was also a perfect, shady spot to enjoy a beer.

the nose; full-bodied; bitter in the finish.

BOCK 6.7% ABV • Bock • Very dark brown; intense buttery nose but surprisingly little body. Roasted malts dominate the aftertaste.

DAS SCHWARZE 5.1% ABV • Dark lager • Mahogany to black; aromas of roasted malts and licorice; very full-bodied but no apparent sweetness.

SPEZIAL

✉ 10 Obere Königstraße, 96052 Bamberg
🖰 www.brauerei-spezial.de

The März family's brewery and down-to-earth tap are just across the street from Fässla (see p.117), near the train station in Bamberg. Spezial focuses on smoked beers that are a bit smoother and less smoky than those of rival Schlenkerla in downtown Bamberg.

LAGERBIER 4.6% ABV • Smoked lager • Reddish-amber; smoked plums in the nose; medium to full body with some applelike flavor and subtle smokiness, balanced by hop aromas in the finish.

MÄRZENBIER 5.3% ABV • Smoked märzen • Chestnut color; smells of yeast and smoke; full-bodied yet refreshing, with a tart aftertaste that is infused with a lot of hoppiness but relatively little smoke.

WEISSBIER 5.3% ABV • Smoked hefeweizen • Pale amber, very hazy; light banana aromas with very little smoke; full-bodied with a refreshing spiciness (cloves, cinnamon) in the finish.

ST. GEORGEN BRÄU

✉ Gg. Modschiedler OHG, Marktstraße 12, 96155 Buttenheim

🖳 www.kellerbier.de

The largest of three breweries in the village of Buttenheim (also famous as the birthplace of Levi Strauss, of blue jeans fame) brews a broad spectrum of beers for the local market while concentrating on export sales of its kellerbier. This is a truly *ungespundetes* beer (matured without pressure on the lagertank) that comes in flip-top bottles. The brewery also makes a distinctive Keller Bier stein with an art deco design.

KELLER BIER 4.9% ABV • Dark lager • Dark amber; very little head and carbonation; aromas of crusty bread, roasted malt, and herbs; full-bodied with an underlying robust bitterness that gives a dry finish.

STAFFELBERG-BRÄU

✉ Am Mühlteich 4, 96231 Bad Staffelstein-Loffeld

🖳 www.staffelberg-braeu.de

The tap of this brewery is a very lively country inn in Loffeld, just southeast of Bad Staffelstein—a former wine-growing center. Beer became important here only in the mid-19th century, when a couple of breweries were founded in the surrounding villages. This

ST GEORGEN BRÄU KELLER BIER

one dates back to 1856 and has been owned by the Geldner family ever since. It has some bottom-fermenting lagers but its most interesting products are the top-fermented beers.

WEIZEN 5.2% ABV • Hefeweizen Extremely pale straw with some haze; pears in the nose; light-bodied and very refreshing; dry in the aftertaste.

URKORN 5.4% ABV • Specialty ale • Amber with little aroma; medium to full body. Intense aromas of pears and nuts in the dry, mildly bitter finish.

TRUNK

✉ Vierzehnheiligen 3, 96231 Bad Staffelstein

🖳 http://vierzehnheiligen. brauereien.bierland-oberfranken.de

The town of Bad Staffelstein is home to a dozen breweries. This one is right behind the popular church of Vierzehnheiligen, a regional pilgrimage center. Formerly the "Alte Klosterbrauerei Vierzehnheiligen," it was acquired by the Trunk family and carefully renovated. The brewery tap is usually very busy but it closes rather early.

NOTHELFER DUNKEL 5.1% ABV • Dark lager Dark copper; aromas of roasted nuts, toasted malt and spicy, herbal hops. Some liquorice complementing the sweetness, the finish is also rather sweet.

NOTHELFER PILS 4.7% ABV • Pilsner • Pale straw color; a hint of yeast in the nose and a citrussy hop aroma; light to medium body and a pronounced bitterness with a lot of hop aroma (Tettnang and Spalter Select) to finish.

SILBERBOCK 6.3% ABV • Bock Golden to amber in color; very full-bodied with a buttery and sweetish overall impression, but one that is well balanced by a herbal hop bitterness and a surprisingly dry finish.

TUCHER

✉ Schwabacher Straße 106, 90763 Fürth

🖳 www.tucher.de

The last large brewery in the Nürnberg-Fürth area was set up as the city of Nürnberg's "Städtisches Weizenbrauhaus" in 1672. When Nürnberg became part of Bavaria in 1806, the brewery became the property of the king of Bavaria and was privatized into the hands of the Tucher family 50 years later. Tucher quickly became the largest beer exporter in Franconia and merged with several other breweries. Now part of the Radeberger group, Tucher also brews the beers of former local rival Lederer, which has an even longer history, dating back to 1471. The crocodile in the Lederer logo is considered one of the oldest trademarks in Germany.

LEDERER PREMIUM PILS 5.1% ABV • Pilsner • Golden, with a firm white head; intense herbal hop aroma; dry and crisp with not too much bitterness in the aftertaste.

TUCHER URBRÄU 4.9% ABV • Pale lager Very pale straw; spicy, floral nose (camomile?); light-bodied and refreshing with just a hint of nutty bitterness.

TUCHER DUNKLES HEFEWEIZEN 5.2% ABV • Hefeweizen • Reddish-brown with a lot of haze; big aroma of very ripe banana; refreshing and dry with roasty notes in the aftertaste.

TUCHER URBRÄU

BELGIUM

Ask a non-Belgian to name three famous Belgians and, even though the list is long (Rubens, Magritte, Jacques Brel, Hergé, Georges Simenon...), there will probably be a painful pause. Ask them to name three Belgian beers, and their performance is likely to improve dramatically.

N estled between the Dutch, Germans, Luxembourgers, and French, the Belgians have adopted three of their neighbors' languages. But when it comes to beer, they are more cautious. From the late 1800s onward, Belgian brewers have stubbornly resisted the pilsner epidemic that threatened to wipe out their regional specialties and replace them with a beer monoculture. Even today, Belgians drink at least 20 percent less pilsner than their neighbors across the border.

What do Belgians drink instead? In Flanders, pale ale (or speciale), developed in the 1920s to compete against pilsner, is still popular, as are witbiers (white beers) and sour red-brown ales. Around Brussels, gueuze, lambic, and kriek are enjoying a resurgence, and Wallonians still enjoy their tart and dry saisons. To be sure, there are Belgian pilsners. Technically they are well-brewed and seem to keep brewery book-keepers happy, but laboratory analysis and consumer organization testing confirms that using less malt and hops results in beers that are thinner, weaker, and seriously lacking in character. Even the "premium"

Belgium's blond ales, refreshing, fragrant, dry, and often deceptively potent, make perfect aperitifs but also sit happily on the dinner table.

brands like Stella Artois can't measure up to supermarket discount brands sold in the Netherlands and Germany.

The biggest single difference between Belgium and other beer-drinking nations is choice. Belgians have more than 25 indigenous styles with countless regional variations, and choose their beers the way the French choose wine. A simple lower-alcohol or fruity ale to quench their thirst, a drier-hopped and more alcoholic beer with a meal or as an aperitif, and a stronger, heavier, darker beer as a digestive or with dessert (called a *degustatie* beer) are only a few of the possibilities.

But while the Belgians were notorious imbibers in the 1970s, at 35 gallons (132 liters) per head per year, the amount of beer they drink has steadily fallen to the current 24-gallon (90-liter) level, giving way to soft drinks. Drinkers going to the local bar for a *pintje* (Belgian slang for a small glass of beer) have seen their choice dwindle by 30 percent in the last decade, and to offset increased costs, the pubs that remain have raised their average beer prices by 40 percent. This has, needless to say, driven many customers to drink… at home! Brewers, on the other hand, have solved this problem by tripling exports and in some cases having their beers locally contract-brewed for foreign markets.

Flanders

West Flanders • East Flanders • Antwerp • Limberg

The majority of Belgians live in Flanders, the northern half of the country. Inhabitants of Flanders are called Flemings, and the language they speak is Flemish, a dialect of Dutch. This stems from when Belgium and the Netherlands to the north were united as one nation.

Flemings produce, per capita, 20–25 percent more than people in other Belgian regions, enjoy a higher general level of education, and have more purchasing power than the average European. This affluence has, unfortunately, had no effect on the brewing sector: there has actually been a decline in breweries over the past 20 years. As a region, Flanders still has Belgium's highest number of breweries but the only real growth has been in brewery museums, as traditional heavy industry has been replaced by tourism and high-tech manufacturing.

Despite such setbacks, it is Flanders that has perfected the greatest variations within a group of beer styles. Flemish brewers tend to shy away from the use of spices, sugars, and exotic

grains and try to maintain the tradition of using locally grown hops. You might think that this Calvinist approach would limit choice, but in fact, even styles that look very similar are separated by nuances in flavour that deserve appreciation.

Some Flemish beers are so distinctive that they have become styles in their own right. Duvel, one of the most famous Flanders brands, has, like Coca-Cola, spawned countless blond-coloured, well-hopped, would-be clones that share devil-themed names. Lucifer, Judas, and Cuveé Diabolique are but three examples from brewers who do their utmost to produce a comparable product and cash in on the quality and fame of the original. The same is true of the region's "other" (just as famous) amber-coloured, hoppy ale, Westmalle.

A waiter serves drinks at a bar in Antwerp. The Belgian café scene is a great place to relax and enjoy a beer.

BLOND BIER   BIERE BLONDE

AUTHENTIC TRAPPIST PRODUCT

Trappist

Achel

Alc 8° Vol   e33cl

ACHEL

✉ St. Benedictusabdij de
Achelse Kluis, Kluis 1, 3930
Hamont-Achel
℧ www.achelsekluis.org

After a hiatus of 80 years,
Trappist brewing finally
returned to the abbey of St.
Benedictus, Hamont-Achel,
in 1999. The income made
by running a religious-article
store and a supermarket was
just not enough to pay for
the upkeep of the abbey and
its 20 monks, so a brewery
was established.

The original plans were
limited to a brewpub, but it
soon became evident that
bottling and selling the beers
(and raising their alcohol
content) could dramatically
improve Achel's revenue, so
the business was expanded
accordingly. Achel beers are
all well-hopped and brewed
using Westmalle yeast.

▮ 5 BLOND (DRAFT) 5.0% ABV •
Belgian bitter • Light blond in
color; nose is hoppy and
slightly fruity; light-bodied
and hoppy palate, with a
fruity-bitter finish.

▮ BLOND 8.0% ABV • Triple
Golden; nose of overripe
bananas is slightly metallic;
the bitter alcoholic and fruity
palate becomes dry and hop-
bitter; highly carbonated.

ALVINNE

✉ Oostrozebeekstraat 114, 8770
Ingelmunster
℧ www.alvinne.be

The Castelein brothers,
Glenn and Jeffry, received
their license to brew in

ACHEL BLOND

December 2004. Their
Alvinne brewery (West
Flanders' smallest) is
located in a wooden
chalet in their brother-
in-law's garden in
Ingelmunster. Glenn,
the brewmaster, runs
homebrew courses and
also gives beer lectures
and holds tastings
throughout Flanders. One
Alvinne beer, Gaspar, claims
a bitterness rating of an
incredible 115 IBUs,
although laboratory analysis
places it at 54 units (still very
high). Alvinne brews eight
beers of its own, in addition
to producing original beers
for a few local pubs.

▮ MELCHIOR 11.0% ABV • Barley
wine • Amber; nose is hoppy,
fruity, and resiny; palate is
complex and bitter, with an
extremely long, mouth-
warming finish. Very British
in character.

ANKER

✉ Guido Gezellelaan 49, 2800
Mechelen
℧ www.hetanker.be

The Anker brewery in
Mechelen has a long history:
it claims to have been
recorded as paying brewing
taxes as far back as 1369.

The company began
brewing Gouden Carolus,
one of its current best-
sellers, in 1960. Despite
losing the Floreffe range to
Lefèbvre (*see p.137*) in 1983,
Anker bounced back with
fine brews such as
Mechelschen Bruynen and
Triple Toison d'Or.

In the 1990s, the brewery
was briefly owned by Riva
and then by John Martin,
and the quality of the beers
suffered. In 1998, ownership
reverted to the descendants
of the Van Breedams, the
family who had owned the
brewery since the late 1870s.
There have since been many
positive changes to the
product range and brewery

site, including a three-star
hotel and restaurant.
▮ GOUDEN CAROLUS CHRISTMAS
10.5% ABV • Christmas ale • Dark
brown; fruit (pineapple) and
herbs (aniseed, coriander,
and grains of paradise) are
evident in the nose; the
palate is sweet with liquorice,
with a full-bodied, warming
alcohol finish.

BAVIK

✉ Rijksweg 33, 8531 Bavikhove
℧ www.bavik.be

The De Brabandere family
founded this brewery near
Kortrijk in 1894. They did
not start using the brand
name Petrus (after St. Peter)
until 1982, when they
relaunched their oak-aged
Flemish brown ale as
Petrus Oud Bruin. This
is a blend of 70 percent
young brown ale and 30
percent pale ale that has
been stored in Calvados
tuns for two to three years.
The latter was bottled on its
own for the first time in 2001
as Petrus Aged Pale.
▮ PETRUS AGED PALE 7.3% ABV •
Stock ale • Golden; nose is a
mixture of wood, horse-
blanket, and mustiness;
sherrylike palate, drying out
into a puckering finish.
▮ PETRUS OUD BRUIN 5.5% ABV •
Flemish brown ale • Dark red;
citric, oaky nose; some
maltiness in the palate,
with a sweetish-sour finish.

BAVIK PETRUS OUD BRUIN

**BOSTEELS
KARMELIET TRIPEL**

BOSTEELS

✉ Kerkstraat 92, 9255 Buggenhout
⌖ www.bestbelgianspecialbeers.be

This sixth-generation family brewery was founded by Jozef Bosteels in 1791. The Pauwel Kwak they launched in 1980 is a Belgian icon. It is served in a coachman's glass that can only remain upright in a custom-built wooden holder (*see below*).

More interesting, however, is Bosteels' multi-grain Karmeliet Tripel. The mixture of malted and unmalted barley, wheat, and oats produces alluring aromas and flavors not normally found in its competitors. In recent years, some production of

Karmeliet Tripel has been moved to the Van Steenberge brewery in Ertvelde.

▣ **BLUSSER** 5.4% ABV • **Urtyp pilsner** • Brewed for Anker (*see p.123*). Light blond; hoppy, slightly sulfury nose; malty, citrus-hoppy, bitter palate; finish is thin-bodied, dry, and bitter.

▣ **KARMELIET TRIPEL** 8.0% ABV • **Triple** • Golden; massive head; spicy mandarin-orange aromas; drying spiciness combined with high carbonation and warming alcohol in the palate; finishes like a Brut (dry) Champagne.

CNUDDE

✉ Fabriekstraat 8, 9700 Eine-Oudenaarde
⌖ www.eine-heemkring.be/ brouwerij_cnudde_index.php

Brouwerij Cnudde is located in the village of Eine, close to the buffalo-adorned Ohio bridge, commemorating the bravery shown here by the Ohio National Guard in World War I. The brewery was founded in 1919 by Alfons Cnudde, and partially restored in 1950.

Three grandsons—Pieter, Lieven, and Steven—now brew every other month on a Saturday to produce just enough beer to supply the

village pubs with draft Cnudde Bruin beer. All three remain in their full-time jobs.

Cnudde Bruin is a simple, thirst-quenching beer brewed from Pilsener malt, sugars, and Northern Brewer hops. It derives its lactic character from "wild" airborne lactic bacteria.

▣ **CNUDDE BRUIN** 4.7% ABV • **Flemish brown ale** • Dark red-brown; lactic-fruity and slightly metallic in flavor; dry and tart, with a thin to medium-bodied finish.

CONTRERAS

✉ Molenstraat 115, 9890 Gavere
⌖ www.contreras.be

Founded in 1818 near Ghent, this brewery has been owned by the Contreras family since 1898. Until recently, they brewed only a pilsner and a couple of session ales. This changed when the brewer, Willy Contreras, who has worked in this pristine brewery for almost 50 years, finally found a successor in his son-in-law. Together they have launched a new range of beers with restyled labels.

▣ **MARS ESPECIAL** 6.5% ABV • **Maarts** • This specialty beer is brewed only in March. Amber; buttery, sourish-

A GLASS FOR EVERY BEER

Belgian bars can be a shock for first-time visitors. Most brewers have a different glass for each style of beer they brew, and a bar may have hundreds of different beer glasses in which to serve their beers. To reduce costs, brewers choose from a range of existing models, adding a label to make each glass unique. Occasionally, a brewer will have a glass custom-made and pay extra for exclusive rights. Famous examples include the Pauwel Kwak glass (*pictured, on left*), made for the Bosteels brewery, and the glasses of De Koninck (the "Bolleke"), Duvel, and Westmalle.

Glass etiquette is taken very seriously in Belgium. If the correct glass is not available, a bartender may refuse to serve a beer.

sweet aromas; slightly tannic and hoppy palate; finishing malty, slightly sour, and bitter, with warming alcohol.

DECA

✉ Elverdingestraat 4, 8640 Woesten-Vleteren
🖰 www.struisebrouwers.be

Since it was set up in 1850, the Deca brewery in West Flanders has had numerous changes of name and ownership, the last of which was in 1991. The brewery is now a bizarre combination of a working museum and drive-through liquor store.

Deca regularly rents out the extra capacity in its brewery to contract-brewers. Many of these contract-brewers make far more successful beers than Deca itself. The newest resident is De Struise Brouwers, which produces a wide range of beers, some for third parties wanting an original brew. Struise Aardmonnik is a blend of 30 percent, 18-month-old, oak-cask-ripened ale and 70 percent young ale.

AARDMONNIK 8.0% ABV • Strong Flemish brown Dark copper; virtually no head; lactic-woody and caramel-sweet aromas; body and sweetness and a puckering feeling in the mouth; sour in the finish with complex tannins.

DE DOLLE BROUWERS

✉ Roeselarestraat 12b, 8600 Esen
🖰 www.dedollebrouwers.be

Architect, artist, and homebrewer Kris Herteleer took over Esen's 145-year-old Costenoble brewery in 1980. With a new range of beers, new labels, a change of name to De Dolle, and an advertising campaign, the brewery rapidly

developed its own cult following. Herteleer's first brew, named Oerbier (meaning "primitive beer"), is a complex variation of the local bruin. Most of Oerbier's character derives from the "old" Rodenbach yeast strain used.

OERBIER RESERVA 13.0% ABV • Strong Flemish brown • Dark amber; a woody, lactic, applelike, caramel nose that continues into the palate with a wave of alcohol and spicy hops, lasting long into the finish. Eighteen months in Bordeaux vats and *Lactobacillus* make this the "Oloroso sherry of beers."

DE GRAAL

✉ Warande 15, 9660 Brakel
🖰 www.degraal.be

This microbrewery was set up in 2002, using second-hand dairy equipment to brew ginger beer in a former marble sawmill. Brewer Wim Saeyens, who keeps his "day" job in the pharmaceutical industry, brews up to three batches on each brewing day. The word *graal* means grail, referring to Saeyens's never-ending search for the "right" name for his brewery. De Graal brews six of its own beers, as well as original beers for customers on a contract basis.

TRIVERIUS 6.8% ABV • Double-wit • Be warned: this beer tastes stronger than is stated on the label! Deep yellow in color; strong coriander aroma; fruity and slightly hoppy palate, with a medium to full body; finishes with well-balanced citrus, fruity, and coriander flavors.

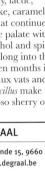
DE DOLLE BROUWERS OERBIER RESERVA

DE KONINCK

DE KONINCK

✉ Mechelsesteenweg 291, 2018 Antwerpen
🖰 www.dekoninck.be

This brewery on the outskirts of Antwerp was founded by the De Koninck family in 1833. Still family-run, it has been in the hands of the Van Den Bogaerts since 1919.

For many years, the brewery produced just one beer—a full-malt ale using Burtonized water and Czech Saaz hop flowers. In 1993, it began experimenting with more fashionable and alcoholic styles. The new brewhouse, which is fully computerized and fitted with stainless-steel equipment, now also produces a blond, a triple, and a seasonal winter beer.

The best way to enjoy De Koninck beers is on draft—ideally in Antwerp's Café Pelgrim, just over the road from the brewery.

DE KONINCK 5.0% ABV • Belgian pale ale • Brilliant amber color; yeasty, fruity, malty palate; medium-bodied; finish is nutty, spicy-hoppy, and lightly toasted.

DE RYCK

✉ Kerkstraat 24, 9550 Herzele
🖰 www.brouwerijderyck.be

De Ryck is a family run brewery dating back to 1886. An De Ryck, who lives with her family on site, is one of Belgium's few female brewers. She was only 24 when she took charge of brewing. The recipe for Special De Ryck pale ale was probably influenced by her father's apprenticeship in England, in Newcastle upon Tyne.

De Ryck became famous for its unpasteurized beers, which it sold in take-away 1¹/₁₀-gallon (5-liter) kegs. In fact, it only started bottling its beers in the 1990s. Of the current range, the classic dry-hopped Special De Ryck and Christmas Pale Ale are the driest, most aromatic, and appetite-inducing.

📙 **CHRISTMAS PALE ALE** 6.3% ABV • Belgian pale ale • Dark amber hue; caramel-hoppy aroma; dry and slightly tannic in flavor; finish is dry and refreshingly spicy-bitter.

DUVEL MOORTGAT

✉ Breendonkdorp 58, 2870 Breendonk-Puurs

🖥 www.duvel.be

The Duvel brewery was set up by the Moortgat family in 1871. With not a hint of copper in sight, there is little romance about Duvel's brewhouse; this will be even more true when its high-tech replacement, which will allow Duvel to more than double production, is on-stream.

Duvel (Flemish for devil) began in 1923 as a dark beer, but went "platinum blond" in 1970. The combination of Burtonized water, Scottish yeast, 32 IBUs, obsessive quality control, and a unique glass makes Duvel the most respected (and imitated) of Belgium's strong blond ales.

📙 **DUVEL** 8.5% ABV • Strong blond ale • Light blond; pearlike and spicy-hop aromas; citrus-bitter, very dry palate; carbonated; bitter, Granny Smith applelike finish.

📙 **MAREDSOUS 8** 8.0% ABV • Double/quadruple hybrid • Dark copper; colalike and slightly metallic nose; slightly hop-bitter palate with notes of caramel, fruit, licorice, and cola; warming alcohol finish.

GAVERHOPKE

✉ Steenbrugstraat 187, 8530 Stasegem-Harelbeke

🖥 http://cmdstud.khlim. be/~hdhulster/gaverhopke/

This weekend pub and brewery was established in 1994 by ex-homebrewer Erik

Ameye, who perfected his brewing techniques at Westvleteren (*see p.131*). He shared his brewhouse with the De Zwingel brewery until it stopped brewing around the turn of the century. Den Twaalf was Ameye's first beer, and he has been perfecting the recipe since he first began brewing it in 1986.

DUVEL

📙 **DEN TWAALF** 12.0% ABV • Quadruple • Quite easy drinking for its strength. Dark copper; the fruity, hoppy, and caramel nose becomes sweeter and slightly mouth-warming; spicy finish with apricot.

GLAZEN TOREN

✉ Glazen Torenweg 11, 9420 Erpe-Mere

🖥 www.glazentoren.be

Jef van den Steen, beer-writer and alderman of Erpe-Mere, started homebrewing in 1988. Years later, he and two partners, Dirk De Pauw and Mark De Nee, converted the building next to his home (originally built to house his RV) into a brewery. Glazen Toren launched its first beer in 2004.

The brewery uses locally grown hops from Aalst and yeast cultures from larger breweries located nearby. Four beer styles are brewed: saison, triple, Scotch ale (for Christmas), and double-wit. All of the Glazen Toren beers are conditioned in 75cl bottles with hand-wrapped labels.

📙 **JAN DE LICHTE** 7.0% ABV • Double-wit Yellow; mixture of strong citrus aromas (Cascade hop and Curaçao); bone-dry and lactic palate, getting even more citric, dry, and puckering in the finish.

KERKOM

✉ Naamsesteenweg 469, 3800 Kerkom-Sint-Truiden

🖥 www.brouwerijkerkom.be

The Clerinx family started brewing in Kerkom in 1878. After World War II, their range consisted of only lemonade and table beers, and they closed in 1968.

Jean Clerinx came back from brewing with Alken to reopen the brewery in 1987. He brewed Bink bitter until he retired and sold the brewery to Marc Limet in 1999. Limet modernized the Kerkom brewery and also expanded the range to four year-round beers and two seasonal brews. He also occasionally contract-brews original beers for third parties. There is a small bar on site, where you can sample Kerkom's beers.

📙 **BINK BLOND** 5.5% ABV • Belgian bitter • Golden; aromas of malt, spices, and citrus fruit; the palate's light fruitiness is overpowered by a resiny-hoppy bitterness that lasts long into the finish.

📙 **ADELARDUS DUBBEL** 7.0% ABV • Double/herb beer • Coppery brown; licorice, herbs, and cherry aromas; full, sweet, mouth-filling, caramel-spice palate, getting slightly drier in the finish.

LIEFMANS

✉ Wontergemstraat 42, 8720 Dentergem

🖥 www.liefmans.be

This beautiful old brewery was founded in 1679 and moved to its current location just prior to World War II. Ex-ballerina Rose Blancquaert was the director's secretary from 1946, until she was named as his replacement after his death in 1972.

Despite a takeover by the English brewery group Vaux in 1974, Blancquaert's business

LIEFMANS KRIEK

CAN I SHOW YOU THE BEER MENU?

There are many more culinary wonders to discover in Belgium than *frieten* (hand-cut fried potatoes) and mayonnaise, Brussels waffles, and pralines. Belgians are as serious about food as they are about their beer, and understand how to match the two together.

Beer is so central to Belgian culture that it is acceptable at the dinner table as wine. And, as with wine, some beers work perfectly with certain foods, bringing the best out of both. Try lambic beers with soft cheese and radishes, Duvel with Parmesan cheese, white beer with steamed mussels; Orval with fish, blond or triple with citrus-based desserts, and Trappist double with pralines.

Beers such as De Ranke XX Bitter, 3 Fonteinen Geuze, or Saison Dupont make an excellent replacement for sherry or white wine as an apéritif, while Liefmans Goudenband makes a superb accompaniment to *carbonade flamand* (a Flemish beef stew), and a

glass of Rochefort 10 effortlessly replaces port as an accompaniment to Stilton cheese.

Belgium is home to more than 300 cheeses of its own, and with at least as many beers, this is a marriage made in heaven. Don't be surprised to receive a small portion of complimentary cheese with your beer. Some Trappist monastery breweries, such as Orval and Chimay, produce their own cheeses, while others, like Rochefort, have cheese produced for them locally.

Belgium has superb restaurants that serve *cuisine à la bière*. The Hof van Cleve in Kruishoutem and Karmeliet in Bruges, for example, are Michelin 3-star restaurants that cook with beer.

Belgium's beers are incredibly varied, and different brands and styles can be matched with dishes to bring out the best in both.

sense and outstanding beers won Liefmans a cult following, and a firm export base.

Blancquaert was part of the De Coster group that repatriated the brewery in 1985. It was bought by nearby rival Riva in 1990. Riva moved the brewing and bottling off-site in 1991 (Liefmans still ferments and lagers) and made the brewery into a museum and restaurant.

📖 **GOUDENBAND** 8.0% ABV • Strong Flemish brown • Dark copper; sourish, fruity nose; slightly lactic and toasted palate; finish is full-bodied and metallic, with warming alcohol.

📖 **KRIEK** 6.0% ABV • Kriek • Dark copper; huge sweet-cherry aroma; tart and slightly tannic cherry palate; mouth-filling and slightly puckering finish.

MALHEUR

✉ Mandekenstraat 179, 9255 Buggenhout

🐾 www.malheur.be

Malheur opened its doors in 1997, on the site of the old Manu De Landtsheer family brewery, which had operated between 1690 and 1938. Starting conservatively with a lower-alcohol blond called Malheur 4, brewer Luc Verhaeghe then brought out "8," "10," and "12," before starting on his Bière Brut project in 1999, using the *méthode originale*. The Brut process starts off using the normal Malheur 10, but the apparatus, bottling (using Champagne-style bottles and a larger dose of sugar), and bottle-conditioning (three times longer than usual, and using *remuage* and *dégorgement*) are the same as those used to produce Champagne.

📖 **MALHEUR 10** 10.0% ABV • Triple (full malt) • Yellowy gold; overripe bananas and

alcohol in the nose; bitter, fruity, warming alcohol palate; the hoppy bitterness increases and lingers long into the finish.

📖 **MALHEUR BIÈRE BRUT** 11.0% ABV • "Champagne" beer • Golden; pear, banana, and alcohol aromas; warming alcohol palate, slightly bitter and yet fruity-sweet; the high carbonation counteracts the sweet, spicy finish.

MALHEUR 10

PAKHUIS

✉ Vlaamse Kaai 76, 2000 Antwerp

🐾 www.pakhuis.info

Antwerp's Pakhuis began in 1996 as one of only a handful of brewpubs in Belgium. High ceilings and concrete give this 1850s multistory warehouse a cool industrial feel, but copper brewkettles near the bar and red-brick walls help to warm up and personalize the building's otherwise cavernous interior.

Pakhuis has brewed three regular beers to date, and occasional seasonal specials. Swing-top bottles can be purchased for take-out, as the beer is not normally sold off the premises. Food receives high priority at Pakhuis, and many menu items are made using the in-house beers.

📖 **ANTWERPS BRUIN** 5.5% ABV • Belgian pale ale • Copper; roasted-caramel and slightly buttery nose; palate is slightly astringent, with rye bread and fruit; finish is nutty, with caramel.

PROEF

✉ Doornzelestraat 20, 9080 Lochristi

🐾 www.proefbrouwerij.com

Proef was set up in 1996 among the azalea nurseries of

PROEF ZOETZUUR

Lochristi, northeast of Ghent. It soon found itself struggling to cope with the demand that flooded in from its satisfied contract-brew customers, so a second, larger brewhouse was built.

The brewery's founder, Dirk Naudts, a former university lecturer in brewing, has brewed using a wide range of ingredients, from shiitake mushrooms to cocoa powder. His beers are regular prize-winners in international competitions.

📖 **VLAAMS PRIMITIEF** 9.0% ABV • Brettanomyces blond • Yellow; hop, citrus, and "barnlike" nose, with sherry and leather notes; bitter, sour, astringent palate; finish is chalk-dry, with warming alcohol.

📖 **ZOETZUUR** 7.0% ABV • Strong Flemish brown • Amber; musty, horse-blanketlike, and tannic aromas; sour-sweet palate, becoming drier, slightly puckering, and more complex in the finish.

📖 **LOZEN BOER ABT** 10.0% ABV • Quadruple • Dark red; raisin, caramel, and bitter-chocolate nose; malty-sweet, warming alcohol palate, with hints of port wine into the finish.

📖 **IKI** 4.5% ABV • Tea beer • Yellowy gold; sweet and citric (fresh-squeezed orange juice) in the nose; sweet, fruity (melon), and slightly tannic palate; finish is dry, slightly bitter, and refreshing.

REGENBOOG

✉ Koningin Astridlaan 134, 8310 Assebroek-Brugge

After working as a teacher and then a printer, Johan Brandt transformed his

printing works (housed in an old smithy on the outskirts of Bruges) first into a shop selling homebrew supplies, and then into a mini-brewery.

Brandt began brewing in 1996, starting with a honey beer. He launched his mustard beer, Wostyntje, in 1999 to celebrate the 130th anniversary of the Torhout-based Wostyn mustard factory.

WOSTYNTJE 7.0% ABV ● Vegetable beer ● Amber to copper in color; hoppy and slightly sour nose; the slightly mouth-puckering, astringent, dry palate continues right through to the aftertaste.

RODENBACH

✉ Spanjestraat 133–141, 8800 Roeselare
🖳 www.rodenbach.be

Alexander Rodenbach bought a distillery-brewery-maltings at Roeselare, West Flanders, in 1820. The business remained in family hands until his great-nephew, Eugene Rodenbach, died in 1889. The Rodenbach brewery then became a public limited company.

Eugene Rodenbach's apprenticeship at a porter brewery in southern England during the 1870s strongly influenced the blending and oak-tun "vinification" process that is still used at Rodenbach today to produce its "sour" red-brown ales. In fact, early advertising even used the slogan "t is wijn" ("It's wine"). Rodenbach ripens its sour beers for up to two years in hundreds of vast oak tuns, some of which are 150 years old.

When Palm (see p.138) took over Rodenbach in 1998, it restored and converted the old listed maltings into a museum and reception hall.

RODENBACH GRAND CRU 6.0% ABV ● Flemish red
Dark copper; sour-apple and cherrylike nose; tannic-sour and sweetish palate;

RODENBACH GRAND CRU

long, complex, puckering finish. To quote the advertising slogan: "You love it or you hate it."

ROMAN

✉ Hauwaart 105, 9700 Mater-Oudenaarde
🖳 www.roman.be

Roman is a family business whose origins lie way back in 1545. Originally known as De Clocke, it began as an inn and farm on the main road from Calais to Cologne, where travelers could rest for the night and exchange their horses. There was also a brewery, where the publican brewed his own ale, as well as a flour mill and a maltings.

In 1930, the brewery was demolished and rebuilt a few yards away from its original site. There have been numerous additions since then, and today the brewery is a large, fortresslike building with an open space in the middle where summer rock concerts are held.

Roman brewed ales until World War II, especially the old brown style of Flemish ale. The post-War years saw it move into pilsners, and its Romy Pils became a Belgian favorite. However, Roman maintained its ale production and built up a global reputation with brews such as the Ename abbey range and Adriaen Brouwer, a traditional old brown ale. The well-water

that Roman uses for brewing has a high iron content, which is especially evident in its range of blond beers. The brewery's Boxer X-Mas is made exclusively for the Colruyt supermarket chain.

BOXER X-MAS 9.0% ABV ● Christmas beer ● Coppery amber; the nose of dried fruit (as in Christmas cake) carries right through to the full-bodied, warming finish.

ST. BERNARDUS

✉ Trappistenweg 23, 8978 Watou
🖳 www.sintbernardus.be

St. Bernardus began in 1930 as a cheese dairy. In 1946, the dairy started brewing a line of St. Sixtus beers for the Westvleteren Trappist monastery (see p.131), and this continued right through to 1992, when its contract with the monastery expired. Shortly thereafter, the Trappists filed a lawsuit against the brewery for its continued use of the St. Sixtus name and the monk's image on the labels. Since losing the case, the brewery has changed the labels of its abbey range no fewer than five times.

St. Bernardus currently exports more than 40 percent of its total production, and brews two versions of Grottenbier for ex-Hoegaarden (see p.137) brewer Pierre Celis.

ABT 12 10.0% ABV ● Quadruple ● Amber to copper; nose of raisins, pears, and bananas; palate is slightly bitter, syrupy, and spicy; coconut- and banana-like in the alcoholic, mouth-warming finish.

GROTTENBIER BRUIN 6.8% ABV ● Spice beer
Dark brown, with spice (grains of paradise?) and banana aromas followed by a drying, almost medicinal resiny palate and a herbal, rooty, and sugar-candy finish.

ST. BERNARDUS
ABT 12

SLAGHMUYLDER

✉ Denderhoutembaan 2, 9400 Ninove

🔗 www.witkap.be

Dating back to 1860, this family brewery started brewing pilsner in 1922. Although the brewery has been moved and rebuilt several times, the brewhouse (with its steam generator) is still 1924-vintage, and now houses a modest museum. The main gate resembles the entrance to a 1920s Hollywood studio.

Slaghmuylder took over the brewing of the Witkap range of beers from the Verlinden brewery (brewer of the first triple in the 1930s) in 1979, and bought the "Witkap Pater = Trappistenbier" brand outright in 1981. This led to a legal battle with Westmalle (*see facing page*) over the use of the term Trappist, and Slaghmuylder has since dropped the name.

SLAGHMUYLDER WITKAP STIMULO

🍺 **WITKAP STIMULO** 6.0% ABV • Blond • Golden-blond; nose is flowery and slightly hoppy; thin-bodied and dry on the palate, with a hoppy, slightly citrus finish.

STRUBBE

✉ Markt 1, 8480 Ichtegem

🔗 www.brouwerij-strubbe.be

Founded in 1830 by Carolus Strubbe, the brewery is currently run by two sixth-generation Strubbe cousins: Marc brews and Norbert does the book-keeping. Strubbe contract-brews for a number of local and foreign customers, and specializes in a wide range of technically challenging beers.

In 1988, almost two years before his larger competitors, Marc Strubbe was the first Belgian brewer to produce alcohol-free beer. In 2001,

he was named laureate of the Fédération des Etudes et Rescherches dans L'Industrie de Fermentation, in honor of his work on hop efficiency and production losses.

🍺 **ICHTEGEM'S GRAND CRU** 6.5% ABV • Strong Flemish brown Coppery; lactic, woody, and caramel nose; tannic and puckering in the palate, becoming more balanced in the finish.

VAN DEN BOSSCHE

✉ St. Lievensplein 16, 9550 Sint-Lievens-Esse

🔗 www.paterlieven.be

This fourth-generation family brewery was established in 1897. Located just off the village square in Sint-Lievens-Esse, the brewery is now a listed monument. The brewhouse pre-dates World War I, but the rest of the brewery has been updated generation by generation, and now includes cylindro-conical fermenters and a modern bottling line.

In 1907, the brewer left a boiling brew unattended to visit Buffalo Bill's traveling rodeo in a nearby village. When he returned, he discovered that the beer had overheated, and had caramelized and evaporated to a higher gravity. His "mistake" was fortuitous, as the resulting beer caught on, and the local specialty called Buffalo was born.

🍺 **KERSTPATER** 9.0% ABV • Christmas beer • Dark red-brown; caramel, spices, dried fruit, and roasted malt in the nose and palate; roasted-malt bitterness and warming alcohol in the long finish.

🍺 **BUFFALO** 6.5% ABV • Specialty beer • Coppery brown; sourish-sweet and roasted malt

nose; slightly sweet in the palate, but more neutral in the short finish.

VAN EECKE

✉ Douvieweg 2, 8978 Watou

🔗 www.brouwerijvaneecke.tk

Located in Watou, in the Westhoek (western corner) region of West Flanders near the French border, Van Eecke began in 1862 as the Gouden Leeuw brewery. Operating from within the grounds of a ruined castle, its first beer was called West-ale.

In 1922, Albert Van Eecke, grandson of the founder, installed a refrigerated cellar, and the brewery made its first bottom-fermented beer, West-Pils. The Kapittel range of abbey beers dates to 1950; it was refined by brewer Jan Van Gysegem (later of De Kluis) in the early 1960s.

In 1967, Van Eecke embarked on a partnership with the Leroy brewery in nearby Boezinge. Van Eecke brews and ferments, while Leroy lagers, bottles, and bottle-conditions the beers.

🍺 **HOMMELBIER** 7.5% ABV • Blond Hommel is local dialect for hop. Yellowy gold; hoppy, pear-like aroma; strong chalky, hop-bitter palate (dry-hopping) that continues long into the aftertaste.

VERHAEGHE

✉ Beukenhofstraat 96, 8570 Vichte

🔗 www.proximedia.com/web/breweryverhaeghe.html

In 1891, Paul Verhaeghe changed the distillery he had bought in 1880 into a brewery-maltings called Vera (Latin for "truth"). In 1934, the brewery installed a refrigeration system and began lagering its new Vera Pils. This was followed in 1960 by the construction of a new brewhouse. More recently, the

VAN EECKE HOMMELBIER

brewery has invested in new cylindro-conical fermenters. Verhaeghe specializes in producing brown ales based on its oak-tun-ripened "stock ale," which varies in age from eight to 18 months. In all but its Vichtenaar ale, the stock is blended with young, sweeter ales, or, in the case of Echte Kriek, infused with cherries.

🍺 **VICHTENAAR** 5.1% ABV • **Flemish brown ale** • Red-brown; slightly metallic, woody nose; sourish-sweet in the palate, finishing sour and dry.

WESTMALLE

✉ Abdij der Trappisten, Antwerpsesteenweg 496, 2390 Malle

🕯 www.trappistwestmalle.be/en/page/brouwerij.aspx

The Westmalle monastery became a Trappist abbey in April 1836, and on December 10, the monks had their first beer with lunch. They initially brewed only enough beer for themselves, but later sales at the gate encouraged the abbey to expand its brewery. Despite subsequent renovations, the brewhouse remains a work of art. Westmalle started selling off-site in 1921. The first

WESTMALLE TRIPEL

recipes for their Tripel and Dubbel were developed using secular help in the early 1930s, and after some fine-tuning in 1956 they have remained virtually unchanged ever since.

🍺 **EXTRA** 5.3% ABV • **Belgian bitter** Yellow; strong hop aromas; resiny-spicy hop palate with a hint of fruit; dry, complex, and long peppery-hop finish.

🍺 **DUBBEL** 7.0% ABV • **Double** Copper-brown; nose of dried fruit, molasses, and bananas; spicy, hoppy, fruity, and slightly roasted palate; finish is cassislike, herbal, slightly bitter, and dry.

🍺 **TRIPEL** 9.5% ABV • **Triple** Yellowy gold; hop and overripe banana aromas; hop-bitter, banana-citrus-

sweet, and alcohol in the palate; pears and some salty bitterness in the finish.

WESTVLETEREN

✉ St. Sixtus Trappistenabdij, Donkerstraat 12, 8640 Westvleteren

🕯 www.sintsixtus.be

Since it began brewing in 1839, Westvleteren has always had the smallest output of any of the brewing Trappists. Located in one of Belgium's last remaining hop-growing regions, Westvleteren brews the hoppiest ales of all the Trappist breweries, using Westmalle yeast. Westvleteren beers are in such demand that customers have to call the monastery and make a reservation to pick up a limited amount of whichever beer is available at the time.

🍺 **BLOND** 5.8% ABV • **Blond** Straw-colored; dried hop-flower and overripe banana aromas; very hop-bitter (41 IBUs), slightly tannic palate; finish is dry and very bitter.

🍺 **12** 10.2% ABV • **Quadruple** Copper; candy sugar and cocoa; hop-bitter palate continues into the mouth-warming finish.

The magnificent brewhouse in Westmalle was built in 1930 to satisfy increasing demand for the monks' Trappist beers.

Liefmans Goudenband is the perfect example of how beer evolution can become revolution. By reducing its sourness, raising its strength from 5.2 to 8.0% ABV, and increasing its body, yet maintaining character, Liefmans created a completely new Flemish ale style.

Brussels and Brabant province

Brussels • Payottenland • Leuven • Opwijk

Brussels is famous as the seat of European government, but has only one brewery, two brewpubs, and a few cafés specializing in beer. Despite its official bilingual status, waiters will address you in *bruxellois* (a local French dialect), then in English, then, as a last resort, in Flemish.

Gastronomy oozes out between the cobblestones in this delightfully chaotic and unpredictable metropole. There are cramped alleyways just off the Grand Place in the Îlot Sacré neighborhood where restaurants flaunt their wares and use sassy waiters to lure in curious tourists. A more relaxed venue that specializes in beer cuisine is Le Bier Circus at Onderrichtsstraat 57, just outside the city center and within walking distance of the Park and Madou metro stations.

West of the city, in Flemish Brabant, lies the Payottenland, a mecca for "wild beer" enthusiasts and worth making a detour to see. Relatively unknown to tourists, it has gained a cult following among serious beer-lovers looking for the world's most authentic and complex beer, gueuze- (or geuze-) lambic. The village pubs in this region that serve this unique style offer a rare glimpse into Belgian culture and beer archaeology. If time is tight, then the best alternative is a visit to the Cantillon brewery-museum in Anderlecht to witness the unique production methods used to produce this style. On the Internet, the nonprofit brewers' association HORAL (www. horal.be) provides useful information.

Cafés and bars on the Grand Place in Brussels stand in the shadow of the great Guild Houses, including that of the city's brewers.

AFFLIGEM

✉ Ringlaan 18, 1745 Opwijk
🖰 www.affligembeer.be

Founded in 1790 by the De Smedt family, this brewery in Opwijk, northeast of Brussels, dates from 1790. It has always specialized in top-fermented ales. The popularity of its Op-Ale (launched in 1935) allowed De Smedt to expand.

When competing brewery De Hertog went bankrupt in 1970, De Smedt bought the rights to its Affligem range of abbey beers. They became so popular that Heineken, which had marketed the beers for De Smedt since the early 1980s, took over the brewery in 2001. The name was changed to Affligem Brewery BDS (Brewery De Smedt).

🍾 **DUBBEL** 7.0% ABV • Double
Copper-colored; fruit, candy sugar; candy palate with grains of paradise; dry finish, with warming alcohol.

🍾 **PATERS VAT** 6.6% ABV • Blond
Gold; hoppy and slightly fruity nose; dry and hoppy palate, followed by a dry, pearlike fruitiness and lingering hop bitterness.

BOON

✉ Fonteinstraat 65, 1502 Lembeek
🖰 www.boon.be

Set up in 1680, this brewery in Lembeek changed hands many times before Frank Boon (who had been blending in nearby Halle since 1975) purchased and renovated it in 1977. When a local factory closed in 1986, Boon bought the site and installed second-hand brewing equipment.

The first batch from the new site appeared in 1990, and today most of Boon's production consists of filtered kriek, but his *oude* (old) beers are far more interesting.

AFFLIGEM
DUBBEL

🍾 **OUDE GEUZE MARIAGE PARFAIT**
8.0% ABV • Gueuze • Light amber; nose of spices and wood; intense astringency and vanilla in the palate; dry and balanced finish.

CANTILLON

✉ Rue Gheude 56, 1070 Brussels (Anderlecht)
🖰 www.cantillon.be

Cantillon, established in 1900, is probably the most authentic gueuze brewery in Belgium, and a real "working museum."

Uncompromising brewer Jean-Pierre van Roy produces dry, intensely sour, complex beers that are as far away from modern beers as one could imagine. Drinkers who are looking for a sweet, mild, or "smooth" beer had better look elsewhere!

Cantillon went organic in 1999, and is well known for experimenting with new ingredients and variations on traditional gueuze and fruit beer styles. Around half of its production is for export.

🍾 **GUEUZE LAMBIC** 100% BIO
5.0% ABV • Gueuze • Golden; hint of ammonia, lactic-wood aromas; lactic sourness and dry tannins in the palate; an astringent finish.

🍾 **GRAND CRU BRUOCSELLA LAMBIC**
5.0% ABV • Lambic
Amber; acetic-lactic and wood nose; lush white wine-cider palate and finish; low carbonation and astringency.

DE BLOCK

✉ Nieuwbaan 92, 1785 Merchtem-Peizegem
🖰 www.satanbeer.com

Louis De Block founded this family-run farm brewery in

CANTILLON
GRAND CRU
BRUOCSELLA

1887. In 1921, he started producing a blend of young and cellared ales with a hint of lambic called Speciale 6, to which a range of lagers was added in the 1960s. Most of these beers were dropped in favor of strong ales when Paul Saerens took over from his father-in-law, Alfons De Block, after his death, aged 86, in 1986.

De Block has Belgium's last coal-fired kettle and brews a Tripel for the Carmelite abbey in nearby Dendermonde.

🍾 **SATAN RED** 8.0% ABV • Quadruple • Dark amber-red; fruity, spicy with roasted bread in the nose; medium-bodied, with a nutty and cola-like palate and an astringent alcohol finish.

DE CAM

✉ Dorpsstraat 67a, 1755 Gooik
🖰 www.decam.be

De Cam is the smallest of the three remaining Belgian *stekers*, which traditionally bought lambic from brewers and then lagered and blended it to produce bottled gueuze or fruit lambic. *Stekers* were common when brewers only sold beer by the barrel, but they virtually disappeared when the brewers began to bottle their own beer for home consumption during the early part of the 20th century.

De Cam, run by Karel Goddeau (the sole employee!) uses the Drie Fonteinen brewhouse (*see p.136*) to brew some of its lambic. Its 264-gallon (1,000-liter) barrels—large by lambic standards—are made from 100-year-old former Pilsener Urquell stock.

🍾 **OUDE GEUZE** 6.5% ABV • Gueuze
Yellowy gold; dry and complex lactic-acetic-peppery aromas; slightly

THE PATRON SAINT OF BREWING

Saint Arnold was born in Tiegem in 1040 and served as a knight under Boudewijn of Flanders, before choosing to live a life of seclusion at the St. Médard monastery in Soissons, France. He was made bishop there in 1081, founded the Oudenburg abbey in 1084, and was canonized in 1121.

He encouraged the local populace to drink beer instead of water. Having been boiled, beer was free of all pathogens and therefore safer to consume. He is often pictured with a straw beehive, which he adopted for use as a filter to improve the quality of beer. St. Arnold's day is celebrated on August 18.

oily-sweet with yellow grapefruit in the palate; woody and tannic finish.

OUDE KRIEK 6.5% ABV • Kriek
Dark copper; complex sour aromas with some fruit on the palate; finish is dry and astringent.

DOMUS

✉ Eikstraat 14, 3000 Leuven
🌐 www.domusleuven.be

Domus, set up by Cyriel Roten and Alfons Swartele in 1985, was one of Belgium's first brewpubs. The beer is tapped out of tanks via a cooled line that runs through an alley between the brewery building and the pub. The installation is well worn and in need of some tender loving care. This could be why production is now restricted to an amber ale (Nostra Domus), a hoppy, unfiltered pilsner (Con Domus), and a winter brew (Nen Engel).

CON DOMUS 5.0% ABV • Urtyp pilsner • Pale gold; complex hoppy nose; very bitter palate with some maltiness; powerful hop-bitter finish.

DRIE FONTEINEN

✉ Hoogstraat 2a, 1650 Beersel
🌐 www.3fonteinen.be

Ex-farmer Gaston Debelder purchased an old pub and lambic-*steker* (*see* De Cam, *p.135*) at Beersel, south of

Brussels, in 1953. The business did so well that he built new premises in the early 1960s, which also included a restaurant. In 1982, Gaston's son Armand took over. When trade was poor, Armand briefly considered stopping his labor-intensive *stekerij* to focus on the more profitable restaurant side of the business. However, supported by local beer-lovers, he decided to install a brewery instead— a gift from Palm (*see p.138*) technical director Willem van Herreweghen. Armand brewed his first lambic in 1999, and currently has the world's largest stock of traditional gueuze beer.

DOMUS
CON DOMUS

OUDE KRIEK 5.0% ABV • Kriek-lambic • Pinkish-red; cellar-like acidic nose, with sour cherry hints; tart and slightly tannic in the palate; dry, astringent finish.

GIRARDIN

✉ Lindenberg 10-12, 1700 Sint-Ulriks-Kapelle

This fourth-generation family brewery dates back to 1874. After experimenting with Ulricher Pilsener in the 1980s, Girardin decided to concentrate on its specialty—lambic. In 1990, a beautiful copper brewkettle was installed next to the old iron one. Girardin rarely grants

brewery tours, has no website, and, despite being the largest traditional lambic brewer, is not especially bothered about exports. It guards its privacy, and its beers deserve respect.

OUDE GUEUZE 1882 5.0% ABV • Gueuze • Golden amber; wood and sherry in the nose; dry, sour-apple palate; bitter and ciderlike finish.

FRAMBOISE 5.0% ABV • Framboise • Light pink; raspberry-syrup aroma; the bitter-dry sour palate is slightly fruity; finish is dry, sour, and rosé-like.

HAACHT

✉ Provinciesteenweg 28, 3190 Boortmeerbeek
🌐 www.haacht.com

Lying southeast of Mechelen, this modern independent brewery—the third largest Belgian brewer—began as a dairy. Beer was first made at the dairy in 1898; four years later the site was converted into a lager brewery.

Haacht was almost taken over by InBev, but bought back its shares and also the rights to brew the Tongerlo brand of abbey beers in the 1990s. Haacht itself bought Dutch brewery De Leeuw in 1990 but, after many cut-backs and product transfers, closed it down in 2005.

Haacht has thousands of tied pubs through which it sells its Primus pilsner, which accounts for most of the brewery's production.

GILDENBIER 7.0% ABV • Double
Copper; salty-roast and caramel aromas; bitter licorice palate and finish.

HAACHT GILDENBIER

INBEV/HOEGAARDEN

✉ Stoopkenstraat 46,
3320 Hoegaarden
⌂ www.inbev.com or http://users.
pandora.be/hoegaarden/

Formed when Interbrew joined with South American brewers AmBev in 2004, this mega multinational has ruffled the feathers of every serious beer-lover worldwide.

InBev's popularity reached rock bottom when, in 2005, it revealed plans to close the Hoegaarden brewery (famous for its white beer and other regional specialties) and move production to a more efficient facility in Wallonia. National and international media had a field day, giving extensive coverage to the resulting strikes, and the wave of negative publicity has fueled anti-InBev sentiment to this day. Despite this, InBev still brews a few decent beers.

🍺 **WIT** 4.8% ABV • Wit • Light straw; tart apple and spicy in the nose; coriander and sweet orange palate that becomes drier in the finish.

🍺 **PIEDBOEF TRIPEL** 3.8% ABV • Lager • Yellow; hop-and-malt nose; dry, with a light hop-bitter palate and finish.

🍺 **CAMPBELL'S SCOTCH ALE** 7.7% ABV • Scotch ale • Dark copper; caramel-candy and spicy-roasted aromas; bitter, with a raisins-in-alcohol flavor; slightly burned finish.

LEFÈBVRE

✉ Chemin du Croly 52,
1430 Quenast
⌂ www.brasserielefebvre.be

Jules Lefèbvre founded a brewery-maltings-farm in Quenast, to the south of Brussels, in 1876. His beers soon became popular with the thirsty workers from the quarry nearby. The brewery moved to its present site in 1922 and focused on brewing the low-alcohol Tafelbier.

In 1960, Lefèbvre launched its first "normal strength" beer, Porph-Ale. This was

followed in 1976 by Bonne Espérance abbey ales, and in 1983 by the Floreffe range. After replacing the old brewhouse, Lefèbvre started production of Barbar honey beer (its current top-seller) in 1996. Exports now account for more than 80 percent of Lefèbvre's production.

🍺 **PRIMA MELIOR** 8.0% ABV • Quadruple • Coppery brown; nose of caramel and dried fruit; palate of raisins, figs, and warming alcohol; finish is complex and spicy.

LINDEMANS

✉ Lenniksebaan 1479,
1602 Vlezenbeek
⌂ www.lindemans.be

The Lindemans family began brewing and farming at Vlezenbeek, near Brussels, in 1809. They produced lambic and sold it to farms and pubs, which then used it to make kriek or faro (a lambic blend with added sugar). In 1930, the family decided to brew on a full-time basis, adding gueuze

and kriek to their range. In the early 1970s, when Schaarbeek cherries were scarce, Lindemans used cherry extract in their kriek instead. In the next decade, they launched their own faro, raspberry, blackcurrant, and peach beers. In 1994, at the request of American importer Charles Finkel, Lindemans began making its Traditional Oude Gueuze.

🍺 **CUVÉE RENÉ** 5.0% ABV • Gueuze Yellowy gold; sour, cellarlike aroma; dry palate with a sherrylike sourness and hints of Champagne and rhubarb in the finish.

MORT SUBITE

✉ Lierput 1, 1730 Kobbegem
⌂ www.alken-maes.be/
PRODUCTEN/NL/mortsubite.php

Although built nearly 200 years earlier, the brewery at Kobbegem did not come into the hands of the

The renowned A la Mort Subite bar in Brussels is full of period character, and serves fine beers.

De Keersmaeker family until 1869. A lambic brewer by tradition, it introduced a pale ale in the 1920s and a pilsner after World War II. These beers were eventually dropped, even though they were far more popular than its lambic and gueuze brews.

In 1970, the brewery bought the famous "A la Mort Subite" bar in Brussels and applied the name to its beers. After various co-operations and takeovers, in 2000 the brewery became part of Scottish & Newcastle. Despite these changes and extensive renovations, the quality of Mort Subite's traditional beers has not been affected.

🍺 **FOND GUEUZE** 6.0% ABV •
Gueuze •Gold-amber; honey and green-leaf nose; acetic, complex, and oily palate, with a dry and sharp finish.

🍺 **OUDE KRIEK** 6.5% ABV • Kriek
Dark copper; lactic and horse-blanket nose; slightly fruity palate; tart cherry finish.

OUD BEERSEL

✉ Laarheidestraat 230, 1650 Beersel

🏠 www.oudbeersel.com

In operation since 1880, this lambic brewery closed its doors in 2003. It was taken over by Gert Christiaens and his partner Roland De Bus, who followed a brewing course at the University of Ghent and secretly continued brewing with the previous owner Henri Vandervelden until late 2005 (they now brew on their own). To help pay for this endeavor and gain publicity, they began selling a contract-brewed triple called Bersalis in 2005. They launched their own traditional gueuze and kriek in March of 2007.

🍺 **BERSALIS** 9.5% ABV • Triple
Gold; faint citrus and aniseed aromas; spicy-fruity

sweetness and mouth-coating palate; hoppy-bitter and alcoholic finish.

🍺 **OUDE GUEUZE** 6.0% ABV •
Gueuze • Yellow-gold; faint sulfur aroma with a mix of lactic-acetic and horse-blanket aromas; dry and astringent with a well-balanced palate and finish.

PALM

✉ Steenhuffeldorp 3, 1840 Steenhuffel

🏠 www.palmbreweries.com

Palm is one of Belgium's largest independent family-owned brewers. Once the market leader, Palm has struggled recently, with casual drinkers demanding more sweetness and serious drinkers more (hop) character.

Palm acquired Steenbrugge abbey ales when it took over Gouden Boom in 2002, and it contract-brews beers for the John Martin group. In 2003, it launched Royal to try to win back serious drinkers.

🍺 **ROYAL** 7.5% ABV •
Blond • Golden; a hop-flower and fruity-malt character prevails, from the nose to the toffeelike finish.

🍺 **JOHN MARTIN'S GORDON FINEST SCOTCH** 8.6% ABV • Scotch ale •
Dark reddish-brown in color; caramel-malt, syrup, and butter in the nose; sweet and spicy palate leads to a sweet alcoholic finish.

MORT SUBITE OUDE KRIEK

SINT-PIETERS/ZENNE

✉ Victor Nonnemansstraat 40a, 1600 Sint-Pieters-Leeuw

🏠 www.zinnebir.be

Former trumpet-player Bernard Leboucq started his one-man brewery in the old premises of gueuze-blender Moriau in 2004. His first beer, named Zinnebir after the Zenne River close by, was of variable quality. He has since

SINT-PIETERS/ZENNE
TARAS BOULBA

added X-Mas, a Christmas beer, and experimented with a wood-barrel lagered version of Zinnebir called Crianza. Taras Boulba, launched in 2006, is one of the best new bitter ales in Belgium—proof that Leboucq has overcome his quality-control problems.

🍺 **TARAS BOULBA** 4.5% ABV •
Belgian bitter • Yellow in color with a hoppy-spicy-resiny nose; dry and hop-bitter (with hints of aniseed) in the palate and finish.

TRIEST

✉ Trieststraat 24, 1880 Kapelle-op-den-Bos

🏠 http://users.pandora.be/label.service/index.htm (the brewer's beer label website)

Stage-lighting technician, breweriana collector (he is currently reputed to have Belgium's largest collection of beer labels and crown caps), and hobby-brewer Marc Struyf has completely renovated a group of buildings on an industrial site into a beer advertising museum-bar and brewery. He currently brews on a small scale to sell on-site and at special beer festivals.

Wood-barrel lagering and exotic spicing are among the techniques that Struyf uses to create his unique beers. They include a double, a triple, and a kriek.

🍺 **TRIEST X-MAS** 11.0% ABV •
Christmas beer • Deep copper; almond and spicy maple-syrup nose; palate of roasted caramel malt; woody-bitter and astringent finish.

Wallonia

Hainaut • Namur • Liege • Luxembourg

Wallonia is Belgium's French-speaking administrative region, occupying its southern half. More rural than Flanders, its economy was formerly based on heavy industry in the north, with farming and forestry in the southeast. Decline in industry has led to diversification.

The bright side of Wallonia's restructured economy is that, encouraged by local and European government subsidies, growth has been steady since the 1980s and is still improving. Brewery growth has been spectacular, and in the province of Hainaut, which enjoys the highest concentration of breweries in Belgium, the industry has doubled in size. In the same period, Luxembourg's breweries have more than tripled in number.

Often located in rural areas, Walloon brewers tend to be more artisanal than their Flemish counterparts. Use of old dairy equipment minimizes startup capital and makes good business sense— many successful Walloon brewers start this way. There also seems to be a definite preference for using more herbs and spices than would be considered

normal in Flanders. The combination works especially well with dark and strong Christmas ales, and some of the best originate here. Rochefort 10, which uses just a hint of coriander, is one of the world's greatest dark barley wines, and started out life as a Christmas beer. Saison, probably the only Belgian style indigenous to Wallonia, illustrates the fact that the use of spices and herbs can have a profound effect without being overpowering. Originally a beer for thirsty peasant farmers, it is now one of the world's most revered styles.

Most of the brewers here do not seem to be as interested in trends or exports as their Flemish counterparts, and only supply local markets. Those searching outside the region may find Walloon beers frustratingly difficult to locate.

The village of Orval is home to a monastery where, to this day, the monks maintain a long and distinguished tradition of brewing.

ABBAYE DE ROCS

✉ Chaussée de Brunehault 37,
7387 Montignies-sur-Roc

🖱 www.abbaye-des-rocs.com

Former tax inspector
Jean Pierre Eloir
set out to prove to
his father-in-law
(a retired brewer) that
brewing really wasn't
that difficult. He
converted an old
washing machine and
other odds and ends
into an 21-gallon (80-
liter) garage brewery,
and officially started
selling his beers in
1979. He built a
1,320-gallon (5,000-liter)
brewery in 1987, and his
daughter Nathalie took over
brewing in the mid-1990s.
Eloir's beers use a wide
range of malts, grains,
and spices (coriander and
licorice are his favorites).

🍺 **BLANCHE DES HONELLES**
6.0% ABV • Doublewit • Yellowy
gold; citrus and yeasty
aromas; coriander and citrus
in the dry palate, becoming
even drier in the finish.

ACHOUFFE

✉ Rue du Village 32,
6666 Achouffe

🖱 www.achouffe.be

Using Pierre Celis and his
Hoegaarden Grand Cru
as their role model, Chris
Bauweraerts and his brother-
in-law Pierre Gobron started
brewing in a pig stall using
two antique washing coppers
in 1982. The unique flavor
of their La Chouffe triple
and the red-hooded bearded
gnome on the label proved
an irresistible combination,
and sales soon took off.
Bauweraerts and Gobron
have replaced and expanded
their brewery six times in the
last 25 years. Achouffe now
exports to more than 20
countries. The company was
taken over by Duvel in 2006.

🍺 **LA CHOUFFE** 8.0% ABV • Triple
Golden hue with a definite

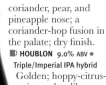

ACHOUFFE
N'ICE CHOUFFE

coriander, pear, and
pineapple nose; a
coriander-hop fusion in
the palate; dry finish.

🍺 **HOUBLON** 9.0% ABV •
Triple/Imperial IPA hybrid
Golden; hoppy-citrus-
spicy and tealike nose;
bitter orange, salty,
and slightly tannic
palate; finish is bitter
and mouth-warming.

🍺 **N'ICE CHOUFFE**
10.0% ABV • Winter beer
Dark copper;
herbal (thyme) and
candy-sugar sweet
aromas; dry cough-
syrupy palate; long
peppery, bitter, and
alcoholic finish.

AUGRENOISE

✉ Chaussée de Bruxelles 184,
7061 Casteau

🖱 www.augrenoise.com

Located alongside St. Alfred,
a home for people with
learning disabilities, this
microbrewery was set up in
2001 with secondhand dairy
equipment. The aim was to
provide residents with an
activity that would have both
social and economic benefits.
Jean-Marie Rock, head
brewer at Orval (see p.144),
has helped with brewing and
quality control from the time
of the first 317-gallon (1,200-
liter) batch. Augrenoise beers
are brewed with malted
barley, malted and unmalted
wheat, Styrian Goldings
hops, and Orval yeast.

🍺 **AUGRENOISE** 6.5% ABV • Blond
Yellow; slight sulfurlike and
fruity aromas; notes of
apple, pear, and white wine
in the palate and finish.
There is no discernible
hop-bitterness.

BINCHOISE

✉ Faubourg Saint Paul 38,
7130 Binche

🖱 www.brasserielabinchoise.be

Binchoise was set up in
1987 by André Graux and
Françoise Jauson on the site

of a centuries-old maltings-
brewery. After experimenting
with various recipes, they
started brewing their flagship
Blonde (50 percent of all
sales) in 1989. Since then,
they have added at least four
permanent and two seasonal
brews. Most Binchoise beers
are spiced with Curaçao, star
anise, or cinnamon.
In 2001, after a change of
ownership, Binchoise moved
its offices down the road,
renovated the historical
maltings into a reception
area, and doubled its output.

🍺 **BELGE** 5.0% ABV • Belgian pale
ale • Golden-amber; nose of
mandarins and hops; slightly
roasted-nutty-malty palate;
dry and light hoppy finish.

BLAUGIES

✉ 435 Rue de la Frontière, 7370
Dour (Blaugies)

🖱 www.brasseriedeblaugies.com

Situated in a farming hamlet
almost on the French border,
Blaugies has been brewing
dry, well-hopped, complex
beer since 1988. The owners,
former teachers Pierre-Alex
Carlier and his wife Marie-
Noëlle Pourtois, stumbled
across their first beer recipe
in an old encyclopedia. They
had a hard time finding
someone to build their 185-
gallon (700-liter) brewhouse,
but finally settled on Walloon
manufacturer Meura.
In order to cope with rising
demand, a new bottling
facility was installed across
the road from the brewery in
1992. A grill and restaurant
were added soon after.

🍺 **LA MONEUSE** 8.0% ABV • Strong
saison • Golden-amber, with

BLAUGIES LA MONEUSE

BELGIAN BOTTLES

Belgian brewers sell their beers in a wide variety of bottle sizes, including the oversized types normally associated with the Champagne industry. Despite the introduction of the crown cap in 1892, many small regional brewers still use swing-top and cork-stoppered bottles, which give an artisanal appearance at the expense of optimum freshness. Brewers of bottle-conditioned beers, such as Duvel, Westmalle, and Orval, have developed strong, heavy bottles that can withstand the internal pressures created by secondary fermentation during transport.

BOTTLE-CONDITIONED BEERS

a huge head; yeasty-citrus-hoppy aromas; bitter but slightly sweet palate; bitter, astringent, alcoholic finish.

MONEUSE SPECIALE NOËL 8.0% ABV • Christmas beer • Amber; yeasty-citrus-pepper nose with caramel hints, and a fruitiness in the palate; finish is astringent (limes), bitter, and slightly warming.

DU BOCQ

✉ Rue de la Brasserie 4, 5530 Purnode
🖥 www.bocq.be

Founded in 1858 by Martin Belot on the banks of the Bocq River, this brewery is still in family hands six generations later. Du Bocq launched its Brune in 1928, but did not round off the La Gauloise range until 1994, when it added the Blonde and Ambrée. Du Bocq inherited Saison Régal and Régal Christmas when it took over Brasserie Centrale in 1967 (closed in 1984), and made Leffe Tripel from 1977 to 1991. Today it brews Corsendonk, St. Feuillien, and many other brands. All Du Bocq beers are well-hopped and heavily spiced.

LA GAULOISE BRUNE 8.1% ABV • Spice beer • Coppery amber; sweet potpourri (aniseed-cardamom-coriander) nose; caramel-sweet palate and finish. A liquid dessert!

RÉGAL CHRISTMAS 9.0% ABV • Christmas beer • Dark copper; nose of allspice, coriander, and cinnamon; a good balance of hoppiness, spiciness, and sweetness in both the palate and finish.

BROOTCOORENS

✉ Rue de Maubeuge 197, 6560 Erquelinnes
🖥 www.brasserie-brootcoorens-erquelinnes.be

Alain Brootcoorens is a self-taught brewer who set up his microbrewery, about 260 ft (80 m) from the French border, in 2000. He brews only on weekends, and has kept his job teaching children with special needs. He uses locally produced malt, tap water, and Styrian Goldings hop pellets in his beers, and adds spices to his Brune.

Brootcoorens decided that it was time to reintroduce hops to Wallonia, so he had 300 hop vines planted across the road from his brewery and has organized an annual hop festival since 2005. It takes place on the second weekend of September.

BELGIAN ANGEL STOUT 5.2% ABV • Belgian stout • Dark brown; cappuccino and cocoa in the nose; mountainous whipped cream head; coffee and licorice palate and finish.

BRUNEHAUT

✉ Rue des Panneries 17–19, 7623 Rongy-Brunehaut
🖥 www.brunehaut.com

Brunehaut was set up using brewkettles from the bankrupt Allard & Grotembril brewery. These were installed in a purpose-built, high-tech brewhouse in 2002.

After being unable to brew enough to sustain the business, the previous owner sold the brewery to Marc-Antoine de Mees in 2006. De Mees's ongoing aim is to invest more in marketing, with the goal of tripling production.

NE KOPSTOOT 7.0% ABV • Spirit beer • Yellow; sweet-fruity-spirit aroma; dry palate is slightly bitter and fruity, finishing slightly sweet. Just a hint of gin.

CARACOLE

✉ Côte Marie-Thérèse 86, 5500 Falmignoul
🖥 www.caracole.be

François Tonglet started brewing 106-gallon (400-liter) batches of beer in a relative's shed in 1990. In 1992, he and his partner bought a disused brewery in Falmignoul. After two years of renovations, they moved there from Namur. Despite all the modernization, Caracole (meaning snail) has perhaps the world's only wood-fired kettles. All the beers are bottle-conditioned, unpasteurized, and unfiltered; and some are organic.

SAXO 8.0% ABV • Triple • Straw-colored; slight ammonia with citrus-spice aromas; hop-bitter, apples and pears; sweeter finish.

CARACOLE SAXO

CAULIER

✉ Rue de Sondeville 134, 7600 Péruwelz

🏠 www.peruwelz.be/fr/commerces/index.php?page=24

After having his La Vieille Bon-Secours contract-brewed for years, Roger Caulier purchased some second-hand kettles from the defunct De Neve brewery and had a brewery-restaurant installed on the second floor of a building that already housed a drive-through liquor store, a supermarket, and a car dealership. Marcel Lebeau of Mort Subite (*see pp.137–8*) assisted with the first brew in 1995. Caulier now exports to at least 10 countries.

▪ **MYRTILLE** 7.0% ABV • **Fruit beer** • This natural-tasting beer is rumored to be contract-brewed. Dark copper; sweet, fresh blueberries in the nose; slightly bitter and astringent palate and finish.

CAZEAU

✉ 67 Rue de Cazeau, 7520 Templeuve

🏠 www.brasseriedecazeau.be

Laurent Agache and Quentin Mariage bought secondhand brewing vessels from Bass in England and local De Ranke of Dottignies and installed them in a brewery—with a history going back to 1753—in which Laurent's father Jean had once brewed.

The new brewery opened in 2002. With advice from Laurent's father and self-study, Agache and Mariage have produced an impressive full-malt blond ale and the dark Tournay de Noël (7.3% ABV), a Christmas beer.

▪ **TOURNAY** 7.2% ABV • **Blond** Yellowy gold in color; wort, (slightly buttery) malt, and hops in the nose; balanced malt and hop palate; nutty-yeasty-hoppy and dry finish.

CHIMAY

✉ Route de Charlemagne 8, 6464 Baileux

🏠 www.chimay.com

Brewing—and cheese-making—started at the Cistercian Trappist abbey of Notre Dame de Scourmont in 1862. After World War II, the Trappists decided to modernize the brewery. Brewer Father Theodore asked advice from Belgian brewing scientist Jean De Clercq, and together they perfected the Dubbel, and designed the Blue (1948) and Tripel (1966). The switch to hop extracts and the addition of wheat starch started around this time.

In 1978, bottling was moved to nearby Baileux, 5 miles (8 km) away. Subsequent improvements have been numerous and include a new brewhouse in 1988, fermentation tanks in 1992, computer automation in 1996, and a new bottling hall in 1999.

CHIMAY ROOD

▪ **TRIPEL** 8.0% ABV • **Triple** Golden; resiny hops and flowers in the nose; highly carbonated cappuccinolike head; bitter-resiny-dry palate, becoming even drier in the finish.

▪ **ROOD** 7.0% ABV • **Double** Coppery amber; dried fruit-spices and candy sugar in the nose; slight hoppiness and roasted malt palate; a finish of figs in alcohol.

DE RANKE

✉ Rue Petit Tourcoing 1a, 7711 Dottignies

🏠 www.deranke.be

After contract-brewing their beers at Deca (*see p.125*) for 11 years, Nino Bavelle and Guido Devos finally started production at their own brewery in an old textile factory in 2005. The fully automated brewery can produce about 925 gallons (3,500 liters) per batch. De Ranke uses local tap water and Brewers Gold and Hallertau hops. Its XX Bitter has earned the reputation of being one of Belgium's bitterest beers.

▪ **XX BITTER** 6.2% ABV • **Belgian bitter** • Yellowy gold; salty and hoppy nose, with a faint hint of ammonia; intense, resiny bitter palate that continues long into the finish.

▪ **GULDENBERG** 6.5% ABV • **Spice beer** • Golden; strong aroma of coriander, with yeasty notes; bitter-tannic-alcoholic and dry palate, with spices in the palate and finish.

▪ **PÈRE NOËL** 7.0% ABV • **Christmas beer** • Amber; hoppy aroma; dry with hoppy, spicy, and cough-syrup flavors; the spicy finish has a complex hop-bitterness.

DUBUISSON

✉ Chausée de Mons 28, 7904 Pipaix-Leuze

🏠 www.br-dubuisson.com

Originating as a brewery-farm in 1769, this business has been under Dubuisson family ownership since the 1890s. The family stopped farming in 1931 to focus on its brewing activities. To compete with popular

DUBUISSON BUSH DE NÖEL

English beers of the time, they launched Bush 12% in 1933. It was joined by Bush Noël in 1991, Blonde in 1998 (when the light-colored 12% was renamed Amber to avoid confusion), Cuvée des Trolls in 2000, and Prestige, their most ambitious beer to date, in 2003.

BUSH AMBER 12.0% ABV • Barley wine
Amber; ripe pear, banana, and slightly buttery nose; alcoholic-tannic and bitter palate; full-bodied; portlike finish.

BUSH DE NOËL 12.0% ABV • Christmas beer • Golden-amber; nose of ripe pears and almond liqueur; bananas, malt, saltiness, and some hops in the palate; finish is full and sherry-like.

BUSH PRESTIGE 13.0% ABV • Wood-aged • Golden-amber; sherry, raspberry, and bourbon aromas; alcohol-astringent in the palate and finish, with some bitterness.

DUPONT

✉ Rue Basse 5, 7904 Tourpes-Leuze
🖱 www.brasserie-dupont.com

This brewery, which dates from 1844, was purchased by Alfred Dupont in 1920. It initially made saison for local farmers at harvest-time, but now brews this style of ale year-round. Dupont added Rédor pils in 1950, and Moinette and Avec les Bons Voeux in the early 1960s. Dupont's choice of hops, multi-strain yeast culture, and fermentation practices produce beers of such unique complexity that it is known worldwide as the benchmark brewer of the saison style. Despite this excellence, Dupont still operates as an artisanal brewer within a working farm that is committed to sustainable agriculture—eggs can still be bought from its "executive offices!"

SAISON DUPONT 6.5% ABV • Saison • Golden; citrus-resiny-hoppy aromas; hop-bitter-citrus and dry palate, with a spicy-grapefruit and spritzerlike finish.

SAISON DUPONT

LA MOINETTE BLONDE 8.5% ABV • Strong saison • Golden; oily-citrus-hoppy aromas; dry-citrus-bitter and sour palate, with increasing bitterness and citrus in the finish.

BONS VOEUX 9.5% ABV • Strong saison • Golden; apples and pears in the nose, with slight cork and cellar flavors added to the palate; bitter-alcoholic and slightly sour finish.

ELLEZELLOISE

✉ Guinaumont 75, 7890 Ellezelles
🖱 www.brasserie-ellezelloise.be

Philippe Gérard already had over 25 years of beermaking experience with different breweries when he bought a farm in 1988 at Ellezelles, a village infamous for the burning of five "witches" in 1610. After transforming the site into a brewery—a process that took no less than eight years—Gérard began production in 1993.

The five regular beers are all made in small batches and lagered for 10 days in German oak casks. Hercule Stout is named after Agatha Christie's detective Hercule Poirot—allegedly a native (if fictional) son of Ellezelles. Unable to find a successor, Gérard sold the brewery to Géants (*see below*) in 2006.

HERCULE STOUT 8.4% ABV • Belgian export stout • Dark brown; licorice aromas; some roasted-bitterness in the palate; finish is roasted-sweet and slightly astringent.

SAISIS WITBIER 5.9% ABV • Doublewit • Golden; limey

yeast and spice aromas; tannic-dry and slightly bitter palate, with some sweetness in the finish.

FANTÔME

✉ Rue Préal 8, 6997 Soy
🖱 www.fantome.be

An eccentrically brilliant homebrewer, Dany Prignon started his brewery in 1988 in an 1830s farmhouse in Soy. Using old dairy tanks, industrial burners, and unbridled creativity (including making an experimental mushroom beer), he started turning out saison-style beers. Prignon has one reasonably consistent year-round brew, Fantôme, and an ever-changing range of seasonal brews called Saison d'Erezée, in which the spices, herbs, and alcoholic strength are constantly altered.

FANTÔME 8.0% ABV • Strong saison • Golden; vegetable-spicy-fruity aromas; faint lactic character, with medium-bodied sweetness in the palate and finish.

GÉANTS

✉ Rue de Castel 19, 7801 Irchonwelz (Ath)
🖱 www.brasseriedesgeants.com

In 1997, brewing engineer Pierre Delcoigne and his wife Vinciane decided to convert a 14th-century medieval castle near the town of Ath (famous for its annual parade of giants) into a brewery. Helped by friends, it took more than three years of intensive work to finish the project, which involved amalgamating recycled brewing equipment from three extinct breweries with brand-new fermenters, lager tanks, and a bottling line. They presented their first beer, Gouyasse, meaning

GÉANTS SAISON VOISIN

"giant" in the local dialect, in August 2000 (it is now named Gouyasse Tradition), and have added a new beer in every subsequent year.

🍺 **SAISON VOISIN** 5.0% ABV •
Saison • Amber; hoppy nose, with hints of sherry; dry-tannic and hoppy palate, with some sourness added to the finish.

🍺 **GOUYASSE TRIPEL** 9.0% ABV •
Triple • Golden; fruity-citrus-bready aromas; medium-bodied, well-hopped, and well-carbonated palate; alcoholic finish.

GRAIN D'ORGE

✉ Centre 16, 4852 Hombourg
🖥 www.brasserie-graindorge.be

Benoit Johnen, an electrician by trade, learned to brew on the job at the Piron brewery in Aubel before it went bankrupt in 1994. After taking a brewing course at Louvain-la-Neuve University, Johnen took over a pub, renovated it, and opened it as Le Grain d'Orge in 1997. It took him another five years to find and install affordable secondhand

brewery equipment on site. He reopened the venue in 2002, complete with brewery, as Brasserie Grain d'Orge.

🍺 **3 SCHTÉNG** 6.0% ABV •
Schwartz • The spices in this beer are added to the lager tank and infused. Brown in color; caramel, toast, and candy aromas, becoming drier, burned, and more coffeelike in the finish.

ORVAL

✉ Abbaye Notre Dame D'Orval, Orval 2, 6823 Villers-devant-Orval
🖥 www.orval.be

There has probably always been a brewery of one kind or another at the abbey at Orval since it was founded 875 years ago. The present brewery was set up in 1931 to generate funds for restoration work. It was a German brewer who (inadvertently) introduced *Brettanomyces* wild yeast to Orval's beer, and a British one who added dry-hopping. Today, Orval and

a "light" version called Petit Orval (brewed for the monks and sold exclusively at the Ange Gardien pub next to the abbey) are, after gueuze, the world's driest, lowest-calorie beers. Sold in "bowling-pin" bottles, Orval reaches its peak at an age of six months.

🍺 **ORVAL** 6.2% ABV •
Brettanomyces blond Golden amber in colour; horse-blanket and hoppy aromas; bitter-resiny in the palate; hoppy and ciderlike finish.

ORVAL

OXYMORE

✉ Rue Verte 1, 6670 Limerlé (Gouvy)
🖥 www.peripleenlademeure.be

Situated in a tiny hamlet, Oxymore was set up in 2001 by a cooperative. The brewery, built with secondhand kettles and tanks, started producing in 2006. Brewer Anne Peters is aided by Orval brewer Jean-Marie Rock, who has been present for every batch. The brewing process uses water tanked in from Houffalize (the local water being unsuitable), malted barley and wheat, unmalted wheat, spelt, and oats, as well as hops and yeast from Orval.

🍺 **OXYMORE** 5.2% ABV • Belgian bitter • Yellow; citrus and hop aromas; bitter and sour palate; thin-bodied and thirst-quenching dry finish.

ROCHEFORT

✉ Abbaye Notre Dame de St. Rémy, Rue de L'Abbaye 8, 5580 Rochefort
🖥 www.trappistes-rochefort.com

This Trappist abbey dates from 1230 and has had a brewery on site since 1595. The abbey closed in 1794 during the French Revolution. It reopened in 1887 and brewing resumed 12 years

The rich color of Rochefort beer hints at the complex flavors and aromas that await the drinker.

later. The abbey extended and modernized the brewery during the 1950s; a picture-perfect copper brewhouse was installed in 1960; a new bottling-line in 1996; and a new reception and meeting center in 2005. Its three beers use essentially the same recipe, but with varying alcoholic strengths.

■ **8** 9.2% ABV ● Quadruple
Dark copper; figs, coriander, and brown sugar in the nose and palate; complex and full-bodied, with a warming alcohol finish.

■ **10** 11.3% ABV ● Quadruple
Coppery amber; figs-raisins-aniseed in alcohol aromas; spicy ripe-pear and caramel palate, with a portlike finish.

RULLES

✉ Rue Maurice Grévisse 36, 6724 Rulles-Habay
🖐 www.larulles.be

In 1998, brewing technician Grégory Verhelst began converting an old farmhouse into a brewery, and his first batch of beer, bottled in 2000, was an overnight success. Verhelst added a warehouse in 2003, and in 2006 replaced his "mix & match" brewhouse with a 800-gallon (3,000-liter) installation, tripling capacity. Inspired by Dupont's La Moinette Blonde (*see p.143*), Rulles beers use American hops and Orval yeast.

■ **TRIPEL** 8.4% ARV ● Triple
Golden-amber; hoppy and slightly fruity nose; bitter and fruity medium-bodied palate, and a long, complex, bitter finish.

■ **ESTIVALE** 5.2% ABV ● Belgian bitter ● Golden-amber; lemon marmalade and hop nose; complex hop-bitter and thin palate continues into the finish.

■ **CUVÉE MEILLEURS VOEUX** 7.3% ABV ● Christmas beer
Coppery amber; sour fruit, caramel, and spicy nose; medium-bodied palate is hoppy, fruity, and spicy; dry and slightly roasted finish.

SILENRIEUX LE PAVÉ DE L'OURS

SILENRIEUX

✉ Rue Noupré 1, 5630 Silenrieux
🖐 http://users.belgacom.net/gc195540/

Originally called Agripur, this brewery was set up as a cooperative by local farmers with help from the brewing science department at the University of Louvain-la-Neuve. By growing and using spelt and buckwheat—relatively unknown and technically challenging ingredients—they were able to generate curiosity and sales in their combined brewpub-store-restaurant.

The cooperative went bankrupt in 1997, and the brewery is now run by a group of businessmen. With the exception of Le Pavé de l'Ours, the beers are typically dry and refreshing.

■ **LE PAVÉ DE L'OURS** 8.0% ABV ● Honey beer ● Golden; full and sweet honey aromas; full-bodied, with some bitterness and astringency added to the palate; finishes sweet.

SILLY

✉ Rue Ville Basse 2, 7830 Silly
🖐 www.silly-beer.com

Named after the farmer who founded it in 1885, the Meynsgrughen brewery was renamed Silly in 1974. Today, Silly brews a wide range of beers using water from its own artesian well, three types of malt, three foreign varieties of hop pellets, and an ale and a lager yeast. The antique

brewhouse was replaced with a secondhand installation from the defunct Aubel brewery in 2000, and there are plans to reopen the old brewhouse as a museum.

■ **SCOTCH** 7.5% ABV ● Scotch ale
Dark brown; buttery caramel and roasted nose; sweet and nutty palate with a metallic mouthfeel; sweet, slightly hoppy finish.

VAPEUR

✉ Rue de Maréchal 1, 7904 Pipaix-Leuze
🖐 www.vapeur.com

The Cuvelier family added a brewery to their farm in 1785 and ran it on a small scale until the seventh-generation brewer (by marriage) Gaston Biset stopped brewing in 1984. History teacher Jean-Louis Dits and his wife took over the brewery and, with the help of local brewer Dupont (*see p.143*), slowly built up a range of heavily spiced and herbed specialties. Despite the tragic death of Dits' wife in an accident at the brewery in 1990, Jean-Louis and his daughter Adeline continue to produce a variety of beers at this "working museum."

■ **SAISON DE PIPAIX** 6.0% ABV ● Saison ● Golden-amber; a musty nose of citrus, pepper, ginger, and aniseed; very complex dry-tart palate and finish.

VAPEUR SAISON DE PIPAIX

BRITISH ISLES

Although more than half the beer consumed in the British Isles is lager, brewing's reputation in England, Scotland, Wales, and Ireland rests on ales. The special genius of the British brewer is to make beers of modest potency that are packed with flavor.

In the British Isles, a greater proportion of beer is consumed on licensed premises (that is, outside the home, in pubs, cafés, clubs, and restaurants) than in any other country. Many historical influences have helped to shape this thriving pub culture. It could be that Britain's high population density—meaning that people's homes are smaller than in many other countries—has led to a tradition of meeting friends in the spacious rooms of a pub, rather than entertaining in one's own home. Certainly, a key influence on Britain's pub culture is the country's long history of socio-economic stability, which fostered a very clearly defined class system. Although this has relaxed in recent years, pubs have always fulfilled a need for a socially neutral area, where lord of the manor and "villein" might mingle on relatively informal terms.

These historical factors have led to a drinking culture in which socializing in the pub, buying beers by the round, and lingering for most of the evening are accepted norms. In light of these customs, the British pub-goer welcomes a beer of modest strength, suited to long sessions.

In a world of mass-market brands, British brewing boasts a wide diversity of styles and pubs, many independent breweries, and a thriving micro scene.

The popularity of pubs as a venue also means that beer enjoys a fast turnover. This enables breweries to deliver beers "unfinished," to reach peak condition in their casks while stored in the pub's cellar. To facilitate this process, cellars must be kept at a temperature of 50–55°F (10–13°C), allowing the beer to undergo a slight secondary fermentation. If properly executed, the result is not the warm, flat beverage of myth, but a gently carbonated beer that is served at a cellar temperature similar to that of a red wine.

The comparison with red wine is perhaps apt, in that the color of many British ales is russet, bronze, or copper. This coloration derives from the types of malt used and should ensure a nuttiness to balance the soft, restrained spiciness of English hops, creating a beer that is ideal for supping during long evenings in the pub. In some former industrial areas, a sweet, malty style of ale known as dark mild endures as an inexpensive restorative. Its companion, bitter ale, is much more common. Visitors to the British Isles often expect to find porters, too. Although this style nearly became extinct in the 20th century, it is enjoying a revival—along with specialties such as oatmeal stout. The world's most famous dry stout, Guinness, remains a best-seller in Ireland, although it is served ever colder to appease the young.

England

The North • The Midlands • Southeast • Southwest

Differences have diminished over the years but there are still some
regional characteristics among the ales of England, whether from the
hop gardens of Kent or the maltings of East Anglia; the Trent Valley,
with its mineral-laden waters; or Yorkshire's slatey tun rooms.

The gentleness of English ales in both
carbonation and temperature highlights
to the full their subtle aromas and flavors.
This delicacy was one of the qualities that
seemed most at risk when an onslaught of
filtration, pasteurization, and chilling was
launched by the big brewers in the 1960s.
The spontaneous public reaction to this
became the Campaign for Real Ale (*see
p.153*). Without CAMRA, it is unlikely
that English ale would have survived at all,
although the industry is far too blinkered
to acknowledge this. CAMRA has been
unable to prevent the implosion of
national brewing firms like Whitbread and
Bass. Nor has it been able to maintain its
early success rate in saving family
breweries, although some have shone in
recent years: Harveys of Lewes is a fine
example, using local hops and reviving

styles like Imperial stout. But recent
decades have also seen the emergence of
startlingly original new microbreweries.
Although trained as a winemaker in
Bordeaux, Sean Franklin, with his
Yorkshire brewery Roosters, has been a
great influence in the more assertive use
of hops, especially varieties from the
USA. An even more eclectic microbrewer
is Alastair Hook, whose education
includes spells at both Weihenstephan in
Bavaria and Heriot-Watt, Edinburgh; he
has judged and tasted widely in the USA.
His Meantime Brewery in Greenwich,
London, offers styles in a diversity
usually found only across the Atlantic.

England's drinking and dining culture may be
becoming more continental, but English beers
remain resolutely true to national traditions.

ADNAMS

✉ Sole Bay Brewery, Southwold, Suffolk IP18 6JW

🌐 www.adnams.co.uk

Within a stone's throw of the lighthouse in Southwold on the Suffolk coast, Adnams was set up 650 years ago as the brewhouse of the Swan Inn. The Adnams brothers, Ernest and George (who was later eaten by a crocodile in Africa), bought the brewery in 1877, and the fourth-generation family is still involved in the company.

Recently refurbished, Adnams claims to be Europe's most energy-efficient brewery. Its new distribution center uses advanced solar-powered technology and rainwater recycling, and has the largest turf roof in the country.

🍺 **BITTER** 3.7% ABV • Bitter Dry and refreshing with a distinctive, fragrantly aromatic hoppiness.

🍺 **EXPLORER** 4.3% ABV • Premium bitter • A blond beer suffused with hop aromas reminiscent of grapefruit.

🍺 **BROADSIDE** 4.7% ABV • Premium bitter • Rich, fruitcake aromas of almonds, citrus zest, and conserved fruit dominate intially, then a balance of hop and malt becomes more apparent.

ARCHERS

✉ Penzance Drive, Swindon, Wiltshire SN5 7JL

🌐 www.archersbrewery.co.uk

This brewery is set in the former weighhouse of the Great Western Railway locomotive works. In 2001, it underwent a massive $4m modernization program, which included a new, state-of-the-art laboratory.

Archers has a huge variety of cask-conditioned ales in its portfolio—190 produced in one year alone—ranging in style from bitters to milds, porters, and stouts.

🍺 **GOLDEN** 4.7% ABV • Premium bitter • A full-bodied, straw-colored ale with an underlying fruity sweetness and a distinct bitter finish.

🍺 **DARK MILD** 3.4% ABV • Mild ale • Malty, roast flavors balanced by a clearly defined hop influence.

ADNAMS EXPLORER

ARKELL'S

✉ Kingsdown Brewery, Swindon, Wiltshire SN2 7RU

🌐 www.arkells.co.uk

Arkell's is one of only about 30 family-run breweries in Britain today. Founded by John Arkell in 1843, it is also among the oldest.

Arkell's still uses the same strain of yeast that it first introduced in the 1930s. Regular Arkell's beers rely on Goldings and Progress hops for bitterness, and Fuggles for aroma.

🍺 **ARKELL'S 2B** 3.2% ABV • Pale ale • A low-gravity session beer with a light, hoppy aroma, a slight tart bite, and a dry hop finish.

🍺 **ARKELL'S 3B** 4.0% ABV • Best bitter • Sweet-scented malt is just perceptible beneath the distinct hoppy aroma. It has a delicate and well-balanced nutty flavor.

BADGER

✉ Hall & Woodhouse, The Brewery, Blandford St. Mary, Dorset DT11 9LS

🌐 www.badgerales.com

The origins of Badger beers go back to 1777, when Charles Hall founded the Ansty Brewery. In 1847, Hall's son Robert took George Woodhouse into partnership, and in 1899 they moved to the brewery's present site, where fifth-generation members of the Woodhouse family continue the brewing tradition. The company plans to build a new brewery on part of the original site.

Badger's seasonal ales include Festive Feasant (4.5% ABV; winter) and Fursty Ferret (4.4% ABV; spring, summer, and fall).

🍺 **BEST** 4.0% ABV • Best bitter Leans heavily on hop bitterness, with underlying malt and fruit flavor.

🍺 **BADGER FIRST GOLD** 4.0% ABV • Bitter • An exceptional, classic golden-brown country ale that uses a single hop—First Gold—for character and flavor. Clean, fresh, and distinctive.

🍺 **TANGLEFOOT** 5.0% ABV • Premium bitter • A light golden ale with a noticeable floral dry hop aroma balanced by biscuit and fruit notes and a rounded, medium bitterness. Hints of lemon and pear on the palate.

BANKS'S

✉ Park Brewery, Bath Road, Wolverhampton, West Midlands WV1 4NY

🌐 www.marstonsbeercompany.co.uk

Now part of Marston's Beer Company (formerly Wolverhampton & Dudley), Banks's merged with Hansons of Dudley in the 1890s. Today, it still occupies its handsome traditional site in central Wolverhampton, although the Dudley brewery has long since shut down.

Original—Banks's best-selling flagship beer—is a fine example of a classic West Midlands mild.

🍺 **ORIGINAL** 3.5% ABV • Bitter • A balanced session bitter, but full-bodied and malty with traces of fruit in the flavor.

BADGER TANGLEFOOT

BITTER 3.8% ABV • Bitter
A full, clean beer with winey, fruit overtones and malt and hop influence on the palate.

BATEMANS

✉ Salem Bridge Brewery, Mill Lane, Wainfleet, Lincolnshire PE24 4JE
🖳 www.bateman.co.uk

Based around the tower of an old windmill which still stands above the building, and overlooking the Steeping River, Batemans is surely one of the most picturesque breweries in the country.

This independent, family-owned brewery was set up in 1874 by the grandfather of the present chairman, although a family rift almost caused its closure during the 1980s. Batemans quickly gained a reputation for "good, honest ales"—a motto that, with the opening of a new brewhouse in 2002, still holds true today.

XXXB 4.8% ABV • Premium bitter
A classic, russet-tan ale with a well-balanced blend of malt, hops, and fruit on the nose and a faintly fruity maltiness in the mouth.

XB BITTER 3.7% ABV • Bitter • A finely balanced session bitter with an apple-influenced hop aroma that lingers in the malty flavor.

VALIANT 4.2% ABV • Best bitter • A clean, crisp, and citrus-fruity golden ale.

BATEMANS XXXB

BATH ALES

✉ Unit 3–7, Plot A2, Caxton Industrial Estate, Tower Road North, Warmley, Bristol BS30 8XN
🖳 www.bathales.com

Established in 1995, Bath Ales occupies a purpose-built site between Bath and Bristol. Its 50-barrel brew-plant is steam-driven. The company has rapidly developed a reputation for

making distinctive ales full of flavor and character, using floor-malted barley, whole English hops, and its own cultured yeast.

SPECIAL PALE ALE (SPA) 3.7% ABV • Pale ale
Uses a pure lager malt for its light-bodied character. It has a prominent citrus-hop aroma and a bitter, malty touch.

GEM BITTER 4.1% ABV • Best bitter • A rich, full-textured ale with a malt, fruit, and hop quality throughout, and a dry, bitter-sweet finish.

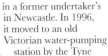
BATH ALES GEM BITTER

BATHAMS

✉ Delph Brewery, Delph Road, Brierley Hill, West Midlands DY5 2TN
🖳 www.bathams.com

This fifth-generation business began in 1877 as a classic Black Country brewery producing mild ales. Brothers Matthew and Tim Batham are the latest owners of the brewery and its attached pub, The Vine. The pub has a quotation on its fascia from Shakespeare's *Two Gentlemen of Verona*: "Blessing of your heart, you brew good ale."

BEST BITTER 4.5% ABV • Best bitter
A straw-colored ale with an initial sweetness soon overtaken by a dry, hoppy flavor.

MILD ALE 3.5% ABV • Mild ale • A dark brown mild; sweet, well balanced, with a hoppy fruit finish.

BIG LAMP

✉ Grange Road, Newburn, Newcastle upon Tyne NE15 8NL
🖳 www.keelmanslodge.co.uk

The oldest microbrewery in the northeast, Big Lamp began brewing in 1982

in a former undertaker's in Newcastle. In 1996, it moved to an old Victorian water-pumping station by the Tyne River. The brewery is organized on the tower principle, in which gravity is used to assist the flow of liquid through the brewing process.

Big Lamp has a popular pub and restaurant attached, and on-site accommodation.

PRINCE BISHOP ALE 4.8% ABV • Premium bitter • An easy-drinking, golden bitter with a full, fruity hop aroma and a spicy bitterness.

SUMMERHILL STOUT 4.4% ABV • Stout • A savory stout with roasted malt character and malty, long-lasting piquancy.

BLACK SHEEP

✉ Wellgarth, Masham, North Yorkshire HG4 4EN
🖳 www.blacksheepbrewery.com

Black Sheep was founded in 1992 by Paul Theakston, a member of Masham's famous brewing dynasty. The brewery's name not only acknowledges the fact that sheep and wool have always contributed to the wealth of the area, but also reflects the idiosyncratic and individual nature of its ales.

The brewery, a former maltings sitting high above the Ure River, has enjoyed sustained growth, resulting in a $10m doubling of capacity in 2006. The magnificent Black Sheep visitor center, bistro-bar, and guided tours draw beer fans and diners from far and wide.

BEST BITTER 3.8% ABV • Best bitter • Well-hopped, light golden in color with a distinctive dry, refreshing tang.

BLACK SHEEP ALE 4.4% ABV • Premium bitter • A full-flavored premium beer with a rich, fruity aroma and bitter-sweet malty taste through to its long, dry, bitter finish.

RIGGWELTER 5.9% ABV • Premium bitter • A strong, fruity bitter with dashes of pear drops and hints of licorice leading to a long, dry finish.

BRAKSPEAR

✉ The Crofts, Eagle Maltings, Witney, Oxfordshire OX28 4DP

🖰 www.wychwood.co.uk

Brakspear was founded in 1779 by a family distantly related to Nicholas Breakspear—better known as Adrian IV, the only British-born pope (1154–9). Following the closure of its brewery at Henley-on-Thames, Brakspear's beers were taken on in 2002 by Wychwood of Witney. Wychwood uses Brakspear's original brewing equipment, including its famous "double-drop" fermenting vessels and its complex yeast strain.

BITTER 3.4% ABV • Bitter
An amber session beer with pleasant fruity hops and malt on the nose. This initial malt and well-hopped bitterness develops into a bitter-sweet and fruity finish.

SPECIAL 4.3% ABV • Premium bitter • Full-bodied, with a hint of sweetness that gives way to a dry hop bitterness; finish is slightly citrus-fruity.

BRAKSPEAR SPECIAL

GLASSWARE: THE NORTH–SOUTH DIVIDE

A beer tour of Britain reveals distinct differences in glassware style. In Scotland and the north, the straight glass, or "nonic" shape, is standard—a fine, tapered glass with a bulge near the top that helps the grip and prevents rims from chipping on the shelves. The dimpled glass with a sturdy handle—the heavy "pot"—is favored in the south, although it is slowly disappearing, despite devotees swearing their beer tastes better out of it. Hands on a glass warm beer up, they say. But the nonic's elegance, head-retention quality and aroma-gathering ability—plus the advertising opportunities it offers on its smooth sides—could make a north–south divide a thing of the past.

A TRADITIONAL "PINT-POT"

BUTCOMBE

✉ Cox's Green, Wrington, Bristol BS40 5PA

🖰 www.butcombe.com

This West Country brewery has doubled in size three times since being set up in 1978 by Simon Whitmore, formerly of Courage and Guinness. Today, Butcombe produces some seven million pints each year. Butcombe's current range of four beers contains no added sugars, colorings, or preservatives, reflecting the brewery's philosophy: "Beer is a natural product… let's keep it that way."

For most of its first two decades of production, Butcombe brewed only bitter, which still accounts for 75 percent of total output. It now produces four cask ales, plus a cold-filtered version of its Blond.

BITTER 4.0% ABV • Bitter
An amber beer that is notably bitter with a citrus-hop, slight sulfur nose, light fruit notes on the palate, and a long, dry, bitter finish.

BLOND 4.3% ABV • Best bitter
A light and fruity beer with a medium bitter finish. The palest English malt is used with Slovenian, Styrian, and Czech Saaz hops to create floral sweetness.

CAINS

✉ Stanhope Street, Liverpool L8 5XJ

🖰 www.cains.co.uk

The Dusanj brothers, Ajmail and Sudarghara, bought the Victorian red-brick Cains Brewery in 2002 and blew a gale of innovation through the business that Irishman Robert Cain had started in 1850. Before being rescued by the Dusanjs, the brewery had passed through several ownerships and even closed for a time. Cains is now one of the fastest-growing breweries in the country.

Cains' portfolio of cask-conditioned ales and keg beers is supplemented by seasonal brews, such as their celebrated Raisin Beer (5.0% ABV; November). The 2008 Culture Beer (5.0% ABV) celebrates Liverpool's year as European City of Culture.

FINEST BITTER 4.0% ABV • Best bitter • A full-bodied yet refreshing bitter with rich, malt flavors and earthy, farmlike aromas from its Goldings hops, leading to a dry finish.

FINEST LAGER 5.0% ABV • Lager
Full in flavor and rich in color, this smooth lager is brewed using Maris Otter malted barley, and follows a three-month cold-maturation regime.

CAMERONS
STRONGARM

CAMERONS

✉ Lion Brewery, Hartlepool, County Durham TS24 7QS
🖰 www.cameronsbrewery.co.uk

Based at the Lion Brewery, Hartlepool, Camerons was founded in 1865. After a number of different owners, it was bought by Castle Eden in 2002 and the company was relaunched as Camerons Brewery Limited.

The brewhouse has superb Italian-marble walls, fine wrought-iron detailing, and its own well, 250 ft (76 m) deep. Camerons has a 500,000-barrel capacity for cask ales, keg beer, and lagers, some of which it contract-brews for Kronenbourg and McEwans. There is also a microbrewery on site for small-scale brews.

▥ **STRONGARM** 4.7% ABV ● Premium bitter ● A well-rounded ruby-red ale with a tight, creamy head and a good balance of malt and hops. Starts fruity in flavor and develops into a pleasant bitterness.

▥ **NIMMO'S XXXX** 4.4% ABV ● Best bitter ● A light golden beer with a malt and hop character and long aftertaste.

CONISTON

✉ The Coppermines Road, Coniston, Cumbria LA21 8HL
🖰 www.conistonbrewery.com

This 10-barrel brewery was set up in 1995 behind the

Black Bull in Coniston. One of the guests at the 400-year-old coaching inn was Donald Campbell, who died trying to break the world water-speed record on Coniston Water in 1967. The flagship beer, Bluebird Bitter, is named after his jet-propelled boat. Coniston also produces the full-bodied Old Man Ale (4.2% ABV) and Bluebird XB (4.2% ABV), made with American Mount Hood hops.

▥ **BLUEBIRD BITTER** 3.6% ABV ● Bitter ● Made with a single variety of hop (Challenger); golden in color, with an inviting hoppy aroma and light, clean palate.

CROUCH VALE

✉ 23 Haltwhistle Road, South Woodham Ferrers, Essex CM3 5ZA
🖰 www.crouch-vale.co.uk

An independent company founded in 1981, Crouch Vale is one of Essex's major craft brewers. The brewery uses traditional methods but always considers new and interesting hop varieties. Crouch Vale produces four regular beers and a number of seasonal brews.

▥ **BREWERS GOLD** 4.0% ABV ● Bitter ● A pale, refreshing, and hoppy ale with aromas of sweet, soft, tropical fruits.

▥ **ESSEX BOYS BITTER** 3.5% ABV ● Bitter Pale brown, with a pleasant malt and citrus hop experience on the nose and a dry finish.

DALESIDE

✉ Camwal Road, Harrogate, North Yorkshire HG1 4PT
🖰 www.dalesidebrewery.co.uk

Established in the mid-1980s, Daleside follows traditional brewing methods, using its own cultured yeast and Harrogate water (the Victorian spa town is famous

for its healing waters). An impressive range of seasonal beers includes Monkey Wrench (5.3% ABV; winter), Greengrass Old Rogue Ale (4.4% ABV; summer), and St. George's Ale (4.1% ABV; spring). Morocco Ale (5.5% ABV) is a resurrection of a 16th-century beer.

▥ **BITTER** 3.7% ABV ● Bitter An amber-colored, well-balanced ale with light and rounded malt, fruity hop properties, and a brush of sweetness.

▥ **BLONDE** 3.9% ABV ● Bitter Distinctively hoppy, with a hint of sherbet and citrus in its delicate flavor and a bitter but short finish.

DURHAM

✉ Unit 5a, Bowburn North Industrial Estate, Bowburn, County Durham DH6 5PF
🖰 www.durham-brewery.co.uk

The Durham Brewery, set up in 1994 by two former music teachers, brews a wide range of bottle-conditioned beers, acknowledged by many to be among the best of their type.

The body and flavor are retained by allowing the beer to mature over time. A large portfolio of some 20 different cask ales complements the bottled range, including many seasonal beers.

▥ **MAGUS** 3.8% ABV ● Bitter ● A pale session beer with lagerlike qualities and aromatic citrus overtones. A complex blend of English, American, Slovenian, and Czech hops provide developing interest on the palate.

DURHAM
EVENSONG

▥ **EVENSONG** 5.0% ABV ● Premium bitter ● A deep ruby-colored bitter based on a 1937 recipe. Its generous hop bitterness is balanced by some sweet fruit and luscious toffee notes with chocolate and coffee nuances.

THE CAMPAIGN FOR REAL ALE

Cask-conditioned beer—cask ale, or "real ale"—is made from fresh, natural ingredients; neither filtered nor pasteurized, it undergoes a secondary fermentation in its container—the cask. The process is not a standardized, uniform one and therein lies its charm and character.

Cask-conditioned beer is a living product, developing as it matures into a drink that is full of natural flavors, influenced in varying degrees by its ingredients of water, malted barley, hops, and yeast. Once it has left the brewery, the beer's final presentation owes a great deal to the skill of the pub landlord who protects and monitors it and chooses the right moment to serve it. In the glass, cask-conditioned beer should be relatively clear, with only the slightest, completely natural carbonation. Temperature is a key factor—beer kept too warm will mature unevenly, and its yeast action will be unworkable if it is chilled too far.

The Campaign for Real Ale can take some credit for the resurgence in England of the ancient art of cooperage, or barrelmaking.

The coveted "Champion Beer of Britain" title is awarded annually by CAMRA to the best real ale.

The term "real ale" was coined by the Campaign for Real Ale (CAMRA), founded in the early 1970s by Michael Hardman, Graham Lees, Bill Mellor, and Jim Makin—who were fed up with the increasingly fizzy and characterless mainstream beer offered around Britain, and concerned by the injudicious takeover and closure of breweries. The movement quickly grew, and membership now exceeds 84,000 individuals who help finance the organization—now the most successful campaigning group in Britain—through more than 200 local-level branches that actively engage with the country's pubs and breweries.

ELGOOD'S

✉ North Brink Brewery, Wisbech, Cambridgeshire PE13 1LN
🖰 www.elgoods-brewery.co.uk

Founded in 1795, the North Brink brewery was one of the first classic Georgian breweries to be built outside London. It came under the control of the Elgood family in 1878, and has remained so ever since.

The superb gardens attached to the brewery cover 4 acres (1.6 hectares). They have been painstakingly restored, complete with original Georgian and Victorian features, forming an attractive backdrop to the 200-year-old brewhouse.

📖 **BLACK DOG** 3.6% ABV
● Mild ale ● A traditional, dark, well-balanced mild with a roasted malt character balanced by a single variety of hop (Fuggles).

📖 **GREYHOUND STRONG BITTER** 5.2% ABV ● Premium bitter ● Full-flavored, opulent, raisiny

ELGOOD'S
BLACK DOG

features are derived from dark sugars, invert sugars, and roasted malt barley.

EVERARDS

✉ Castle Acres, Narborough, Leicestershire LE19 1BY
🖰 www.everards.co.uk

Beer was first brewed by Everards in Leicester in 1849. Current chairman Richard Everard is the fifth generation of the family to run the business. Brewing moved to Burton upon Trent in 1892, but the company returned to its native Leicestershire in 1979. All of Everards' principal beers are dry-hopped and conditioned for a full week at the brewery.

📖 **TIGER** 4.2% ABV ● Best bitter ● Some spicy hop and toffee on the nose; a classic example of a balance of sweetness and bitterness. Crystal malt gives the beer its rounded, toffeed quality.

📖 **ORIGINAL** 5.2% ABV ● Premium bitter ● A smooth, copper-hued and full-bodied premium ale with aromas of toasted caramel and port and a rich, fruity flavor.

EXMOOR

✉ Golden Hill Brewery, Wiveliscombe, Somerset TA4 2NY
🖰 www.exmoorales.co.uk

Exmoor, Somerset's largest brewery, was set up in the defunct Hancock's Brewery at Wiveliscombe, near Taunton, in 1980. A steady stream of brewing-industry awards has since flowed Exmoor's way, and the company has expanded. Exmoor's seasonal beers include Wild Cat (4.4% ABV; fall) and Beast (6.6% ABV; winter/spring).

📖 **GOLD** 4.5% ABV ● Best bitter A golden best bitter with powerful earthy hop, lemon, and juicy malt aromas. A fruity butterscotch sweetness on the palate gives way to a satisfying and memorable bitter finish.

📖 **EXMOOR ALE** 3.8% ABV ● Bitter A pale-colored, medium-bodied session bitter with

Hops are poured into one of the coppers at Fuller's Griffin Brewery in west London.

some malt and hop in the aroma and a bitter, hoppy aftertaste.

FULLER'S

✉ Griffin Brewery, Chiswick Lane South, Chiswick, London W4 2QB

🖰 www.fullers.co.uk

Fuller, Smith & Turner's brewery has stood on the same site near the Thames River for more than 350 years. Direct descendants of the founding families are still involved in its running and, despite its national profile, Fuller's retains the spirit and drive of a small company. Its beers are among the most consistent in the country.

In 2005, Fuller's took over the Hampshire brewer George Gale, transferring production of Gale's beers to its own Chiswick brewery.

🍺 **LONDON PRIDE** 4.1% ABV • Premium bitter • The best-selling premium cask bitter in Britain. It has a fruity, sweet malt nose and a floral, spicy, hoppy presence and marmalade undercurrents before a lingering, dry finish.

🍺 **ESB** 5.5% ABV • Extra special bitter • Complex aromas with the house-style orangey fruit nestling comfortably with tangy hops and some roasted malt. A multi-award winner.

🍺 **VINTAGE ALE** 8.5% ABV • Old ale Introduced in 1997 as an autumn-bottled beer using different varieties of malt and hops (at the discretion of the head brewer). Each year's brew can be dramatically different, but all are dark and intriguing.

GREENE KING

✉ Westgate Brewery, Bury St. Edmunds, Suffolk IP33 1QT

🖰 www.greeneking.co.uk

This company has been active in Bury St. Edmunds since 1799, when Benjamin

GREENE KING
ABBOT ALE

Greene first opened his brewery. The rival King Brewery opened nearby in 1868, and the two companies merged in 1887. In recent years, Greene King has bought up and closed Ridley's, Morland, Ruddles, Belhaven of Dunbar, and Hardys & Hansons of Nottingham, with each takeover stirring up controversy in the craft-brewing world.

🍺 **ABBOT ALE** 5.0% ABV • Premium bitter • A biscuit malt and spicy hop aroma, with a tangy fruit and malt bitter-sweetness on the palate.

🍺 **IPA** 3.6% ABV • India pale ale Distinctly copper-colored with a clean, fresh hop savoriness and subtle, sweetish malty nose.

🍺 **RUDDLES' COUNTY** 4.3% ABV • Best bitter • A premium ale with a fruity sweetness and a definite hoppy, dry finish.

🍺 **OLD SPECKLED HEN** 5.2% ABV • Premium bitter • Rich and intense with savory, spicy malt and fruity sweetness.

HAMBLETON

✉ Melmerby Green Road, Melmerby, North Yorkshire HG4 5NB

🖰 www.hambletonales.co.uk

Nick Stafford started the Hambleton Brewery in 1991 in the hamlet of Holme-on-Swale, North Yorkshire. Now relocated a few miles south to Melmerby, near Ripon, the brewery turns out 100 barrels a week.

The horse graphic on the logo and labels is inspired by the giant White Horse carved into the side of the nearby Hambleton Hills. Hambleton's distinctive portfolio of regular and special brews includes

HAMBLETON
STALLION

the first gluten-free ale (GFA) and lager (GFL) to be produced in Britain.

🍺 **STALLION** 4.2% ABV • Bitter A malty character, with a hint of nuttiness, and the generous hopping that, for some, is the definition of a true Yorkshire bitter.

🍺 **STUD** 4.3% ABV • Bitter A straw-colored ale with a delicate hop flavor that enhances its robust, full-bodied character.

HARVEYS

✉ The Bridge Wharf Brewery, Cliffe High Street, Lewes, East Sussex BN7 2AH

🖰 www.harveys.org.uk

Harveys is an independent, seventh-generation family brewery first established in 1790. With its brewhouse and tower (1880), Harveys is a fine example of a country brewery in the Victorian Gothic style. The cellars and fermenting room remain structurally unaltered, even though they now house modern equipment. Major additions in the 1980s (built in a similar Gothic style) greatly increased the brewing capacity.

🍺 **SUSSEX BEST BITTER** 4.0% ABV • Best bitter • A full, well-hopped bitter with a pungent, grassy hop character, biscuit malt and citrus fruit, then a dry aftertaste.

🍺 **ARMADA ALE** 4.5% ABV • Best bitter • A hoppy, amber-colored best bitter with a well-balanced blend of fruit and hops on the palate.

HAWKSHEAD

✉ Staveley Mill Yard, Staveley, Cumbria LA8 9LR

🖰 www. hawksheadbrewery.co.uk

This microbrewery relocated from its original premises at Hawkshead, in "Beatrix Potter country," in 2006 to

THE VICTORIAN ENGLISH BREWERY

The Victorian tower brewery developed as the science of engineering provided new answers to architectural problems, and was an effective combination of function with form. Simple and efficient, the system uses gravity as its driver: raw materials enter at the top and drop down or across at various stages of the brewing process, limiting the need for pumps. The liquor (water) tank is at the highest level with a mash-tun below, fed by a grist mill, with a copper in the center and casking at ground level. Good examples are Hook Norton in Oxfordshire and Wadworth in Wiltshire.

Wadworth's six-story Northgate Brewery in Devizes, Wiltshire (*see also p.166*) still uses much of its original, 1885-vintage equipment.

a state-of-the-art plant and visitor center in Staveley. The old brewery, a former milking parlor, is still used for small runs and experimental brews.

Hawkshead beers are brewed using Maris Otter malted barley. They are all distinctly bitter, with a hop character produced by careful blending and balancing of different varieties.

🍺 LAKELAND GOLD 4.4% ABV ● **Premium bitter** ● Hoppy and uncompromisingly bitter with complex fruit flavors from a blend of English First Gold and American Cascade hops. Branded in bottles as Hawkshead Gold.

🍺 RED 4.2% ABV ● **Best bitter** A bitter-sweet red ale whose color comes from dark crystal malt. It is malty

HIGHGATE DAVENPORTS ORIGINAL

and spicy on the palate and a juicy, woody aroma from the Fuggles hops leads to a long, dry finish.

HIGHGATE

✉ Sandymount Road, Walsall, West Midlands WS1 3AP
🖐 www.highgatebrewery.com

This imposing red-brick brewery was built in 1898 to supply mild ale to the Midlands. It still uses most of the original Victorian equipment, including wooden mash tuns (now lined with stainless steel) and coppers topped off by "Chinese hat" funnels. Some modern technology and a laboratory have been added in recent years. Ownership of Highgate has changed several times since James A. Fletcher founded the business in the 19th century, passing to Mitchells & Butlers, Bass (when it was the smallest brewery in the group), and, most recently, to Aston Manor.

🍺 DARK MILD 3.6% ABV ● **Mild ale** ● A typical Black Country mild, with a complex aroma of dark fruit and chocolate, traces of spicy hops on the palate, and a long malt finish.

🍺 DAVENPORTS ORIGINAL 4.3% ABV ● **Best bitter** ● A full-bodied, copper-colored ale with ample malt and fruit, balanced by a satisfying bitter finish.

HOG'S BACK

✉ Manor Farm, The Street, Tongham, Surrey GU10 1DE
🖐 www.hogsback.co.uk

A modern but traditional-style brewery built into 18th-century farm buildings, Hog's Back began brewing in 1992. The popularity of Hog's Back ales has since led to expansion.

Seasonal beers, such as Summer This (4.2% ABV) and Autumn Seer (4.8% ABV), complement the range of commemorative ales and bottle-conditioned beers, culminating in the mighty barley-wine-styled A over T (9.0% ABV).

🍺 TRADITIONAL ENGLISH ALE (TEA) 4.2% ABV ● **Bitter** ● A pale brown, well-crafted, malty bitter with a hoppy and slightly fruity aroma, some bitter-sweetness, and a long, dry finish.

🍺 HOP GARDEN GOLD 4.6% ABV ● **Best bitter** ● A pale and malty golden best bitter with hints of banana and pineapple teased out of a finely balanced aroma with bittering hops. Long, dry, hoppy finish.

HOLT

✉ **Derby Brewery, Empire Street, Cheetham, Manchester M3 1JD**

🖥 www.joseph-holt.com

This brewery was founded by Joseph and Catherine Holt in 1849. Joseph had previously been a carter at Harrison's Strangeways brewery in Manchester. Holt's is still in family hands four generations later. Expansion and investment continue steadily on Holt's 3-acre (1.2-hectare) site, with the latest addition being a 30-barrel brew-plant.

🍺 **MILD** 3.2% ABV • Mild ale
A dark brown beer with a fruity and malty nose, roasted malt, chocolate, licorice, and some fruit flavors. There is also a welcome strong bitterness to the finish.

🍺 **BITTER** 4.0% ABV • Bitter
Very bitter indeed. Pungently spicy hops dominate the aroma and its aggressive tart fruitiness is eventually tempered by malt biscuit and bitter-sweet fruit.

HOOK NORTON

✉ **Brewery Lane, Hook Norton, Oxfordshire OX15 5NY**

🖥 www.hooky.co.uk

The Hook Norton brewery near Banbury dates back to 1849, when it was founded by John Harris, a Cotswolds farmer and maltster. The current building, erected in 1900, is a fine example of a Victorian tower brewery. The machinery is still steam-driven, with a series of belts, cogs, and shafts supplying power from the 25-horse-power engine. Water is drawn from wells under the brewery. A museum displays

HOOK NORTON OLD HOOKY

highlights from the brewery's long history, but Hook Norton is not stuck in the past: recent installations include a new copper mash tun and fermenters.

🍺 **OLD HOOKY** 4.6% ABV
• Premium bitter
A beautifully balanced beer with a fruity nature and a suggestion of malt on the palate.

🍺 **HOOKY BITTER** 3.6% ABV • Bitter
A subtly balanced bitter with a definite hoppy nose, followed by some malt and a lingering hop finish.

HOP BACK

✉ **Units 22–24, Batten Road Industrial Estate, Downton, Salisbury, Wiltshire SP5 3HU**

🖥 www.hopback.co.uk

John and Julie Gilbert took over The Wyndham Arms, on the outskirts of Salisbury, in 1986. John began brewing beer on site for sale in the pub. Awards soon followed. In order to meet the rising demand, the Hop Back company was set up and the brewing was moved to more modern premises in Downton in 1992.

🍺 **SUMMER LIGHTNING** 5.0% ABV • Premium bitter
A straw-colored ale with a terrific fresh, hoppy aroma, and some malt on the palate. This, coupled with an intense bitterness, leads to a good long, dry finish.

HYDES

✉ **46 Moss Lane West, Manchester M15 5PH**

🖥 www.hydesbrewery.com

This family-run concern is one of the top 10 regional breweries in the UK. The Hyde brewing dynasty began in 1863, when

Alfred and Ralph Hyde acquired a small brewery from their grandfather, Thomas Shaw.

Contract-brewing of the Boddingtons brand for InBev has meant expansion, and this has enabled Hydes itself to brew more occasional and experimental beers.

🍺 **TRADITIONAL BITTER** 3.8% ABV • Bitter • A pale brown ale with a malty-nosed earthiness leading to a long, bitter finish.

🍺 **DARK MILD** 3.5% ABV • Mild ale
A dark, reddish-brown beer with a fruit and malt nose and a complex flavor that meanders through berry fruits, malt, and a hint of chocolate.

JENNINGS

✉ **Castle Brewery, Cockermouth, Cumbria CA13 9NE**

🖥 www.jenningsbrewery.co.uk

The Jennings brewery sits in the lee of Cockermouth Castle, in the northern Lake District. Established as a family concern in 1828, it is now owned by Marston's Beer Company, which has made huge investment to secure the brewery's future. The brewing process uses Lakeland water drawn from Jennings's own well. Seasonal beers include Crag Rat (4.3% ABV) and Redbreast (4.5% ABV).

🍺 **CUMBERLAND ALE** 4.0% ABV • Bitter
A golden-colored, hoppy beer with a dry aftertaste.

🍺 **SNECK LIFTER** 5.1% ABV • Premium bitter
A strong, intriguing dark brown with a complex aroma and a flavor developing through fruit, malt, and roasted notes.

🍺 **COCKER HOOP** 4.6% ABV • Best bitter
Styrian Goldings hops give an unmistakeable resiny aroma with a sweet malty quality.

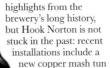

HOP BACK SUMMER LIGHTNING

A specialty of northern England, from Yorkshire's oldest brewery, Samuel Smith's Nut Brown Ale (5.0% ABV) is a relatively dry brown ale, with a rich, malty color that corresponds to its palate of malt, beechnut, and sweet-and-sour walnut. It makes an ideal dining companion.

JOHN SMITH'S

✉ The Brewery, Tadcaster, North Yorkshire LS24 9SA

🖥 www.johnsmiths.co.uk

John Smith, from the same family as Samuel Smith (*see p.164*), began brewing in 1847 to cater for the local mill trade. The enterprise was bought by Courage in 1970, and later absorbed by Scottish & Newcastle. John Smith's is the UK's top-selling bitter, with over a million pints drunk each day.

■ **JOHN SMITH'S ORIGINAL**
3.8% ABV • Bitter • A moderate-bodied, fruitily flavored bitter with a short hoppy finish. A cask-conditioned version is known as John Smith's Cask.

■ **JOHN SMITH'S MAGNET** 4.0% ABV
Best bitter • A balance of bittersweet flavors including caramel and licorice make for an easy-drinking, full-flavored beer.

KELHAM ISLAND

✉ 23 Alma Street, Sheffield S3 8SA

🖥 www.kelhambrewery.co.uk

The Kelham Island Brewery was purpose-built in 1990 on land adjoining the renowned Fat Cat pub in Sheffield, although it later relocated to premises nearby. The original Kelham Island building now serves as a visitor center.

With the closure of all four of Sheffield's large breweries —Bass's Hope & Anchor and Stones breweries, Wards, and Whitbread's old Tennents brewery—Kelham is now the city's largest brewery. Its five regular beers are augmented by special monthly brews.

■ **PALE RIDER** 5.2% ABV • Premium bitter • A straw-colored, strong and delicately fruity ale using American hops.

■ **EASY RIDER** 3.8% ABV • Pale ale • A subtle, easy-drinking,

premium-strength pale ale. Its initial crisp bitterness gives way to a lingering, fruity finish.

KELHAM ISLAND PALE RIDER

LEES

✉ Greengate Brewery, Middleton Junction, Manchester M24 2AX

🖥 www.jwlees.co.uk

Founded by retired cotton manufacturer John Lees in 1828, this brewery remains a family concern today, six generations on. John Willie Lees, the founder's grandson, designed the current brewery in 1876. Lees' seasonal beers include the rich, limited-release Lees Vintage Harvest Ale (11.5% ABV), which can be laid down to mature like a wine.

■ **LEES BITTER** 4.0% ABV • Bitter Amber in color and distinctly malty in flavor, with a citrus fruit finish.

■ **GB MILD** 3.5% ABV • Mild ale A malt and fruit aroma balancing chocolate, malt, and dried fruit flavors.

McMULLEN

✉ The Hertford Brewery, 26 Old Cross, Hertford SG14 1RD

🖥 www.mcmullens.co.uk

With a history dating back to 1827, this handsome red-brick brewery faced closure in 2003 because of a family dispute, but recovered sufficiently to open a new brewhouse in 2006. McMullen's beers are made using water drawn from an on-site artesian well.

■ **COUNTRY BEST BITTER** 4.3% ABV • Best bitter • A full-bodied and well-balanced bitter, with a hint of citrus fruit and an apricotlike aroma.

■ **AK MILD** 3.7% ABV • Mild ale A full-bodied mild with floral and spice notes and a malt-heavy flavor.

MARSTON'S

✉ Shobnall Road, Burton upon Trent, Staffordshire DE14 2BW

🖥 www.marstonsdontcompromise. co.uk

Marston's is one of the great traditional breweries based in Burton upon Trent, "the home of British beer." The brewery, founded by John Marston in 1834, moved to its current site when it merged with Thompson's in 1898. It is now part of Marston's Beer Company, along with the Banks's, Jennings, and Mansfield brands.

Marston's Pedigree is a premium ale that is still brewed in the oak casks of the Burton Union—the unique yeast-cultivating system (*see box, p.163*) that has preserved the character of Pedigree yeast since the early 1800s.

■ **PEDIGREE** 4.4% ABV • Premium bitter • A British classic. Sweet and hoppy with the slight sulfur aroma characteristic of Burton ales.

■ **BURTON BITTER** 3.8% ABV
• Bitter • Malty biscuit flavors with a delicate hop nature and the distinctive sulfurous aroma.

■ **OLD EMPIRE**
5.7% ABV • India pale ale A stylish, copper-colored IPA with a well-balanced hop and fruit character and a dry, extra-hoppy finish.

McMULLEN COUNTRY BEST BITTER

MEANTIME

✉ The Greenwich Brewery, 2 Penhall Road, London SE7 8RX

🖥 www.meantimebrewing.com

When Meantime began brewing in 2000, brewmaster Alastair Hook's mission was to "demonstrate the full flavor that beer has to offer, and to engage the drinking public with those flavors." Meantime specializes in innovative recreations of traditional ale and beer styles. One of its most notable brews is Coffee Beer, brewed with fair-traded coffee beans from Rwanda.

🍺 **INDIA PALE ALE** 7.5% ABV • India pale ale • Extremely hoppy, with aromas and flavors alternating between grassy and earthy and rich orange marmalade.

🍺 **CHOCOLATE BEER** 6.5% ABV • Premium bitter • A silky smooth, vanilla-infused, and complex "suppertime" beer that uses dark malts and dark chocolate to create a rich, warming, and powerful character.

MELBOURN BROTHERS

✉ All Saints Brewery, 22 All Saints Street, Stamford, Lincolnshire PE9 2PA

🖥 www.merchantduvin.com (US importer's website)

Melbourn Brothers' stone-built brewery has a cobbled yard, grist mill, steam engine, wooden tanks, and coppers that hark back to the early Industrial Revolution. Originally opened in 1825,

the brewery was bought by Herbert Wells Melbourn in 1869. It ceased trading in 1974, but was revived by Samuel Smith of Tadcaster (*see p.164*) in 1998, to make a range of fruit beers. The lambic-style brews are spontaneously fermented by airborne wild yeasts, and then bottled with the addition of fruit juices.

🍺 **APRICOT** 3.4% ABV • Fruit beer Deliciously dry, tartly fresh, and well balanced.

🍺 **STRAWBERRY** 3.4% ABV • Fruit beer • Clean and fresh, with ripe fruit flavors.

🍺 **CHERRY** 3.4% ABV • Fruit beer Matured for a year, it is delicate and spicy with a fine balance of sweetness and astringency.

MOORHOUSE'S

✉ Moorhouse Street, Burnley, Lancashire BB11 5EN

🖥 www.moorhouses.co.uk

Established in 1865 by William Moorhouse, this brewery originally produced mineral water and a hop-flavored soft drink. Some of the equipment used in the

brewing process today dates back nearly a century. Cask-ale production has risen steadily over the past 30 years, with more national and international awards gained than any other brewer of a similar size.

🍺 **BLACK CAT** 3.4% ABV • Mild ale A dark, complex ale with a distinct chocolate malt flavor, nuances of licorice and fruit, and a smooth, hoppy finish.

🍺 **PENDLE WITCHES BREW** 5.1% ABV • Premium bitter A distinctive, amber-colored, full malt-flavored beer with a strong, fruity hop aftertaste.

MORDUE

✉ D1/D2, Narvik Way, Tyne Tunnel Trading Estate, North Shields, Tyne and Wear NE29 7XJ

🖥 www.morduebrewery.com

The original Mordue brewery, at Wallsend near Newcastle, was a 19th-century enterprise. The name was revived in 1995 when microbrewing brothers Garry and Matthew Fawson discovered that they were living in the old head-brewer's

John Smith's classic Victorian industrial buildings have been cleaned and refurbished.

house. Several expansions later, Mordue has a strong local customer base and a growing national reputation.

WORKIE TICKET 4.5% ABV • Best bitter • A complex, well-constructed bitter with a good malt and hop level throughout and a long, satisfying bitter finish.

GEORDIE PRIDE 4.2% ABV • Bitter • A well-balanced, amber-hued bitter with a hop and fruit aroma that is echoed on the palate, with a long bitter finish.

NEWCASTLE FEDERATION

✉ Dunston Industrial Estate, Lancaster Road, Gateshead, Tyne and Wear, NE11 9JR

🖳 www.scottish-newcastle.com

This Gateshead brewery was built by the now-defunct Federation Brewery in 1980, and was bought by Scottish & Newcastle in 2004. Situated beside the Tyne river, 2 miles (3 km) from Newcastle city center, the 33m-gallon (1.25m-hectoliter) brewery has been the home of Newcastle Brown Ale since 2005. The world-famous beer, the company's flagship, was first brewed in 1927. Today, "Newkie Broon," as it is affectionately known, is the UK's best-selling premium bottled ale.

NEWCASTLE FEDERATION NEWCASTLE BROWN ALE

NEWCASTLE BROWN ALE 4.7% ABV • Brown ale A premium brown ale, full-bodied with a caramel and fruity character. and a sweet aftertaste.

NEWCASTLE EXHIBITION ALE 4.3% ABV • Best bitter • A full-bodied pale ale; hoppy aroma continues in the flavor; sweet rather than bitter, with a dry finish.

NORTH YORKSHIRE

✉ Pinchinthorpe Hall, Pinchinthorpe, Guisborough, North Yorkshire TS14 8HG

🖳 www.nybrewery.co.uk

This secluded brewery is housed in the old dairy at Pinchinthorpe Hall—a 17th-century listed manor house (now a hotel) set in a moated estate in the North Yorkshire Moors National Park. The organic beers are made with Maris Otter malt, Goldings and Northdown hops, and water from the estate's own spring.

FLYING HERBERT 4.7% ABV • Premium bitter • Well balanced and full-flavored; malt and fruit-influenced dry finish.

FOOL'S GOLD 4.6% ABV • Premium bitter • A hoppy, pale-colored premium beer with bitter-sweet citrus notes.

OAKHAM ALES

✉ 2 Maxwell Road, Woodston, Peterborough, Cambridgeshire PE2 7JB

🖳 www.oakhamales.com

Now on its third site since starting out in 1993, Oakham has grown from a homebrew-sized operation into a brewery turning out 700 barrels a week. A preference for floral American hops, such as Willamette and Mount Hood, is Oakham's signature. Its seasonal beer range includes Black Hole

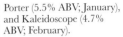

OAKHAM ALES JEFFREY HUDSON BITTER

Porter (5.5% ABV; January), and Kaleidoscope (4.7% ABV; February).

JEFFREY HUDSON BITTER 3.8% ABV • Bitter • A straw-colored ale with a big, citrus-hoppy aroma, which unfolds into a fruity and grassy bitter-sweetness.

WHITE DWARF 4.3% ABV • Wheat beer • This English-style wheat beer has a piercing bitter character with citrus fruit overtones and a dry bite of a finish.

O'HANLON'S

✉ Great Barton Farm, Whimple, Devon EX5 2NY

🖳 www.ohanlons.co.uk

O'Hanlon's was established in 1995 under railway arches at Vauxhall Station, London, as a brewing offshoot of a pub of the same name. In 2000, it relocated to Devon, and now brews hand-crafted beers using water from its own well.

O'Hanlon's has recreated Thomas Hardy's Ale (11.7% ABV), formerly brewed by Eldridge Pope of Dorchester. Powerfully hoppy, strong, and infused with preserved-fruit flavors, it is made in annual "editions" of individually-numbered bottles that can be laid down for 25 years.

FIREFLY 3.7% ABV • Bitter A crisp, amber session bitter with an alluring hop aroma; fruitily orangey on the palate.

YELLOWHAMMER 4.2% ABV • Best bitter • Well balanced, with hop and fruit aromas and a dry, bitter afterglow.

OKELLS

✉ Falcon Brewery, Kewaigue, Douglas, Isle of Man IM2 1QG

🖳 www.okells.co.uk

Founded in 1850 by Dr. William Okell in Douglas, Isle of Man, Okells moved to its Falcon Steam Brewery, which Dr. Okell had designed himself, in 1874. At the time, the use of steam led it to be regarded as one of the world's most sophisticated breweries.

In 1994, Okells relocated to a purpose-built plant just outside Douglas. All beers are produced under the Manx Brewers Act, which permits only the use of water, malt, sugar, and hops.

🍺 **BITTER** 3.4% ABV • Bitter
A light and complex golden-colored beer with a malt and hop aroma, hints of honey, and a long-lingering dry finish.

🍺 **MILD** 3.4% ABV • Mild ale
A fine example of a dark, reddish-brown mild reveling in rich maltiness and a hint of Seville oranges.

PALMERS

✉ **The Old Brewery, West Bay Road, Bridport, Dorset DT6 4JA**
🖥 **www.palmersbrewery.com**

Dating from 1794, Britain's only thatched brewery is located in a designated Area of Outstanding Natural Beauty on the Dorset coast. It is run by the Palmer family, whose great-grandfather bought it in 1896. Central to its beers are Maris Otter malted barley and Goldings hops.

🍺 **COPPER ALE** 3.7% ABV • Bitter
A fruity, hoppy session beer with a hint of caramel and a bitter-sweet finale.

🍺 **BEST BITTER** 4.2% ABV • Best bitter • An IPA-style beer with a pronounced hop character and fruit and malt undertones.

RINGWOOD

✉ **138 Christchurch Road, Ringwood, Hampshire BH24 3AP**
🖥 **www.ringwoodbrewery.co.uk**

Ringwood was started in 1978 by Peter Austin, the "father of microbrewing," in a former bakery. In 1986, it moved to its present location, the site of the old Tunks' Brewery, which had closed in

RINGWOOD
OLD THUMPER

1821. Today, Ringwood is a 30,000-barrel-a-year regional brewery. New fermenting vessels and conditioning tanks have been installed in recent years, and further development is planned.

🍺 **BEST BITTER** 3.8% ABV • Best bitter • A tempting hop and fruit aroma with a slightly tart, dry, and fruity flavor supported by an underlying malt sweetness.

🍺 **OLD THUMPER** 5.6% ABV • Premium bitter • A peppered spice aroma with a touch of apples that unfolds into a well-balanced, rounded malt and caramel flavor with some fruit in the finish.

ROBINSON'S

✉ **Unicorn Brewery, Stockport, Cheshire SK1 1JJ**
🖥 **www.frederic-robinson.com**

In 1865, Frederic Robinson joined his father at Stockport's Union Inn to brew beer, inaugurating a business that is still in family hands today.

Now one of Britain's largest regional brewers, Robinson's continues to develop while remaining true to traditional brewing methods. Its state-of-the-art bottling facility handles beers for many different customers.

🍺 **UNICORN BEST BITTER** 4.2% ABV • Best bitter • A golden ale with some spicy hop and malt on the nose balanced by a bitter-sweet flavor.

🍺 **OLD TOM STRONG ALE** 8.5% ABV • Premium bitter • Full-bodied and dark with a combination of fruit, malt, and chocolate in the aroma. A beautiful complexity develops through more defined malt, port wine, and fruit flavors.

ROOSTER'S

✉ **Unit 3, Grimbald Park, Wetherby Road, Knaresborough, North Yorkshire HG5 8LJ**
🖥 **www.roosters.co.uk**

Brewery owner Sean Franklin is a devotee of hops and their influence on beer's aromas and flavor, and has a special fondness for American hops. Franklin makes no apology for his beers' aromatic individuality!

🍺 **YANKEE** 4.3% ABV • Bitter
A straw-colored beer with a delicate, fruity aroma and slightly sweet balance of malt and hops.

🍺 **YORKSHIRE PALE ALE** 4.3% ABV • Bitter • Pale gold in color with a medium bitterness and fruity, raspberry aroma. Gold medal winner at the

YORKSHIRE SQUARES AND BURTON UNIONS

Two fermentation methods creating distinctly flavored beers are the Yorkshire Square system and the Burton Union. Marston's Pedigree (see p.160) is believed to be the only beer now produced on Burton Union, while Samuel Smith (see p.164) and Black Sheep (see p.150) still use Yorkshire Squares—shallow, double-decked chambers traditionally made from Welsh slate. Fermenting beer is pumped from the bottom over the yeasty head to keep it mixed in for mellowness and balance. The Burton Union is a series of 24 oak casks with a long trough above. Pedigree's special yeast, which does not separate easily from the beer, is trapped in the trough and recovered for subsequent brews.

World Beer Cup 2006 in Seattle, Washington.

LEGHORN 4.3% ABV • Premium bitter • Four aromatic hops combine to produce tropical fruit and floral characteristics. Full-tasting and well balanced.

ST. AUSTELL

✉ 63 Trevarthian Road, St. Austell, Cornwall PL25 4BY

🖰 www.staustellbrewery.co.uk

Founded by Walter Hicks in 1851 at a cost of £1,500, St. Austell became one of Cornwall's largest companies, running 164 pubs and hotels and employing more than 1,000 people. Hicks's great-great-grandson is the current MD. The brewery is a glorious combination of Victorian grandeur and Cornish vernacular architecture.

IPA 3.4% ABV • India pale ale • Full of flavor for such a low-strength beer, and packed with fresh hoppiness; a full-bodied palate with touches of caramel.

TRIBUTE 4.2% ABV • Best bitter • Uses the brewery's own Cornish Gold malt, which imparts a rich, biscuity aroma. An intense fruitiness also envelops the nose and palate, balanced by malt and fruit flavors.

ST. PETER'S

✉ St. Peter's Hall, St. Peter South Elmham, Bungay, Suffolk NR35 1NQ

🖰 www.stpetersbrewery.co.uk

Set up in 1996 in listed agricultural buildings at St. Peter's Hall in Suffolk, this brewery makes classic English ales using water from its own borehole, local malted barley, and Kentish hops. While St. Peter's bottled beers, with their distinctive 1770-vintage flask

shape, have been its hallmark, the brewery has also developed a range of cask ales. The 13th-century Hall itself is now a busy bar and restaurant.

BEST BITTER 3.7% ABV • Best bitter • Distinctly fruity, with caramel notes developing into a complex and full-bodied ale with a dry, hoppy finish.

GOLDEN ALE 4.7% ABV • Premium bitter • Full-bodied and robust with a strong hop bouquet and a distinct balance of malt and fruit; reminiscent of a Czech lager.

SAMUEL SMITH

✉ The Old Brewery, High Street, Tadcaster, North Yorkshire LS24 9SB

🖰 www.merchantduvin.com/ pages/5_breweries/samsmith. html (US importer)

ST. AUSTELL TRIBUTE

Yorkshire's oldest brewery, dating from 1758, Samuel Smith's remains independent and family-owned. Beers are fermented in traditional roofed fermenting vessels called Yorkshire Squares (*see box, p.163*). The brewery's original well, 85 ft (26 m) deep, draws on a plentiful supply of limestone water. Some ales are still supplied in wooden casks.

OLD BREWERY BITTER 4.0% ABV • Bitter • A fine example of a northern malty bitter with a dash of hops and fruit in the flavor.

NUT BROWN ALE 5.0% ABV • Brown ale • A hazel-colored northern specialty with a palate of beech nuts, almonds, and walnuts.

SHEPHERD NEAME

✉ 17 Court Street, Faversham, Kent ME13 7AX

🖰 www.shepherdneame.co.uk

England's oldest continuously operated brewery, Shepherd Neame is still fed by the same

SHEPHERD NEAME SPITFIRE

well used for its first brews in 1698. The Neame family has been involved in running the company since 1864.

The cask beers are brewed using Kentish hops and locally malted barley. Russian teak mash tuns installed in 1914 are still in daily use. In 2005, a $6.1m investment boosted ouput to more than 200,000 barrels a year.

SPITFIRE 4.5% ABV • Premium bitter • Combines an underlying depth of maltiness with a subtle hint of toffee and boldly fruity citrus hops.

BISHOP'S FINGER 5.0% ABV • Premium bitter • Generously fruity, with banana and pear coming to the fore, a biscuit-rich maltiness, and a dried fruit flavor.

MASTER BREW BITTER 3.7% ABV • Bitter • A distinctly hoppy, well-balanced session beer with a dusting of sweetness and a slight bitterness to the finish.

SPRINGHEAD

✉ Old Great North Road, Sutton on Trent, Nottinghamshire NG23 6QS

🖰 www.springhead.co.uk

Springhead was set up in 1990 in a tiny outbuilding adjoining the brewer's house in the village of Sutton on Trent in Nottinghamshire. Named after a nearby bend in the Trent River, it was at the time England's smallest microbrewery (2.5 barrels). In 2004, two expansions later, it moved into a new

50-barrel plant. Most beers have names relating to the English Civil War, which was bitterly fought in this area.

BITTER 4.0% ABV • Bitter
A copper-colored, easy-drinking hoppy ale with malt on the nose complemented by a slight fruitiness and long bitter finish.

PURITAN PORTER 4.0% ABV •
Porter • A dark beer that looks heavier than it tastes. Well-rounded, smooth, with a lingering roast-barley finish.

TETLEY

✉ PO Box 142, Hunslet Road, Leeds, West Yorkshire LS1 1QG
⌂ www.carlsberg.co.uk

This historic Leeds brewery, with its traditional open Yorkshire Square fermenters, has been synonymous with high-quality ales since Joshua Tetley bought it in 1822. In 1960, Tetley merged with Walker Cains to form Tetley Walker. It later became the main cask-ale brewery for Allied Brewers, and is now owned by Carlsberg. As well as Tetley beers, the Leeds brewery produces brands from the Carlsberg portfolio.

TETLEY'S CASK BITTER 3.7% ABV
• Bitter • Amber-colored with a slight malt and hop aroma and a touch of fruit on the palate. The finish is dry and bitter.

Tetley's beers are the pride of Leeds and the brewery itself is a prominent local landmark.

TETLEY'S MILD 3.3% ABV •
Mild ale • A light malt and caramel aroma and a well-balanced malt structure, which develops a good level of bitterness.

THEAKSTON

✉ The Brewery, Masham, North Yorkshire HG4 4YD
⌂ www.theakstons.co.uk

This brewery began life in 1827, when Robert Theakston took a lease on The Black Bull Inn and brewhouse at Masham. The current brewery was built in 1875 by Robert's son, Thomas. After numerous ownership changes, the brewery is now independent again and back in family hands, with three Theakston brothers at the helm. Its logo is the seal used by the Official (chairman) of a local, historic ecclesiastical court— the Peculier Court of Masham—set up in the 12th century.

XB 4.5% ABV •
Premium bitter
A premium-strength, ruby-colored, well-

balanced ale that has a complex aroma and full-bodied flavor.

OLD PECULIER 5.5% ABV •
Premium bitter • Rich, dark, and strong with a deep ruby color, fruity, mellow aroma, and malty, full-bodied flavor.

THORNBRIDGE

✉ Thornbridge Hall, Ashford-in-the-Water, Derbyshire DE45 1NZ
⌂ www.thornbridgebrewery.co.uk

Based in an old stonemason's and joiner's workshop in the grounds of Thornbridge Hall in Derbyshire, this brewery made its first beer in 2005. It rapidly gained a reputation for innovative beers with an emphasis on flavor. The aim at the 10-barrel plant is to brew a small number of regular beers while continuing to develop new styles.

JAIPUR IPA 5.9% ABV •
India pale ale • Complex but well balanced, with an emphasis on citrus-hoppiness. Its powerful, lingering flavors lead to a bitter finish.

LORD MARPLES
4.0% ABV • Bitter • An easy-drinking bitter with hints of honey and caramel and a long, bitter afterglow.

THEAKSTON
OLD
PECULIER

THWAITES

✉ Star Brewery, Syke Street, Blackburn, Lancashire BB1 5BU

🖳 www.thwaites.co.uk

Thwaites, the seventh-largest brewer in Britain, dates from 1807. Staunchly independent, it is still run by descendants of its founder, Daniel Thwaites. Traditional open fermenting vessels are used, although the brewery is fully automated. Contract-brewing makes up a significant amount of Thwaites' output.

🍺 **LANCASTER BOMBER** 4.4% ABV • Best bitter • An inviting malty aroma crossed with floral hop and a full-bodied flavor, plus some fruit in its malty firmness.

🍺 **ORIGINAL** 3.6% ABV • Bitter A clean, dry-tasting session bitter with a glowing amber appearance. Maris Otter malted barley and a blend of Goldings and Fuggles hops contribute its citrus crispness and firm malted base.

TIMOTHY TAYLOR

✉ Knowle Spring Brewery, Keighley, West Yorkshire BD21 1AW

🖳 www.timothy-taylor.co.uk

This classic English brewery has been family-owned since its inception in 1858. Its attractive stone premises were built in 1863 to make use of the pure Pennine hills water from a nearby spring. Timothy Taylor is the only brewery to use Golden Promise barley, specially grown in Scotland and widely used in the malt whisky industry. A recent $2m expansion program added a new brewhouse to the site.

🍺 **LANDLORD** 4.3 ABV • Strong pale ale • This world-renowned classic strong pale ale has a complex hoppy aroma and a well-balanced spice and citrus

TIMOTHY TAYLOR LANDLORD

fruit flavor tinged with biscuit malt.

🍺 **BEST BITTER** 4.0% ABV • Best bitter • A full measure of malt in its well-balanced flavor and a citrus-fruit hoppiness to the aroma.

TITANIC

✉ Unit 5, Callender Place, Lingard Street, Burslem, Stoke-On-Trent, Staffordshire ST6 1JL

🖳 www.titanicbrewery.co.uk

Founded in 1985, Titanic was named after the famous but ill-fated passenger ship, whose captain, John Edward Smith, had lived nearby. A new 50-barrel plant was installed in 2005, and Titanic now brews more than 17 million pints of beer each year.

🍺 **BEST BITTER** 3.5% ABV • Best bitter • A straw-colored ale with a hint of sulfur in its aroma and a floral hop flavor that persists to a dry finish.

🍺 **STOUT** 4.5% ABV • Stout A full-roast and preserved-fruit aroma and a malt-influenced palate that balances fruit and licorice nuances.

WADWORTH

✉ Northgate Street, Devizes, Wiltshire SN10 1JW

🖳 www.wadworth.co.uk

Wadworth is a family business dating back to 1875. The imposing red-brick Northgate Brewery was designed and built by Henry Wadworth in 1885. It is a fine example of a Victorian tower brewery (see p.156), in which ingredients were fed into the top of the tower and moved through the brewing process under gravity. Some of the original equipment, such as the open copper,

TITANIC STOUT

remains in use today, and wooden casks are still used for deliveries. A full-time cooper—one of only five left in the country—and a team of dray horses continue traditional customs.

🍺 **WADWORTH 6X** 4.3% ABV • Premium bitter • Exhibits a malt and fruit nose with a restrained hop character that develops in intensity on the palate through to a lingering malt finale.

🍺 **JCB** 4.7% ABV • Premium bitter Hints of tropical fruit in the aroma; a rich, malty flavor with some nutty sweetness.

WELLS & YOUNG'S

✉ Eagle Brewery, Havelock Street, Bedford, Bedfordshire MK40 4LU

🖳 www.wellsandyoungs.co.uk

Draft beer was produced on the site of Young's Wandsworth Brewery in southwest London from 1581 until 2006. Young's has now combined its brewing operations with Bedford-based Charles Wells to create a major new force in the industry: Britain's third-largest supplier of cask ale.

Both are family businesses, with Young's dating back to 1831 and Charles Wells to 1876. All of Young's beers are now brewed in Bedford alongside the Charles Wells brand. Both firms jointly own the Eagle Brewery, but operate as entirely separate entities.

🍺 **WELLS BOMBARDIER** 4.3% ABV • Premium bitter A powerful citrus hop aroma is balanced by traces of malt and dried fruit that impart a rich complexity and a final bitterness to the taste.

🍺 **EAGLE IPA** 3.6% ABV • India pale ale • This refreshing, amber-colored session beer is packed with malt flavors and has a ripe apple sweetness that belies its relatively low alcoholic strength.

YOUNG'S BITTER 3.7% ABV • Bitter • Well balanced, with fruity citrus hop notes combining with enough malt to create a pleasing flowery and bready finish.

YOUNG'S SPECIAL 4.5% ABV • Premium bitter • A sweet citrus hop aroma, but a robust malt and hop combination persists with layers of toffee and dry bitterness.

WOODFORDE'S

✉ Broadland Brewery, Woodbastwick, Norwich, Norfolk NR13 6SW

⌂ www.woodfordes.co.uk

Established in 1981 by homebrewers Ray Ashworth and David Crease, Woodforde's has developed through three changes of location and continues to produce high-quality, consistent beers. A major expansion in 2002 doubled production and created a visitor center. Woodforde's also make homebrew kits that are popular nationwide.

WHERRY BITTER 3.8% ABV • Bitter • Floral and citrus fruit aromas open up a malt-

Woodforde's brewery tap, the Fur and Feather Inn, is next to the brewery and visitor center.

infused flavor that carries through to a sustained finish.

NORFOLK NOG 4.6% ABV • Old ale • Deep red in color with a roasted malt character that develops through licorice nuances and dried-fruit flavors.

WYCHWOOD

✉ Eagle Maltings, The Crofts, Witney, Oxfordshire OX28 4DP

⌂ www.wychwood.co.uk

WELLS BOMBARDIER

Wychwood was established in 1990 in the maltings that once served Witney-based Clinch's Brewery. The name comes from the ancient Wych Wood forest nearby. Today, Wychwood produces 50,000 barrels a year, and proclaims itself "the UK's No. 1 brewer of organic ales." There is now a separate brewhouse for the Brakspear brand (*see p.151*), following the takeover and closure of Brakspear's brewery in 2002.

HOBGOBLIN 5.0% ABV • Premium bitter • A powerful, full-bodied, copper-red, well-balanced beer, strong in roasted, chocolate, and toffee malts with

a moderate hoppy bitterness and fruit character.

FIDDLER'S ELBOW 4.5% ABV • Bitter • Brewed with added English wheat malt and Styrian Goldings hops for a citrus and floral aroma, tart citrus flavors, and a long, hoppy, fruity finish.

YORK

✉ Toft Green, Micklegate, York, North Yorkshire YO1 6JT

⌂ www.yorkbrew.co.uk

The first working brewery within York's city walls for four decades began making beer in 1996. It is now an award-winning 20-barrel brew-plant with its own visitor center, bar, and shop. The visitors' gallery gives a bird's-eye view of the brewing process, including the five 20-barrel fermenters and 10 conditioning tanks.

YORKSHIRE TERRIER 4.2% ABV • Bitter • An assertive bitterness tempered by its fruit and hop aroma that extends into the refreshing flavor and full hop finish.

CENTURION'S GHOST ALE 5.4% ABV • Premium bitter • Dark ruby, warming, mellow, and roasted malt character livened by autumn fruit.

Scotland

Edinburgh • Lothian • Perth • Highlands and Islands • Borders • Central

Although new breweries are developing their own styles, traditional Scottish ales retain a heavy malt accent from the days when hops were expensive to import from the south of England, and barley—grown primarily for the whisky trade—was freely available in Scotland.

Global brewing giants, such as Scottish & Newcastle, may no longer have a brewing presence in the country, but the Scottish microbrewing sector is witnessing something of a boom, with an increasing number of sustainable businesses created in recent years. The day may come when the likes of Aviemore, Black Isle, Arran, Orkney, and Harviestoun develop in the same confident way that the Youngers and McEwans in Edinburgh, the Tennents in Glasgow, and George Younger in Alloa once did.

Some breweries have resurrected age-old recipes that used bittering substances other than hops. Scots monks and alewives brewed using cereals, wild herbs, and ripe fruits and now the Heather Ale company, for example,

is producing beers from spruce needles and pine-cones as well as heather flowers, seaweed, and gooseberries.

The hard water of Edinburgh from its "Charmed Circle" of wells is particularly suitable for brewing pale ale, and 40 breweries once operated in the city. Caledonian Brewery, brewers of the award-winning Deuchar's IPA, is the sole survivor, and likens itself to a living, working, thriving museum. It is also the last brewery in Britain to use direct-fired coppers, which, it claims, boil the liquid properly rather than it being "stewed."

In 1827, the Austrian Emperor chose Belhaven beers for his cellar, referring to them as "the Burgundy of Scotland, and, as famed as Bavaria is for its strong beer, it cannot produce the like."

The tiny Traquair brewery once made beer for the Laird's household and estate workers; today, it is one of Scotland's best-known micros.

BELHAVEN

✉ Dunbar, East Lothian
EH42 1RS

🖳 www.belhaven.co.uk

Scotland's largest and oldest regional brewer, Belhaven was founded in 1719. It has had several owners in recent times and was bought by Greene King in 2005.

Belhaven uses locally grown barley, which is floor-malted in the traditional manner. There is evidence that Benedictine monks were brewing in this coastal town in the 14th century and water is still drawn from the wells they sunk. Despite Belhaven's reputation as a producer of cask ale, the style represents only a small percentage of its output.

🍺 **ST. ANDREW'S ALE** 4.9% ABV • Premium bitter • Alternates in flavor between roasted malt, hints of caramel, and tart fruit, while a spicy hop aroma continues through to its dry finish.

🍺 **BEST** 3.2% ABV • Bitter A honey-colored session beer, well-balanced with some malt and fruit on the palate. Belhaven's best-seller.

🍺 **80/-** 4.2% ABV • Heavy A classic Scottish brew, with huge malt influences in its aroma and flavor—though some hoppiness and fruit breaks through as well.

BROUGHTON

✉ Broughton, Biggar, Peeblesshire
ML12 6HQ

🖳 www.broughtonales.co.uk

Founded in 1979 in a former sheep abattoir in the Scottish Borders, Broughton now has 11 beers in its portfolio, three of which are organic. Its production goes mainly into bottles, for domestic and export markets, and it makes own-label beers for selected retailers. All are suitable for vegetarians and vegans. Its beers are named after literary characters with a local connection, and historic national heroes.

BROUGHTON
GREENMANTLE
ALE

🍺 **GREENMANTLE ALE** 3.9% ABV • Heavy A typical Scottish "80-shilling" ale (*see box, p.170*), dark copper in color with a rich fruit and bitter-sweet flavor, hints of gooseberry, and a hop-bitter finale. The brewery's flagship.

🍺 **BLACK DOUGLAS** 5.2% ABV • Premium bitter • A dark ruby-red ale with a rich, full-bodied maltiness and overtones of preserved fruit.

CAIRNGORM

✉ Dalfaber Estate, Aviemore,
Highlands PH22 1ST

🖳 www.cairngormbrewery.com

Established in 2001 in the shadow of some of Scotland's highest mountains, Cairngorm expanded in 2005 to take fermentation capacity to 90 barrels. Its beers, particularly Trade Winds, have been the recipients of several industry awards. Innovation is to the fore: Blessed Thistle Ale (4.5% ABV) actually uses the emblematic Scots plant for bitterness, with some hops and ginger aiding its complexity.

CAIRNGORM TRADE WINDS

🍺 **TRADE WINDS** 4.3% ABV • Wheat beer • A light golden wheat beer, which, through its blend of Perle hops and elderflower, offers up an intense bouquet of fruit with a bitter-sweet finish.

🍺 **CAIRNGORM GOLD** 4.3% ABV • Bitter • A pale and light-bodied Continental-style beer. Saaz hops provide an initial zestiness while Styrian Goldings hops furnish delicate late aromas.

CALEDONIAN

✉ The Caledonian Brewery,
Slateford Road, Edinburgh EH11 1PH

🖳 www.caledonian-brewery.co.uk

This impressive red-brick brewery was originally founded by Lorimer and Clark in 1869, and operated under their names until it was sold to Vaux of Sunderland in 1919. It was saved from closure in 1987 by a management buy-out, and although "The Caley" is still run as an independent company, Scottish & Newcastle purchased the brewery site, together with a small percentage of the business, in 2004.

The only survivor of the city's 40 breweries, Caledonian still draws its brewing water from a series of natural wells known as the Charmed Circle. The last brewery in Britain to use direct-fired coppers, it suffered two huge fires in 1994 and 1998.

🍺 **DEUCHAR'S IPA** 3.8% ABV • India pale ale • A multi-award-winning pale ale. Deuchar's has a strident hop aroma with citrus-fruit notes and a degree of maltiness in the flavor that never gives up. Its long, well-balanced finish is bitter with a flourish of biscuit malt.

🍺 **80/-** 4.2% ABV • Heavy Russet-brown in color, typically malt-led with an underlay of raspberry fruit and a suggestion of chocolate, leading to a late hoppy finish.

HARVIESTOUN

✉ Alva, Clackmannanshire FK12 5DQ
🖰 www.harviestoun-brewery.co.uk

Harviestoun, in the tiny county of Clackmannanshire, started off in farm buildings in 1985 with a five-barrel brewplant and an emphasis on quality and hop flavors and aromas. This approach has been instrumental in winning some of the country's top brewing awards. A new 50-barrel brewery was built a few miles away from the original location in 2004. The original owners have retired and the business is now operated by Caledonian Brewing (*see p.169*).

🍺 **BITTER & TWISTED** 3.8% ABV •
Bitter • A refreshing blond beer with grapefruit- and lemon-influenced hop aromas, and maltiness that is retained in the finish. Voted Beer of Britain in 2003.

🍺 **SCHIEHALLION** 4.8% ABV • Lager
An unusual cask lager with a distinctive floral nose, an unyielding maltiness throughout its palate, and a bitter finish.

SCOTTISH STYLES

Scottish customers still ask for beer by names such as "light," "heavy," and "export:" distinct styles graded by strength and labeled with the 19th-century cost of a hogshead of the beer—thus light, heavy, and export are known alternatively as 60/-, 70/-, and 80/- (60-, 70-, and 80-shilling) ales. Heavy is quite different in taste to an English bitter, being a more robust, sweeter beer with less of an edge.

INVERALMOND

✉ Inveralmond Way, Perth, Perthshire PH1 3UQ
🖰 www.inveralmond-brewery.co.uk

INVERALMOND
OSSIAN

This was the first brewery in Perth for more than 30 years when it opened in 1997. The countryside here is renowned for its natural mineral springs and the company builds on that by using only the finest ingredients available. An extension of floor space in 2005 doubled brewing and fermentation capacity, and there are plans for further expansion.

🍺 **OSSIAN** 4.1% ABV • Bitter
First Gold, Perle, and Cascade hops create a spicy and orange-zest aroma, while the flavor develops through nutty tones and a further fruitiness.

🍺 **INDEPENDENCE**
3.8% ABV • Bitter
Malty, full-bodied, with subtle hints of mixed fruit and spice. Pilgrim and Saaz hops round off the flavor balance with earthy and spicy notes.

ORKNEY

✉ Quoyloo, Stromness, Orkney
🖰 www.orkneybrewery.co.uk

This micro was established in 1988 in a former school, with equipment sourced from England, Wales, and France. New buildings and equipment followed in 1995 to allow for a 120-barrel capacity, and further expansion with a visitor center is planned. Beers are brewed under strict ecological guidelines, with waste water, for example, being treated before it is returned to two nearby lakes that support wildlife.

🍺 **DARK ISLAND** 4.6% ABV •
Premium bitter • The brewery's leading brand. Full-bodied, dark ruby in color, and intriguing, with blackcurrant fruit on the nose and roasted malt on the palate.

🍺 **SKULL SPLITTER** 8.5% ABV •
Old ale • A forceful nose with hints of apple and spice from its definite hop edge. There is some nut in the complex flavor that builds to a long, dry finish.

WILLIAMS

✉ Kelliebank, Alloa FK10 1NU
🖰 www.fraoch.com

Bruce and Scott Williams started brewing Heather Ale in 1993 in the west of Scotland to an old recipe they had translated from Gaelic. An impressive range of indigenous historical ales followed, and the business now operates a 40-barrel plant at the Forth Brewery in Alloa – once the brewing capital of Scotland. Mixing traditional styles and modern techniques is a company hallmark, and each year, wild ingredients are harvested in season to add their individual characters to the beers, including heather, myrtle, pine, spruce, seaweed, and gooseberries. It is said that the actor Mel Gibson flew 20 cases of Heather Ale to Los Angeles to celebrate winning an Oscar for the film *Braveheart*.

WILLIAMS
FRAOCH
HEATHER ALE

🍺 **FRAOCH HEATHER ALE** 4.1% ABV
• Bitter • Floral in aroma and flavor, with a spicy, minty character, a whiff of peat, a full-bodied maltiness, and a dry, applelike finish.

🍺 **KELPIE ORGANIC SEAWEED ALE**
4.4% ABV • Best bitter
A recreation of a 19th-century coastal ale: rich, dark, herb-like, and powerfully malty, with notes of single-malt whisky.

Wales

Cardiff • Swansea • Carmarthen

The Welsh brewing industry was bolstered in the 19th century by the thirst of miners and steelworkers in the heavy industries of the valleys. However, strong temperance movements led by religious groups ensured that the "demon drink" was denounced to every congregation.

Welsh beer was brewed for drinking in quantity, so a typical ale was—and to a certain extent still is—low in gravity compared to its English equivalent. Temperance pressures also kept beer's strength—and profile—low. Wales is, however, known for its pale ales and dark milds. The main independent Welsh brewer is SA Brain, which now also brews the much-admired Buckley's range at its Cardiff brewery. Among several craft breweries that are thriving in recent years are Tomos Watkin, Plassey of Wrexham, and Breconshire.

Tourism has replaced heavy industry in much of Wales, and visitors now enjoy its traditional ales in picturesque surroundings (here at Caernarfon).

BRAINS

✉ The Cardiff Brewery, Crawshay Street, Cardiff CF10 1SP
🖰 www.sabrain.com

Samuel Arthur Brain founded Brains with his uncle, Joseph Benjamin Brain, in 1882, and it has remained in family ownership ever since. The brewery's beers are produced in Cardiff at a site formerly used by Hancock's, acquired from Bass in 1999. Brains now has more than 250 pubs across South Wales, anchoring it deep in the region's culture.

🍺 **BITTER** 3.7% ABV •
Bitter • Rich amber; subtle malt and crisp hop aromas. Well balanced in flavor, some bitterness, marked at the finish.

🍺 **DARK** 3.5% ABV • Mild
A classic mild: treacle-colored and -flavored with a blend of chocolate, crystal, and brown

BRAINS SA GOLD

malts. A hoppy backdrop to a sweet, mellow palate with hints of dark chocolate, liquorice, and coffee.

🍺 **SA GOLD** 4.7% ABV • Golden ale
Pale straw in color; citrus, pine, and honey palate with a bitter edge provided by Target hops. Styrian Goldings and Cascade varieties add complexity. Refreshing.

FELINFOEL

✉ Felinfoel, Llanelli, Carmarthenshire SA14 8LB
🖰 www.felinfoel-brewery.com

The brewery, built in 1878, is still family-run, operating from Grade II-listed buildings in the village of Felinfoel. It was modernized in the 1970s, when wooden fermenting squares were replaced with stainless steel equivalents and a new copper was installed in place of the old coal-fired vessel.

🍺 **DOUBLE DRAGON ALE** 4.2% ABV •
Best bitter • Fruit-based hop and malt in the aroma, with maltiness that continues into the smoothly balanced flavor to a malt and fruit finish.

TOMOS WATKIN

✉ The Hurns Brewing Company Ltd., Phoenix Brewery, Swansea Enterprise Park, Swansea SA6 8RP
🖰 www.hurnsbeer.co.uk

Established in a converted garage in Llandello in 1995, Tomos Watkin moved to Swansea in 2000, increasing capacity from 10 barrels to 50. In 2002, the company was purchased by the Hurns Brewing Company; plans are under way to build a visitor center with a brewery tap.

🍺 **CWRW BRAF** 4.5% ABV • Best bitter • Amber-colored with a gentle hop aroma, a light bitterness, and some malt.

🍺 **BREWERY BITTER** 4.5% ABV •
Best bitter • Pale amber in color with a floral hop aroma, light fruity bitterness, and a full malt palate.

Republic of Ireland

Dublin • County Kilkenny • County Cork

Brewing in Ireland has a long history—Saint Patrick is reputed to have employed a brewer, and medieval monasteries continued the custom. Irish brewing later developed from a cottage industry into a global enterprise led by one all-conquering brand: Guinness.

Irish brewing is dominated by the stout style. Its most famous expression, Guinness, has become not only an internationally famous brand, but an icon of Irish culture. Its success derives from a fortuitous alteration of an existing style. When Arthur Guinness established his Dublin brewery in 1759, he initially brewed bitter, then switched to producing porter, a style that originated in London. He began using unmalted roasted barley (mainly to avoid a tax on malted barley), and later increased the hop rate dramatically, making the beer more bitter and dry. His adaption of the porter style proved so popular that by the turn of the 20th century, Guinness was the largest brewer in the world, exporting its products to dozens of countries.

The story of Irish brewing does not begin and end with its most famous style, however. Although best-known for stouts, Ireland's brewers also produce some excellent ales. These are typically softly rounded, with a characteristic reddish tinge from the barley-roasting process.

In recent years, a number of notable brewpubs have emerged in Ireland, adding diversity and vigor to the beer-making scene. The Porterhouse Brewing Company in Dublin, founded in 1989, led the way and inspired contemporaries from Biddy Early in County Clare to Franciscan Well in County Cork.

The Guinness brewery at St. James's Gate, Dublin. More than 10 million glasses of their famous stout are drunk every day across the globe.

BEAMISH

✉ South Main Street, Kilkenny, County Kilkenny

🖥 www.diageo.ie

Beamish is said to be the most ancient porter brewery in Ireland, originating in 1792 in premises that are believed to have served as a brewery from the mid-1600s. By 1805 it was producing 100,000 barrels, making it the largest in the country and the third-largest in the British Isles. It has had several owners in recent years and is now run by Scottish & Newcastle.

The brewery's step-gabled tower and half-timbered facade are architectural features of merit, as is the entrance hall, which is galleried in the style of an Elizabethan theater.

🍺 **BEAMISH IRISH RED** 4.1% ABV • Bitter • Malt-accented and well-rounded with a distinct soft-sweet fruitiness and a rust-red tinge that is characteristic of the style.

GUINNESS

✉ St. James's Gate, Dublin 8

🖥 www.guinness.com

Guinness can rightly claim to be the most special beer ever brewed. When young Arthur Guinness was left £100 in a will in 1756, he bought a small brewery in County Kildare. In 1759, he took a 9,000-year lease on a dormant brewery at St. James's Gate in Dublin. By 1833 it was the biggest brewery in Ireland and in 1881 production surpassed one million barrels per annum, making it the largest anywhere in the world.

Innovations in chemistry, product, packaging, and advertising have kept Guinness well ahead of its rivals. In 1997, Guinness entered into a $47 billion

GUINNESS
FOREIGN
EXTRA
STOUT

merger with another drinks group, Grand Met, to form the multinational Diageo.

🍺 **DRAUGHT** 4.1% ABV • Stout Some hop influence apparent above the milky, burned malt aroma. The fruit and cream flavors are balanced by bitterness, with liquorice and dark toffee emerging toward the dry finish.

🍺 **FOREIGN EXTRA STOUT** 7.5% ABV • Stout • Has a leafy hop aroma with notes of burned toast and flavors of rich malt, bitter coffee, and liquorice. Sourness in the finish softens its hefty alcoholic kick.

KINSALE

✉ The Glen, Kinsale, County Cork

🖥 www.kinsalebrewing.com

The port of Kinsale has a brewing tradition that dates back to the 18th century. Records show that in 1708 the frigate *Duke* set sail for the island of Juan Fernandez, off the coast of Chile, to rescue Alexander Selkirk (the real-life model for Robinson Crusoe), carrying "18 butts of Kinsale beer" among its stores. Kinsale operates from a brewery built in the 1700s, which was restored to working condition in 2001.

🍺 **IRISH LAGER** 4.3% ABV • Lager A biscuit malt nose, fresh in flavor with a crisp hoppiness and a smooth, creamy, malty character.

MURPHY'S

✉ Lady's Well, Leitrim Street, Cork, County Cork

🖥 www.murphys.com

James J. Murphy founded his brewery in 1856 along with his brothers William, Jerome, and Francis. By the start of the 20th century it was

producing 100,000 barrels. English brewer Watneys held a 51-percent stake by 1969, but pulled out two years later, and the company was rescued by the Irish government to be part-run by a cooperative of publicans. The company entered receivership in 1982 and was bought by Heineken of Holland in 1983. Murphy's now exports to more than 70 countries.

🍺 **IRISH STOUT** 4.0% ABV • Stout Has a beguiling aroma of roasted malt, caramel, coffee, and chocolate. Malt throughout with a smooth, peaty bitterness and a dry sourness.

🍺 **IRISH RED** 5.2% ABV • Premium bitter • Amber-bronze in color with nut, bread, and chocolate aromas balanced by a creamy, rich mid-palate and a degree of hoppiness toward the dry finish.

SMITHWICK'S

✉ St. Francis Abbey, Kilkenny, County Kilkenny

🖥 www.diageo.ie

Franciscan monks began brewing in Ireland's smallest city during the 14th century, and today the ruins of St. Francis's Abbey form part of the Smithwick's brewery grounds. It is the country's oldest operating brewery, founded in 1710 by John Smithwick, and produces the biggest-selling Irish ale brand—a distinction Smithwick's Draught has enjoyed since the 1920s. The company is now part of the Diageo group, which also includes Guinness and Harp.

🍺 **DRAUGHT** 3.5% ABV • Bitter • A red ale with a malt, bread, and lightly-fruited aroma wrung out of its combination of four hop varieties. Dried fruit is apparent on the palate.

MURPHY'S
IRISH STOUT

OTHER EUROPEAN COUNTRIES

Classic beer culture is most likely to be found in Europe's northern, central, and western countries. But outside these temperate areas, even in warmer, wine-making areas, many great brewers producing both traditional and innovative beers can be found.

The Czech Republic (*see pp. 74–9*) and its pilsner aside, the rest of eastern Europe can still claim a proud place in the history of beer. This region is, after all, home to many of the world's great hop varieties—Saaz from Bohemia, Styrians from Slovenia, and Poland's Lublin. It is also where several great beer styles originated—including Imperial stout. Today, Poland has a thriving beer culture, and Estonia and Hungary have long-established breweries that have earned their place in beer history and remain vibrant. However, in other parts of eastern Europe, a 21st-century beer culture has yet to evolve, and companies owned by international brewers dominate the markets.

Austria is famous for its amber-red style of Vienna lager, first brewed by Anton Dreher in 1841, which has been revived in recent years by New World brewpubs. The country is now home to Samichlaus, one of Europe's strongest beers. In Switzerland, where the plans for Europe's oldest brewery are housed reverently in a museum, a small band of microbrewers pride themselves on the quality and variety of their beers.

Scandinavia is home to the oldest lager brewery in northern Europe, Carlsberg in Denmark – a country that also has a new generation of microbrewers. In Sweden, too, the microbrewery scene is vibrant and growing. Norway has some excellent brewpubs and Finland is home both to sahti, one of the world's oldest surviving beer styles, and a growing number of new micros.

The Netherlands produces some blander international beer brands; however, in recent years a wave of new brewers has begun to develop a range of more interesting beers. Luxembourg lacks its own beer style, but it does have a number of good brewers influenced by those of Belgium, France, and Germany. France, better known for wine, has some exciting brewpubs around Lille in French Flanders. And Brittany is experiencing an explosion of new and imaginative brewers, many of whom own cafés where they experiment with beer cuisine.

In Italy, beer is now the drink of sophistication, and there are many stylish brewpubs with extensive beer and food menus. In other parts of southern Europe, long-established brewers today make thirst-quenching beers for a hot day. In Spain, Portugal, Cyprus, Malta, and even the tiny island of Corsica can be found brewers making beers of merit.

Denmark may have sent its Carlsberg around the world, but in Copenhagen pubs, such as this old-world bar, more varied Danish beers can be had.

The Netherlands

North Brabant • North & South Holland • Gelderland • Overijssel • Limburg

Famous for its Heineken and Grolsch pilsners, the Netherlands has only recently started to resurrect the more interesting beer styles that were lost when lager production superseded traditional Dutch ale brewing during the second half of the 19th century.

Almost half of the country's 60-odd breweries and contract-brewers came into being in the last decade. Most are influenced by popular Belgian ales that have been imported throughout Holland since the 1970s. However, try as they might, few have managed to emulate the quality of the beers brewed by their neighbors on the other side of the border. Regional brewers in the south have had more success with German- and Czech-style lagers, and pilsner now accounts for around 90 percent of all Dutch beer consumption.

The current specialty beer market in Holland probably owes its existence to the consumer organization PINT (Promotion and Information over Traditional beers). PINT was founded by beer-lovers in 1980, using the British organization CAMRA (*see p.153*) as a model. As well as informing the public of national developments via its magazine, PINT organizes beer festivals and holds monthly beer tastings across the country. In 1986, one of PINT's founders set up the ABT (Alliance of Beer Tappers), which promotes good beer pubs and cafés, and encourages correct storage and service of specialty beers.

If there is one beer style that the Dutch embrace and (incorrectly) call their own, it is bock, which has enjoyed a meteoric rise in popularity: in 1980 there were just five bocks on the market, but today there are more than 60. The annual three-day-long Bock Beer Festival in Amsterdam is further testimony to its national appeal.

A bar in Amsterdam, where bock-style beers are a popular menu item, when in season. Specialty beers are gaining ground in the Netherlands.

BUDELS

✉ Nieuwstraat 9, 6020 AA Budel
🖰 www.budels.nl

Dating back to 1870, this small, family-run brewery is based in Budel, in North Brabant, a stone's throw from the Belgian border. Budels recently replaced its copper brewkettle with stainless steel tanks, but it retains its traditional brewing methods, which ensure malty, well-hopped and well-balanced beers. Some of Budels' unorthodox interpretations of classic styles raise eyebrows among purists. One classic style they do brew well is bock!

🍾 **BOCK** 6.5% ABV • Bock
Dark copper in color; malty roasted caramel aromas and palate, with some hoppiness in the finish.

🍾 **MEI BOCK** 6.5% ABV• May-blond bock • Golden color; malty butterscotch aromas; medium bodied; warming alcohol; bitter-sweet finish.

DE BEKEERDE SUSTER

✉ Kloveniersburgwal 6–8, 1012 CT Amsterdam
🖰 www.debekeerdesuster.nl

Brouwhuis Maximiliaan was founded by ex-homebrewer Albert Hoffmann on the site of Amsterdam's Saint Maria Magdalena convent in 1992, but went bankrupt in 2002. It was reopened by the Beiaard group in 2003 and renamed De Bekeerde Suster (The Reformed Sister), in memory of Maria Magdalena van Bethanien, a prostitute in the Middle Ages who saw the error of her ways and joined the church. The Bavarian-style copper brewkettle was made in southern Holland, and the house beers are tapped using a unique system that

forces the beer out of large plastic bags using compressed air. A sprawling multi-level pub, with lots of nooks and crannies, surrounds the brewery.

The first brew, Blonde Ros, was produced in November 2004. It has recently had its recipe tweaked by former La Trappe monastery brewer Harrie Vermeer.

🍾 **BLONDE ROS** 6.0% ABV • Blond Golden; citrus (East Kent Goldings hop), malt, and fruit aromas; evolves from sweet fruitiness to a spicier (Saaz hop) and drier finish.

DE HEMEL

✉ Franseplaats 1, 6511 VS Nijmegen
🖰 www.brouwerijdehemel.nl

Having sold his successful Raaf brewery in Heumen to Oranjeboom, craft brewer Herm Hegger set up De Hemel in 1996 in one of Nijmegen's oldest buildings—the 12th-century De Commanderie van St. Jan. De Hemel makes a wide range of beers, including some for local pubs and others on contract. It combines its brewing with distilling and making vinegar and mustard, and B&B rentals. Nieuw LIGT is brewed annually and laid down to ripen and improve for at least 12 months before sale.

🍾 **NIEUW LIGT GRAND CRU** 10.0% ABV • Barley wine Copper; fruity, tealike aromas; a slight lactic note changes to rum-raisin and resiny hop flavors; the finish is long and dry.

DE SCHANS

✉ Schans 21, 1421 BA Uithoorn
🖰 www.schansbier.nl

De Schans is located in the village of Uithoorn, on the Amstel River, just outside Amsterdam. Drawing on his

DE HEMEL NIEUW LIGT GRAND CRU

DE SCHANS VAN VOLLENHOVEN & CO'S EXTRA STOUT

experience in engineering and automation, self-taught brewer Guus Roijen bought three 18th-century buildings —a former barber shop and family house on a street called Schans—and renovated them into a brewery, reception area, and a beer store, which also stocks a good selection of Dutch gins. Roijen designed his own 53-gallon (200-liter) brewkettle and had it custom-built by a local dairy equipment manufacturer. Since its opening in 1998, the brewery has experimented very widely, making beers that draw inspiration from Belgium, Germany, and Britain. Few can dispute that Roijen has successfully embraced the technical challenge of developing beers across a wide range of styles.

🍾 **SAISON** 7.0% ABV • Saison Brilliant gold; nose citrussy, acetic, and spicy; palate is dry, hoppy, and bitter; has plenty of carbonation.

🍾 **VAN VOLLENHOVEN & CO'S EXTRA STOUT** 7.0% ABV • Stout Almost black; roasty, burned-sugar, and rye breadlike aromas; bitter and liquorice-like in the palate; finish has hints of burned raisin bread.

GROLSCH

✉ Brouwerslaan 1, 7548 XA Enschede
🖰 www.grolsch.nl

Founded in 1615, Grolsch is Holland's second-largest producer of pilsner (after

Heineken) and its green, swing-top bottle is easily recognized in at least 50 foreign markets. Grolsch recently transferred all production to a new site, just outside Enschede. Having experimented over the last decade with everything from fruit essences to Champagne yeast, Grolsch finally regained its senses and started brewing a classic Bavarian weizen in 2005.

🍺 **PREMIUM WEIZEN** 5.5% ABV ● Weizen ● Golden-amber; aromas of cloves and yeast; medium-bodied, with a high carbonation; finishes with malt and spices.

GULPEN

✉ Rijksweg 16, 6271 AE Gulpen
🖳 www.gulpener.nl

Ale-brewers since 1825, Gulpen acquired steam power in 1884 and began brewing lager. They now produce a wide range of beers, including some made in cooperation with Grolsch, its major shareholder. Gulpen's unpasteurized beers are increasingly brewed with a percentage of locally grown organic barley and hops. They also brew sweet beers for the youth market.

🍺 **DORT** 6.5% ABV ● Dortmunder (Dutch variation) ● Amber; very

malty, sweet aroma with a slight hoppiness; full-bodied and sweet, with a mouth-warming alcohol finish.

🍺 **MESTREECHS AAJT** 3.5% ABV ● Old brown (original Dutch version) Dark copper; nose of winey-oak, caramel, and fruit; thin and astringent in the mouth, with a short, sour-sweet finish.

HEINEKEN

✉ Burgermeester Smeetsweg 1, 2382 PH Zoeterwoude
🖳 www.heineken.nl; www. amstel.nl; www.brand.nl

Heineken currently owns more than 130 breweries in at least 65 countries and employs a staggering 64,000 people. With a portfolio of more than 170 beers and an annual production of around 3.2bn gallons (122m hectoliters), it is the fourth-largest brewing company in the world—and a true behemoth among brewers.

🍺 **AMSTEL BOCK** 7.0% ABV ● Bock Copper; caramel and liquorice aromas; slight bananalike flavor, with a cocoa-bitter finish.

🍺 **BRAND URTYP** 5.5% ABV ● Urtyp pilsner ● Golden; floral hop

and malt aromas; full bodied, with an amazingly long, resiny hop finish.

HERTOG JAN

✉ Kruisweg 44, 5944 EN Arcen
🖳 www.hertogjan.nl

HERTOG JAN GRAND PRESTIGE

Stoombierbrouwerij de Vriendenkring in Arcen was bought by Allied Breweries in 1968. When Allied planned to close the brewery in 1980, ex-brewmaster Toon van de Reek was allowed to buy it as long as he did not produce pilsner. Over the next 12 years, his Arcense Stoombierbrouwerij developed a successful range of specialty ales, in addition to a range of Hertog Jan lagers brewed by Dommelsch. After another brief period under Allied (1992–5), Interbrew took over, and in 1998 changed the name to Hertog Jan Interbrew; it has been experimenting with the beer range ever since.

🍺 **GRAND PRESTIGE** 10.0% ABV ● Barley wine ● Dark copper; nose of currants soaked in alcohol; roasted caramel and liquorice palate, finishing with a wave of alcoholic warmth.

THE HEINEKEN STORY

In 1863, Gerard A. Heineken purchased Amsterdam's Den Hoybergh brewery (founded 1592) and replaced its ale with lager. In 1933, just three days after the repeal of prohibition in the US, Heineken delivered a shipload of beer to New York. From that moment on, Heineken has been America's premium import pilsner. The company set up its specialty brewery in Den Bosch in 1958, and opened its main facility in Zoeterwoude in 1975. Production ceased in 1988 at the Amsterdam brewery, which is now the interactive Heineken Experience. Heineken bought out Amstel in 1968 and Brand in 1989.

The Heineken brewery in Amsterdam, home of one of the world's most famous pilsners. Heineken products are sold across the globe.

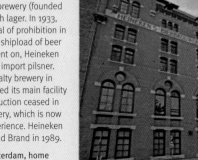

JOPEN EXTRA STOUT

JOPEN

✉ R. Peereboomweg 13 achter,
2031 BC Haarlem
🖰 www.jopen.nl

This contract-brewery run
by Michel Ordeman started
reintroducing extinct Dutch
beer styles in 1994. Jopen's
seven beers, produced under
the guidance of its brewer-
consultant Cris Wisse, are
currently produced at various
Dutch and Belgian breweries.
In 2006, Jopen purchased
a vacant Haarlem church,
where it plans to open its
own brewpub-restaurant.

🍺 **EXTRA STOUT** 5.5% ABV • Export
stout • Dark red-brown; nose
of roasted sweetened coffee;
drying, astringent, roasted
palate is followed by a short
and quenching aftertaste.

LINDEBOOM

✉ Engelmanstraat 54, 6086 BD Neer
🖰 www.lindeboom.nl

Dating from 1870, this family-
run south Limburg brewery
was one of the last to change
over from ale to lager
production in 1924. The
quality of its beers won it
the title of brewer "By
Appointment to the Royal
Family" in 1996. Five years
later, the brewery began
changing its emphasis from
lagers to ales, and took over
production of Venloosch Alt
from the Leeuw brewery.

🍺 **VENLOOSCH ALT** 5.0% ABV • Alt
Dark amber-red; aromas of
butterscotch and spice; palate
is very hoppy (three German
varieties), finishing with a
dry roastiness.

MOMMERIETE

✉ Holthornerweg 9, 7779
De Holthorne
🖰 www.mommeriete.nl

Mommeriete is situated in
a renovated farmhouse on
an estate in the rural
province of Overijssel. The
gleaming 53-gallon (200-
liter) Kaspar Schulz copper
brewkettle is not just for
show. Proprietors Gert and
Karina Kelder make this
installation earn its keep by
producing a brilliant range
of ales and lagers using
mostly German ingredients.

🍺 **VROUWE VAN GRAMSBERGH**
10.0% ABV • Quadruple • Dark
copper; overripe fruit and
caramel malt nose; malty-
sweet and spicy-hop palate
gives way to rum-and-raisin.

SINT CHRISTOFFEL

✉ Metaalweg 10, 6045 JB Roermond
🖰 www.christofelbier.nl

Sint Christoffel was set-up in
1986 by Leo Brand (of the
Brand brewery family).
Brand left the brewery in
2004, a year after it had been
bought by an advertising
company. Sint Christoffel
makes three bottom-
fermented beers, with its
flagship Blond being the
main seller. The Blond recipe
has changed many times
since 2001, reflecting Sint
Christoffel's attempts to
market it as a specialty
beer for the guest
taps of pubs run
by the larger
Dutch brewing
groups.

🍺 **BLOND** 6.0% ABV
• Urtyp pilsner
Golden-amber
and cloudy;
sulfury-hoppy
nose; the very

bitter (almost salty) palate
becomes drier and assertively
hoppy in the finish.

SNAB

✉ Postbus 204, 1440 AE Purmerend
🖰 www.snab.nl

Founded in 1991, one of
Snab's goals is to introduce
Dutch beer-lovers to styles
that have never previously
been brewed in Holland.
Snab develops its own recipes
and then has them contract-
brewed elsewhere. Of its
seven beer styles, the top-
fermented bocks are
consistent prize winners. The
Ice Bock won a Silver Award
at the 2006 World Beer Cup.

🍺 **PALE ALE** 6.3% ABV • American
red ale • Amber-red; nose of
grapefruity hops; bitter,
malty palate; the hoppy
character gives it a dry,
slightly metallic feel.

🍺 **IJSBOK** 9.0% ABV • Ice bock
Copper; cocoa nose; caramel
malt and bitter-currant
flavors; warming alcohol
and a hop- and malt-bitter,
blackberrylike aftertaste.

TEXELSE

✉ Schilderweg 214b, 1792 CK
Oudeschild
🖰 www.speciaalbier.com

Originally set up by Harry
Bonne on the island of Texel
in 1994, Texelse closed in
1998, only to be reopened a
year later by Jaap van der
Weide. Since then, various
brewers have come and
gone, and there have been
many additions, including
a secondhand German
copper brew-kettle. Now
under a new group of
owners, Texelse
produces 66,000
gallons (2,500
hectoliters)
each year.

🍺 **TEXELS BOCK**
7.5% ABV • Double bock
Copper; roasted
malt aromas;
stoutish palate;
blackcurrant finish.

TEXELS BOCK

Eastern Europe

The Baltic • Poland • Russia • Hungary • The Balkans • Slovakia

Eastern Europe has produced some of the world's greatest beer styles, but years of Communist government stifled investment in the brewing industries of former Eastern Bloc states. When the Cold War ended, multinational companies snapped up many of the surviving brewers.

Eastern Europe is home to many superb hop varieties, including the renowned Bohemian Saaz, and the region has an illustrious brewing heritage that is now being revived in many countries formerly aligned with the Soviet Union.

Poland has over 70 brewpubs and micros, some of which are planning to reintroduce *grodziskie*—a top-fermented, smoked wheat beer. A pre-lager style, it was last brewed in Grodzisk in the 1990s.

In the Baltic region, the Estonians have their own version of the Finnish sahti beer (*see p.195*), although it is not brewed commercially. This is definitely one for the inquisitive. Further examples of elusive rural brewing are the winey, malty-tasting farmhouse beers of Latvia and Lithuania. These are particularly

prevalent in the Lithuania's Biržai region, where malt grists are sometimes supplemented with peas, which allegedly confer a richer mouthfeel. The most resilient style in the region is a Baltic variety of porter that is known in the West as Imperial stout. These dark beers are usually bottom-fermented, but can nonetheless pack some powerful flavors.

Despite the continued existence of regional specialties, industrial brewing conglomerates have a commanding presence in Eastern Europe. In Slovakia, SABMiller runs Pivovar Šariš and Topvar, while Gemer and Zlatý Bažant belong to Heineken. Hungary's major breweries are all owned by multinational companies: Dreher (SABMiller), Borsod (InBev), and Union Hungaria (Heineken).

A grand square in Kraków, Poland, lined with cafés and bars where visitors can sample national brews.

ALDARIS

✉ Tvaika 44, Riga LV-1005, Latvia
🖱 www.aldaris.lv

Founded in 1865, Aldaris is not only the biggest brewery in Latvia but also one of the largest in the Baltic. It is owned by Baltic Beverages Holding, which is itself a jointly owned asset of Scottish & Newcastle and Carlsberg. The brewery produces more than 12 types of light and dark lager, many of which are quite sweet.

🍾 ALDARA GAIŠAIS
4.5% ABV • Light lager • A pale beer with a fresh aroma of hops and a softly bitter taste; not too challenging, but refreshing to drink.

🍾 ALDARA ORIĢINĀLAIS 5.0% ABV
• Pilsner • Amber-colored, with a light aroma of caramel and a pleasingly bitter taste of hops.

ALDARIS
ALDARA GAIŠAIS

APATINSKA PIVARA

✉ Trg Oslobođenja 5, Apatin, Serbia 25260
🖱 www.inbev.com

Apatinska Pivara is based in the town of Apatin in Serbia, and has been brewing since 1756. Today, it is the largest brewer in the Balkans and the undisputed king of beermakers in Serbia, commanding a 40 percent share of the domestic market and producing 87.2m gallons (3.3m hectoliters) of beer every year. Interbrew, now part of the InBev group, bought the company in 2003.

Apatin is situated next to the Danube River, in the fertile agricultural province of Vojvodina, and has always sat at a crossroads between cultures. The Sarmates, Huns, Slavs, Croats, and Hungarians have all helped to shape the present-day character of the area.

🍾 JELEN PIVO 5.0% ABV • Lager
Light yellow in color, with a white, wispy head. It has hints of grass and grain.

BALTIKA

✉ 6 Proezd, Parnas 4, 194292 St. Petersburg, Russia
🖱 http://eng.baltika.ru

Baltika is the largest brewer in Russia and all of Eastern Europe. The company was established in St. Petersburg in 1990, and since 1996 it has been the dominant force on the Russian beer market. Baltika operates 10 breweries across the Russian Federation, with a total annual capacity of 977m gallons (37m hectoliters). Its beers are exported to 38 countries around the world, and it makes the two most popular domestic brands: Baltika and Arsenalnoye.

The company is jointly owned by brewing giants Scottish & Newcastle and Carlsberg Breweries.

🍾 No. 6 PORTER 7.0% ABV • Porter
A well-balanced beer with a smoothness that belies its strength. Dark roasted malt, chocolate, and molasses flavors fill the glass, overlaid by a good hop finish.

BERE ROMANIA

✉ Str. Mănăştur 2–6, Cluj Napoca, Romania
🖱 www.sabmiller.com

This is Romania's second-largest brewer, with a national market share of 22 percent. The company is now owned by SABMiller and operates four breweries, in Cluj-Napoca, Buzău, Timişoara, and Brasov, with a total annual capacity of 79m

BALTIKA No. 6
PORTER

gallons (3m hectoliters), and a combined workforce of more than 1,300 employees.

The brewery began production in 1878 and its main brand, Ursus, is promoted under the slogan *"Regele berii în România,"* which means "King of Beers in Romania." The town is situated in the heart of Transylvania and hosts an annual beer festival in September.

🍾 URSUS PREMIUM PILS 5.0% ABV
• Lager • Pale golden, with a lively carbonation; has a malty aroma with a hint of fresh hops and bread. Lemony notes grace the finish; dry aftertaste.

BEOGRADSKA INDUSTRIJA PIVA

✉ Bulevar Vojvode, Putnika 5, 11000 Beograd, Serbia
🖱 www.bip.co.yu

Before Yugoslavia's breakup in the 1990s, Belgrade was the capital of the most advanced nation in the old Eastern Bloc. Beer has been produced in Belgrade since 1839, and the city's first modern, high-capacity brewery was built in 1872, by industrialist Ignat Vajfert. After World War II, the brewery was nationalized under the name "July 7th," in memory of the date when a Serbian uprising ended German military occupation. The company still exists, but now trades as Beogradska Industrija Piva. It modernized its product range in 2003, with the launch of Belgrade Beer (BG), and visitors can sample this brand, amongst others, at Belgrade's annual beer festival, which takes place every August at the foot of Kalemegdan fortress.

BG BEER 5.0% ABV • Lager
This beer has a pleasant bitterness, and its soft aroma hints at sweetcorn and bread. It is sparkling gold in color.

BRAU-UNION ROMANIA

✉ Str. Harghita 100, Miercurea-Ciuc, Romania 4100
🖑 www.brauunion.ro

Owned by Heineken since 2003, Brau-Union Romania is the main player on the country's beer market, controlling a 34 percent share. It employs 1,600 people and operates breweries in Bucuresti, Constanța, Craiova, Hateg, and Miercurea-Ciuc.

Heineken is currently investing $109 million in Romania, much of which is to be spent on improving brewing plants. Many people buy beer in plastic bottles in Romania, and Heineken has earmarked $10.7 million to boost production of these products at the Constanța brewery in the Dobrogea region, where two-thirds of national beer sales are made.

CIUC PREMIUM 4.8% ABV • Lager • A golden lager with a decent head. Dry flavor with little hop character gives way to a sweet aftertaste.

CĒSU ALUS

✉ Aldaru laukums 1, Cēsis, Latvia 4101
🖑 www.cesualus.lv

Beer has been brewed in the town of Cēsis since 1590. The Cēsu Alus brewery was founded there in 1879, making it the oldest in Latvia, and in 1999 it was bought by Estonian brewer A. Le Coq (*see facing page*). It is the second-largest brewer in the country and recently built a new brewhouse.

Cēsis is 56 miles (90 km) from the Latvian capital, Riga, and hosts popular events, including a beer festival, open-air theater performances, and a jousting tournament. Cēsis Castle, now a majestic ruin, was the medieval stronghold of the Livonian knights, who once ruled over most of Latvia and Estonia.

CHOCOLATE PORTER 6.8% ABV • Porter • Has a slightly bitter flavor of chocolate malt and a nice, not overly sweet taste.

DREHER

✉ Magladi ut 17, Budapest, Hungary 1106
🖑 www.dreher.hu

Anton Dreher (*see p.186*), the son of the brewery's founder, studied his trade in England and Germany and is said to have stolen samples of beer yeast from breweries there, smuggling them out in a hollow walking stick. He developed the technology to ferment beer at low temperatures in around 1840, and devised a new kind of malty amber beer, called Vienna lager. These achievements, and others,

The Dreher brewing name survives, but much of Hungary's brewing heritage has been lost.

earned him the enduring title of "King of Beer." The company that takes his name is now owned by SABMiller.

CLASSIC 5.5% ABV • Pilsner
With a crisp, fresh aroma, this bitter, golden-yellow pilsner contains a hint of hops and a wisp of malt.

ELBREWERY

✉ Ul. Browarna 71, Elbląg, Poland
🖑 www.grupazywiec.pl

The Elbrewery Company is Poland's largest beermaker and belongs to the Żywiec Group, established in 1998 after Zaklady Piwowarskie Żywiec SA and Brewpole BV merged. The Group has four main breweries: Żywiec, Elbrewery, Leżajsk, and Warka, and is owned by Heineken.

Elbrewery was founded in 1872 as the Brauerei Englisch Brunnen Elbing, in honor of close trade links with Britain at that time.

EB 5.4% ABV • Pilsner • A pale and somewhat thin, pilsner-type beer. Its lack of depth belies its strength, however – and this is a potent brew.

PORTER 9.2% ABV • Porter
A porter in the Baltic style;
dark and reddish-brown in
color. It is smooth on the
palate and has a warming
aftertaste.

HEINEKEN HUNGARY

✉ Sörgyárak Nyrt 9400 Sopron,
Vándor Sándor st. 1, Hungary
🖰 www.brau.hu

The Hungarian beer
market is dominated by
three closely matched
breweries: Dreher,
Heineken Hungary
(formerly known as
Brau Union Hungária),
and Borsod (owned by
InBev). Each brews
an annual output
of between 55 and
60m gallons (2.1–
2.3m hectoliters)
of beer, for a joint
market share of
30–33 percent.
Pécs, the fourth
member of the
Association of
Hungarian Brewers,
produces some
10.5m gallons
(400,000 hectoliters)
annually, representing just
under 5 percent of the
market share.

Heineken Hungary has
breweries in Sopron and
Martfu. Its brands include
Soproni Ászok, Heineken,
Amstel, Kaiser, and Gösser.

A number of small micro-
breweries have emerged in
Hungary in recent years,
including Ilzer and Blonder.

SOPRONI ÁSZOK 4.5% ABV •
Lager • Light to taste, this
beer is crisp on the palate
and very refreshing.

KALNAPILIS

✉ Taikos Avenue 1, LT-5319
Panevėžys, Lithuania
🖰 www.kalnapilis.lt

AB Kalnapilis is the most
modern and rapidly growing
brewery in Lithuania,
though its history stretches
back to 1902. A landowner

of German origin, Albert
Foight, founded a brewery
in Panevezys and named it
Bergschlösschen, which
means "small castle on the
hill." This was later changed
to Kalnapilis. Over the
years, the brewery grew and
saw many changes. Between
1970 and 1990, the company
underwent a long process of
modernization, in which
almost all obsolete equipment
was replaced. After
Lithuanian independence
was restored in 1991,
Kalnapilis Brewery
became a joint-stock
company.

ORIGINAL 5.0% ABV •
Lager • Pale golden
yellow; has a
sweetcorn aroma
and a hint of hops.

KARLOVAČKA
PIVOVARA
KARLOVAČKO
PIVO

KARLOVAČKA
PIVOVARA

✉ Dubovac 22,
Karlovac, Croatia 47000
🖰 www.karlovacko.hr

The city of Karlovac
is situated in the very
heart of Croatia,
where valleys and hills
surround the confluence of
the Korana, Kupa, Mrenica,
and Dobra rivers. A brewery
was founded there in 1854; it
was privatized as Karlovačka
Pivovara in 1992, then
bought in 1994 by the Luksic
Group, a Chilean company
owned by Andróniko Luksic
(a Chilean of Croatian
descent). It was eventually
sold to Heineken in 2003.

With a market share of
19 percent and an annual
output of 22.5m gallons
(850,000 hectoliters),
Karlovačka Pivovara is the
second-largest brewery in
Croatia, and visitors can try
its products during an
annual beer festival held in
the city's pretty central
square in August.

KARLOVAČKO PIVO 5.4% ABV •
Lager • A golden-yellow beer,
with a refreshing bitterness.
The brand is a favorite with
travelers to Croatia.

LAŠKO

✉ Trubarjeva ulica 28,
SI-3270 Laško, Slovenia
🖰 www.pivo-lasko.si

Nestled peacefully beneath
the hill of Hum, in the
commanding presence of
Tabor castle, is the ancient
Slovenian settlement of
Laško—the "town of beer
and flowers." Brewing there
can be traced back more
than 170 years to humble
origins in a gingerbread
bakery. Today, however,
Laško's brewery is a large
joint-stock company owned
by 10,000 Slovenian
shareholders. It produces
more than 34m gallons
(1.3m hectoliters) of beer
every year.

Laško's annual Beer and
Flower Festival is very
popular and attracts more
than 120,000 visitors to the
town's inns and hostelries
during the month of July.

ZLATOROG LAGER 4.8% ABV •
Lager • The aroma has a hint
of sweet malt and hops;
bitter to the finish.

A. LE COQ

✉ Tähtvere 56/62,
50050 Tartu, Estonia
🖰 www.alecoq.ee

This brewery, founded in
1826, was bought in 1913
by the A. Le Coq company,
which was based in London.
It was looking
for a brewery
in the Russian

A. LE COQ
PORTER

TOASTING TRADITION

Some Hungarians consider it bad luck to clink beer glasses together when making a toast. This superstition dates back to a failed rebellion against the Hapsburg empire in 1849. Austrian gaolers toasted the capture of 13 Hungarian generals, later executed for their part in the attempted coup, with glasses of beer—gleefully clinked together. Many Hungarians still avoid the gesture, and simply raise their glasses and say "*egészségedre*" ("to your health.")

The customary Hungarian toast to "health" should be pronounced carefully, as the word sounds somewhat similar to "backside."

Empire where it could produce Imperial stout locally, rather than export it from England.

During the Russo-Japanese War, A. Le Coq made generous donations of porter to Russian military hospitals, and was granted the right to supply the Imperial Court with its beers as a reward.

Production ceased during the 1960s, but was revived again in 1999. A small museum housed in the brewery's former maltings is open to group visits by appointment.

▣ PORTER 6.5% ABV ●
Porter ● A strong, dark beer that can rightfully be considered to be a descendant of the the world-famous Imperial extra double stout style. Its mature character and color are derived from the use of extra-dark caramel malt. Despite its strength, it has a mellow taste.

OKOCIM

✉ Ul. Browarna 14,
32–8–Brzesko, Poland
🖰 www.okocim.com.pl

Brzesko lies to the east of Kraków in Poland. The town is home to two of the region's finest buildings: the palace

of Baron Jan Goetz, and the Okocim brewery, which was founded in 1845 when the region was still a province of the Austrian Empire.

The brewery itself is well preserved, although closed conical fermenters have been installed and the premises expanded. As one of the few remaining Austrian breweries from this period, it is an important heritage site in terms of the modern history of beermaking. Carlsberg increased its share in Okocim to 85 percent in 2003.

▣ ZAGLOBA 4.8% ABV ●
Lager ● Pale in color, with a yeasty, biscuity zest, and a hint of spicy hops; light-bodied.

▣ OKOCIM PORTER
9.0% ABV ● Porter
A porter in the northern Baltic tradition, it has a soothing, almost medicinal taste with hints of cinnamon.

OKOCIM
PORTER

SAKU ÕLLETEHASE

✉ 75 501 Saku, Estonia
🖰 www.saku.ee

This is the largest brewery in Estonia, and is owned by Baltic Beverages Holding, itself a jointly owned subsidiary of Carlsberg and Scottish & Newcastle. The roots of the Saku brewery

stretch back to the beginning of the 19th century. At that time, the Saku estate was owned by count Karl Friedrich Rehbinder, who built a distillery and a brewery there. Its existence was first documented in October 1820, and it is believed that the production of beer intended for sale to pubs and taverns began during the fall of that year. Today, the main product of Saku Brewery is Saku Originaal, Estonia's best-selling beer.

▣ ORIGINAAL 4.6% ABV ● Lager
A light, straw-colored beer; mild-mannered on the palate with hints of sweetcorn on the nose.

HEINEKEN SLOVENSKO

✉ Novozámocká 2, 947 12
Hurbanovo, Slovakia
🖰 www.heineken.sk

Since Heineken entered the Slovak market in 1995, the multinational company has invested more than $165 million in buying and improving breweries there, but now operates only one plant, the former Zlatý Bažant (Golden Pheasant) brewery at Hurbanovo. The group's current market share in Slovakia is more than 45 percent, and it operates the biggest malt plant in central Europe, which is also based in Hurbanovo.

Heineken Slovensko produces more than 45m gallons (1.7m hectoliters of beer) every year from these facilities.

Slovakia's largest beer festival, the Junefest, takes place in Bratislava's Incheba exhibition center in June.

ZLATÝ BAŽANT 5.0% ABV •
Pilsner • Clear and golden in color, this is a simple beer. It is easy-drinking and without any complexities.

SUN INBEV

✉ Vorontsovsky Park, 6 Moscow, Russia
🖥 www.suninterbrew.ru

Sun InBev is one of the leading brewing companies in Russia. The company was set up in 1999 as a strategic partnership between InBev and the SUN Group, which has operated in the region since 1958, and in the beer sector since the beginning of the 1990s.

It has breweries in Klin, Ivanovo, Kursk, Omsk, St. Petersburg, Perm, Saransk, Volzhsky, Novocheboksarsk, and Ukraine, employing more than 8,000 people in total.

Brazilian beers are proving popular in Russia and the Brahma lager brand, also owned by InBev, is now being brewed in Klin.

TOLSTIAK DOBROYE 5.0% ABV •
Lager • A pale beer with a smooth sweetness and pleasant hop bitterness.

ŠVYTURYS-UTENOS ALUS

✉ Kulių Vartų g. 7 Klaipėda, Lithuania
🖥 www.svyturys.lt

There is an old Lithuanian tradition of bringing beer to relatives and neighbors on special occasions. Thus, beer has always been a symbol of friendship and kinship in that country. The first

brewery in Klaipėda was established by Merchant J. W. Reincke in 1784. The brewery was destroyed during the war, but was rebuilt in 1946, after which production resumed. At first, the brewery's beer was sold in wooden casks to bars in the Klaipėda area, but the company installed a bottling system in 1950 and widened distribution.

Švyturys-Utenos is today part of Baltic Beverages Holding, a jointly owned subsidiary of Carlsberg and Scottish & Newcastle.

ŠVYTURYS-UTENOS ALUS EKSTRA

EKSTRA 5.2% ABV •
Dortmund lager • Clear and golden, with a firm white head; has an intense aroma of hops and a slight hop bitterness. Lithuania's best-selling brand.

TOPVAR

✉ Krusovska cesta 2092 Topol'čany, Slovakia
🖥 www.topvar.sk

One of the largest breweries in Slovakia, Topvar was bought by SABMiller in 2005 for $14.3 million. Located in the city of Topol'čany in western Slovakia, the company today produces more than 15.8 million gallons (600,000 hectoliters) of beer each year. In 2000, the brewery launched a beer called Brigita, which was named after the Slovak finance minister Brigita Schmögnerovà. It is still on sale, despite the fact that she has since quit.

The Šariš brewery in Velký Šariš, bought by SABMiller in 1997, has now been merged with the company.

SVETLÉ 5.2% ABV •
Lager • Displaying a sunburst of yellow

colors, this beer has a thin white head and an attractive nose, with notes of fruit.

UNION

✉ Ljubljana, Pivovarniška ulica 2, 1000 Ljubljana, Slovenia
🖥 www.pivo-union.si

Brewing in Ljubljana has a history dating back at least 400 years, and the city's archives contain a document showing that an innkeeper was paying tax on beer as early as 1592. Union was founded in 1864 by Peter Kozler and his brother and sister, using money that they inherited from their father. A museum celebrating its history was established in 1987 in the attic of the old malt-house.

Pivovarna Union is one of the largest joint-stock enterprises in Slovenia. The Cutty Sark pub and As restaurant, both in Knafljev Prehod, are good places to try their beers.

LAGER 5.0% ABV • Lager
Golden, with a good head and sweet overtones.

ZAGREBAČKA PIVOVARA

✉ Ilica 224, Zagreb, Croatia
🖥 www.ozujsko.com

Zagrebačka Pivovara was established in 1893. In 1994, Interbrew (now InBev) bought 23 percent of the company and later became the majority stakeholder.

The brewery makes Tomislav Pivo, one of the strongest beers in Croatia at 7% ABV. The use of dark chocolate malted barley gives this dark lager its full taste and spicy aroma.

OŽUJSKO PIVO
5.2% ABV • Lager •
A golden lager with a large white head; a sweetcorn and malt nose gives way to a fruity finish.

ZAGREBAČKA PIVOVARA OŽUJSKO PIVO

Austria

Vienna • Salzburg • Linz • Graz

At its height, the Austro-Hungarian Empire produced beers that influenced brewing traditions all around the world, from Mexico to Bohemia. The country's most famous brewer, Anton Dreher, is still remembered today in the name of a well-known Hungarian brewery.

What put Austria on the beer map in the 19th century was the Vienna lager style. This reddish lager, first brewed by Anton Dreher in 1841, has been revived in recent years by small brewpubs. Dreher did not invent bottom-fermentation (and thus lager beer) as many claim. He did, however, pioneer the use of vast cold-maturation cellars for his lager in the winter of 1840. Dreher and his fellow brewers in the Austro-Hungarian Empire were also responsible for standardizing the malting process and were instrumental in the introduction of pale pilsner and caramel malts. In 1862, Anton Dreher went on to found a brewery in Budapest, now the capital of modern Hungary, which still operates today (*see p.182*).

Just as Austria's chefs often adapt recipes from neighboring countries, so do its brewers. Hence, beers in Vienna and eastern parts of the country tend to be less hoppy and more full-bodied than those in western provinces, where many brewing styles are rooted in the traditions of Germany and Bohemia. For much of the 20th century, a cartel of breweries made sure that regional beers had restricted distribution—many of today's national brands and even styles were strictly regional 30 years ago. Bavarian-style wheat beer, for example, became available in eastern Austria only after the cartel was terminated in the late 1970s.

In recent years, a few dozen brewpubs and a handful of micros have broadened the spectrum of specialty beers on offer, brewing in most international styles and using a greater diversity of ingredients, including honey, fruit, and even beets.

The fresh air and Alpine scenery of Austria's mountainous regions provide the perfect setting in which to enjoy a new generation of Austrian beers.

1516 BREWING COMPANY

✉ Schwarzenbergstraße 2, 1010 Vienna

Established in 1999, this American-style brewpub has pioneered Belgian-style ales, porters, and stouts in Vienna. Owner Horst Asanger often plays host to professional guest brewers from around the world, and he regularly adds interesting brews to his ever-changing portfolio of beers. At least one lager and one wheat beer are on tap all the time, and Hop Devil IPA, his interpretation of a similar brew from Victory Brewing (*see p.220*) in Pennsylvania, is also available year-round.

🍺 **HOP DEVIL** 6.5% ABV • India pale ale • Intense grapefruit-like aroma; very full-bodied and, at 65 IBUs, arguably the hoppiest beer in Austria.

🍺 **PEARL JADE STOUT** 5.0% ABV • Foreign extra stout • Rich and full-bodied, with an intense hop aroma (Nelson Sauvin) and coffeelike notes.

🍺 **WEDDING BELLS** 5.0% ABV • Vienna lager • Seasonal amber-colored summer lager; lemony and almond aromas, a hint of roastiness from the malts, and a dry finish.

EDELWEISS

✉ Hofbräu Kaltenhausen, 5400 Kaltenhausen

🖰 www.edelweissbier.at

Hofbräu Kaltenhausen, established in 1475 as the official brewery of the Archbishop of Salzburg, lies 15 miles (25 km) south of the city. It is partly built into the caves of a mountain on the Bavarian border. This provides natural cooling for the fermenting cellars, which are used to make a wide variety of wheat beers (and some lager sold under the Kaiser brand) for BrauUnion/Heineken.

EDELWEISS HOFBRÄU

AUSTRIA'S MÄRZEN

Märzen literally means "beer made in March," and was traditionally the last brew to be cooled with natural ice in spring. It was brewed strong to have a longer storage life. Due to this strength it was adopted as a festival beer in Germany, where legal requirements stipulate that *festbiers* have to be slightly stronger in alcohol than standard lagers. Thus, a typical German märzen will have 5.5% ABV or more, but an Austrian märzen will be below 5.0% ABV. Märzen beers in Austria are medium-bodied lagers and account for more than half of the country's annual 238 million-gallon (9 million-hectoliter) output. Popular commercial brands include Gösser Märzen (*see below*) and Stiegl Goldbräu (*see p.188*).

GÖSSER MÄRZEN

🍺 **HOFBRÄU** 4.5% ABV • Hefeweizen • Dark amber; spicy, clovelike aromas, with less banana notes than in other wheat beers; spritzy and refreshing, with not too much body or sweetness.

🍺 **GAMSBOCK** 7.1% ABV • Weizenbock • Dark gold; intense banana aromas and a refreshing fruity sourness almost make one forget its strength. Some apparent bitterness in the aftertaste adds to the unusual overall dryness of this wheat bock.

🍺 **BERNSTEIN** 4.1% ABV • Lager An amber lager with a strong malty character, some caramelly sweetness, but no apparent hop aromas.

FORSTNER BIERE

✉ Dorfstraße 52, 8401 Kalsdorf bei Graz

🖰 www.hofbraeu.at

Formerly Hofbräu Kalsdorf (which is still the name on the tap), Gerhard Forstner's brewpub was voted the best in Austria in 2004. Housed in an old school building, it produces a variety of distinctive, small-batch beers. The "Slow" range, which uses organically grown ingredients, is named after the Slow Food movement,

which aims to counter fast-food culture.

🍺 **SLOW 2** 5.6% ABV • Amber ale A light ale based on rye malts. Very hoppy nose (Malling hops from Mühlviertel) with citrus aromas, and a spicy bitterness. It is medium-bodied, but very little malt character is evident.

🍺 **STYRIAN ALE** 5.6% ABV • Bitter ale • Dark burgundy, almost black; roasty aromas, slightly tart, and very refreshing; medium bitterness. There are intense grapefruitlike hoppy aromas (from Cascade hops) when the beer is very fresh. It ages well in the bottle and loses some of the hoppiness as it develops an astringent character like a tart rosé wine.

🍺 **WUNDER BIER** 6.5% ABV • Strong ale • Reddish-brown; walnut and roasted hazelnut aromas; a light sweetness and a tartness in the palate that increases when the beer is aged as recommended.

GÖSSER

✉ Brauhausgasse 1, 8707 Leoben

🖰 www.goesser.at

Austria's best-known beer brand is produced by this former abbey brewery in the southern province of Styria. Parts of the original abbey buildings still exist and house a small brewing museum. Gösser has commercial links with two breweries in Graz: Puntigamer and Reininghaus. The latter is now closed, but Puntigamer produces its former brands. Gösser and Puntigamer are both owned by Heineken, and they share the same head brewer.

All Reininghaus, Gösser, and Puntigamer beers are bottom-fermented. The portfolio includes light beers as well as bocks and sweetened dark lagers.

GÖSSER MÄRZEN 5.2% ABV • Austrian märzen • Pale gold, with remarkably good head-retention. Intense baked-apple and malt nose; full-bodied, with a robust bitterness. (The unfiltered Zwickl-version of this beer is slightly less hoppy.)

REININGHAUS JAHRGANGSPILS 5.3% ABV • Pilsner • Very pale gold; a fine white foamy head and herbal hop aroma. Aroma and bitterness levels vary from batch to batch, as Jahrgangspils is meant to be a vintage beer that boasts the characteristics of each year's hop vintage.

SCHLOSS EGGENBERG

✉ Eggenberg 1, 4655 Vorchdorf
🖐 www.schloss-eggenberg.at

This brewery specializes in bock-strength beers. Located halfway between Salzburg and Linz, Schloss Eggenberg has been owned by the Forstinger-Stöhr family for

SCHLOSS EGGENBERG SAMICHLAUS

more than 200 years. There are more than 10 beers in its portfolio, plus a shandy, an alcohol-free beer, and three "distilled beer" spirits. It is the urbock, however, that has proven to be the brewery's real treasure.

When the Hürliman brewing company of Switzerland stopped the production of Samichlaus in 1997, after merging with beverage producers Feldschlösschen, the brewery acquired the production rights for this beer, which is brewed only on December 6, St. Nicholas's (Samichlaus) Day.

SAMICHLAUS 14.0% ABV • Lager Reputedly the world's strongest lager. Deep copper coloration; no discernible head. Intense malty aroma, with noticeable alcohol. Sweet and fruity taste, with notes of dried cherries, plums, and figs. This beer has very little hop aroma or bitterness.

URBOCK 23 9.6% ABV • Dunkel eisbock • Bright gold, with little lacing. Slightly malty nose, with hints of red apples and pears. Very full-bodied palate; the sweetness is well balanced by some bitterness in the aftertaste.

HOPFENKÖNIG 5.1% ABV • Pilsner • Very pale gold, with a firm head; haylike spicy hop aromas. The very light body is followed by some dry bitterness.

SCHWECHATER

✉ Mautner Markhof-Straße 11, 2320 Schwechat
🖐 www.schwechater.at

The Schwechater brewery is situated on the eastern outskirts of Vienna. The modern new brewhouse was built by current owners Heineken in only 2006, but it stands on the site of a historic brewery founded by Peter Descrolier (valet and

SCHWECHATER ZWICKL

paymaster to Archduke Matthias) in 1632. Franz Anton Dreher bought the brewery in 1796, and it was here that his son, Anton Dreher (see p.186), brewed the first Vienna lager in 1841. Today, Schwechater brews several pale lagers, but it no longer produces the beer style that made the city famous throughout the brewing world.

ZWICKL 5.5% ABV • Pilsner • A very light, whitish-yellow color; very cloudy, with a firm head. Lemon-zest and herbal hop aromas; the extremely soft mouthfeel is offset by a constant peppery hoppiness.

STIEGL

✉ Kendlerstraße 1, 5017 Salzburg
🖐 www.stiegl.at

Founded in 1492, Stiegl is Austria's largest independent brewery. Their märzen beer (see box, p.187), Stiegl Goldbräu, accounts for more than 90 percent of Stiegl's output, making it the single best-selling beer in Austria.

Stiegl's Salzburg site has recently been graced by a new brewhouse. The old maltings was extensively refurbished and transformed into a museum (Stiegl's Brauwelt), which holds proof that the great composer Wolfgang Amadeus Mozart was a Stiegl drinker in his time! Draft Stiegl beers, and a beer of the month brewed in the facility's pilot brewery, can be enjoyed on site in the cosy braustube (brewing room) of the museum.

GOLDBRÄU 4.9% ABV • Austrian märzen • Golden to pale amber, with a firm head; aromas of malt and bread-crumbs, and also some hops; slightly sweet on the palate but well balanced; some floral hoppiness in the aftertaste.

Austria's culinary tradition encompasses both wine and beer, with the blessing of patron saint Leopold.

TRUMER

✉ Brauhausgasse 2, 5162 Obertrum am See
🖱 www.trumer.at

Situated north of Salzburg close to a lake, this 400-year-old family brewery specializes in producing pilsner lagers. The brewery's history dates back to 1601, when it began producing Bavarian-style beers. It was later purchased by hop merchant Josef Sigl. With the introduction of pilsner lager, the Sigl family saw the potential and concentrated on perfecting brewing in the pilsner style.

Although the brewery has been refurbished in recent years, Trumer adheres strictly to its traditional brewing processes, including open fermentation. The head-brewer, Axel Kiesbye, produces some adventurous special brews in a micro-brewery located in a tavern across the street from the main brewery.

In 2003, having linked up with San Antonio-based brewers Gambrinus in the US, Trumer set up a second brewery in Berkeley, California. The water in Berkeley is apparently almost identical to that used by the Trumer brewery in Salzburg.

🍺 **PILS** 5.0% ABV • Pilsner
Light straw in color, with an extremely stable foamy head and an intense herbal hop aroma. Possesses just enough body to dominate the dry aftertaste.

ZIPFER

✉ 4871 Zipf 22
🖱 www.zipfer.at

Zipfer is the only large brewery in Austria that still uses whole hops. Founded in 1858 by Viennese banker Franz Schaup, this country brewery is located in a bucolic setting in the province of Upper Austria. Zipfer specializes in making very pale lagers, including seasonal bock beers for Christmas and Easter, with Urtyp (introduced in 1967) being their best-selling beer. The company has changed hands several times throughout its history, and it is now part of the Heineken group, which is currently responsible for more than half of all beer production in Austria.

🍺 **URTYP** 5.0% ABV • Pilsner
Straw-colored, with a stable head; some hay and citrus aromas; crisp and refreshing, with a medium-bodied palate.

🍺 **PILS** 5.2% ABV • Pilsner
Pale gold in color, with intense (Tettnang) hop aromas, and a noble bitterness. Floral hop aromas predominate in the aftertaste, which underlines the overall dry impression.

🍺 **SPARKLING** 5.0% ABV • Dry beer • Very pale gold in color; a hint of peach in the nose, but generally little aroma. An extremely refreshing beer owing to high carbonation, and extremely dry with virtually no aftertaste. It is worth noting that the term "sparkling" denotes a dry beer in the German brewing tradition.

ZIPFER PILS

Switzerland

Bern • Zurich • Gräubunden • St Gallen • Thurgau

Most of Switzerland's mainstream beers are now brewed by Heineken and Carlsberg, and lack distinctive character. But while not all Swiss beers are as spectacular as the scenery, there are still hidden gems to discover. Switzerland also produces a number of low-alcohol brands.

By rights, Switzerland should have a proud and prominent position in the history of European brewing, as the Stifts library in the town of St. Gallen holds the oldest-known brewery plans. Dating from the 9th century, they outline three brewhouses that produced beer for the monks and guests at the nearby abbey. While the abbey no longer makes beer, the town still possesses the admirable Schützengarten brewery.

Switzerland is a divided beer nation, with French-speaking cantons in the west-embracing Belgian, French, and even British styles, and the German-speaking cantons in the east favoring German-style lagers. Despite Swiss beer's reputation for being somewhat bland, there are some interesting breweries, micros, and brewpubs to be found. One of these, BierVision Monstein, is the highest brewery in Europe, at 5,400 ft (1,650 m). The brewery claims that its elevated position means that the beer is just one step from heaven!

Switzerland once boasted the highest-strength beer in Europe. Samichlaus, which was brewed at the Hürlimann brewery in Zurich, had an ABV of 14%, but production ceased in the 1990s. Fortunately, it is not goodbye to this idiosyncratic beer, as it is now brewed in Austria by Schloss Eggenberg (*see p.188*).

One of Switzerland's more unusual brews is a beer that is intended to taste of corn—and it does. Called Maisgold, it is 5% ABV and the grain mixture contains 30 percent corn; this is almost unheard of in Europe, but not uncommon in the US. Maisgold is produced by the Rosegarten Brewery of Einsieden.

Diners enjoy beers and food beneath the snowy peaks of the Swiss Alps.

ALTES TRAMDEPOT

✉ Grosser Muristalden 9, 3006 Bern
🕭 www.altestramdepot.ch

Based in a former tram garage and situated near the city's famous (or infamous) bear pits, this bar, restaurant, and microbrewery gives fantastic views over the old town of Bern. Brewing takes place right in the middle of the restaurant, with fermentation cellars beneath. In addition to its three highly drinkable Tram house brews (Helles, Märzen, and Weizen) the Tramdepot produces up to 10 seasonal beers, including an English-style bitter, an Easter bock, and a smoked ale.

📺 **TRAM-HELLES** 4.7% ABV • Pale lager • Brewed with Pilsener and caramel malts; non-filtered, bottom-fermented, and mildly hopped.

📺 **TRAM-MÄRZEN** 4.9% ABV • Amber lager • Brewed with Wiener, Pilsener, and dark caramel malt, plus Saaz hops. It is bottom-fermented and has a malty taste.

BIERVISION MONSTEIN

✉ Monstein, 7278 Davos
🕭 www.biervision-monstein.ch

The BierVision brewpub is located in the mountain village of Monstein, 8 miles (13 km) from Davos— a winter sports center, and the base for the World Economic Forum. Andreas Aegerter, who had previously worked for the brewpub group Back und Brau ("Bake and Brew") fell in love with this mountain paradise and set up his brewpub in the most "modern" building in the village—a 100-year-old former dairy. He brews using Bamberg malt, Monstein spring water, and Stammheim hops. The brewkettle works like a pressure cooker in order to overcome the problems of low atmospheric pressure at high altitude.

📺 **MONSTEINER WÄTTERGUOGE-BIER** 4.5% ABV • Amber lager
An unfiltered lager brewed using a small amount of smoked malt, which imparts a light smoky flavor throughout.

SCHÜTZENGARTEN

✉ St. Jakobsstrasse 37, 9004 St. Gallen
🕭 www.schuetzengarten.ch

This independent brewery is the country's oldest. Founded by John Ulrich Tobler in 1779, the business was bought by the Billwiller family in 1825. The installation of state-of-the-art equipment has turned the historic Schützengarten into one of the most modern Swiss breweries, as well as an eco-friendly one. Schützengarten makes its own electricity, using turbines on a nearby river, and attempts to source raw materials for its malt from local farmers. Its portfolio of around a dozen products, mainly German-style beers, includes the alcohol-free Schützengold. The brewery houses a bottle museum with more than 2,000 exhibits from 260 breweries.

📺 **LAGERBIER** 4.8% ABV • Pale lager • This easy-drinking, unpasteurized lager is brewed from barley, wheat, and maize. Light-bodied, with just a hint of spice and a crisp taste.

STERNEN

✉ Hohenzornstraße 2, 8500 Frauenfeld
🕭 www.brauhaussternen.ch

Some of the most exciting Swiss beers, including Belgian-style abbey ales, are brewed by Sternen. The owner, Martin Wartmann, sold his share in Frauenfeld's Aktienbrauerei (producer of

Ittinger Klosterbräu) to Heineken 12 years ago. But he yearned to own a brewery again, and in 2003 he opened a microbrewery in the by-then defunct Aktienbrauerei buildings. Sternen's beer range includes a chocolate stout, a barley wine, and an English-style bitter.

Martin Wartmann says he can "make people's beer dreams come true" if they attend one of Sternen's regular brewery tours with the master-brewer, or sign up for a one-day course on how to brew beer.

**BIERVISION MONSTEIN
MONSTEINER
WÄTTERGUOGE-BIER**

📺 **HEFE-WEISSBIER HELL** 5.0% ABV • Wheat beer
Medium-bodied; sweet, with a light acidity and a creamy mouthfeel; finish is dry with wheaty notes.

📺 **HONEY BROWN ALE** 6.0% ABV • Brown ale • Hazy amber-orange in the glass; light and sweet, with a hint of fruit and a soft hoppiness; some honey in the finish.

TURBINENBRÄU

✉ Badenerstraße 571, 8048 Zurich
🕭 www.turbinenbraeu.ch

Zurich's only stand-alone brewery, Turbinenbräu is located in the city's industrial area. Established in 1997, following the closure of the city's Hürlimann brewery, Turbinenbräu moved to its current site in 2002. It uses modern brewing technology to brew traditional beers, usually to German purity-law standards. As the beers are unpasteurized, the brewery recommends that they are drunk within two months of brewing.

📺 **START** 5.0% ABV • Pale wheat beer Unfiltered; easy on the eye and light on the palate.

📺 **REKORD** 5.2% ABV • Amber lager Unfiltered; uses dark Munich malt, which gives it an orange hue.

Scandinavia

Denmark • Norway • Sweden • Finland

Farmhouse-brewing is a community ritual in Europe's far north. The Finns emphasize rye and juniper. The Scandinavians speak of Viking yeasts. And when the midnight sun has vanished, Russian and Scottish influences are evident in warming porters like Koff and Carnegie.

Despite a recent history of prohibition and tight controls on the sale of alcohol, Scandinavia is surprisingly beer-friendly. The Danes, of course, are second only to Germany in popularizing lager brewing. In the 1840s, Carlsberg founder J. C. Jacobsen brought jars of bottom-fermenting yeast 600 miles (950 km) from Munich to Copenhagen. Carlsberg now owns breweries across the region. But Denmark has also seen a rapid growth in craft breweries in recent years: it now has more than 70 micros and brewpubs. In Copenhagen, one of the newest is the Kobenhavn, selling not only its own beers but others from Danish micros, while Apollo brews a light, tart, unfiltered lager; Brewpub Norrebro has an eclectic list of homebrews; and Cafe Plan B sells craft beers from all over the world.

Norwegian breweries operate under the strictest regulations of any in Europe. Ringnes, the country's largest brewery, is now owned by Carlsberg. Norway has a handful of brewpubs, including Oslo's Mikro Brygerri, which brews in British and American styles, and Møllebyen Mikrobryggeri in Moss, whose range features a strong Belgian triple.

Carlsberg is also a big player in Sweden, where it owns Falkenberg and Pripps. The dynamic Swedish micro scene helps to keep alive Sweden's 200-year-old tradition of porter-brewing. Jämtlands, one of the newer breweries, has a fine oatmeal stout.

Although Finland is not, technically, a Scandinavian country, it makes sense to include it here. Once part of Russia, it lies along the trade route that took dark ales known as Imperial stouts from England to Russia. The Helsinki Beer Festival, held each April in the famous Cable Factory in Ruoholahti, is a great chance to sample beers from Finland's 30 microbreweries.

Named after J. C. Jacobsen's young son Carl, the Carlsberg brewery was where the technique for isolating a single yeast strain was developed.

AASS

✉ Postboks 1530, 3007 Drammen, Norway
🖱 www.aass.no

Established in 1834, Aass (pronounced "orse" in Norwegian) is the oldest brewery in Norway. It stands on the banks of the Drammen River, in the city of the same name, in the same spot it has occupied since its earliest days. The brewery is named after Poul Lauritz Aass, who bought the business in 1860. Since then it has remained in Aass family hands, and is today run by Poul's fourth-generation descendants. Aass produces around 2.6m gallons (100,000 hectoliters) of beer each year, in a wide range of styles, as well as soft drinks and mineral waters.

🍺 **AASS BOCK** 6.5% ABV • Dark bock • A dark bock brewed from Munich malt and Hallertau hops. It is lagered for at least three months.

AHLAFORS

✉ Box 3060, 449 15 Alafors, Sweden
🖱 www.ahlafors.se

Quite appropriately, this microbrewery is located in the Swedish region of Ale! One of Sweden's new breed of micros, Ahlafors was set up in 1996 by a group of homebrewers as an antidote to the "dumbed-down" international lagers that dominated the market. Its beers have won several prizes at the Swedish homebrewing championships.

🍺 **AHLE SLÄTTERÖL** 3.5% ABV • Lager • A hazy, bottom-fermented beer flavored with elderflower.

🍺 **AHLE ALE JULÖL** 4.5% ABV • Ale A dark, top-fermented ale hopped with Goldings. One for Christmas.

BRØCKHOUSE

✉ Høgevej 6, 3400 Hillerød, Denmark
🖱 www.broeckhouse.dk

Allen Poulsen used to be an IT engineer, but in 2002 his success as a homebrewer led him to give up his day job and move from being a mere beer hobbyist to a full-time brewer. Increasing sales meant that he had to find new premises in 2003. Poulsen is renowned for his adventurous beer styles, picking the best examples from Britain, Germany, and Belgium.

BRØCKHOUSE IPA

🍺 **IPA** 6.0% ABV • India pale ale • A powerful, top-fermented ale. Three hops—Northern Brewer and Fuggles from England, and American Cascade—give the beer an assertive quality.

🍺 **OLD ALE** 6.5% ABV • Dark lager A blend of new and two-year-old beer. The long storage time adds a sherry note; there are also tones of coriander, cloves, and rich, ripe fruit.

CERES

✉ Cerea Allé 1, 8100 Århus C, Denmark
🖱 www.ceres.dk

Part of Royal Unibrew, Denmark's second-largest brewing group, Ceres (named after the Roman goddess of fertility) began in 1856, when it was one of seven brewers in Århus. In 1914, the brewery was made Purveyor to the Royal Danish Court.

Also in Århus is the St. Clements brewpub, unrelated but well worth a visit. It is to be found in the Old Town—an open-air museum consisting

FINLANDIA SAHTI STRONG

of 75 historic buildings, some from the 1500s, collected from all over Denmark. Customers can admire the shining copper vats as they dine and sip beer that has been brewed on site.

🍺 **ROYAL STOUT** 7.7% ABV • Stout Made from lager malt, Munich malt, and black malt, the taste is softened by the addition of some unmalted grain. Best drunk at room temperature, it improves with age.

FINLANDIA SAHTI

✉ Suokulmantie 237, 31110 Matku, Finland
🖱 www.finlandiasahti.fi

Finlandia is a commercial producer of sahti (*see box, p.195*)—a beer style that was traditionally homebrewed. Every May there is a sahti festival at Helsinki's St. Urho's Pub (Museokatu 10), which includes the pioneering Lammin Sahti, Joutsan Sahti, and Finlandia Sahti. In fact, St. Uhro's is an excellent place to sample Finlandia brews year-round.

Finlandia's sahti beers are brewed on a farm in Matku, north of the town of Forssa, which is equidistant from Helsinki, Turku, and Tampere. The farm adjoins an RV park and horse-trekking stables.

🍺 **TAVALLINEN** 8.0% ABV • Sahti A deep chestnut color, with a heavy juniper nose and a hint of blackcurrant.

🍺 **STRONG** 10.0% ABV • Sahti Sweet and somewhat oily on the palate, the juniper nose giving way to a bubblegum aftertaste.

GOTLANDS

✉ St. Hansgatan 47, 621 56 Wisby, Sweden

📠 www.gotlandsbryggeri.se

The tiny town of Wisby with its 13th-century walls has two spectacular ruined churches at its center. Across from them is a 1700s building that once housed a Methodist church and, from 1850 to 1910, a brewery that made porter and dark lager. Now smartly restored, it opened in 1995 as the Gotlands microbrewery. Owned by Spendrups, one of Sweden's largest brewers, Gotlands produces many experimental brews, including Klosteröl, an oatmeal stout made with yeast from Maclays of Scotland.

📦 **WISBY KLOSTERÖL** 5.0% ABV • Oatmeal stout • Uses Scottish top-fermenting yeast; Pilsner, Munich, and wheat malts; and German hops. Orangey and unfiltered, with yeasty flavors balanced by peachy fruitiness and honey hints.

📦 **WISBY MEDELTIDSÖL** 6.0% ABV • Amber ale • Flavored with honey, this unfiltered beer has subtle hints of hops.

HANSA

✉ Kokstaddalen 3, 5061 Bergen, Norway

📠 www.hansabeer.com

Hansa was founded in 1891 by Waldemar Stoud Platou. Its name reflects Bergen's history as one of the trading cities of the Hanseatic League, which maintained a trading monopoly over the Baltic region between the 13th and 17th centuries. Hansa merged with Borg in 1997 to form Hansa Borg Bryggerier, Norway's largest independent brewing group. Its breweries in Sarpsborg,

A vintage poster for Hansa, whose Norwegian beers have a following in the US.

Kristiansand, and Bergen supply about one quarter of the Norwegian beer-drinking market.

📦 **PILSNER** 4.5% ABV • Pilsner A crisp, light lager with a lemon finish.

📦 **BAYER** 4.5% ABV • Dark lager • Dark malts give this lager a toffeelike finish.

JACOBSEN

✉ 1799 København V, Copenhagen, Denmark

📠 www.carlsberg.com

The visionary brewer J. C. Jacobsen set up Carlsberg in 1847. His brewery, just outside the old city ramparts of Copenhagen, pioneered steam-brewing, refrigeration techniques, and the propagation of a single yeast strain. Today, most Carlsberg beer is produced in Fredericia, and the Copenhagen site now brews only specialty beers, with the Jacobsen brewhouse itself being the centerpiece of a visitor attraction and museum.

📦 **BRAMLEY WIT** 4.6% ABV • White ale • A Belgian-style beer flavored with fresh orange peel and apple juice.

JACOBSEN BRAMLEY WIT

📦 **SAAZ BLONDE** 7.1% ABV • Belgian ale • Extract of angelica adds a juniperlike flavor, which complements the fruity taste of the yeast.

JÄMTLANDS

✉ Box 216, 840 58 Pilgrimstad, Sweden

📠 www.jamtlandsbryggeri.se

Established in 1996 in a village in northwest Sweden, Jämtlands' beers are inspired by brews from Germany, Britain, and the Alsace region of France. Its range covers a broad spectrum, from fruit beers and a Baltic porter to English strong ale and a Vienna lager. The brewing is imaginative, but production runs are small; the brewer says he wants to concentrate on quality, not quantity. His beers regularly win awards at the Stockholm Beer Festival.

📦 **PRESIDENT** 5.2% ABV • Pilsner This bottom-fermented beer in pilsner style has a medium bitterness and the soft aroma of Czech Saaz hops.

📦 **OATMEAL PORTER** 5.8% ABV • Porter • An unfiltered and top-fermented porter with a ruby-black color. Espresso in a glass!

KRÖNLEINS

✉ Bryggaregatan 7–9, 302 43 Halmstad, Sweden

📠 www.kroenleins.se

Krönleins is one of Sweden's largest independent breweries. It was founded in 1836 by Anders Julius Appeltofft, who bought an old half-timbered hospital, or *curhuset*, in Halmstad and converted it into a café-bar. For the first decade he made *svensköl*, a traditional sweet, low-alcohol beer.

In the 1920s, Anders Krönleins took a controlling stake, and today the brewery is run by his grandsons. Krönleins currently produces a huge range of beverages, from beer, cider, and spirits to soft drinks.

THREE HEARTS STOCKHOLM FINE FESTIVAL BEER 7.2% ABV • Strong ale • Light in color, heavy in alcohol. A malty aroma; finishes long and warm.

MACK'S

✉ Storgata 4, 9005 Tromsø, Norway
🖥 www.mack.no

Founded in 1877 by Ludvig Mack, this Norwegian brewery still claims to be the most northerly brewery in the world, despite the fact that in 2000 a microbrewery called Nordkapp was set up even closer to the North Pole in Honningsvåg. Nordkapp's first brew was a lager called Sorry Mack, a joke at Mack's expense. From mid-May to mid-June, Mack's serves its beer with seagull eggs.

ARCTIC BEER 4.5% ABV • Pale lager • Pale golden in color, with a hint of hops on the nose and a dry finish.

OLVI

✉ Olvitie I–IV, 74100 Iisalmi, Finland
🖥 www.olvi.fi

Olvi, which dates from 1878, owns A. Le Coq in Estonia, Cēsu Alus in Latvia, and Ragutis in Lithuania. After Hartwell and Sinebrychoff ("Koff"), it is the third-largest brewer in Finland.

The brewery and a museum, and the company's headquarters and soft drinks' plant, can be found in forested countryside in Iisalmi. Olvi is involved with the organization of Oluset,

SINEBRYCHOFF PORTER

Finland's biggest beer festival, held in Iisalmi every July.

SAAREMAA TUULIK 5.2% ABV • Ale • Golden; aromas of woody juniper and malt; malty, hoppy palate, with some juniper coming in toward the finish.

TULPAPUKKI 8.5% ABV • Pale doppelbock • Rich in malt and hops. A spicier version is produced for Christmas.

SINEBRYCHOFF AB

✉ Sinebrychoffinaukio 1, 04201 Kerava, Finland
🖥 www.koff.fi

Finnish Beer Day is held each year on October 13. Behind this tradition is the founding of the Sinebrychoff brewery in 1819 by a Russian, Nikolai Sinebrychoff. The brewery, usually abbreviated simply to "Koff," was bought by Carlsberg in 1998.

Sinebrychoff has had a porter in its range of beers from the earliest days, except during a period of prohibition at the start of the

20th century. The current porter is brewed using a recipe developed in 1957.

PORTER 7.5% ABV • Porter Energetic and brimming with coffee flavors, this beer has a long, warming finish.

STADIN PANIMO OY

✉ Kyläsaarenkatu 14/101, Helsinki, Finland
🖥 www.stadinpanimo.fi

Founded in 2000, Stadin Panimo Oy is Helsinki's only micro-brewer. It produces a wide range of beer styles including stouts and porters, Belgian white beers, German wheat beers, a strong India pale ale, and some British-style cask-conditioned ales. The two award-winning brewers, Kari Likovuori and Ari Järmälä, have an almost unrivaled knowledge of specialty beers.

ORIGINAL PORTER 4.1% ABV • Porter • Dark, with hints of gold and caramel; wonderful bitter overtones.

WITBIER 4.8% ABV • White ale A Belgian-style beer flavored with coriander and orange peel. Refreshing.

THISTED

✉ Bryggerivej 10, 7700 Thisted, Denmark
🖥 www.thisted-bryghus.dk

Located in northwestern Jutland, Thisted has become well-known in Denmark for its range of organic beers. The brewery was founded in 1899, went bust and was re-established in 1902; its shares are still owned by 1,800 local people. Thisted first began brewing organic beers in 1995 with Thy Pilsner, at 4.6% ABV. It now produces four others, including robust Easter and Christmas seasonals.

THY JULE REN 7.9% ABV • Strong ale • A seasonal Christmas beer that is pale yellow in color, and includes a spicy and smoky, perfumed aroma.

SAHTI

The Finnish specialty sahti is brewed with rye and sometimes oats. The juniper bushes that grow locally perform a number of functions. The branches are typically used to form a filter base in the mash vessel. Thus, when the mash is run off, not only is sediment trapped by the bed of twigs, but the wort also picks up flavors from the berries. The hops that would be used in a normal beer might be replaced or augmented by juniper berries. Juniper wood might also be used to boil the kettle, although this step is not always taken. In some places, a juniper tea is made to disinfect the brewing vessels.

France

Paris • Alsace • Brittany • Flanders

France is famed as the gourmet capital of the world. The French love their food, wines, spirits, and liqueurs. But they also love their beers, and scores of craft brewers are using their skills with locally grown ingredients to strengthen regional and cultural identities.

A hundred years ago, there were well over 1,000 breweries in France, but two World Wars, rural depopulation, and a lack of investment saw most close. Fortunately, a handful of smaller breweries survived, and today they are joined by a new wave of brewers. France has two main brewing regions: the east, centered on Strasbourg, and the north, especially French Flanders around Lille. While brewers can now be found spread thinly across much of rural France, a third distinct brewing area is developing in Brittany.

Brewers around Strasbourg tend to make lighter versions of German-style lagers, while most around Lille specialize in bière de garde (*see box, p.198*), a style similar to some Belgian ales across the border. Bières de garde can be bought direct from the brewery or are for sale in local bars. Lille is a great city for beer-lovers who like to bar-hop and enjoy local brews. Les 3 Brasseurs, opposite Lille's train station (18–22 Place de la Gare), is an ideal place to sample the region's three main styles— blonde, ambrée, and brune—which tend to be packed with spice and hops.

Brittany now has a score of brewers. Being both Celtic and Gallic, Bretons love the taste of barley beer, or *cervoise*, and are perhaps reviving old brewing traditions as a way of affirming their 21st-century identity. One thing is for certain: the French beer revolution is underway, and its only limitation is imagination.

Culture and cuisine intertwine in Paris. Diners at Les Deux Magots enjoy food and beer in the former haunt of Jean-Paul Sartre and Ernest Hemingway.

ANNOEULLIN

✉ 5 Grand Place, 59112 Annoeullin

Established in 1905, this tiny, rustic brewery is run by members of the Lepers family, who can trace a history of hop-growing and brewing through five generations back to the 1880s. The wheat beer L'Angélus, Annoeullin's best-known brew, was first produced in 1988. The label is a reproduction of Jean-François Millet's masterpiece *L'Angélus* (1857). The brewery also produces a beer for La Tireuse café in Toulouse.

🍺 **L'ANGÉLUS**

7.0% ABV • Wheat beer
Wonderfully aromatic and unmalted, with just a hint of syrup.

CASTELAIN
CH'TI BRUNE

BAILLEUX

✉ Café-Restaurant Au Baron, 2 Rue du Piémont, 59570 Gussignies
🖰 www.lachope.com/baron.html

Brasserie Bailleux is in the hamlet of Gussignies, on the banks of the Hogneau River. It is a small microbrewery attached to the restaurant that Roger Bailleux opened in the 1970s. The brewery followed in 1989. Its beers are unpasteurized and unfiltered, and make a glorious accompaniment to the grilled fish and meat served in the restaurant.

🍺 **CUVÉE DES JONQUILLES** 7.0% ABV • Bière de garde
Named after the daffodils that throng the village in spring, this beer is full of tropical fruit flavors and citrus zests.

CASTELAIN

✉ 13 Rue Pasteur, 62410 Benifontaine
🖰 www.chti.com

Yves and Annick Castelain succeeded their parents in 1978 at this independent, traditional brewery. They say they love the life of turning water into beer! Opened in 1926, the brewery is situated in northern France, close to Flanders and Artois.

Castelain's beers are sold under the name Ch'ti, which is local patois for a northerner. Some of its Christmas beers are brewed in August and September and then bottle-aged *sur lie* (on a yeast sediment) for at least two months.

🍺 **CH'TI BRUNE** 6.4% ABV
• Bière de garde • Dark chocolate color; well balanced, with port-like notes, hints of tropical fruit, and a long, sweet finish.

🍺 **CH'TI AMBRÉE** 5.9% ABV
• Bière de garde • Lots of fruit flavors; the finish is long, crisp, and rich in malt.

LA CHOULETTE

✉ 16 Rue des Écoles, 59111 Hordain
🖰 www.lachoulette.com

La Choulette, which takes its name from a game that was a forerunner to lacrosse, is a charming farmhouse brewery whose beers are classics of the bière de garde style. The brewery dates back to 1885. Alain and Martine Dhaussy bought it in the 1970s, determined to revive traditional brewing methods. Today, La Choulette's bières de garde rank among the world's greatest beers. The basement of the brewery houses a tiny museum.

🍺 **LA BIÈRE DES SANS CULOTTES** 7.0% ABV • Bière de garde
Champagnelike aroma, with a subtle hint of aniseed; the elegant finish is dry and bitter.

🍺 **FRAMBOISE** 7.0% ABV • Fruit beer • An amber bière de garde flavored with

LA CHOULETTE
LA BIÈRE DES
SANS CULOTTES

natural raspberry extract. Slightly nutty, it has a hint of cherry.

DEUX RIVIÈRES

✉ 1 Place de la Madeleine, 29600 Morlaix
🖰 www.coreff.com

Christian Blanchard and Jean François Malgorn are part of France's new wave of beer producers. After consulting the famous English brewer Peter Austin, founder of the Ringwood brewery (*see p.163*), they opened Deux Rivières in 1995. The brewery is named after two rivers, the Jarlot and the Queffleuth, which flow through Morlaix in Brittany. Beer is brewed according to traditional English methods. Visitors to the brewery are welcomed throughout July and August (by appointment at other times).

🍺 **COREFF AMBRÉE** 5.0% ABV • Ale • An *entente cordiale* of French and English malts; full-bodied, with a hint of redness; a complex beer tinged with quinine and lemony citrus notes.

DUYCK

✉ 113 Route Nationale, BP 6, 59144 Jenlain
🖰 www.duyck.com

The son of Flanders brewer Léon Duyck, Félix Duyck set up his own farmhouse brewery in Jenlain, near Valenciennes, in 1922. That same year he brewed his first beer, which would later become the spicy Jenlain—the best-known of the bières de garde. In 1950, the company began bottling in recycled Champagne bottles. Today Duyck, no longer a farmhouse brewery but still in family hands, produces food-friendly beers that work superbly both as ingredients and

WHAT IS BIÈRE DE GARDE?

Bière de garde means "beer for keeping," referring to the custom on farms in northern France of brewing batches of beer during the cooler months to be kept (lagered or *gardée*) for summer, when warm weather and wild yeasts make brewing difficult. With the industrialization of brewing, bière de garde almost disappeared, but small brewers kept the style alive in rural areas. Many filled bottles directly for customers, using Champagne bottles sealed with corks. Originally a top-fermented, strong, bottle-conditioned brew, today bière de garde may be both bottom-fermented and filtered.

as accompaniments. They are best enjoyed with crusty bread and bold meat dishes.

🍺 **JENLAIN** 6.5% ABV ● Bière de garde ● Sweet-and-syrupy orange spice notes slip away to a long dry finish. Pours with a large head.

🍺 **JENLAIN BLONDE** 7.5% ABV ● Bière de garde ● A complex top-fermented ale; bold malts combine well with citrus hops and a potpourri of aromatic spices.

FERME-BRASSERIE BECK

✉ Rue Eeckelstraete, 59270 Bailleul
🖥 www.fermebeck.com

Being at one with nature is important to the Beck family. Quality, not quantity, is the guiding principle on their small cereal and hop farm.

The Becks began brewing at the farm in 1994, and produce two beers, both seasonal. Hommelpap is made in time for the annual hop festival in September, which celebrates the end of the Flanders hop harvest.

🍺 **HOMMELPAP** 7.0% ABV ● Bière de garde ● Use of fresh hops gives the beer assertive and dominant lemon and orange fruit flavors.

FISCHER

✉ 7 Rue de Bischwiller, 67300 Schiltigheim, Strasbourg
🖥 www.brasseriefischer.com

This sizeable lager brewery is situated in Alsace—the part of Europe that bridges

the best of France and Germany. Jean Fischer founded the business in 1821, in the center of Strasbourg, and the brewery moved out to Schiltigheim in 1854. In 1922, Fischer absorbed its neighbor, the brewery Adelshoffen, and formed the Groupe Pêcheur. Heineken purchased the company in 1996, along with Saint-Arnould, another French family brewer in the north of France.

🍺 **FISCHER TRADITION** 6.0% ABV ● Amber ale ● A medium-bodied beer with a moderate dryness in the mouth. It has hints of lemon and lime. Very refreshing.

🍺 **ADELSCOTT** 5.8% ABV ● Smoked beer ● Known as "The Different Beer," it is flavored and colored by a peat-smoked whisky malt. Full of sinuous smoky notes, this beer is a classic.

GAYANT

✉ 63 Faubourg de Paris, BP 89, 59502 Douai
🖥 www.brasseurs-gayant.com

Gayant is a small brewery in Douai, in French Flanders. For many years, Gayant has claimed to brew the world's strongest golden lager, Bière du Demon, at 12% ABV.

Founded in 1919, Gayant remains a traditional, family-run, independent company. The beers are brewed with

the same care and attention given to fine wines. Gayant's blond beer Terquieros is tequila-flavored.

🍺 **LA DIVINE** 8.5% ABV ● Bière de garde ● Fruity, woody, and caramel aromas; a warming bitterness on the palate and a smooth, delicate finish.

🍺 **LA GOUDALE** 7.2% ABV ● Bière de garde ● Golden; flavored with hops from Flanders, this dense beer is long in the mouth, with an overlay of apricots.

LANCELOT

✉ Site de la Mine d'Or, 56460 Le Roc St. André
🖥 www.brasserie-lancelot.com

Established in 1990 in an old manor house, the Lancelot brewery relocated to larger premises just a decade later to meet the demand for its beers. It is now housed in the 19th-century buildings of a disused tin and gold mine. Archaeological evidence shows that the seams were worked as far back as Neolithic times.

Lancelot is a sponsor of the Interceltique Festival of Lorient, which is held every August. The festival is a celebration of Brittany's culture and music, and a great chance to try Lancelot beers with the crêpes that are sold in the bars and cafés of Lorient.

🍺 **CERVOISE LANCELOT** 6.0% ABV ● Ale ● Copper-colored; orange fruit notes dominate, before giving way to honey and spice.

FISCHER TRADITION

MOR BRAZ

✉ St.-Léonard Nord, 56450 Theix
🖥 www.morbraz.com

Opened in 1999, this Breton brewery is situated on the coast between Vannes and Theix. The brewery claims to have "married beer to the sea," and its two main beers, Mor Braz and L'Ocean, are actually brewed with sea water pumped from a depth of 65 ft (20 m) off the island of Groix. The brewery welcomes visitors, and its shop sells beer "jam" and beer confectionery.

MOR BRAZ 6.0% ABV • Belgian ale • Blonde, slightly ambrée, with a beautiful dense, creamy, and persistent head. With a soft perfume of delicate malt, it is said to have the aroma of sea air.

PELFORTH

✉ Zone Industrielle de la Pilaterie, 59370 Mons en Baroeul, Lille
⌂ www.pelforth.fr

This brewery near Lille is owned by Heineken. One of its best-known beers, Pelforth George Killian's, was inspired by the Ruby Ale made by the G. H. Lett Brewery in Enniscorthy, County Wexford, Ireland. The brewery closed in 1956, but in 1972, George Killian Lett licensed the beer to Pelforth in France and Coors in the US to maintain the tradition. The French interpretation of George Killian's has a wonderfully smoky flavor.

Pelforth produces speciality beers, in addition to their basic blonde and brune brews.

PELFORTH GEORGE KILLIAN'S 6.5% ABV • Ruby ale Golden-apple coloration; notes of toffee and licorice, finished with a smoky dryness.

PELFORTH PELICAN 4.5% ABV • Lager Light-bodied, with just a hint of spice; easy-drinking and refreshing.

ST. SYLVESTRE

✉ 141 Rue de la Chapelle, 59114 St.-Sylvestre Cappel
⌂ www.brasserie-st-sylvestre.com

This classic artisanal brewery in Flanders is set amid hop country between Steenvorde and Hazebrouck, close to the Belgian border. According to records held in the local town hall, a brewery has existed at Saint Sylvestre Cappel since before the French Revolution. Many of St. Sylvestre's bottled beers are sealed with a cork that must be drawn with a corkscrew—unlike other artisanal beers, which use Champagne-style corks.

BIÈRE NOUVELLE 7.5% ABV • Bière de garde • This bottle-conditioned beer is made with the first hops and malt from the previous year's harvest, and is fresh and feisty.

ST. SYLVESTRE
TROIS MONTS

TROIS MONTS 8.5% ABV • Bière de garde • This wonderfully bitter golden beer is unpasteurized and very robust.

THIRIEZ

✉ 22 Rue de Wormhout, 59470 Esquelbecq
⌂ www.ifrance.com/brasseriethiriez

The village of Esquelbecq is situated 12 miles (20 km) from Dunkirk, right in the heart of the Flanders countryside. In 1996, Dainel Thiriez set up his brewery here in an old farm building. Thiriez is a passionate brewer who produces beers of great quality and is obviously influenced by Belgian beer styles. Much of Thiriez's beer is sold directly from the brewery. Thiriez made its name with Blonde d'Esquelbecq, the first beer it produced.

BLONDE D'ESQUELBECQ 6.5% ABV • Bière de garde • Made with locally grown two-row barley and hops. Robust, with aromas of tart fruit, bread, and cereal.

WARENGHEM

✉ Route de Guingamp, 22300 Lannion
⌂ www.distillerie-warenghem.com

Founded in 1900 by Leon Warenghem, this distillery produces various kinds of spirits, including a Breton whisky. It has recently started to make beer in a plant next door to the distillery, and it currently offers a blonde, a blanche, and an ambrée. Warenghem brews using whisky malts, which give the beers a husky, peaty feel. It is open to visitors during the summer months.

BIER BREIZH BLANCHE 6.0% ABV • Belgian white • A distinct hint of whisky malt; notes of apple and even blackcurrant, along with orange.

Grand Duchy of Luxembourg

Luxembourg City • Bascharge • Ardennes

Bordered by the brewing powerhouses of Germany, Belgium, and the Alsace (France), Luxembourg has no distinctive beer style. The largest brewer, Mousel-Diekirch (part of InBev) makes a pale pilsner, but it lacks the vitality of a Belgian brew or the purity of a German beer.

At one point in Luxembourg's history, 36 brewery chimneys poured their smoke into the sky, but today its brewing industry consists of just a handful of producers. However, these brewers show a healthy commitment to not only sourcing brewing ingredients locally, but also selling locally produced foods in their brewpubs and restaurants. Look out for their smoked pork dishes, which work well with the less assertive pilsner styles that predominate. Café du Coin in Rumelange, 15 miles (24 km) southwest of Luxembourg City, offers an excellent range of local beers.

Visitors to Luxembourg City can enjoy local and international beers and wines and sample the local cuisine in the many cafés and bars.

BEIERHAASCHT

✉ Avenue de Luxembourg 240, 4940 Bascharge
🖰 www.beierhaascht.lu

Tradition and the 21st century meet head on in this hotel-cum-brewpub 9 miles (15 km) from Luxembourg City. Beierhaascht's customers can sample the beer in the bar-restaurant while sitting alongside the gleaming brew kettles. All the beers are produced to German purity rules. The menu features a range of regional specialties, as well as dishes made with beer. The hotel, which offers comfortable three-star accommodation, has been awarded Luxembourg's EcoLabel for sustainable tourism. Beierhaascht also has a traditional butcher shop on site.

🍺 BIÈRE MEESCHTERBÉIER 5.0% ABV • Lager • Pale orange; a light, thirst-quenching beer produced during the summer months.

CORNELYSHAFF

✉ Maison 37, 9753 Heinerscheid
🖰 www.cornelyshaff.lu/

Standing in a nature park, this bar, restaurant, and hotel brews its own beers and also showcases a range of produce from local farms. It was established by a cooperative of farmers who were intent on reducing their dependence on subsidies.

Visitors to Cornelyshaff can tour the modern, stainless-steel, automated brewery, which opened in 2003. The brewery is extremely energy-efficient: the cooperative prides itself on minimizing the brewery's impact on the environment. Cornelyshaff, which currently produces four beers, has strong links with Wiltz's Simon brewery (*see right*).

🍺 KORNELYSBÉIER 4.2% ABV • Ale A top-fermented rye beer. The spicy aroma gives way to a deep, strong, earthy taste produced by the use of rye grain.

SIMON

✉ Rue Joseph Simon 14, 9550 Wiltz
🖰 www.brasseriesimon.lu

The Simon brewery of Wiltz —Luxembourg's third largest brewery—lies in the hilly, forested Ardennes region. This brewery has operated within sight of the church in Lower Town Wiltz since 1824. It once produced beer for the Grand Duke of Luxembourg, and it still uses traditional open fermenters and copper brew kettles, which can be seen through the brewery's windows. Simon produces five beers of its own—Pils, Régal, Dinkel, Nöel (a Christmas beer), and Prestige—and in 2007 it relaunched Okult No1, a white (wheat) beer previously brewed by the brewery at Rédange, which closed in 2005.

🍺 SIMON DINKEL 4.5% ABV • Lager A pale beer with a soft, fruity aroma. Brewed from 70-percent barley and 30-percent unmalted spelt.

Italy

Piedmont • Lombardy • Veneto • Friuli-Venezia Giulia • Latium

Italy is the fastest-growing microbrewery market. Ten years after the first brewpubs were set up, "Made in Italy" is a real mark of brewing quality, and craft beers are now on the menus of the best restaurants. Beer in Italy is, at last, receiving the same respect as Italian wine.

Serious brewing in Italy dates back to the 19th century, when far-sighted brewing entrepreneurs from Austria and Germany began arriving in northern Italy. Most famous were Franz Wührer (who moved from Salzburg to Brescia in 1829), Anton Dreher (Vienna to Trieste, 1870), and Heinrich Von Wunster (Baden-Württenberg to Bergamo, 1879). The brands they created still exist, but today these brands, along with the homegrown names Peroni and Moretti, are owned by multinational brewing giants such as Heineken, Carlsberg, and SABMiller, which produce mass-market lagers.

With the establishment of the first brewpubs by former homebrewers in the mid-1990s, the Italian beer-scene underwent a radical transformation. Consumers began to discover unfiltered, unpasteurized beers whose rich flavors injected new life into their flat tastebuds. To meet the tremendous surge of interest in beer culture, Unionbirrai (the union of craft brewers) arranged tastings, courses, homebrewing contests, and food-pairing events throughout Italy. Today, the country has more than 150 micros and brewpubs, which turn out original and interesting new beers that are enjoyed both at home and abroad.

The new breweries are often found off the beaten track, using pure water and local ingredients, such as fruits, chestnuts, herbs, and spices. The brewers often find common ground with local farmers and with craft-workers making cheese, cold meats, chocolate, honey, and other produce. From this collaboration, new beers and new foods are born, as well as cultural events focused on developing an exciting new beer-gastronomy.

Le Baladin is Italy's best-known brewpub, and its creative head brewer, Teo Musso, has inspired a generation of new producers.

32 VIA DEI BIRRAI
OPPALE

32 VIA DEI BIRRAI

✉ Via Cal Lusent 41, 31040 Onigo di Pederobba, TV (Veneto)
🖱 www.32viadeibirrai.com

Born into a brewing family, Fabiano Toffoli was destined to devote his life to beer. Having been a brewer and subsequently a brewing consultant, he founded his own microbrewery, 32 Via dei Birrai, in 2006.

Strong on Belgian-style ales, Toffoli's brews use pure water from several springs, hops imported by Toffoli himself from Poperinge in Belgium, malts from Belgium, Britain, and Germany, and yeasts cultured in the brewery.

📖 **OPPALE** 5.5% ABV ● Belgian blond ale ● A refreshing, easy-drinking cloudy ale, with a pleasant bitter finish of chives.

📖 **AUDACE** 8.4% ABV ● Belgian strong golden ale ● Rich in estery flavors; warming, spicy, and very dry in the mouth, with a long, bitter, citrus-fruit finish.

ALMOND 22

✉ Via Colle di Mezzo 25, 65125 Pescara (Abruzzo)
🖱 www.birraalmond.com

Swedish–Italian beer-lover Jurij Ferri founded this microbrewery in 2003 in the seaside town of Pescara, in central Italy's Abruzzo region. Ferri brews British- and Belgian-style ales,

along with some notable experimental beers.

📖 **FARROTTA** 6.9% ABV ● Spelt ale Cloudy golden ale brewed with barley and local spelt; easy-drinking and thirst-quenching.

📖 **TORBATA** 6.9% ABV ● Barley wine This peated ale has a smoky flavor similar to a Scotch whisky; easy to drink, despite its strength.

BABB

✉ Via San Martino del Carso 6, 25025 Manerbio, BS (Lombardy)
🖱 www.babb.it

Opened in Manerbio, near Brescia, in 2004, Babb was voted Best Italian Craft Brewery of 2006. This ultra-modern brewpub proves that, rather than being "retro," microbreweries can be at the cutting edge of contemporary culture.

Swiss-born Maurizio Cancelli, a modest yet supremely talented brewer, produces a range of high-quality, interesting beers. These can be sampled on draught or bottles in Babb's stylish restaurant.

📖 **OMNIA** 5.5% ABV ● Pilsner A generously hopped pilsner, with a Czech-like full body, but with a German-style dry finish.

📖 **RUBINIA** 7.0% ABV ● Bock Seven different malts and three types of hop are used in this award-winning amber lager. Caramel, toffee, and roasted notes in the nose; dried fruit and cherry flavors on the palate; and a surprisingly long, bitter finish.

BARLEY

✉ Via Cristofero Colombo, 09040 Maracalagonis, CA (Sardinia)
🖱 www.barley.it

With six years of home-brewing under his belt, Nicola Perra felt ready to set up his own microbrewery, founding Barley in 2006 in Maracalagonis, southern Sardinia. He obviously likes

a challenge, as the region has the highest consumption per head of mass-market lager in the entire country.

Undaunted by the task, Perra embarked on brewing ales in his own distinctive style. His gamble paid off, and Barley beers have won an appreciative audience, not only throughout the island, but also on mainland Italy.

📖 **SELLA DEL DIAVOLO** 6.5% ABV ● Belgian amber ale ● Herbal, hoppy nose with caramel and notes of plum and morello cherry; roasty and slightly smoked in the mouth; intense bitter finish.

📖 **TOCCADIBÒ** 8.4% ABV ● Belgian strong golden ale ● A warming ale; spicy, hoppy, and dry, and with intriguing almondy notes of amaretto.

BEBA

✉ Viale Italia 11, 10069 Villar Perosa, TO (Piedmont)
🖱 www.birrabeba.it

The lager specialist Beba has a broad portfolio of regular and seasonal brews. This microbrewery near Turin was set up in 1996 by two brothers, Alessandro and Enrico Borio.

In the adjoining taproom, you can enjoy fine food and all the house beers on draft. The local food specialty is *gofri*, a crispy, waferlike bread cooked in a cast-iron pot and served with meats, cheeses, or preserves.

📖 **TALCO** 4.2% ABV ● Rye lager This seasonal brew is an unusual rye weizen-lager.

BEBA MOTOR OIL

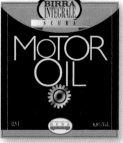

Thirst-quenching and easy-drinking, it is perfect for a hot summer's afternoon.

MOTOR OIL 8.0% ABV • Strong dark lager • This ebony-colored, full-bodied lager is as viscous as its namesake, with strong notes of licorice and roasted coffee, with a long, bitter finish.

BI-DU

✉ Via Confine 26, 22070 Rodero, CO (Lombardy)

🖥 www.bi-du.it

This brewpub was founded in 2002 in the tiny village of Rodero, just a few miles from the Swiss border. It is named after an ancient Sumerian beer used to pay workers.

BI-DU LEY LINE

Beppe Vento, one of the best and most often awarded Italian brewers, produces a range of interesting beers—but only to the styles he loves! He is very fond of German kölsch (see p.53), and Rodersch is his version of the style.

RODERSCH 5.1% ABV • Kölsch A cloudy, fresh digestif, with a lovely bitterness that is typical of Vento's philosophy.

ARTIGIANALE 6.2% ABV • Bitter ale • This celebrated strong, bitter ale strikes a good balance between malt and hops; caramel and fruity flavors; long, bitter finish.

LEY LINE 6.0% ABV • Honey ale Brewed with malt and hops from England and Germany, malt and yeasts from Belgium, and bitter Sardinian *corbezzolo* honey.

BIRRA DEL BORGO

✉ Via del Colle Rosso, 02021 Borgorose, RI (Latium)

🖥 www.birradelborgo.it

Birra del Borgo is a brewpub set in a small village about 60 miles (100 km) northwest of Rome. It was founded in 2005 by Leonardo

Di Vincenzo. After gaining experience at a brewpub in Rome itself, Di Vincenzo left his secure job as researcher to embark on an exciting—if uncertain—adventure in the world of microbrewing. So far, it has paid off. Di Vincenzo makes fine ales, often inspired by British styles, and also experiments with ingredients such as tobacco.

KETO REPORTER 5.5% ABV • Tobacco porter • This unusual but pleasant porter is infused with Kentucky Toscano tobacco. Despite strong peppery and smoked flavors, it is surprisingly well balanced and easy to drink.

RE ALE 6.0% ABV • India pale ale Inspired by India pale ale and hopped with Goldings and Cascade varieties, this is the brewery's flagship beer. Its relatively high 65 IBU rating offsets the strong, sweet caramel notes, leaving a well-balanced beer.

IL BIRRIFICIO DI COMO

✉ Via Pasquale Paoli 3, 22100 Como (Lombardy)

🖥 www.ilbirrificio.it

This large brewpub-cum-restaurant was set up in 2004 not far from Lake Como by the Orsenigo family, who own the Frey silk clothing company. Beers are produced under the Malthus brand by brewer Andrea Bravi, a food technologist. There are regular blond, amber, black, and wheat beers, plus seasonal brews using unusual ingredients.

ROXANNE 5.8% ABV • Bock • This coppery-amber lager has great character, with its sweet notes of caramel balanced by a dry, bitter finish.

BALUBA 6.9% ABV • Flavored strong lager • A coffee-dark Christmas lager flavored with rue (more traditionally added to grappa) and with dried fruits. Baluba is served in the brewpub along with delicious ginger cookies.

BIRRIFICIO ITALIANO

✉ Via Castello 51, 22070 Lurago Marinone, CO (Lombardy)

🖥 www.birrificio.it

Homebrewer Agostino Arioli "saw the light," and his destiny, during a visit to the Grenville Island Brewery in Vancouver, Canada. After gaining experience at brewpubs in Freiburg and Konstanz, he returned to Italy to work in quality control at the Von Wunster brewery in Bergamo. In 1994, he set up Birrificio Italiano at Lurago Marinone, between Milan and Como, with his brother Stefano and some friends.

Arioli, one of Italy's most knowledgeable brewers, began by brewing German-inspired lagers, and his pils and bock soon achieved cult status among Italian drinkers.

As Arioli's own beer tastes widened, so did the brewpub's portfolio, which now includes a sparkling blackcurrant lager, a sour cherry ale, a light ale flavored with flowers, and a cask-conditioned ale spiced with cinnamon and ginger.

Birrificio Italiano's restaurant is famous for its excellent regional food, as well as live concerts featuring world-renowned musicians.

FLEURETTE 3.7% ABV • Flavored light ale A light beer brewed with barley, wheat, and rye, and flavored with petals of rose and violet, elderberry juice, black pepper, and citrus honey.

BIRRIFICIO ITALIANO FLEURETTE

TIPOPILS 5.2% ABV • Pilsner
This excellent dry pils is well-hopped with four varieties: Hallertauer Magnum, then Perle, Hersbrücker, and Saaz, before a final dry-hopping with Saaz again. Voted the world's best pils on ratebeer.com.

SCIRES 7.0% ABV • Cherry ale
A fantastic sour beer brewed with black Vignola cherries, lactic bacteria, wild yeast, and wood chips.

CITTAVECCHIA

✉ Z.A. Stazione di Prosecco 29/E, 34010 Sgonico, TS (Friuli-Venezia Giulia)

✍ www.cittavecchia.com

This microbrewery is situated in the wine-producing village of Prosecco, between Trieste and the Slovenian border. It was founded in 1999 by Michele Barro, an eager homebrewer and former designer. His first beers were a pale lager and an amber lager, both in the Vienna style. Barro's lagers and ales are mainly sold to quality restaurants and bars in the Trieste area.

SAN NICOLÒ 6.0% ABV • Spiced ale • An amber ale brewed once a year for Saint Nicholas's Day. Despite its strength, it is dry and easy to drink, with aromas of peach and apricot, and a powerful punch of cardamom.

FORMIDABLE 8.0% ABV • Belgian strong dark ale • Georges Simenon's fictional sleuth Maigret was always asking for a *formidable* (two-pint/one liter) tankard of his favorite beer. Michele Barro used this as inspiration to name this ale, which is strong in fruity and liquorice notes.

GRADO PLATO

✉ Viale Fasano 36/bis, 10023 Chieri, TO (Piedmont)

✍ www.gradoplato.it

Sergio Ormea established this brewpub, which lies about 12 miles (20 km) east of Turin, in 2003. Ormea's son Gabriele helps him to run the pub, which is famous for its food—in particular, snails cooked in more than 20 different ways! Ormea plans to open his own micromaltery in the near future.

STICHER 6.5% ABV • Sticke Dark amber to copper in color, this rich beer is an award-winning interpretation of Sticke, a strong altbier brewed twice yearly by Uerige of Düsseldorf, Germany (*see p.102*). It uses locally grown barley.

STRADA SAN FELICE 8.0% ABV • Chestnut strong lager • An amber seasonal ale made with local chestnuts, which lend it a gentle smoked aroma and a marked taste of chestnuts; finish is slightly bitter.

Grado Plato beers (*below, left*) typify the eclectic, adventurous side of Italian brewing.

LAMBRATE

✉ Via Adelchi 5, 20131 Milan (Lombardy)

✍ www.birrificiolambrate.com

The first (and still the best) brewpub in Milan, Lambrate was founded in 1996 by brothers Davide and Giampaolo Sangiorgi and their friend Fabio Brocca, after a visit to 't IJ Brewery in Amsterdam. They produce 264 gallons (1,000 liters) per day of their seven top-fermented beers. A happy hour (6–8 pm, Monday to Friday) features reduced-price draft beer and a free buffet.

LAMBRATE GHISA

MONTESTELLA 4.9% ABV • Bitter blond ale
A delicious, thirst-quenching, hoppy blond ale, with fresh aromas of hay and hops.

The long, dry finish cleanses the mouth—ready for another glass!

GHISA 5.0% ABV • Smoked ale Lambrate's flagship brew, this ebony-colored beer has a foamy, cappuccino-like head. It is slightly smoked, easy to drink, and well balanced, with plum notes and a long, hoppy finish.

LE BALADIN

✉ Piazza V Luglio 15, 12060 Piozzo, CN (Piedmont)

🍺 www.birreria.com

Always the nonconformist, Teo Musso left Piozzo, his home village in one of the world's most celebrated wine-producing regions (home of Barolo, Barbera, and Barbaresco) to learn the art of brewing in Belgium. He was fortunate to have such great teachers as Christian Vanhaverbeke (Chimay, Grimbergen, and Achouffe) and Jean-Louis Dits (Vapeur Brewery).

Back in Italy in 1986, Musso initially opened Le Baladin as a pub, turning it into a brewpub 10 years later. He specializes in personal interpretations of such traditional Belgian styles as blond, brune, blanche, and saison, but has recently added some new ales—which he calls "my raptures"—made using wine and whisky yeasts. The inventive Musso has even made beer-filled chocolate pralines and beer candies.

NORA 6.8% ABV • Spiced ale Brewed to a recipe inspired by Ancient Egypt, using kamut (a Mesopotamian grain), ginger, and myrrh. Using the minimum amount of hops allowed by Italian law, its bitterness comes from Ethiopian resins.

ELIXIR 10.0% ABV • Belgian strong "whisky" ale • A sparkling *demi-sec* strong ale made with Islay whisky yeasts. Brewed

only during solstices and equinoxes, followed by long bottle-ageing. Musso says it's best served frozen!

XYAUYÙ 12.0% ABV • Experimental barley wine • The result of extensive research on oxidation to obtain "solera"-type flavors (the method used in sherry production). Warming and velvety; a great nightcap or "sofa beer"—one to enjoy after a hard day's work. Already a classic.

MONTEGIOCO

✉ Frazione Fabbrica 30, 15050 Montegioco, AL (Piedmont)

🍺 www.birrificiomontegioco.com

In 2006, Riccardo Franzosi left the family construction business to follow his passion: beer. He set up his micro-brewery in a tiny village in Montegioco, lower Piedmont. Franzosi is one of the most modest, yet eclectic and promising brewers in Italy. He believes in "building" beers through careful selection of malts, and currently brews three regular and seven seasonal ales in a variety of styles, often using local products, such as coriander from his neighbor's garden.

QUARTA RUNA 7.0% ABV • Peach ale • Fresh Volpedo peaches are oven-heated then added to the fermentation to maximize the "peachiness" of this autumn brew. No lactic bacteria or wild yeasts are added: the beer's natural sourness comes from wild yeasts already present in the skin of the peaches.

DRACO 11.0% ABV • Blueberry barley wine Rich, fruity, and complex; fermented three times and flavored with

fresh organic blueberries. A calming nightcap, it could also, served hot, make a perfect winter warmer.

PANIL (TORRECHIARA)

✉ Strada Pilastro 35/a, 43010 Torrechiara, PR (Emilia-Romagna)

🍺 www.panilbeer.com

This microbrewery near Parma was set up in 2000. The founder, graduate in biology Renzo Losi, got his break in brewing when his father gave him permission to make beer at the family's winemaking business.

Losi brews under the Panil brand, producing some excellent ales inspired by Belgian styles. His first beer, Panil Ambrè (6.5% ABV) was an abbey-style ale. True to his winemaking roots, Losi's beers are aged in wooden barrels or fermented with *spumante* yeasts.

PANIL BLACK OAK 4.0% ABV • Oak barrel-aged ale • Steam-boiled in a wooden half-barrel and then fermented directly in situ. Tannins from dark malt and wood give this beer an intriguing aroma of *gianduiotto* chocolate praline, with hint of *panna cotta*.

PANIL BARRIQUÉE SOUR 8.0% ABV • Flemish sour red • Based on Panil Brune and aged for three months in 60-gallon (225-liter) *barriques*, this uncompromisingly sour and vinous beer was the winner in a UK contest against the world classic Rodenbach Grand Cru (*see p.129*).

PICCOLO BIRRIFICIO

✉ Via IV Novembre 20, 18035 Apricale, IM (Liguria)

🍺 www.piccolobirrificio.com

Lorenzo Bottoni and Roberto Iacono set up this microbrewery in 2005 in an old

LE BALADIN
XYAUYÙ

MONTEGIOCO
QUARTA RUNA

olive-oil mill in the lovely medieval village of Apricale, near the French border. The pair brew a range of fine beers under the brand Nüa ("naked"), including some ales using local fruits and plants. Many are Belgian in style. The pair also import Hanssens' Oude Gueuze, Oude Kriek, and Oudbeitje from Belgium, selling them under different names.

CHIOSTRO 5.0% ABV • Spiced ale An unusual ale spiced with *Artemisia absinthium* (wormwood) and then fermented with Trappist yeasts to give complex aromas and flavors.

SESON 6.5% ABV • Spiced ale • A prize-winning saison-style beer matured in Chardonnay barrels with spices and local chinotto peel (from a small, bitter citrus fruit produced by the chinotto, or myrtle-leaved orange tree).

TROLL

✉ Strada Valle Grande 15/A, 12019 Vernante, CN (Piedmont)

🖥 www.birratroll.it

The village of Vernante is famous for its painted houses, which show scenes from the tale of Pinocchio. Located in the middle of "snowhere" in a beautiful Alpine valley close to the French border, Vernante is also home to the Troll brewpub. Beer enthusiast Alberto Canavese turned his pub into a brewpub in 2002, ably assisted by Andrea Bertola and Daniele Meinero, two passionate homebrewers trained by Teo Musso of Le Baladin (*see p.205*). Troll's beers are well known for their clever use of unusual herbs and spices, often collected from the "haunted" woods around Vernante.

Troll's restaurant and grill offer regular and seasonal beers on draft, and the menu

PICCOLO BIRRIFICIO SESON

includes some very fine meat dishes cooked with beer.

DAÙ 3.9% ABV • Belgian saison-style ale • This thirst-quenching, dry summer ale is spiced with two kinds of pepper and a "secret" local plant.

SHANGRILA 8.5% ABV • Spiced ale • An astonishing deep amber ale brewed with six types of malt and English hops, and enlivened by a mixture of Himalayan spices. The result is a beer with exotic scents and an intense flavor.

TURBACCI

✉ Via della Mezzaluna 50, 00013 Mentana, RM (Latium)

🖥 www.birraturbacci.it

This brewpub was founded in 1995 in Mentana, near Rome, by Giovanni Turbacci, who learned the brewer's art at the Prinz Luitpold brewery in Bavaria. Assisted by his sons Marco and Stefano, Turbacci produces four regular beers—Weisse, Lager, Black, and Super—as well as seasonal brews. All his beers are available on draft in the large pub, where relaxed customers can watch skating on the ice rink downstairs while they enjoy their food and drink.

EROICA 5.0% ABV • Scottish wee heavy • As a young man, Giovanni Turbacci lived in Scotland, where he fell in

TURBACCI EROICA

love with local beers and his future wife! Eroica is his interpretation of a Scottish wee heavy; full-bodied with low hop flavor.

ZAHRE

✉ Via Razzo 50, 33020 Sauris di Sopra (Friuli-Venezia Giulia)

🖥 www.zahrebeer.com

Sauris, a mountain village in the Friuli region close to the Austrian and Slovenian borders, was known as Zahre in ancient times—hence the name of this microbrewery, which is currently enjoying great success in Italy. Brewer Sandro Petris produces his highly appreciated lagers using pure water taken from a local mountain spring.

AFFUMICATA 6.0% ABV • Smoked lager • A dark red lager; well-rounded, with a persistent and unmistakable aroma of smoked barley malt.

CANAPA 5.0% ABV • Flavored lager • Smooth and easy-drinking, this surprisingly elegant pils is flavored with Carmagnola hemp flowers.

UNIONBIRRAI

The Italian Union of Brewers was founded in 1998, two years after the birth of the first Italian brewpubs, by a group of pioneers who had been impressed and inspired by what they saw on trips abroad. They were struck by pubs serving fresh, "living" beers, brewed on the premises. Initially an organization for professional brewers, Unionbirrai soon opened its doors to homebrewers and beer enthusiasts, and became an active member of the EBCU (European Beer Consumers Union). The union aims to promote craft-beer culture through tastings and courses, and educates via its own magazine and website.

Southern Europe

Spain • Portugal • Malta • Cyprus

Wine reigns in the south of Europe, but beer is no stranger to the region, and for some young people, beer is the drink of style and sophistication —wine is for their parents! An added attraction is that most beers, at about 5% ABV, are far less intoxicating than the average wine.

Light pilsner styles dominate in southern Europe, as do the brewing giants Heineken, Carlsberg, and Inbev, which own many local producers. Spain has some dry pilsners and strong lagers in the Dortmunder export and bock styles. Also of note is Keo, a full-bodied pilsner from Cyprus. However, the star is Malta's Simonds Farsons Cisk brewery, which produces fine ales and lagers. The region is also home to interesting variants, such as Corsican chestnut-flavored beer, and Portuguese beer cocktails made of dark lager, chocolate, and Madeira!

The streets of Madrid in Spain are home to a lively café culture. On hot summer evenings in the city, beer offers a refreshing alternative to wine.

DAMM

✉ Roselló 515, 08025 Barcelona, Spain

🖥 www.damm.es

Auguste Kuentzmann Damm brought Alsace-style lager-brewing to Barcelona in 1876. This auspicious occasion is commemorated by the company's AK Damm, at 4.8% ABV, which was first brewed in 2001. Also included in the company's portfolio is Bock Damm, a 5.4% ABV stout brewed in the Munich style, and Voll Damm, a complex beer of 7.2% ABV. In 2006, the company introduced a new gluten-free beer called Estrella Damm. In 2002, Interbev bought a 12 percent stake in Damm.

📖 **ESTRELLA DAMM** 5.4% ABV • Lager Refreshing and light, with a rather dry and bitter taste.

SIMONDS FARSONS CISK

✉ The Brewery, Notabile Road, Mriehel, BKR 01, Malta

🖥 www.farsons.com

This wonderful brewery was set up in 1928 to make beer for British troops stationed on Malta. Rebuilt in a grandiose, art-deco style in 1946, it is soon to be redeveloped again, with old brewing vessels becoming the centerpiece of a new museum. All of its beers are worth sampling: Lacto, a genuine milk stout; Blue Label, a darkish mild ale; Hopleaf, a hoppy dry ale; and two refreshing lagers, Cisk and Cisk Export. The brewery also makes the potent XS (10% ABV) brand for the Italian market.

📖 **LACTO** 3.8% ABV • Milk stout • Soft on the tongue, this is a classic milk stout, with lactose added after fermentation.

SIMONDS FARSONS CISK LACTO

📖 **HOPLEAF EXTRA** 5.2% ABV • Ale • English malt and hops (Challenger and Target) produce a beer of great complexity, with a strong, long, refreshing bitter finish.

SOCIEDAD CENTRAL DE CERVEJAS

✉ Estrada da Alfarrobeira 2625–244 Vialonga, Portugal

🖥 www.centralcervejas.pt

This brewery was formed in 1977 by the nationalization of the Sociedade Central de Cervejas and the Companhia de Cerveja de Portugal. It was sold by the Portuguese state to the Colombian brewer Bavaria in 1990, and then taken over in 2000 by the British group Scottish & Newcastle. Its Sagres range draws on Bavarian and Danish influences, with both dark and light lagers.

📖 **SAGRES DARK** 4.3% ABV • Dark Munich lager • Mahogany to dark brown; light cocoa palate, with hints of toffee, chocolate, and caramel.

US

There is a startling new world of beer in the US. An inventive generation of brewers now makes the world's most intense-tasting beers in a country once known for the blandest, and the US now has more breweries and produces beers in more styles than any other nation.

Just as the ascent of New World wines began on the West Coast, the revival of American brewing first took root in Northern California. American wines enjoy an excellent reputation among connoisseurs, and the nation's beers now command equal respect. The commercial success of New World wines on the international market has yet to be achieved by New World beers, but it is within sight.

The godfather of the US beer renaissance is Fritz Maytag, who bought a controlling stake in the Anchor Brewing Company in 1965 to keep it from closing and thus saved the unique "steam" style of beer from extinction. By the 1970s, other boutique breweries began to join Anchor. Jack McAuliffe founded the short-lived New Albion Brewing Company in 1977, and Sierra Nevada Brewing followed in 1979.

In an important parallel development, President Jimmy Carter signed a bill in 1978 that made it legal to brew beer at home, and Charlie Papazian founded the American Homebrewers Association (AHA) in Colorado in the same year.

Homebrewers swelled the ranks of commercial beermakers in the decades that followed, while the AHA evolved into the Brewers Association, which still serves smaller brewers today.

The beer map of the US changed dramatically in little more than two decades. One drawn in 1984 would have shown just 83 breweries, most of which were located east of the Mississippi River. The majority of those have since closed, but they have been replaced by more than 1,400 new breweries. Many businesses that were originally known as micro-breweries outgrew their "micro" status, and the term "craft brewery" came into use. However they are described, the defining feature of such breweries is that they exist to provide alternatives to mainstream lager beers. Their products are often inspired by beers from classic brewing nations, and many faithfully replicate Old World styles or even beers that had become extinct in Europe, such as oatmeal stout—a British specialty. American brewers have also embraced diversity: few settle for selling a limited range, instead brewing a dozen or more styles over the course of a year, including ales of their own invention. As a result of this revolution in brewing, American consumers now have access to the widest variety of beers in the world.

Brooklyn Brewery in New York is one of a new breed—strong on community spirit and charity fundraising, 100 percent powered by renewable energy, and with a wide portfolio of beer styles.

Northeast

New York • Pennsylvania • Massachusetts • Maine • Vermont • Delaware

For more than 200 years, American brewers produced only ales. Most of their products were based on British styles, until ales were usurped by lagers in the 1840s. Thus, it shouldn't be a surprise that many British-inspired beers survive to this day, especially in the Northeast.

The Northeast has many reminders of its ale-drinking past, including Longfellow's Wayside Inn near Sudbury, Massachusetts, which received its tavern license in 1716, and Fraunces Tavern in Manhattan, where George Washington drank. However, the region is also rich in "old-line" regional lager breweries, many of whose buildings are today historic and architectural landmarks. Before the global and national brands of the brewing giants overwhelmed the US beer scene, the beers of the old-line breweries were the foremost regional tipples.

The old-line breweries may have had to reinvent themselves to survive, but most still produce lagers. Perhaps that explains why traditional and nouveau reside together more comfortably in this region than in most (only the Midwest would be comparable). The breweries of Pennsylvania are a case in point, with old-line Lion reinvigorating its Stegmaier line, and small breweries such as Penn, Stoudt's, and Victory producing outstanding traditional lagers.

Vermonters are fierce advocates of their local brews, and Long Islanders of theirs, but most beer-drinkers now accept that beer styles have broken out of their former regional boundaries. You are just as likely to find a Northwest hop-influenced beer in Washington as you are in Pennsylvania. And while Brewery Ommegang in upstate New York is known for its Belgian-style beers, so too is Flying Fish in New Jersey. Tradition and change go hand in hand in the Northeast.

Nestled in the rolling countryside outside Cooperstown in upstate New York, the Ommegang brewery brings a taste of Belgium to the Northeast.

ALLAGASH WHITE

ALLAGASH

✉ 100 Industrial Way,
Portland, ME 04103
🖰 www.allagash.com

Inspired by his first taste of
Celis White (*see p.230*), Rob
Tod set up Allagash in 1994
as a one-man operation
selling a single beer—the
classic Allagash White, which
remains the flagship beer. All
Allagash beers are inspired by
Belgian traditions, but as the
company has expanded, its
portfolio has moved beyond
the basic dubbel–tripel–quad
line-up. Tod's brewing
experiments have included
ageing beer in whisky and
wine barrels, and cultivating
his own strain of wild yeast.

◗ **WHITE** 5.0% ABV ● **Witbier**
Hazy; fruity and refreshing,
with coriander and Curaçao
orange peel remaining nicely
in the background.

◗ **INTERLUDE** 9.5% ABV ● **Belgian
strong ale** ● Oaky and playfully
tart, with a lactic character
balanced by fleshy and
citric fruits.

BERKSHIRE

✉ 12 Rail Road Street South,
Deerfield, MA 01373
🖰 www.berkshirebrewingcompany.
com

With the help of friends and
family, Gary Bogoff and
Chris Lalli transformed an
old cigar factory into what
has become the local

brewery for western
Massachusetts. Production
began at the Berkshire
Brewing Company in 1994;
despite three expansions and
increased output, Bogoff and
Lalli have managed to
maintain their commitment
to the freshness of their
unfiltered, unpasteurized
beers. The company handles
almost all distribution, with
most of its beer being sold on
draft, and much of the rest in
64-ounce growlers (jugs).

◗ **DRAYMAN'S PORTER** 6.2% ABV ●
Porter ● A big, chocolatey,
roasty nose with hints of
coffee promises freshness;
rich-tasting, with a
moderately dry finish.

◗ **IMPERIAL STOUT** 8.5% ABV ●
Imperial stout ● Smells like
double-chocolate, chocolate-
chip cookies right out of the
oven and just a little burned,
followed by molasses,
caramel, and hints of smoke.

BLUE POINT

✉ 161 River Avenue,
Patchogue, NY 11772
🖰 www.bluepointbrewing.com

Long Island's Blue Point
Brewing grew into a regional
brewer less than eight years
after beer sales began in
1998. Pete Cotter
and Mark Burford
built their brewery
in a former ice
factory using
equipment
acquired from
defunct breweries,
much of it from
Maryland's Wild
Goose Brewery.
Cotter and Burford
removed the brick
surround of the Peter
Austin-system brew-
kettle by hand, then
reassembled it around the
kettle in their own premises.
  Although its flagship beer
is a lager (Toasted Lager),
Blue Point also produces a
range of traditionally made
ales. Its draft beer, easily
found on tap all over Long
Island and into New York

City, is brewed in Patchogue;
bottled-beer production is
contracted out.

◗ **TOASTED LAGER** 5.3% ABV ●
Vienna lager ● "Toasted" refers
to the fact that the brewing
kettle is direct-fired, but it
also describes the final
toasty-nutty impression of
this balanced, smooth, easy-
drinking lager.

BROOKLYN

✉ 1 Brewers Row, 79 North 11th
St., Brooklyn, NY 11211
🖰 www.brooklynbrewery.com

Brooklyn was once home to
48 breweries, but they had
all closed by the time
homebrewer Steve Hindy, a
former news correspondent,
and Tom Potter, his banker
neighbor, set up the
Brooklyn Brewery in 1987.
Matt Brewing in Utica
(*see* Saranac, *p.216*) brewed
their first beer under
contract and still produces
the bulk of it. In 1996, the
duo opened their own
brewing premises, which
became the city's first
commercial building to
derive 100 percent of its
electricity from wind-power.
Now a neighborhood fixture,
the brewery is a Friday
night community-
gathering spot
where locals bring
their families for
happy hour. As
well as brewing
specialty drafts in
Brooklyn, the
brewery recently
introduced a line
of Belgian-inspired,
bottle-conditioned
ales sold in corked
750 ml bottles.
Brewmaster Garrett
Oliver's book, *The
Brewmaster's Table*, has
become a bible for those
promoting the role of beer
at the dining table.

BROOKLYN
BROWN

◗ **BROWN** 5.6% ABV ● **Brown ale**
Caramel, chocolate,
and perhaps plum; a hint
of smoke and a coffee-
dry finish.

BLACK CHOCOLATE STOUT

10.6% ABV • Imperial stout
A pitch-black, viscous mixture of dark fruits, port, and, of course, chocolate.

BROOKLYNER WEISSE 5.1% ABV
• Hefeweizen • Effervescent and fruity (mostly banana), with spicy cloves. Refreshing.

CLIPPER CITY

✉ 4615 Hollins Ferry Road, Suite B, Baltimore, MD 21227
🖥 www.clippercitybeer.com

In 1989, Hugh Sisson opened Baltimore's first brewpub, Sisson's, after successfully lobbying the Maryland legislature to make brewpubs legal. He sold Sisson's in 1995 to start Clipper City. Operating as a stand-alone brewery, Clipper City began with the Heavy Seas and Chesapeake brands. In 1998, it acquired Maryland craft brewery Oxford Brewing and its popular Oxford Raspberry Wheat Beer, and also produces beer under contract for other breweries.

HEAVY SEAS SMALL CRAFT

WARNING 7.5% ABV • Strong lager
Packing a considerable punch for a pale beer, Heavy Seas' malt sweetness is quickly overtaken by a sturdy bitterness.

HEAVY SEAS LOOSE CANNON

7.3% ABV • India pale ale
A hops cocktail; this is a perfectly composed beer.

CLIPPER CITY HEAVY SEAS
SMALL CRAFT WARNING

Reminiscent of toasted bread that has been slathered in orange marmalade.

DOGFISH HEAD

✉ 6 Cannery Village Center, Milton, DE 19968
🖥 www.dogfish.com

Founder Sam Calagione has been one of the most influential figures in the US craft-brewing movement since starting the Dogfish Head Brewing and Eats brewpub in Rehoboth Beach in 1995. Dogfish Head has since built a packaging brewery, then a bigger one, then expanded that.

The brewery is true to its motto: "Off-centered ales for off-centered people." It brews beers with unusual components or "extreme" amounts of ingredients, creates novel brewing devices, such as the "organoleptic hop transducer module" (which adds hop flavor to its beer as it is dispensed), and offers a Dogfish 360-Degree Experience weekend at the brewery for those who want to immerse themselves completely in the world of Dogfish beers.

MIDAS TOUCH 9.0% ABV •
Historic beer • Brewed to a recipe based on pottery from King Midas's tomb. The ingredients—white Muscat grapes, honey, and saffron—all show themselves; sweet, but not excessively so; hints of wine.

90 MINUTE IMPERIAL IPA

9.0% ABV • India pale ale
Hopped continuously for 90 minutes. Brimming with hop flavor and quite bitter.

WORLD WIDE STOUT 18% ABV •
Imperial stout • Rightfully compared to port; dark fruits and ripe berries mingle with a solid dose of alcohol; chocolate, roasted malt, even tar. A warming stout.

FLYING FISH

✉ 1940 Olney Avenue, Cherry Hill, NJ 08003
🖥 www.flyingfish.com

Flying Fish founder Gene Muller launched his brewing company on the Internet. Muller's idea was not only to generate publicity, but also to let visitors to his website see how a craft brewery is put together and give them a chance to get involved. By the time the first beers went on sale in 1996, his cyber-fans had helped to name beers and design T-shirts and labels; asked to be taste-testers; and applied for jobs at the brewery.

FLYING FISH
ESB

DUBBEL 7.3% ABV •
Double • Chocolate mingled with dark fruit, delivered with a pleasant whiff of alcohol; finish is on the sweet side of dry.

ESB 5.5% ABV • Extra
special bitter • Fruity nuttiness blended with caramel; medium-dry finish.

D. L. GEARY

✉ 38 Evergreen Drive, Portland, ME 04103
🖥 www.gearybrewing.com

Before founding D. L. Geary Brewing in Portland in 1986, David Geary worked in a number of small commercial breweries from the south coast of England to the Highlands of Scotland in order to research and learn the brewing craft. One of these was Scotland's Traquair House brewery, whose founder, Peter Maxwell Stuart, was Geary's mentor.

D. L. Geary was the 13th microbrewery to open in the US. Geary brought in English brewing consultant Alan Pugsley to set up the brewery. For many years, the only products produced year-round were the flagship Pale Ale and the rich

AMERICA'S MOST FAMOUS

Since artist John Sloan immortalized McSorley's Old Ales House (15 East Seventh Street) with a series of paintings between 1912 and 1930, this New York City saloon has become America's most famous. Founded in 1854 by John McSorley as The Old House at Home, it has changed little since Sloan's time and is rich in history. Prohibition was openly flaunted here; Woody Guthrie once chatted with regulars; and it took a lawsuit to end the bar's century-old policy against serving women. The line to get inside can be ridiculously long on weekends; a weekday afternoon visit is more pleasant.

McSorley's can claim the accolade of being New York City's oldest continuously operated drinking establishment.

London Porter, a modest 4.5% and 4.2% ABV.

■ HAMPSHIRE SPECIAL ALE
7.0% ABV ● Strong ale ● No longer brewed "only when the weather sucks." Complex balance of slightly burned caramel, light fruits, and warming alcohol; traditional bitter finish.

■ PALE ALE 4.5% ABV ● Pale ale
A showcase for the Ringwood yeast. Fruity with underlying caramel, and slick over the tongue.

HARPOON

✉ 306 Northern Avenue, Boston, MA 02210
🖰 www.harpoonbrewery.com

The Harpoon brewery was founded on Boston's waterfront in 1987 as the Mass Bay Brewing Company. It later reinvented itself as Harpoon, acquired the defunct Catamount Brewery in Windsor, Vermont, and built a glistening new brewhouse at its original location.

Harpoon's five beer festivals—three in Boston each year and two at its Windsor brewery—are all huge events that draw thousands of beer-

HARPOON
UFO
HEFEWEIZEN

drinkers. The brewery also recently began a popular 100 Barrel Series, in which a Harpoon brewer picks a style, writes a recipe, and brews a single batch of 100 barrels for a one-off sale.

■ UFO HEFEWEIZEN 5.0% ABV ●
US Hefeweizen ● Unfiltered and cloudy; straightforward and refreshing; meant to be served with a slice of lemon.

■ MUNICH DARK 5.5% ABV ●
Dunkel ● Rich, almost sweet, with hints of toast, then chocolate; restrained hops; long, smooth finish.

HIGH FALLS

✉ 445 St. Paul Street, Rochester, NY 14605
🖰 www.highfalls.com

Genesee Brewing, founded in Rochester, New York, in 1878, renamed itself High Falls in 2000. It continues to produce beers under the Genesee name, as well as the J. W. Dundee brand and several others. The brewery also keeps busy with contract-brewing, operating near its capacity of 3.5 million barrels per year.

■ GENESEE CREAM ALE 4.9% ABV ●
Cream ale ● Pale in color; faintly sweet with cooked-corn flavors, but smooth and easy-drinking.

IRON HILL

✉ Multiple locations
🖰 www.ironhillbrewery.com

Iron Hill opened its first brewery-restaurant in Newark, Delaware, in 1996. It now has six such establishments, and plans to open at least five more in the Mid-Atlantic states. The balance between dining-room and bar varies from location to location, but the focus on beer never wavers. Brewing across a wide range of styles, some rather esoteric, Iron Hill's brewers have been medal-winners at the Great American Beer Festival for 10 years in succession.

■ PIG IRON PORTER 5.4% ABV ●
Porter ● Roasty, rich, and complex; coffee blended with prunes and dark cherries.

LION

✉ 700 North Pennsylvania Avenue, Wilkes-Barre, PA 18705
🖰 www.lionbrewery.com

With a brewing tradition dating back to 1857, the Lion Brewery survived

WHERE BEER IS THE STAR

In few other establishments in the world can a beer drinker sit down and sample as many of the world's great beers as in an American "multi-tap." Most often these bar-pub-restaurants offer scores of draft choices and even more beers by the bottle.

While today you could fill a directory with multi-taps, little more than 20 years ago they simply did not exist. Then the multi-tap pioneers began to emerge everywhere, from the Horse Brass Pub (*see p.238*) in Portland, Oregon, to the Great Lost Bear in Portland, Maine. These watering holes give beer-drinkers a chance to taste what is coming out of the world's most heralded brewing centers and to find out what is new in the US. Never has education from a glass been so easy! Notable Northeast multi-taps include the Brickskeller in Washington, DC, with an amazing bottle menu; Clark's Ale House (Syracuse, NY), with a perfect pub setting, a great roast-beef sandwich, and well-kept beer; and the

At one count Manhattan's popular d.b.a. bar was offering more than 125 beers, 50 tequilas, and 130 single malt Scotch whiskies.

Stoudt's from Pennsylvania is just one of a huge range of beers offered at Max's, a Baltimore institution.

aforementioned Great Lost Bear, devoted to Maine beer and other brews of the region. In Massachusetts, Sunset Grill in Allston, one of the original multi-taps, is known for its generous food portions; Moan and Dove in Amherst is smallish, but has an outstanding mix of world favorites and regional beer. The well-kept beer at d.b.a. in Manhattan (also in New Orleans) is augmented by a massive spirits menu, and Spuyten Duyvil in Brooklyn can surprise even beer aficionados with its selection. Max's On Broadway has the widest selection in Baltimore's pub-friendly Fells Point area (consider also the nearby Wharf Rat), while Monk's Cafe in Philadelphia is where all brewers of Belgian-inspired beer want their efforts showcased.

against the odds while a host of other regional breweries in northeast Pennsylvania went to the wall. One of these was the nearby Stegmaier Brewery, whose portfolio of beers Lion purchased in 1974 when Stegmaier closed its doors. Lion managed to keep brewing at close to capacity by contract-brewing, producing nonbeer drinks, and adding new beer brands. More recently it has upgraded its brewhouse and released a new line of popularly priced Stegmaier seasonal beers.

STEGMAIER PORTER 5.5% ABV • Porter • Mildly roasty, medium body, with chocolate and dark fruits.

STEGMAIER BREWHOUSE BOCK 6.2% ABV • Bock • Part of the new Stegmaier line. Rich, moderately bready; smooth and balanced.

LONG TRAIL

✉ Junction Route 4 and 100A, Box 168, Bridgewater Corners, VT 05035
🖥 www.longtrail.com

Specializing in German-style ales, Long Trail was founded in 1989 in the basement of the Bridgewater Woollen Mill. It soon developed into a dominant regional brand, selling more draft beer than any brewery in Vermont. In 1995, Long Trail moved into its new brewery, which dominates the tiny town of Bridgewater Corners in the Green Mountains. Popular in winter with off-piste skiers, it is best to visit during summer, so that you can sample the Long Trail brews on the streamside patio.

LONG TRAIL ALE 5.0% ABV • Altbier • Deep copper; smooth malt aromas and hop spiciness, but without the incessant hop bitterness of the German alts.

MAGIC HAT

✉ 5 Bartlett Bay Road, Burlington, VT 05403
🖥 www.magichat.net

MAGIC HAT #9

Favoring "non-style" beers with esoteric names and unique packaging, Magic Hat seems to be the brewing equivalent of the mold-breaking ice-cream makers Ben & Jerry's (another of Vermont's success stories). Everything associated with the brewery reminds drinkers that Magic Hat aims to be "alternative"—and that includes a brewery tour akin to stepping into a cartoon!

#9 4.6% ABV • Pale ale Straightforward flagship beer; apricot-infused, with other subtle stone-fruit flavors; dry finish.

HEART OF DARKNESS STOUT 5.3% ABV • Sweet stout • Smoky, roasty, thick, and a tad oily; chocolate aftertaste.

OLD DOMINION

✉ 44633 Guilford Drive, Ashburn, VA 20147
🖥 www.olddominion.com

Jerry Bailey, a former government employee, founded Old Dominion Brewing in 1989. He began by producing German-inspired beers before developing a strong range of brands across all styles. Old Dominion also makes several award-winning contract beers for other companies. The brewery was recently sold to Coastal Brewing, a joint venture of Fordham Brewing and Anheuser-Busch. Fordham operates the Rams Head taverns in Maryland as well as its own brewery.

TUPPERS' HOP POCKET 6.0% ABV • Pale ale • Hop pockets are sacks for transporting hops. Flowery nose; crisp malt middle; long, spicy-citrus bitter finish.

OMMEGANG

✉ 656 County Highway 33, Cooperstown, NY 13326
🖥 www.ommegang.com

Originally a partnership between Belgian and American companies, Ommegang was designed to resemble a Belgian farmhouse brewery, and has brewed in that spirit since opening in 1997. In tribute to the quality of its output, brewmaster Randy Thiel became the first American brewer "knighted" by the Belgian brewers' organization Knights of the Mashing Fork.

Duvel Moortgat took full control of operations in 2003, even brewing some of Ommegang's beer at its Belgian brewery while Ommegang expanded production capacity.

HENNEPIN 7.7% ABV • Saison Spicy-peppery throughout, playing against various fleshy fruit flavors.

OMMEGANG 8.5% ABV • Abbey ale • The flagship beer, Ommegang is produced in the spirit of a Christmas beer; rich and chocolatey, with underlying licorice and festive-season spices.

THREE PHILOSOPHERS 9.8% ABV • Belgian strong ale • A dark, strong beer blended with Lindemans Kriek (a cherry lambic); smooth one moment, tart the next; dry, dark fruits, then ripe, red fruits.

OMMEGANG HENNEPIN

OTTER CREEK

✉ 793 Exchange Street,
Middlebury, VT 05753
🖥 www.wolavers.com

The Otter Creek brewery
was founded by Lawrence
Miller in 1991. The Wolaver
family bought the business in
2002 to brew its own line of
nationally distributed
organic beers, which were
previously made under
contract at several sites.
As well as Wolaver beers,
the brewery continues to
produce the German-style
Otter Creek brands. The
recent introduction of
"World Tour" beers allows
the brewery to sell a wider
range of styles.

■ OTTER CREEK COPPER ALE
5.4% ABV ● Altbier ● Rich,
complex, malty nose and
palate, giving way to a well-
balanced, smooth finish.

■ WOLAVER'S OATMEAL STOUT
5.9% ABV ● Oatmeal stout
Creamy, chocolate nose;
roasty and grainy in the
mouth; slightly creamy finish.

PENN

✉ 800 Vinial Street,
Pittsburgh, PA 15212
🖥 www.pennbrew.com

The Pennsylvania Brewing
Company's founder, Tom
Pastorius, can trace his roots
back to Franz Daniel
Pastorius, who led the first
German settlers to America.
His company has stuck to
traditional German beer

Penn occupies an older brewery's
buildings in a part of Pittsburgh
once known as "Deutschtown."

since 1986, when it opened
in the former Eberhardt and
Ober Brewery (cooling caves
remain in the neighboring
hillside). Its on-site restaurant
has a separate beer hall, beer
garden, and *rathskeller*.

■ WEIZEN 5.0% ABV ● Hefeweizen
Bavarian all the way—
bubble-gum, banana, and
fruit, enlivened by cloves
and almost peppery spices.

SAMUEL ADAMS

✉ 30 Germania Street,
Boston, MA 02130
🖥 www.samadams.com

Founded in 1985 by Jim
Koch, who comes from a
family of brewers, the
Boston Beer Co. is best
known for Samuel Adams
Boston Lager, although its
brewers manage to explore
or invent new styles each
year. The company sells
more beer than the next
three largest American craft
breweries put together.

Initially, Koch had his
beer made under contract
at old-line breweries with
excess capacity. Today, the
company produces much of
its own beer at its breweries
in Boston and Cincinnati.
The Boston operation is
housed in the old Haffenreffer
brewery building, where beer
buffs can take the popular
brewery tour or visit the
Boston Beer Museum,

which gives an insight into
the city's brewing history.

■ BOSTON LAGER 4.9% ABV ●
Vienna lager ● Complex nose
of pine and flowers; full-
bodied; caramel in the middle
and a satisfyingly dry finish.

■ BLACK LAGER 4.9% ABV ●
Schwarzbier ● Roasted but
smooth, with a coffee
bitterness that lingers.

■ UTOPIAS 25.6% ABV ● Strong ale
The world's strongest beer
just keeps getting stronger!
A wish-list of warming
(alcohol) flavors; well-
integrated, although not
very beer-like.

SARANAC

✉ 811 Edward Street,
Utica, NY 13502
🖥 www.saranac.com

The producer of Saranac
beers, Matt Brewing, began
as the West End Brewing
Company in 1888. By the
early 1990s, it was an old-
line brewery in decline.
The company decided to put
familiar brands such as Utica
Club in the background to
focus on its Saranac line of
craft beers, starting with
Traditional Lager. This bold
step paid off. With its
Saranac beers, contract-
brewing, and on-going

THE ETERNAL TAP

Imagine walking into a
brewery and pulling yourself
a free glass of beer any time
(during business hours).
That's the Straub Brewery's
Eternal Tap. Located in
Pennsylvania's Allegheny
Mountains (303 Sorg Street,
St. Mary's) since 1872,
Straub is the smallest of the
old-style breweries left in the
US, producing just two lager
beers and selling 60 percent
of its production in the town
where it is brewed. They do
appreciate it if you rinse out
your glass when you are
done at the tap!

production of "family beers" such as Utica Club, Matt is now one of the largest craft breweries in the US.

⬛ **SARANAC BLACK & TAN** 5.3% ABV • Blend • A blend of Irish stout and German lager. Imagine chocolate and roast beef with a dash of caramel.

⬛ **SARANAC PALE ALE** 5.5% ABV • Pale ale • Fruity yeastiness complemented by crisp, citrussy hops; sneakily bitter.

SHIPYARD

✉ 86 Newbury State, Portland, ME 04101

🍺 www.shipyard.com

Co-founder and brewer Alan Pugsley set up numerous breweries around the world before he and Fred Forsley became partners at Shipyard Brewing in 1994. The following year, they sold a stake in the business to Miller Brewing, gaining a national presence and receiving a quick lesson in larger-scale production before buying back full control of the operation three years later. Although Shipyard's beers are widely available throughout the US, it mostly focuses on selling its products in New England and Florida. The Shipyard brand

was born in nearby Kennebuck at Federal Jack's Brew Pub, which still brews on site. Shipyard also owns the Sea Dog brand.

⬛ **EXPORT ALE** 5.1% ABV • Golden ale Shipyard's flagship; sweet honey and fruits at first; light and crisp.

⬛ **OLD THUMPER** 5.9% ABV • Extra special bitter • At its best on cask, Old Thumper is brewed under license from Ringwood in the UK (*see p.163*). Fruity, with balanced bitterness.

SMUTTYNOSE

✉ 225 Heritage Avenue, Portsmouth, NH 03801

🍺 www.smuttynose.com

Peter Egelston was already busy with the Portsmouth and Northampton brewpubs when he bought a defunct brewery at auction. Thus Smuttynose Brewing was born in 1994, and it has since grown into a regional brewery with a range of noteworthy ales and lagers. In 1998, Smuttynose launched its Big Beer Series

of specialty beers released seasonally in very limited quantities. Smuttynose beers are brewed with a sensibility that has twice earned them the award of "Best American Beer" at the Great British Beer Festival.

SMUTTYNOSE SHOAL'S PALE ALE

⬛ **SHOAL'S PALE ALE** 5.0% ABV • Pale ale First produced at the Portsmouth pub. The fruity cookie palate gives way to a crisp American hop finish.

⬛ **ROBUST PORTER** 5.7% ABV • Porter • Rich dark fruits, some chocolate; a roasty, satisfying bitterness through to the finish.

SOUTHAMPTON

✉ 40 Bowden Square, Southampton, NY 11968

🍺 www.publick.com

Southampton Publick House is first and foremost a brewery-restaurant, giving brewmaster Phil Markowski the chance to experiment across a wide range of styles. Many of his single-batch beers, some bottled and for sale only at the brewery, have achieved cult status. Southampton also distributes

A fourth-generation family firm, Matt Brewing, producer of Saranac beers, was founded by an ambitious young German immigrant in 1888.

beer produced under contract at other breweries.

📖 **SAISON** 6.5% ABV • Saison
Fruity, tart, earthy, and refreshing. A ringing endorsement for Markowski's book *Farmhouse Ales*.

📖 **SECRET ALE** 5.1% ABV • Altbier
Slightly sweet caramel at first; firmly bitter in the middle through to the finish.

📖 **IMPERIAL PORTER** 7.2% ABV •
Baltic porter • Intoxicating, rich aromas of dark fruit and chocolate, then coffee; pleasantly bitter finish.

STOUDT'S BREWING CO.

✉ 2800 North Reading Road, Route 272, Adamstown, PA 19501
🖳 www.stoudtsbeer.com

Pennsylvania's first micro-brewery, Stoudt's was founded by Carol and Ed Stoudt in 1987. Although they established one of the first outstanding local beer festivals in the US and have won scores of brewing medals, they are perhaps best known as advocates of the importance of brewing tradition. Carol's first beers were German-influenced, but she was also one of the first in the country to explore Belgian brewing styles.

📖 **PILS** 4.8% ABV • Pilsner
Flowery up front, spicy in the middle, and long and dry at the finish.

📖 **FAT DOG STOUT** 9.0% ABV •
Imperial stout • Rich maltiness and assertive hoppiness of an Imperial stout; luscious,

STOUDT'S FAT DOG STOUT

with bittersweet coffee notes, hints of smoke, prunes, and molasses at the finish.

TRÖEGS

✉ 800 Paxton Street, Harrisburg, PA 17104
🖳 www.troegs.com

Brothers John and Chris Trogner founded Tröegs Brewery in 1997, giving it their family nickname. Its esoteric beers, such as Mad Elf (brewed with cherries and a Belgian yeast) and Nugget Nectar, have earned attention from many beer-trading enthusiasts, but it is local demand for its more conventional brews, such as the flagship Hopback Amber Ale, that has fueled Tröegs' continuing expansion.

📖 **HOPBACK AMBER ALE** 5.6% ABV
• Amber ale • Caramel-sweet fruit character with floral-spicy hops.

📖 **NUGGET NECTAR** 7.5% ABV •
India pale ale • Essentially an amped-up version of Hopback Amber Ale; an American hop experience.

VICTORY

✉ 420 Acorn Lane, Downingtown, PA 19335
🖳 www.victorybeer.com

Victory Brewing's restaurant and brewery are located in an old bakery-products factory that takes a map to find. After gaining experience at other breweries, childhood friends Bill Covaleski and Ron Barchet opened Victory in 1996, leaning on German training and brewing across a wide range of styles. During a recent expansion, Victory installed a modern brewhouse designed to produce almost any style in a traditional manner. Its restaurant-bar remains the best place to sample its beers, many of which are sold only on draft, such as Victory's varietal pilsners.

VICTORY PRIMA PILS

📖 **HOPDEVIL** 6.5% ABV • India pale ale • Spicy hops announce this beer's intentions, with hop flavor and bitterness throughout, with a solid malt backbone.

📖 **PRIMA PILS** 5.3% ABV • Pilsner
Fresh flowery nose; cookielike palate and solidly bitter-rough finish.

📖 **GOLDEN MONKEY** 9.5% ABV •
Triple • Spicy, initial hints of banana followed by light pepper. Gently alcoholic, with some sweetness and a dryish finish.

YUENGLING

✉ Fifth and Mahantongo Streets, Pottsville, PA 17901
🖳 www.yuengling.com

This is the oldest brewery in the US. David G. Yuengling built the Eagle Brewery in 1829, and rebuilt it after a fire in 1831. It survived as a struggling regional brewery into the 1980s, when Yuengling managed to successfully reposition itself outside the mainstream. Growth has been constant since the brewery introduced its Traditional Lager in 1987. Yuengling built a second brewery near the original and also bought a former Stroh brewery in Florida. All three now produce more than half a million barrels annually.

📖 **TRADITIONAL LAGER** 4.9% ABV •
American lager • Slightly sweet and floral, with hints of caramel and a crisp underlying bitterness.

South

N & S Carolina • Georgia • Alabama • Florida • Louisiana • Mississippi • Texas

Although the region lags behind the rest of the nation in embracing the craft-beer movement, the growth of microbreweries and the work of beer activists have nevertheless created the widest range of locally produced beers ever available south of the Mason–Dixon line.

The South has long been home to some of the country's most active homebrewers, but consumers have been slow to mirror their enthusiasm. Even so, regional enthusiasts recently played a leading role in getting alcohol limits for beer raised above 6% ABV in Georgia and North and South Carolina, and similar campaigns are planned in Alabama. Curious alcohol laws still permeate the region. Some states do not permit beer to be bought at the brewery door; draft beer is illegal in many Mississippi counties; and in Oklahoma, beer stronger than 4% ABV (called "three-two" beer because it is 3.2 by weight) cannot be sold "to go." Texas remains a patchwork of "wet" and "dry" townships; it can even be legal to sell beer on one side of the street and not the other. Against this backdrop, many breweries stuck with light-colored, light-flavored beers they knew Southerners would buy. Only over time have breweries like the smallish Live Oak found a market. The Austin brewery brews a true-to-tradition Czech-style pilsner, which the Ginger Man chain of pubs serves on tap. Similarly, the Summits Wayside Taverns near Atlanta offer local Sweetwater beers, and pub-restaurants in North Carolina's Raleigh-Durham area sell regional beers from Highland Brewing. The gap between the beer tastes of the South and the rest of the US is closing.

The bottling line at Abita. The company is one of the oldest craft breweries in the US, although the South is not a traditional brewing heartland.

ABITA

✉ P.O. Box 1510,
Abita Springs, LA 70420
🖱 www.abita.com

Across the US, drinkers reach for Abita beers when they celebrate Mardi Gras, eat Cajun food, or dance to zydeco music. Since opening at Abita Springs on the north side of Lake Pontchartrain in 1986, Abita Brewing has made its name synonymous with Louisiana and New Orleans. While the brewery sells 60 percent of its beer in New Orleans, it also ships beer to more than 30 states.

Having relocated out of town, Abita now operates a brewpub-restaurant on its original brewery site (72011 Holly Street). Here you can sample the full range of beers, as well as a few special seasonal brews.

🍶 **TURBODOG** 6.1% ABV • **Brown ale** • Rich; long on toffee and chocolate; finishes with a coffeelike bitterness.

🍶 **PURPLE HAZE** 4.8% ABV • **Fruit ale** • A wheat beer infused with raspberry purée. Sweet, but light enough to refresh even in stifling Louisiana humidity.

ATLANTA

✉ 2323 Defoor Hills Road, NW
Atlanta, GA 30318
🖱 www.atlantabrewing.com

In 1993, Greg Kelly, a former Guinness employee, set up Atlanta Brewing in an old red-brick printing works, using brewing equipment brought over from Ireland. Although it was a popular gathering spot in Midtown, Atlanta Brewing had to move to make way for a new highway, settling into bigger quarters with expanded brewing capacity, fuelling plans to distribute beer throughout the South. Many travelers

**ABITA
PURPLE HAZE**

Atlanta's Red Brick Summer Brew is an unfiltered hefeweizen made using German wheat.

know the brewery's beers because of its Red Brick Tavern in Atlanta's airport.

🍶 **RED BRICK ALE** 6.5% ABV • **Brown ale** • The flagship beer—and the brewery's strongest. Caramel and toffee up front, followed by lesser notes of chocolate and coffee.

BOSCOS

✉ Multiple locations
🖱 www.boscosbeer.com

Billed as "The Restaurant for Beer Lovers," the Boscos chain of brewery-restaurants is a regional trend-setter, introducing many drinkers in the mid-South to Old World brewing traditions. Founding partner and brewer Chuck Skypeck uses hot stones from the restaurant's wood-fired ovens to heat the brewkettle for his Famous Flaming Stone Beer, which is brewed in the manner of German stein beers. Boscos pubs also feature English-inspired cask-conditioned ales, and customers are invited to participate as cellarmen. Boscos, first opened in 1992, operates brewpubs in Memphis, Nashville, and

Little Rock. The company built a stand-alone brewery in Memphis to produce beers for nonbrewing Boscos franchises.

FAMOUS FLAMING STONE BEER
4.8% ABV • Steinbeer • Toffee, caramel, and nutty character throughout, with a smoky, sour, and dry finish.

CAROLINA

✉ 110 Barley Park Lane, Mooresville, NC 28115
⌂ www.carolinablonde.com

The Carolina Beer & Beverage Co. opened in 1997, and today it is North Carolina's only regional brewery. Fuelled by sales of its mainstream beers, Carolina Blonde and Carolina Light, the brewery bought well-known brands from Cottonwood Brewery in 2000, including Low Down Brown, in order to expand its consumer base. Carolina also launched a High Cotton–High Gravity series after North Carolina lifted its alcoholic-strength limit on beer.

CAROLINA BLONDE 5.0% ABV •
Golden ale • Pale gold in color; sweet and grainy; at its best when fresh.

DIXIE

✉ 2401 Tulane Avenue, New Orleans, LA 70119

Dixie Brewing began its centennial year, 2007, with a fight for survival, although it has faced similar struggles in the past. Back in 1975, the brewery had to give away 60,000 six-packs of beer after a bad batch went on sale, hoping to prove to consumers that the blunder was a fluke. Even after the closure of its New Orleans competitors, Falstaff and Jackson (Jax beer), Dixie still slipped into bankruptcy

during the 1980s. In the end, it was the magic of its Blackened Voodoo dark lager that helped the brewery to get back on its feet.

The most recent calamity to befall Dixie occurred in 2005, when Hurricane Katrina flooded the old red-brick brewery, which was then looted. A year later, its owners secured financing to install a new state-of-the-art brewery and arranged for Dixie beer to be brewed elsewhere under contract. First opened in 1907, the old brewery still aged some of its beer in 1912-vintage Cyprus wood tanks, although Dixie phased out their wooden fermenters in 1987.

BLACKENED VOODOO
5.0% ABV • Schwarzbier
This dark lager was briefly banned in Texas because of its voodoo references. Chocolate and toffee notes; smooth and light-bodied for Southern drinking.

CAROLINA BLONDE

HIGHLAND

✉ 12 Old Charlotte Highway, Asheville, NC 28802
⌂ www.highlandbrewing.com

Highland Brewing started up in the basement of Barley's Tap Room, Asheville, in 1994, using adapted dairy equipment to lay the cornerstone for a vibrant craftbrewing scene in this fast-growing town in the Blue Ridge Mountains. After struggling to keep up with demand, the brewery moved from its downtown location to its current site at the end of 2006. Barley's itself (also a pizzeria) remains an excellent spot to sample Highland and other Asheville-brewed beers.

GAELIC ALE 5.8% ABV • Amber ale • Its caramel character gives a nod toward Scotland, but the resiny hop finish is American.

PETE'S

✉ 14800 San Pedro Avenue, San Antonio, TX 78232
⌂ www.petes.com

Pete Slosberg, founder of Pete's Brewing, was one of microbrewing's most visible celebrities in the early days of the movement. Pete's, which produced its beers under contract at various breweries, briefly enjoyed a position as the nation's second-largest craftbrewing company before declining precipitously. San Antonio-based Gambrinus now owns the brand, which is still brewed under contract.

WICKED ALE 5.3% ABV • Brown ale • This was the defining American brown ale when it was brewed to Slosberg's original homebrew recipe. It sadly lost its bite when the hopping rate was halved.

REAL ALE

✉ 231 San Saba Court, Blanco, TX 78606
⌂ www.realalebrewing.com

Like the legendary Belgian brewer Pierre Celis (see p.230), who located his Celis brewery in nearby Austin because of the quality of the water, the founders of Real Ale Brewing set up in the tiny Hill Country town of Blanco in 1996 so that they could brew with water from the Blanco River. Having outgrown their basement brewery on the main square,

REAL ALE
FULL MOON PALE RYE

Real Ale Brewing Company
Blanco, Texas

Full Moon Pale Rye Ale
A distinctive pale ale with a touch of rye malt
Brewed and Bottled by Real Ale Brewing Co. Blanco, TX
12 FLUID OZ. (355 ml)   5.6% ALC.BY VOL.

CHOC: AN INDIGENOUS AMERICAN BEER

In the early 1900s, Indians from the Choctaw Nation taught many Italian immigrants, including Pete Prichard (born Pietro Peigari), how to make native beer. Prichard sold his illegal, homebrewed Choc beer when he opened Pete's Place in Krebs, Oklahoma, in 1925. This eventually led to his arrest in 1932, but Choc soon returned to the menu at Pete's, and he continued to flaunt state law until a local newspaper exposed his brewing activities in 1981. Production resumed on a legal basis in 1995 when Pete's, run by Pete's grandson Joe, became a licensed brewpub. The wheat-based Choc beer is now so popular that Pete's also distributes it in cans.

they recently moved into a larger facility to the north of the town.

■ FULL MOON PALE RYE 5.6% ABV • Pale ale • Distinct rye character, balanced by fruitiness in the middle and a lively citrus-hop finish.

■ SISYPHUS 11.0% ABV • Barley wine • A rich, mahogany-colored beer that varies in strength with every vintage. Complex and viscous, it improves with age.

SAINT ARNOLD

✉ 2522 Fairway Park Drive, Houston, TX 77092
🖑 www.saintarnold.com

Brock Wagner and Kevin Bartol, two refugees from the world of investment banking, established Saint Arnold Brewing in 1994. Shortly afterward, their first brew-kettle blew up and the man assembling their bottling line died. To bring better luck, they hung a picture of the patron saint of beer, Austrian-born St. Arnold, who gave the brewery its name.

With its luck changed, Wagner—now the majority owner—has seen Saint Arnold become the oldest surviving and largest craft brewery in Texas. Although based in an industrial park, Saint Arnold has its own loyal community of beer-drinkers. All its fermenters are

labeled with the names of saints, while other pieces of brewing equipment are named after friends of the brewery who donated money for their purchase. The brewery also trades beer and beer-gear for recycled six-packs.

■ AMBER 5.5% ABV • Amber ale • A beer to find locally on cask. Soft fruit and biscuit malt is balanced by bracing citrussy American hops.

■ ELISSA IPA
6.6% ABV • India pale ale Delightfully hoppy throughout; as floral as it is bitter, big, and juicy.

■ CHRISTMAS ALE
7.0% ABV • Strong ale Seasonal beers are Saint Arnold's bestsellers. Their first festive brew hints at English Christmas cake.

SHINER
HEFEWEIZEN

SHINER

✉ 603 Brewery Street, Shiner, TX 77984
🖑 www.shiner.com

The Spoetzl Brewery looked in 1990 to be another regional brewery that might shut down, with annual sales at just 36,000. Then Texas, and eventually much of the US, discovered Shiner Bock. Replacing Lone Star and Pearl—both of

which closed their breweries—it became the foremost Texas beer, with sales rising nearly tenfold.

The brewery traces its roots back to the Shiner Brewing Association, founded in 1909 and catering to residents of German ancestry. Some locals still talk about the dark Bavarian-style beer that Spoetzl made into the 1960s, and recently Shiner has added to its line of German-influenced beers. Shiner launched Bocktoberfest in 1994 to celebrate reaching sales of one million cases of beer, and it has grown into one of the largest one-day music festivals in Texas.

■ SHINER BOCK 4.4% ABV • Dark lager • A dark lager, rather than a true German bock. Hints of caramel sweetness, and low on hops.

■ HEFEWEIZEN 5.3% ABV • Hefeweizen • Cloudy; brewed in the Bavarian style, but with the addition of a little honey.

SWEETWATER
420 EXTRA
PALE ALE

SWEETWATER

✉ 195 Ottley Drive, Atlanta, GA 30324
🖑 www.sweetwaterbrew.com

Sweetwater Brewing has emerged as the dominant regional craft brewery in Georgia and Florida, with high demand fueling growth of more than 30 percent per year. Even after 10 years of selling beer, Sweetwater still successfully presents an "alternative" image. The name of its flagship beer, 420, has marijuana connotations, while the delivery trucks are painted to look tie-dyed.

■ 420 EXTRA PALE ALE 5.2% ABV • Pale ale • Its appearance lives up to its extra-pale billing; citrussy hops and honeyed malt flavors.

Midwest

Illinois • Indiana • Michigan • Minnesota • Missouri • Ohio • Wisconsin

Northern European immigrants (mostly Germans) brought with them a thirst for beer, and the skill to make it, that helped to establish the Midwest as the center of US beer production by the late 19th century. Breweries have prospered in St. Louis and Milwaukee ever since.

The US was not really a beer-drinking nation until those breweries capitalized on the popularity of German lagers, then exploited a preference for lighter-flavored beers, and finally used new technologies to grow into the first national breweries. Although two (Anheuser-Busch in St. Louis and Miller in Milwaukee) eventually triumphed and the US was left with just three dominant brewing companies, the Midwest continued to support local breweries from Dubuque, Iowa, to Evansville, Indiana, until they dropped off one by one in the 1980s and '90s. By then smaller craft brewers managed to tap

The Boulevard Brewing Company was founded in Kansas City in 1989, and is now one of the region's largest producers of specialty beers.

into the same local pride, and have themselves grown larger. The region still has many outstanding German restaurants offering German beers, as well as lagers from small American breweries—in fact, some of the best examples of traditional lagers come from the Midwest—and away from the larger cities these are often the best places to find a better range of beers.

That link to tradition hasn't inhibited Midwest brewers. For example, lagers used to represent 70 percent of Goose Island's production, but now the brewery is known for a variety of ales. "We in the Midwest bemoan the fact that we lagged behind everybody," says founder John Hall, "but the nice thing is, we got to learn from other's mistakes."

ANHEUSER-BUSCH

✉ One Busch Place,
St. Louis, MO 63119
🖰 www.anheuser-busch.com

Ever since Adolphus
Busch married the
daughter of Eberhard
Anheuser in 1861, the
Busch family has been
directly involved with
the running of
Anheuser-Busch,
the world's largest
brewing company
(based on revenues).
Almost half the beer
sold in the US is
produced by A-B's
12 regional breweries.

The company has
been an innovator in
all facets of the beer
business since it
introduced the Czech-
style Budweiser in
1876, particularly in
distribution, recently striking
deals to sell popular
imported beers. While
clinging to some traditions,
such as ageing beer on
beechwood, the company
has tested scores of new
products in recent years.
These include a pumpkin
beer, two aged with bourbon
barrel slats and vanilla, and
traditional all-malt beers.

🍺 **BUDWEISER** 5.0% ABV • US
pilsner • Sweet, grainy nose,
with green apples; a light,
balanced body, but without
distinct flavors. Budweiser is
one of the world's top 30
brands, but Bud Light (4.2%
ABV) now outsells it.

🍺 **MICHELOB** 5.0% ABV • US lager
Promoted as A-B's premium
beer since 1896, it returned
to its all-malt roots in 2007.
Spicy nose, with a light malt
middle and a dry finish.

AUGUST SCHELL

✉ 1860 Schell Road,
New Ulm, MN 56073
🖰 www.schellsbrewery.com

German-born August Schell
founded this brewery in
1860, and it has remained

in family hands to this day.
The brewery grounds,
developed in the 1880s as
vineyards, include a deer park
and ornamental gardens
decorated with statues of
gnomes; the old carriage
shop is now a museum.

Schell produces several
well-made traditional
styles under its own
name, and has brewed
many popular craft
beers under contract.
It boosted production
significantly when it
acquired the iconic
Grain Belt Premium
Brand. Its annual
February Bockfest
includes a "Bock
Hunt" in the
surrounding woods.

ANHEUSER-
BUSCH
BUDWEISER

🍺 **CARAMEL BOCK**
5.8% ABV • Bock • Rich
caramel start; rummy,
with a lingering
sweetness to the finish. Its big
brother Doppel Bock (6.8%
ABV) is available in winter.

BELL'S

✉ 8938 Krum Avenue,
Galesburg, MI 49053
🖰 www.bellsbeer.com

Larry Bell began selling his
beer in 1985, which makes
this business, formerly called
Kalamazoo Brewing, the
oldest surviving craft brewery
west of Boulder, Colorado.
Bell brewed in 18-gallon
(68-liter) soup kettles and
bottled by hand. The
brewery has expanded
several times, relocated
twice, and now operates
as Bell's Brewery in the
town of Galesburg,
just outside
Kalamazoo.
Although it sells
mostly wheat beer,
Bell's remains famous
(or infamous) for its
assertive barley-based
beers, including an
array of stouts.

Bell's runs the aptly
named Eccentric
Café (355 East
Kalamazoo Avenue,

Kalamazoo), which opened
as the brewery taproom in
1991. Each December it
hosts Eccentric Day—an
event to which Bell's fans
return annually.

🍺 **OBERON** 5.8% ABV • US wheat
beer • Zesty, with orange rind
in the aroma and spiciness
behind that, and a crisp,
tart finish. A thirst-quenching
summer refresher.

🍺 **TWO HEARTED ALE** 7.0% ABV •
India pale ale • Amplified hops,
with an initial rush of orange
and grapefruit mingling with
fresh flowers. Perfectly
balanced, it exhibits a
persistent bitterness.

🍺 **EXPEDITION STOUT** 11.5% ABV •
Imperial stout • An intense blast
of dark fruit (figs and plums)
blends with chocolate, port,
and roasted coffee. Almost
graceful, despite the obvious
alcohol and viscous body.

BOULEVARD

✉ 2501 Southwest Boulevard,
Kansas City, MO 64108
🖰 www.blvdbeer.com

Having staked out America's
heartland, Boulevard Brewing
has grown into the largest of
the new craft breweries in
the Midwest. Boulevard has
undertaken three major
expansions since it began
selling beer in 1989, most
recently building a new
brewery and packaging
facility that allowed
a near six-fold increase
in capacity.

Boulevard's core
brands, particularly the
Pale Ale and Wheat,
have fueled growth,
but head-brewer
Steven Pauwels
(recruited from
Belgium) has recently
begun to roll out a
wider range of beers,
Belgian-inspired and
otherwise. The
brewery's tours are
justifiably popular.

🍺 **UNFILTERED WHEAT**
4.5% ABV • US wheat beer
Cloudy and lightly

BOULEVARD
UNFILTERED
WHEAT

grainy, with refreshing citrus notes throughout.

BULLY PORTER 5.4% ABV • Porter
Roasted coffee aroma, with chocolate emerging on the palate; rich and slightly sweet, balanced by a subtle hop flavor and finish.

BOB'S 47 5.5% ABV • Vienna lager • A smooth and almost creamy beer. Warm toast on the nose (with honey?); sweet malt in the middle; clean and just a little nutty.

CAPITAL

✉ 7734 Terrace Avenue, Middleton, WI 53562
🖥 www.capital-brewery.com

At the heart of Capital Brewery's system are copper kettles taken from a defunct brewery in Germany and an efficient cooling system to facilitate the production of lagers. Most of Capital's beers are German-influenced, although some step outside any style categories, such as the superb Autumnal Fire—a cross between an Oktoberfest beer and a doppelbock.

Capital's premises are located just outside the city of Madison, Wisconsin. Their beers can be sampled in the beer garden and Bier Stube (beer room) bar, although both have limited opening hours, and food is not available.

MUNICH DARK 5.5% ABV • Dunkel • Malt-accented, with early hints of caramel and nuts, building richness with some chocolate and toffee. Classically smooth and clean.

CITY BREWERY

✉ 1111 South 3rd Street, La Crosse, WI 54601
🖥 www.citybrewery.com

The "world's largest six-pack" (six lagering tanks big enough to hold 7.3 million cans of beer) was repainted to represent LaCrosse Lager instead of Old Style when City Brewery took control of

the mothballed G. Heileman facility in 1999. As well as brewing its own beer, City packages not only beer from other breweries, but also tea, energy drinks, and alcopops. In 2007 it acquired the defunct Latrobe plant in Pennsylvania, where Rolling Rock was brewed, to make similar products for East Coast distribution.

FESTBIER 5.7% ABV • Oktoberfest/Märzen
A seasonal beer made for the LaCrosse Oktoberfest, one of America's largest and longest-running Bavarian-style beer celebrations. City Brewery's Festbier is sweeter and less assertive than more traditional versions.

GOOSE ISLAND

✉ 3535 North Clark Street, Chicago, IL 60657
🖥 www.gooseisland.com

This brewery takes its name from a neighborhood on the only island in the Chicago River, located near the original Goose Island brewpub (1800 North Clybourn), and its distinctive long-necked-goose tap handles can be found in hundreds of taverns across the city. Goose Island Beer Co. operates two brewpubs (the second is at 3535 North

Clark, near Wrigley Field), and also opened a production facility in 1995 that ships beer across the Midwest.

Maintaining tradition from the period when brewmaster Greg Hall brewed scores of styles at the original pub (which opened in 1988), the brewery offers a wide range of beers. Ten different Goose Island beers have won medals at the Great American Beer Festival in the last decade.

GOOSE ISLAND INDIA PALE ALE

312 URBAN WHEAT 4.2% ABV • US wheat beer
Unfiltered and hazy; the citrussy, almost sweet hop nose announces that this is a US beer. Tart and fruity, with an underlying creaminess. Satisfyingly thirst-quenching.

INDIA PALE ALE 5.9% ABV • India pale ale
Juicy, with pineapple and grapefruit notes; full of hop flavor. Fruit and malt backbone balances persistent hop bitterness.

MATILDA 7.0% ABV • Belgian strong ale • Brewed in a style that pays homage to Belgium's Orval. Wild, lively hopsack aroma; earthy, with rich fruits (pineapple predominates again) and a firm, dry characterful finish. Vintage-dated, with good reason.

GREAT LAKES

✉ 2516 Market Avenue, Cleveland, OH 44113
🖰 www.greatlakesbrewing.com

Befitting its location near Cleveland's historic West Side Market, Great Lakes Brewing has been an industry leader in environmentally sustainable practices since opening in 1988. Producing highly regarded lagers and ales, the brewery has undergone multiple expansions. It now occupies six buildings, three of which were once part of Schlather Brewing Co., one of 30 breweries that existed in Cleveland before Prohibition. Visitors to the Taproom are directed to the Tiger Mahogany bar and shown bullet holes said to have been made by Eliot Ness, the lawman who brought down gangster Al Capone.

🍺 **EDMUND FITZGERALD PORTER**
5.8% ABV • Porter • Perfectly balanced, with chocolate mocha notes throughout; delightful fresh quality and dry coffee finish.

🍺 **DORTMUNDER GOLD** 5.8% ABV • Dortmunder • Aromas of fresh grain and new-mown hay blend with bright noble hops. Robust and crisp.

🍺 **ELIOT NESS** 6.2% ABV • Vienna lager • Bold and hoppy for the Vienna style, with creamy maltiness and brisk hoppiness nicely balanced. Late notes of oak linger on the palate.

GREAT LAKES EDMUND FITZGERALD PORTER

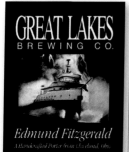

GREAT LAKES
BREWING CO.

Edmund Fitzgerald
A Handcrafted Porter from Cleveland, Ohio

HUBER

✉ Minhas Craft Brewery, 1208 14th Avenue, Monroe, WI 53556
🖰 www.minhasbrewery.com

Ravinder Minhas bought the former Joseph Huber brewery in 2006. Most of its beer is sold under the Mountain Creek label in Canada, but the brewer also produces the Berghoff brand for sale in the Midwest as well as other beers long associated with the brewery. Founded in 1843, it was initially known as the Blumer Brewing Co. It became the Joseph Huber brewery in 1947, and produced many popular regional beers, including the highly acclaimed Augsburger.

🍺 **HUBER BOCK**
5.4% ABV • Bock
Toasty and dry; notes of caramel. Best consumed at Baumgartner's Cheese Store & Tavern around the corner from the brewery, along with a Limburger cheese sandwich (with a breath mint on the side).

LAKEFRONT

✉ 1872 North Commerce Street, Milwaukee, WI 53212
🖰 www.lakefrontbrewery.com

Opened in 1987 beside the Milwaukee River, Lakefront makes a wide range of robust beers, from traditional lagers like Eastside Dark to beers infused with cherries and coffee.

Already known for its outstanding tours, Lakefront Brewing added the chalet and slide used by "Bernie the Brewer," mascot of the Milwaukee Brewers baseball team, to its décor when co-founder Jim Klisch bought it at auction after Brewers Stadium closed. Lakefront recently experienced a boost in sales by introducing New

Grist, a beer brewed with sorghum and rice for gluten-intolerant drinkers.

🍺 **NEW GRIST** 5.0% ABV • Sorghum ale • A bit of lemon and orange zest to start; light palate, hints of fruit. Mildy astringent and tart.

LEINENKUGEL

✉ 1 Jefferson Avenue, Chippewa Falls, WI 54729
🖰 www.leinie.com

Leinenkugel's has maintained its northwoods image since the days when Jacob Leinenkugel began selling beer to lumberjacks in 1867. Although Miller bought a controlling interest in 1988, brothers Jake, Dick, and John remain the faces of the brand.

"Leinie" beers lean mainly on German tradition, but also include fruit styles. Most of them are produced at the Chippewa Falls brewery, where the malthouse and an old horse barn date back to the 19th century. Leinenkugel also operates a brewery with a smaller output on 10th Street in Milwaukee.

LEINENKUGEL
CREAMY DARK

🍺 **SUNSET WHEAT** 4.9% ABV • US wheat beer • Light but complex beer, almost a fruit salad of aromas and flavors; some wheat tartness and definite spiciness (coriander).

🍺 **CREAMY DARK** 4.9% ABV • US dark lager • Creamy as promised, with chocolate from start to finish, some coffee and cream character, and a dryish finish.

MILLER

✉ 3939 West Highland Boulevard, Milwaukee, Wisconsin 53208
🖰 www.millerbrewing.com

Although it has a long history—German-born Frederick Miller bought the

RETRO BEERS

In 2003, weeks before Miller Brewing closed their legendary Olympia Brewery in Tumwater, anxious customers began showing up at Washington stores. One man bought 22 cases of Olympia in stubbies, so he could enjoy his favorite beer packaged the way he loved it.

When production of Olympia beer moved to a plant in California it meant the end of the brand's familiar "stubby" format, because the squat bottles slowed down production lines. Moves like this signaled the end of an era for many established names on the US beer market. Only four of the 10 largest US brewing companies in 1970 continued to operate into the 21st century, and one of them—Pabst—no longer brewed its own beer. Yet the brands live on, produced under contract. A loyal few still drink Ballantine, Lone Star, Old Style, Lucky Lager, Schlitz, Hamms, Natty Bo, Blatz, Rheingold, Pearl, Narragansett, and a variety of others, keeping these fading household names alive.

Pabst owns more than two dozen old brand-name beers, with most of these brewed under contract by Miller. Other than the popular Old Milwaukee, they tend to be available only in limited regions. However, Pabst's own Blue Ribbon (known as "PBR" by its friends) managed a revival, with a rise in sales during 2002 and 2003 that halted 25 years of decline (although leaving it one-tenth its earlier size).

In the craft brewery hub of Portland, Oregon, a backlash movement began championing Pabst Blue Ribbon.

The trend was soon dubbed "retro-chic," with urban hipsters adopting it as an "anti-brand." It was often the "cheap beer" of choice at places that otherwise sold new-wave beers.

The most recent of the old-line brands to go looking for a new home was Rolling Rock. Brewing giant InBev sold the brand to another brewing giant, Anheuser-Busch, in 2006, and the Latrobe, Pennsylvania brewery where it was made to City Brewery (*see p.227*). Anheuser-Busch now brews Rolling Rock in New Jersey.

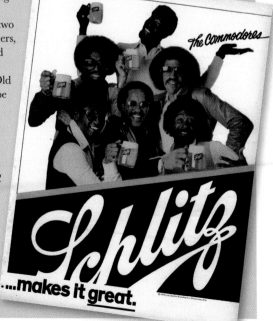

Celebrity endorsements, such as this classic ad featuring The Commodores, helped to make Schlitz a leading '70s brand.

WANDERING WIT

Despite his diminutive frame, Belgian brewer
Pierre Celis casts a giant shadow over US
brewing, although he made beer there for only
a few years. After saving the "white" beer style
in Belgium, Celis brought it to Texas in 1991,
introducing Americans to what then seemed
exotic beer flavors. Impressed, brewing giant
Miller bought a stake in Celis Brewery, then the
whole enterprise. A few years later it closed the
operation and sold the brands to a Michigan
company. In 2006, Texans hoped that Celis,
who is still involved in Belgian brewing, would
return, but legal hassles scuttled the plan.

Pierre Celis was the originator of the enduringly
popular white beer Hoegaarden (*see p.137*),
which is now manufactured by InBev in Belgium.

Plank Road Brewery in 1855
and was one of Milwaukee's
brewing pioneers—it was
only after conglomerate
Philip Morris acquired
Miller Brewing in 1969 that
the company quickly rose to
become a dominant force
(behind Anheuser-Busch)
nationally. Using advertising
and promotion like no other
brewery before, Miller was
the first to cash in on the
popularity of low-calorie
beer. It bought the rights to
Meister Brau Lite in 1972
and turned that into Miller
Lite. South African Breweries
bought Miller in 2003,
renaming the combined
company SABMiller.

MILLER LITE 4.2% ABV • Low
calorie lager • No hop aroma;
lightly sweet malt, no fruit or
bitterness; crisp at finish.

NEW GLARUS

✉ County Trunk West and Highway
69, New Glarus, WI 53574
🖱 www.newglarusbrewing.com

New Glarus Brewing enjoys
fame that reaches far beyond
this storybook village of
2,000 inhabitants—
a remarkable achievement,
given that it does not sell its
beer outside Wisconsin.

Brewery president Deborah
Carey raised the money to
start the business in 1993,

and her husband Dan
brewed beers that fueled
demand for ongoing
expansion. A new $19
million plant constructed in
2007 has a decidedly Old
World German feel. The
Careys' fruit beers earned
the brewery acclaim, and
beer aficionados plead for
distribution of New Glarus
beer aged in wood barrels.
It was the best-selling
Spotted Cow, however, that
drove astonishing growth,
with its name and packaging
reflecting the brewery's
setting in dairy country.

WISCONSIN BELGIAN RED
5.1% ABV • Fruit beer • Jammed
with Wisconsin-grown
Montmorency cherries that
dominate the aroma and
flavor, balanced by just-right
sourness and acidity.

NEW GLARUS
WISCONSIN BELGIAN RED

Bittersweet almond adds to
the cherry impression, with
oaky undertones.

SPOTTED COW 4.8% ABV • Cream
ale • Billed as a Wisconsin
farmhouse ale, and featuring
a little corn in the recipe.
Faintly fruity (fresh peaches),
a tad grainy, light on the
tongue, and refreshing.

YOKEL 4.7% ABV • Zwickel
Unfiltered lager in the
Bavarian zwickel tradition.
Bready, yeasty, fresh, and dry
at the finish. The brewery
suggests that drinkers "Buy
Local, Drink Yokel."

NEW HOLLAND

✉ 690 Commerce Court,
Holland, MI 49423
🖱 www.newhollandbrew.com

Before its Tulip Time
Festival became popular,
Holland, Michigan, was
best-known as the "City of
Churches" because of the
170 churches in its town of
35,000. Only recently did
the city even permit the sale
of beer on Sundays, but
New Holland Brewing has
found an audience for "Art
in Fermentation Form."

Beyond a range of ales in
more familiar styles, the
brewery regularly offers
barrel-aged beers (it has up
to 75 wood barrels lagering
beer at any time). New

Holland operates a pub restaurant in downtown Holland (66 Eighth Street).

THE POET 6.5% ABV • Stout
Features an abundant combination of coffee, chocolate, and dark, rummy fruits from the nose to the back of the mouth. Full-bodied and creamy enough to balance the coffee start.

SCHLAFLY

✉ 2100 Locust Street, St. Louis, MO 63103
🖱 www.schlafly.com

The "other" brewery in St. Louis began as a brewpub in 1991, then built a separate production facility. It makes a wide range of seasonal beers beyond its six regular brews, with up to 30 different beers on offer each year. Officially called Saint Louis Brewery, its original downtown pub is better known as the Taproom, the beers as Schlafly (after co-founder Tom Schlafly), and its production brewery and restaurant on Locust Street in Maplewood as Bottleworks. This was the first brewery-restaurant in the country to serve a sorghum-based beer for the gluten-intolerant.

PALE ALE 4.4% ABV • Pale ale • The brewery's flagship product. Well-balanced, with biscuit and fruit aromas and flavor. Dry, and not-too-bitter finish. The stronger American Pale (5.5% ABV) is dry-hopped and is particularly fresh and bright when served direct at the brewery's bars.

SCHLAFLY PALE ALE

OATMEAL STOUT 5.7% ABV • Oatmeal stout • A complete breakfast in a glass: coffee and cream balanced by a slight oiliness from the oatmeal. Smooth, with hints of smoky chocolate.

SPRECHER

✉ 701 West Glendale Avenue, Glendale, WI 53209
🖱 www.sprecherbrewery.com

Randy Sprecher, formerly a brewing supervisor at Pabst, founded Sprecher in downtown Milwaukee in 1985, later moving to the company's current suburban location. Known from the start for its traditional approach, exemplified by beers such as Black Bavarian, Sprecher continues to experiment. After brewing a special beer for the African World Festival in 2006, the brewery released two African-inspired beers. One was made with sorghum, the other with bananas.

BLACK BAVARIAN 5.9% ABV • Schwarzbier • Dark; sweet molasses nose, with hints of coffee and caramel. Medium-bodied, clean, balanced bitterness through the finish.

SUMMIT

✉ 910 Montreal Circle, Saint Paul, MN 55102
🖱 www.summitbrewing.com

Since 1986, when Mark Stutrud and his employees rolled their first keg out of the brewery and across the street to the bar where it would be served, Summit's focus on the local market has been unmatched by any of the other 20 largest craft breweries in the country. Almost all of its beer is sold within 50 miles (80 km) of the Twin Cities brewery. In 1998, Summit built the state's first new brewery in 100 years.

EXTRA PALE ALE 5.1% ABV • Pale ale • Distinctive but not overpowering citrus nose;

SUMMIT EXTRA PALE ALE

firm, fruity middle; dry finish, disappearing with a scent of lemon.

GREAT NORTHERN PORTER 4.8% ABV • Porter
A satisfying session beer. Coffee and chocolate bitterness merge with herbal hops and balance sweet caramel-toffee flavors.

THREE FLOYDS

✉ 9750 Indiana Parkway, Munster, IN 46321
🖱 www.threefloyds.com

Three Floyds Brewing began in 1996 in a warehouse in Hammond, Indiana, using the slogan "It's not normal," and living up to it. In the early days Nick Floyd (one of three family founders) brewed the flagship Alpha King Pale Ale in open stainless-steel fermenters he dubbed "Hammond Squares" in homage to Samuel Smith's Yorkshire Squares (*see p.163*). Hops immediately became Floyd's signature ingredient; he once quipped "I love the smell of hops in the morning. It smells like victory."

The brewery has since moved to bigger quarters in Munster that include a brewpub. Many of its beers, most notably the Dark Lord Russian Imperial Stout and Dreadnaught Imperial IPA, have developed a devoted cult following.

ALPHA KING 6.0% ABV • Pale ale
Opens with a rush of grapefruit, followed by other citrus fruits and fresh hop oils. A firm malt backbone retains some balance, although the final impression is one of citric bitterness.

GUMBALLHEAD 4.8% ABV • US wheat beer • Unique among wheat beers, with distinct citrus and orchard fruits on the nose, followed by wheat tartness and apparent hops throughout. Almost challenges a drinker not to be refreshed.

Mountains

Colorado • Arizona • Montana • Nevada • Utah

Miners and cowboys once hung out in the saloons of the Rocky Mountain frontier, but today's customers are more likely to be outdoors enthusiasts, such as skiers and rock-climbers, and many drink craft beer. Colorado, especially, is a key region in the American beer revolution.

Before 1988, Colorado had only three breweries, yet today it has more than 90—only California has more. The American Homebrewers Assocation was founded in Boulder in 1978. The Brewers Association, which represents the nation's small and not-so-small breweries, shares the same offices. Nearby Denver hosts the annual Great American Beer Festival (*see p.236*), is home to the esteemed Falling Rock Tap House, and in 2003 elected Wynkoop Brewing founder John Hickenlooper as its mayor.

The same venturesome attitude permeates the whole region. In Flagstaff, Arizona—another hub for outdoors devotees—three brewery-restaurants are only a 10-minute walk apart. In New Mexico, the state's breweries have an annual competition in which consumers pick the best India pale ale in the state (and in 2006 an Imperial IPA from Chama River in Albuquerque won). Grand Teton Brewing in Idaho takes credit for reviving the use of takeaway "growlers" (half-gallon jugs), now a staple in brewpubs across the country.

The region can still be conservative when it comes to the law. Colorado allows supermarkets to sell no beer stronger than 4% ABV. Liquor stores can, but must close on Sunday. Utah limits the alcohol content of beer sold in taverns, brewpubs, supermarkets, and convenience stores to 4% ABV. Stronger beer is sold warm in state liquor stores.

New Belgium's brewery in Fort Collins stands as testament to the company's remarkable success story (*see p.236*).

AVERY

✉ 5763 Arapahoe Avenue,
Boulder, CO 80303
🖰 www.averybrewing.com

Family-run Avery Brewing
has made much-admired
beers since 1993. But the
company's popularity really
surged after the launch of its
stronger beers in series of
threes. The first series was
the "Holy Trinity" of Hog
Heaven, The Reverend, and
Salvation—the latter two
being respectively dark and
light strong ales, brewed
using the same Belgian yeast.
Among those that followed
were the Demons of Ale
(The Beast, Mephistopheles,
and Samael's, averaging
more than 15% ABV each)
and the Dictator series.

📖 **HOG HEAVEN** 9.2% ABV • **Barley
wine** • Intensely malty and
hoppy at the same time,
with rich caramel fruitiness
and hints of whisky malt.
A distinctly chewy feel in the
mouth, with long legs that
coat the glass.

📖 **INDIA PALE ALE** 6.3% ABV • **India
pale ale** • Piney, almost oily
nose, with grapefruit and
orange from the start
through to the finish.
Unapologetically bitter.

📖 **SALVATION** 9.0% ABV • **Strong
golden ale** • Prominent fleshy
fruits, particularly apricots;
sweet spicy aromas and
flavors, a hint of honey.
Leaves a lingering
impression of
perfume.

AVERY HOG
HEAVEN

BIG SKY MOOSE DROOL

BIG SKY

✉ 5417 Trumpeter Way,
Missoula, MT 59808
🖰 www.bigskybrew.com

Since opening its doors in
1995, Big Sky's growth into
a regional brewery has been
driven principally by its
flagship brown ale, Moose
Drool. Its unusual name
comes from a painting made
by the mother of one of the
brewery's founders for
possible use on the beer
labels. On seeing the
painting—which depicted
a moose lifting his head from
a pond—one of the brewers
said, "Let's call it Moose
Drool." The name stuck, but
not to universal approval:
Big Sky had to defend their
right to use the name Moose
Drool in the courts when it
was challenged by Canadian
brewer Moosehead.

📖 **MOOSE DROOL** 5.3% ABV •
Brown ale • Dark fruits and
nuts mingle with chocolate
aromas and flavors. Medium
body; sweetness moderated
by earthy hop tones.

BOULDER BEER

✉ 2880 Wilderness Place,
Boulder, CO 80301
🖰 www.boulderbeer.com

Colorado's first microbrewery,
Boulder was founded in 1979
by two college professors
working from a goat shed
outside Longmont, near
Boulder. With a helping
hand from brewing giant
Coors, they sold their first
beers in 1980 and made
a high-gravity brew for the
first Great American Beer

Festival in 1982. Boulder
made another special beer to
celebrate the festival's 25th
anniversary. The brewery
has used several names over
time, finally settling on
Boulder Beer in 2005.

📖 **PLANET PORTER** 5.1% ABV •
Porter • One of Boulder's first
beers, although originally
produced under a different
name. Dark fruit in the nose,
subdued roast in the middle,
bitterness at the finish.

BRECKENRIDGE

✉ 471 Kalamath Street,
Denver, CO 80204
🖰 www.breckbrew.com

Breckenridge Brewing began
in 1990, and is still there as a
brewpub, in the ski resort of
the same name. A second
brewpub was added in
Denver (2220 Blake) just two
years later. The company
tried to run brewpubs in
several other states, although
all eventually closed. Its
production brewery,
however, has thrived since
opening in 1996.

📖 **AVALANCHE ALE** 5.4% ABV •
Amber ale • The flagship since
the beginning. Fruity, tart,
balanced toward the sweet
side, with underlying
caramel and honey.

COORS

✉ 311 10th Street, Golden,
CO 80401
🖰 www.coors.com

Coors was the cult US beer
of the 1970s—a notoriety
achieved through both its
limited availability (at the
time, it could be bought only
west of the Mississippi) and
its starring role in the box
office hit film *Smokey and the
Bandit*. Uniquely among
large brewers, Coors stopped
pasteurizing its beer in 1959,
and still makes little use of
pasteurization today.
  Operating the largest
single-site brewery in the
world, Coors merged with
Canadian brewer Molson in

The Coors brewery in Colorado is a giant facility that produces popular American light beers.

2005 to form the world's fifth-largest brewing company. Coors Light, not much different from other best-selling light beers, has been its flagship for nearly 30 years.

◗ BLUE MOON WHITE ALE 5.4% ABV • Witbier • This successful beer was developed in a brewpub at Denver's Coors baseball stadium. Citrussy-sweet nose (even without the suggested garnish of an orange slice); spicy, with notes of celery. Some wheat-inspired tartness, finishing on the sweet side.

FLYING DOG

✉ 2401 Blake Street, Denver, CO 80205
🖰 www.flyingdogales.com

Flying Dog made its debut at US beer festivals in 1991, memorably asking customers to bark for their beer. The canine theme is still part of the company ethos—Weihenstephan-trained Eric Warner calls himself "lead dog" rather than president—and the brand leans heavily on an edgy image cultivated by associations with the late "gonzo" journalist Hunter S. Thompson and the British illustrator Ralph Steadman, who creates the brewery's label artwork.

Flying Dog opened as a brewpub in Aspen, but left the ski resort long ago for Denver. The brewery here reached full capacity in 2006, at which point Flying Dog bought a brewery in Maryland to produce beer for the East Coast.

◗ GONZO IMPERIAL PORTER 9.0% ABV • Porter • Rummy, chocolate, almost sweet before dry cocoa flavors and solid hop bitterness kick in. Intense, somewhat boozy.

◗ DOGGIE STYLE PALE ALE 5.3% ABV Pale ale • A fragrant mixture of fresh fruits to start. Citrus sharpens a fruity middle, balanced by cookie malt. Clean-dry finish.

FOUR PEAKS

✉ 1340 East 8th Street, Tempe, AZ 85281
🖰 www.fourpeaks.com

Housed in a marvelous 19th-century creamery building, Four Peaks Brewing favors beers of British heritage—such as its award-winning Kiltlifter Scottish-style ale and the easy-drinking Eighth Street Ale (a 4.5% ABV bitter). However, the brewery also offers a range of specials, including some rather esoteric products. Blind Date Ale is made with Arizona-grown Medjool dates; the brewery also made a version that was aged for three months in Jim Beam

Bourbon oak barrels. Opened in 1997, Four Peaks uses a reverse-osmosis process to treat the odiferous Phoenix Valley water, then adds the brewing salts needed to recreate water profiles of classic brewing areas. The brewery also operates a restaurant at 15730 North Pima Road in nearby Scottsdale.

◗ KILTLIFTER 6.0% ABV • Scottish ale • Decidedly and richly malty, with caramel emerging on the palate. Complex, with just a bit of smokiness.

GREAT DIVIDE

✉ 2201 Arapahoe Street, Denver, CO 80205
🖰 www.greatdivide.com

Brian and Tara Dunn opened Great Divide in 1994 in an old brick dairy at the north end of an area that has become Denver's "brewing corridor." The brewery now features an inviting tasting bar at the front of the premises, making it another great place to stop for a drink when visiting the city. In the 14 states in which it sells its beer, Great Divide is perhaps best known for its hoppier, stronger creations, although the brewery's real strength lies in the thoughtful balance of all its beers, including the "big" ales, such as Oak Aged Yeti Imperial Stout.

◗ HIBERNATION ALE 8.1% ABV • Old ale • Complex, earthy nose packed—at first—with chocolate, roasted nuts, and freshly baked molasses cookies. Intensely flavored, with a fleeting mineral character and a drying hop bitterness. Well-integrated flavors.

◗ DENVER PALE ALE 5.4% ABV • Pale ale Mildly robust, with a solid English malt presence and orchard fruits. Evident but well-balanced hops.

GREAT DIVIDE HIBERNATION ALE

BREWPUBS: MAKING BEER LOCAL AGAIN

Most Americans live within 10 miles (16 km) of a brewery—a statistic for which brewery-restaurants (also known as brewpubs) are largely responsible. The movement began only 25 years ago, but today nearly 70 percent of America's 1,400-plus breweries are brewpubs.

The products of brewpubs account for about only nine percent of craft-beer sales but their impact has been more substantial, as they have helped to introduce consumers to classic styles, while inventing new styles of their own.

Innovative ales are adding flavor to the brewpub scene. The US now leads the way in developing new styles.

Bert Grant opened America's first brewpub in Yakima, Washington, in 1982. Like many that followed, Grant's (now closed) grew into a distributing brewery. Some emerging brewpubs accented the brewing arm of their business; others the restaurant. Small or large, there was no standard blueprint for success, although many embraced innovation, both inside and outside of the glass. For example, Oskar Blues Grill & Brewery broke a taboo in 2002 when it installed a canning line. "Our goal is to change the perception in the (craft)

Drinkers relax in a branch of the Pyramid Alehouse chain. The rise of such enterprises has helped to popularize craft ales in the US.

industry about what you can sell in cans," said owner Dale Katechis. His flagship, Dale's Pale Ale, did just that. By 2006, he was selling 8,200 barrels a year—a 13-fold increase in sales. Dozens of other small breweries began to offer their beer in cans.

A later success story is that of the Rock Bottom brewpub chain, which opened its first outlet in 1990. Today, Rock Bottom operates more than 30 brewery-restaurants—together producing more than 40,000 barrels annually—across the country, as well as 50-plus Old Chicago restaurants that offer more than 30 beers each on tap. Initially, each member of the chain brewed essentially the same beers, but by the late 1990s, the chain gave its pub brewers more freedom, particularly with seasonal beers.

LEFT HAND

✉ 1265 Boston Avenue,
Longmont, CO 80501
🖰 www.lefthandbrewing.com

Founders Dick Doore and
Eric Wallace met as cadets
at Colorado's Air Force
Academy in the early 1980s,
were reunited in 1993, and
soon started homebrewing in
the nearby town of Niwot.
They named their brewery
after the Arapahoe Indian
Chief Niwot, whose name
translates as "left hand."
Brewing in a former sausage
factory, they began selling
mostly English-inspired ales
in 1994, and in 1998 merged
with Tabernash—a Denver
microbrewery that also
started in 1994 and had
earned a reputation for its
Bavarian-inspired beers.
Today, the brewery, with its
distinctive red left-hand
logo, is simply called Left
Hand Brewing.

🍾 **BLACK JACK PORTER** 5.2% ABV •
Porter • Chocolate and
liquorice aromas, medium
body, hints of chocolate-
covered dark cherries, and
a smooth dry finish.

🍾 **HAYSTACK WHEAT** 5.0% ABV •
Hefeweizen • Spicy nose, with
a hint of bubblegum. Clovey,
banana-dominated fruit
flavors, with a yeasty-wheat
presence. Refreshing.

LEFT HAND
BLACK JACK
PORTER

🍾 **SAWTOOTH ALE** 4.8% ABV •
Special bitter • A properly
balanced beer that begs to
be served on cask. Floral at
the start, with baked fruit in
the middle and a persistent
but restrained bitterness.

NEW BELGIUM

✉ 500 Linden Street,
Fort Collins, CO 80524
🖰 www.newbelgium.com

Set up in a basement in
1991, New Belgium grew
within a dozen years into the
third-largest craft brewery in
America—an achievement
all the more remarkable
because it distributes very
little east of the Mississippi.
Founders Jeff Lebesch and
Kim Jordan and Belgian-
born brewer Peter Bouckaert

are best-known for their
flagship Fat Tire amber ale,
but New Belgium's output
includes many beers that
defy easy classification into
recognized styles.

The company's thoroughly
modern brewery combines
cutting-edge technology with
Old World tradition, such as
the 10 wooden tanks used to
create beers like La Folie.
New Belgium was the first
brewery in the US to be
entirely powered by wind
and has been an industry
leader in sustainable
practices. Its expansive
tasting room is a mecca for
travelers seeking special
beers that seldom make it
outside the brewery.

🍾 **FAT TIRE** 5.3% ABV • **Amber ale**
Biscuity, malty nose, with
toasted caramel in the
middle and a balanced finish
on the sweet side of dry.

🍾 **LA FOLIE** 6.0% ABV • **Flemish
sour** • Complex combination
of tart fruits on the nose,
oak, sometimes vanilla.
Distinct but balanced acidity,
with a mouth-puckering
finish. Vintages vary, both in
the fruits that come through
and the degree of sourness.

🍾 **BIER DE MARS** 6.2% ABV • **Bière
de garde** • A spring seasonal
that changes as the seasons
pass, with early fruit giving
way to more spices and
barnyard flavors as it ages.

THE GRANDDADDY OF BEER FESTIVALS

Starting out modestly in 1982 with 20
breweries serving 35 beers in a Boulder,
Colorado, hotel room, the Great American Beer
Festival has grown into the greatest beer
showcase anywhere. In 2006, 41,000 beer
drinkers attended four sessions (three of them
sold out) at the Colorado Convention Center in
Denver, with 384 breweries offering 1,668
beers. In a competition associated with the
festival, an international panel of judges
evaluated 2,404 beers from 450 breweries.
Almost 2,700 volunteers worked more than
41,000 hours to put on the GABF.

Beer-lovers from all over the US converge on
Colorado every year to browse the stalls and
exhibits at the Great American Beer Festival.

UINTA

✉ 1722 South Fremont Drive,
Salt Lake City, UT 84104
📱 www.uintabrewing.com

Uinta became the first Utah brewery to grow officially bigger than a microbrewery when its sales exceeded 15,000 barrels in 2005. Beyond its range of 4% ABV beers, the brewery crafts a distinctive and potent anniversary barley wine at 9.8% ABV, which is available all year round in state-licensed stores.

🍺 **KING'S PEAK PORTER**
4.0% ABV ● Porter ● Has a coffee and cream sweetness that is restrained by dark fruit on the palate, with a peppery and cocoa dryness at the finish. Has won numerous awards as a German-style schwarzbier.

UTAH BREWERS

✉ 1763 South 300 West,
Salt Lake City, UT 84115
📱 www.utahbeers.com

The Utah Brewers Cooperative was founded in 2000 as a partnership

between Schirf Brewing Co. and Salt Lake Brewing Co., although these two breweries each continue to own brewpubs that are separate from their joint brewing operation. Schirf Brewing opened in 1986 in Park City and makes the Wasatch range of beers, including Polygamy Porter, whose irreverent marketing has riled Utah's Mormon population, while Salt Lake, with its Squatters beers and brewpubs, was established in 1989. Both breweries' beers can be found in an increasing number of outlets outside Utah, and both companies license their names to pubs based in Salt Lake City airport.

🍺 **WASATCH POLYGAMY PORTER** 4.0% ABV ● Porter "Why have just one?" the brewery asks of drinkers of this dark session beer. Chocolate dominates, with some coffee and a short, dry finish.

🍺 **SQUATTERS PROVO GIRL PILSNER** 4.0% ABV ● Pilsner ● Flowery hops keep the bready nose fresh and distinctive. Light-bodied and a little sweet with a dry, bracing finish.

UTAH BREWERS
SQUATTERS
PROVO GIRL
PILSNER

The Squatters brewpub in Salt Lake City, Utah, owned by Salt Lake Brewing Co.

WYNKOOP

✉ 1634 18th Street,
Denver, CO 80202
📱 www.wynkoop.com

John Hickenlooper, an unemployed geologist, and the late Russell Schehrer, a former National Homebrewer of the Year, opened the first brewpub in the Rockies in 1988, well before their "LoDo" (Lower Downtown of Denver) neighborhood became fashionable.

Wynkoop Brewing has influenced brewpubs as far east as New York by providing consultancy and also by briefly investing in an "unlinked" chain of brewpubs—several of which now prosper individually. In addition to its own achievements, the brewpub has sponsored a national search for a Beerdrinker of the Year since 1997.

🍺 **WIXA WEISS** 5.4% ABV ● Hefeweizen ● Begins with aromas of banana, orchard fruits, and bubblegum. Tart wheat notes on the tongue, with clove flavors that linger in the throat.

Pacific Northwest

Alaska • Oregon • Washington

Portland and Seattle are the top two craft-beer markets in the world. The big names have changed—once-dominant Blitz-Weinhard, Rainer, and Olympia have all closed—but beer-drinkers in the Northwest still support regional breweries with unmatched enthusiasm.

Craft beer accounts for less than 4 percent of US beer sales, but constitutes 11 percent of sales in Oregon, where the state's breweries rank second only to California in craft production. Half of the country's 10 largest craft breweries operate in the Northwest region. "The provincialism of beer-drinkers in Oregon is unmatched anywhere else," remarks one regional beer distributor.

Drinking locally made beer became part of the culture of the Northwest soon after the first German-trained brewers arrived in the 1850s. The climate was suitable for cultivating the ingredients necessary for brewing beer—the Yakima Valley (Washington) and Willamette Valley (Oregon) produce most of the hops in the US, and barley is grown in both states—

and proved conducive to beer drinking. "People were ready, the pipeline was here," says Don Younger, who has operated Portland, Oregon's, venerable Horse Brass Pub since 1976. Although Oregon's first small brewery (Cartwright) failed, the second (BridgePort) was a success, and scores more have followed. Younger, and other publicans who followed his lead, nurtured many of them.

Perhaps because the beer-importer Merchant du Vin was located in Seattle, that city's restaurants were among the first in the nation to add specialty beers to their menus. In Portland, Higgins is one of America's best beer-friendly restaurants. Both cities are full of refurbished alehouses where locals take great pleasure in drinking local beers.

A gleaming copper takes pride of place at a brewpub in Portland, Oregon.

ALASKAN

✉ 5429 Shaune Drive,
Juneau, AK 99801
🖰 www.alaskanbeer.com

When Geoff and Marcy
Larson opened their
brewery in 1986, it was one
of only 67 in the country
and stood alone in Alaska.
Geoff, a qualified chemical
engineer, dumped 19 batches
of the Amber Ale that would
become their flagship beer
before he considered it ready
to sell. The recipe was based
on one used by the Douglas
City Brewing Co., which
operated on the other side of
the Gastineau Channel from
Juneau from 1899 to 1907.

Each of the beers that
Alaskan produces emphasizes
its regional roots, from the
justifiably famous Smoked
Porter, made with malt
smoked at a local fishery, to
the Big Nugget barley wine
aged in an old mine shaft. Its
beers are on sale throughout
the gigantic state, even in
National Park souvenir
shops, and in a growing
number of other US states.

🍺 **SMOKED PORTER** 6.5% ABV •
Porter • Alder-smoked;
presents chocolate, roast,
burned fruit, and other
luscious flavors. Smoky
from the beginning through
to a satisfying finish.

🍺 **AMBER** 5.0% ABV • Alt
Clean caramel nose,
brightened by spicy hops;
smooth and malty.

🍺 **WINTER ALE** 6.4% ABV • Old
ale • Spruce intertwines with
fruit at the start, followed by
rich, thick maltiness and a
woody finish.

ALASKAN WINTER ALE

BRIDGEPORT

✉ 1313 Northwest Marshall Street,
Portland, OR 97209
🖰 www.bridgeportbrew.com

Oregon's oldest
operating craft
brewery, first
known as
Columbia River
Brewery, was
founded by the
Ponzi winemaking
family. BridgePort
Brewing became a
community anchor
in the Pearl District
after opening in
1984. San Antonio-
based Gambrinus
bought the brewery
in 1995, funding
several brewery
expansions, widening
distribution, and successfully
promoting the flagship IPA.

Since the return of
BridgePort's original brewer,
Karl Ockert, their ales are
promoted as naturally
conditioned in the bottle and
on draft. As well as having a
brewpub-bakery at the
brewery, BridgePort operates
an alehouse in the
Hawthorne neighborhood.

🍺 **INDIA PALE ALE** 5.5% ABV • India
pale ale • Begins with a citrus
blast, grapefruit, and pine.
Offers a solid malt backbone,
delicate fruits (peaches and
apples), and then a complex
hoppy finish.

🍺 **BLACK STRAP STOUT** 6.0% ABV •
Stout • A full-bodied blend of
molasses, chocolate, and
coffee. Excellent with cookies
baked using the stout.

DESCHUTES

✉ 901 Southwest Simpson Avenue,
Bend, OR 97702
🖰 www.deschutesbrewery.com

Deschutes Brewery began as
a brewpub in 1988, taking its
name from a local river and
featuring regional landmarks
on its labels. After only five
years it opened a separate
production brewery, its
flagship Black Butte,

DESCHUTES
BLACK BUTTE
PORTER

capturing 90 percent of the
Northwest porter market.
With continued expansion,
the brewery has grown into
one of the 10 largest craft
producers in the country.

Deschutes still
operates its
brewpub at 1044
NW Bond, and
more recently
opened a pub in
Portland. Its well-
received Bond
Street Series of
special releases
features beers that
began "at the pub."

🍺 **BLACK BUTTE PORTER**
5.2% ABV • Porter
A roasty, coffee nose;
a rich and nutty
palate; spicy hops
and a dry finish.

🍺 **MIRROR POND PALE ALE**
5.3% ABV • Pale ale • Grapefruit
and fresh flowers at the
outset, with a clean, lightly
malty middle and a
restrained bitterness.

🍺 **INVERSION IPA** 6.8% ABV • India
pale ale • A swirl of hop
aromas (orange zest); solid
biscuity malt holds its own
against bracing bitterness.

ELYSIAN

✉ 1221 East Pike Street,
Seattle, WA 98122
🖰 www.elysianbrewing.com

Since opening in 1996,
Elysian Brewing has earned
a reputation that exceeds its
modest beer production. Its
brewery, in Seattle's Capitol
Hill neighborhood, doubles
as a popular restaurant and
destination for beer events,
such as its pumpkin beer
festival. Co-founder and
brewer Dick Cantwell is well
known in the craft industry,
and while Elysian sells most
of its beer in the Seattle
area, bottles are also found
in far-flung states.

Elysian operated a small
brewery inside a downtown
video arcade for four years.
After that closed, it opened
a brewpub in the Greenlake
neighborhood, then another

located not far from Seattle's grandly historic Pioneer Square.

DRAGONTOOTH STOUT
7.2% ABV • Stout • A rich nose, with dark fruit, chocolate, molasses, and liquorice, carrying through to a slightly oily palate. Decadent.

PERSEUS PORTER 5.4% ABV •
Porter • Campfire memories on the nose; roast and chocolate, joined by rich coffee/bitter flavors.

FISH

✉ 515 Jefferson Street Southeast, Olympia, WA 98501
🖱 www.fishbrewing.com

Fish Brewing sells organic ales brewed broadly in an English style, German-inspired lagers, and cider. The brewery opened in 1993, but has since acquired Leavenworth Brewing (the lagers) and Spire Mountain Cider (the ciders). It is best-known for its distinctively hopped Fish Tale Organic Ales. A portion of the profits from each beer in the line goes to support an organization working to protect aquatic habitats.

FISH TALE ORGANIC IPA
5.5% ABV • India pale ale • Has the fresh taste of Northwest hops, piney and citrussy. Crisply rich, although hops dominate, lasting well beyond the beer's clean, bitter finish.

A colorful mural gives a clue to the location of the Fish Brewery, based in Olympia, Washington.

FULL SAIL

✉ 506 Columbia Street, Hood River, OR 97031
🖱 www.fullsailbrewing.com

Few breweries in the world can offer visitors views as striking as those from the deck at Full Sail Brewing, looking out over the Columbia River Gorge with its kiteboarders and windsurfers. The brewery opened in an abandoned fruit-pressing factory in 1987 and was one of the first in the Northwest to ship its beer in bottles. It became employee-owned in 1999. As well as making its

FULL SAIL AMBER

own beers, Full Sail brews some of the Henry Weinhard's line for Miller. The company also runs a small brewery at the Pilsner Room in Portland, Oregon.

AMBER 5.5% ABV • Amber ale
Citrus and spice quickly balanced by underlying sweetness; seamless through to a clean finish.

SESSION LAGER 5.1% ABV •
US lager • Designed as a throwback to beer produced before Prohibition; clean and malt-accented.

HAIR OF THE DOG

✉ 4509 Southeast 23rd Avenue, Portland, OR 97202
🖱 www.hairofthedog.com

This still-tiny brewery sold its first beer, Adam, in 1994. Its recipe was inspired by the work of well-known beer writer Fred Eckhardt, who returned the compliment by buying the first bottle. Chef-turned-brewer Alan Sprints has continued to craft unique, very strong bottle-conditioned beers, including one called Fred, honoring Eckhardt. Hair of the Dog puts a batch number on each label, encouraging buyers to cellar their beers.

ADAM 10.0% ABV • Historic ale
Patterned after the adambier style formerly made in Dortmund, Germany. Rich and complex; dark fruits, bread, chocolate, smoked peat and more, neatly unified.

HALE'S

✉ 4301 Leary Way Northwest, Seattle, WA 98107
🖱 www.halesales.com

Founder Mike Hale began his brewing education at Gale's Brewery in 1982, while he was living in England. Within a year he opened Hale's Ales in western Washington, moving the brewery to Spokane in 1991, and on to Seattle in 1995. Although Hale's is best known for its English ales,

HALE'S ALES

which can be enjoyed in the inviting English-style pub at the brewery, it also offers a range of seasonal beers.

PALE ALE 5.2% ABV • Pale ale
Rounded biscuit malt on the nose and in the mouth, nicely balanced by citric, earthy hops.

MAC & JACK'S

✉ 17825 Northeast 65th Street, Redmond, WA 98052

Founders Malcolm Rankin and Jack Schropp began their business on a small scale, brewing in a garage by night and delivering their beer during the day, first selling kegs in 1994. They named their flagship ale African Amber at the suggestion of the owner of the first pub to sell their beer, which was located near Seattle's Woodland Park Zoo. Although Rankin and Schropp's company has grown well beyond its original

"microbrewery" status, it still sells only draft beer.

AFRICAN AMBER UNDISCLOSED ABV
• Amber ale • Dry-hopped and brimming with citrussy, floral hop aromas and flavors; complex caramel in the mouth, with a medium-dry finish.

McMENAMINS

✉ Multiple locations, Oregon and Washington
🖰 www.mcmenamins.com

The McMenamin brothers, Mike and Brian, operate more than 50 pubs in the Northwest, some of them with breweries, some with their names on them, and some with neither. They are the chamaeleons of the pub-world, blending seamlessly into their neighborhoods. Their venues may be large and historic, such as Kennedy School in Portland, Oregon, or simpler, like their first pub, the Barley Mill, which opened in 1983.

The company brews much of its beer at Edgefield Manor, outside Portland—a bed and breakfast establishment that also makes wine, has extensive gardens, and operates a small golf course.

HAMMERHEAD 6.0% ABV • Pale ale • The best-selling beer across the chain; toasted malt battling to balance the citrussy/floral hops.

PIKE

✉ 1415 First Avenue, Seattle, WA 98101
🖰 www.pikebrewing.com

Charles and Rose Ann Finkel reacquired Pike Brewing in 2006, returning to the brewing business after a nine-year absence. The Finkels founded the brewery in 1989, later moving it to the current location and adding a restaurant decorated with brewing-related items. Charles Finkel started the beer-importing business Merchant du Vin in 1978 and was responsible for introducing classic European styles to many Americans.

PALE ALE 5.3% ABV • Pale ale
Rich and creamy, with juicy hops playing well off a fruity, biscuity, medium body; lingering nutty, dry finish.

PYRAMID

✉ 1201 First Avenue South, Seattle, WA 98134
🖰 www.pyramidbrew.com

Pyramid traces its history to the founding of Hart Brewing in the logging town of Kalama, Washington, in 1984. It first brewed its Wheaten Ale in 1985 and its Hefeweizen in 1993, and today introduces itself primarily as a wheat-beer brewery. It officially changed its name to Pyramid in

---

AMERICA'S BREWING CAPITAL

With four of the nation's 10 largest breweries within its city limits, Milwaukee was known as the "Beer Capital of the World" in the 19th century, holding the crown for nearly 100 years. These days Portland, Oregon, lays claim to the title of "US Brewing Capital." Known as "Beervana", the city had 28 breweries at the start of 2007, with more planned. Portland hosts one of the nation's best beer events each July, the four-day Oregon Brewers Festival, in a riverfront park.

The Pacific Northwest is now the hub of craft brewing in the US. Festivals draw thousands of beer-lovers to the region each year.

1996, opening a brewery in Berkeley, California, the following year. The brewery-restaurant on First Avenue in Seattle is one of four alehouses that Pyramid operates under its own name. Pyramid bought Portland Brewing in 2004, and now produces the Portland and MacTarnahan brands, as well as owning MacTarnahan's Taproom in Portland.

📖 **HEFEWEIZEN** 5.2% ABV • US hefeweizen • Cloudy; slightly grainy with a distinctive wheat tartness, balanced by earthy hop flavors.

📖 **APRICOT WEIZEN** 5.1% ABV • Fruit beer • Looks and tastes like apricot; a light-bodied summer refresher.

REDHOOK

✉ 14300 Northeast 145th Street, Woodinville, WA 98072
🖱 www.redhook.com

The oldest craft brewery in the Northwest, Redhook operates on both coasts with state-of-the-art breweries in Woodinville and in Portsmouth, New Hampshire. Gordon Bowker, a founder of Starbucks, recruited Paul Shipman from the wine business when they started Redhook in 1981. They sold their first beer, Redhook Ale, in 1982 but with little success as locals quickly labeled the fruity Belgian-inspired ale a "banana beer." But the successful introduction of Ballard Bitter in 1984 and the flagship ESB in 1987 started the company on a track that ultimately affected small breweries across the nation.

Redhook built a new brewery in 1989, but soon outgrew that. Work had begun on another expansion in 1994 when a deal was struck to sell part

of the company to brewing giant Anheuser-Busch and expand distribution, which is now national. Other breweries have since done the same.

📖 **REDHOOK ESB** 5.7% ABV • Extra special bitter • Hop-accented and slightly grassy; underlying butterscotch-biscuit-caramel flavors.

ROGUE

✉ 2320 OSU Drive, Newport, OR 97365
🖱 www.rogueales.com

This brewery takes its name from the Rogue River, which flows through southern Oregon—where Rogue Ales first established a brewpub in Ashland in 1988. Its iconic beers immediately attracted drinkers who call themselves part of the Rogue Nation.

Since taking charge of the brewery in Newport in 1989, self-effacing brewer John Maier has come to represent the Rogue-ish attitude. He was the first to win the Brewers Association annual award for brewing innovation, using unique ingredients (such as hazelnut and chocolate) and also creating beers known for their depth of malt and aggressive hop character.

As well as operating a restaurant at its Newport brewery, Rogue owns a number of "micro-meeting halls" (breweries and/or restaurants) in several other cities, including Portland and San Francisco.

📖 **DEAD GUY ALE** 6.6% ABV • Heller bock Has complex, clean malt aromas, with rich and fruity notes; bright, bitter-hop flavors combine to create an overall dry and spicy impression.

ROGUE DEAD GUY ALE

📖 **SHAKESPEARE STOUT** 6.0% ABV • Stout • Dark roasty chocolate-coffee mingles with dark fruit and husky malt. Substantial hops balance an oily, creamy smooth finish.

📖 **BRUTAL BITTER** 6.2% ABV • Extra special bitter Aromatic and flowery hops early on, becoming juicy on the palate, before a long and bitter finish.

WIDMER

✉ 929 North Russell, Portland, OR 97227
🖱 www.widmer.com

When brothers and brewery founders Kurt and Rob Widmer delivered their first kegs of beers in 1985, using an old 1970 pickup truck bought from their father, they planned to sell German-style beers, starting with their distinctive altbier. But from the time they first offered their cloudy Hefeweizen, also created—almost by accident—in 1985, it became the best-selling beer in the nation's most craft-beer-crazy city. Flashing its distinctive American hops, it outsold Budweiser on tap in Portland, perhaps explaining why Anheuser-Busch decided to buy a stake in the brewery and now distributes Widmer beers nationwide.

Widmer Brothers Brewing produces a full range of beers, including specialties in collaboration with local homebrewers. Widmer also operates the Gasthaus Pub just down the street from the brewery.

📖 **HEFEWEIZEN** 4.7% ABV • US hefeweizen • Citrus (particularly lemon zest) aromas and flavor, matched against clean bready-yet-tart wheat. Long, citrussy finish.

📖 **BROKEN HALO** 6.0% ABV • India pale ale • Grapefruit and other notes of citrus and pine dominate; a bitter edge mellowed by caramel.

WIDMER HEFEWEIZEN

California and Hawaii

San Francisco • San Diego • Hawaii

America's 20th-century beer revolution started in Northern California, at a time when the state was helping to rekindle interest in fine food and wine. The key players were Jack McAuliffe, Fritz Maytag, Ken Grossman, Paul Camusi, and the Cascade hop.

The regional movement that lifted wine and food above the bland standards of the 1950s also elevated beer. At about the same time in the early 1970s that Fritz Maytag was turning Anchor Brewing in San Francisco into a modern enterprise (*see p.244*), Alice Waters opened Chez Panisse across the bay in Berkeley, serving dishes that began to define "California cuisine." Jack McAuliffe founded New Albion Brewing in Sonoma County in 1976, the year that local vintners celebrated the victory of their wines over France's best in the famous "Judgment of Paris" tasting.

New Albion closed in 1982, but by that time, other craft breweries had arrived on the scene. Ken Grossman and Paul Camusi opened Sierra Nevada Brewing (*see pp.247–9*) in 1980, making use of the Cascade hop variety

Lost Abbey's Cuvee de Tomme (*see p.247*) is one of the beers that changed perceptions about Southern California brewing.

for its flavor and aroma, as well as for its bittering qualities. Since then, craft brewers have continued to find new ways to infuse beers with the intense flavors of hops from the Pacific Northwest.

California had just five breweries when New Albion opened, but it is now home to more than 220. Beers made in the state's south have their own unique appeal, but the highest concentration of brewpubs and drinking venues is in the north. San Francisco is the third-largest market for craft beers in the US, and is a hub for beer-appreciation in California—with the Toronado pub at its center. Established in 1987, this beer emporium hosts a legendary barley wine festival each February.

FRESH HOP BEERS

The *Wall Street Journal* labeled so-called "wet hop beers"—ales brewed with hops picked fresh from the vine and rushed directly to the kettle—as "beer nouveau." West Coast breweries, situated close to where hops are grown, lead the way in the style, but other brewers across the country also produce these "harvest ales." In the fall of 2006, O'Brien's American Pub in San Diego hosted a festival featuring 35 wet hop beers. Why? Fresh flavors—bright, floral, and citrussy—are lost when hops are dried and compacted before shipping or being turned into pellets. Wet hop beers retain these lively flavors.

FRESH HOPS

ALESMITH

✉ 9368 Cabot Drive,
San Diego, CA 92126
🖰 www.alesmith.com

AleSmith is one of several breweries to open in the San Diego area in the mid-1990s, producing innovative beers that quickly changed the public perception of Southern California as a brewing wasteland.

Founded by an avid homebrewer in 1995 and sold to another in 2002, AleSmith Brewing still emphasizes its amateur roots. Although demand for its beers outstrips production, even after expansion, AleSmith continues to make several small specialist batches that are frustratingly hard to obtain outside the brewery's own tasting room.

🍺 **IPA** 7.3% ABV •
India pale ale • Hops dominate the citric salad aromas and appear again on the palate, alongside flavors of mango and pineapple.

🍺 **SPEEDWAY STOUT** 12.0% ABV •
Imperial stout • Roasted coffee beans throughout, matching a broad imperial palate of chocolate, toffee, currants, and oily nuts.

ANCHOR

✉ 1705 Mariposa Street,
San Francisco, CA 94107
🖰 www.anchorbrewing.com

Anchor's history dates back to the 1850s, but the brewery was producing just 600 barrels annually when Fritz Maytag bought a controlling share in 1965. While Maytag famously preserved the Steam beer indigenous to San Francisco, Anchor just as famously ignited the microbrewery revolution—inspiring and aiding scores of other small breweries. It introduced, or reintroduced, Americans to many traditional styles, brewing the Cascade hop-laden Liberty Ale as a holiday beer; making its Our Special Ale, brewed with spices, a regular holiday release; beginning production of a barley wine in 1975; brewing the first American wheat beer in modern times; then becoming the world's first brewery with its own in-house distillery.

ANCHOR
LIBERTY ALE

🍺 **ANCHOR STEAM** 4.9% ABV •
Steam beer • Signature woody, minty nose; caramel flavors with a crisp finish.

🍺 **LIBERTY ALE** 5.9% ABV • Pale ale
Introduced many Americans to the citrussy Cascade hop, with an aromatic nose, biscuit and hop oils on the tongue, and a memorable dry finish.

🍺 **OLD FOGHORN** 9.0% ABV •
Barley wine • Rich malt augmented by earthy, apricot-citrus hops with an intense, flowery dryness.

BALLAST POINT

✉ 5401 Linda Vista Road,
San Diego, CA 92110
🖰 www.ballastpoint.com

Founder Jack White opened Home Brew Mart in 1992 to raise money for a brewery, and four years later built Ballast Point Brewing behind the store, naming it after a local landmark. The success of the light but flavorful Yellow Tail Ale, brewed in the style of a German kölsch, fueled growth, while the brewery earned "street cred" with its more assertive beers.

🍺 **DORADO DOUBLE IPA** 9.6% ABV
• Imperial India pale ale • Pine and grapefruit throughout; melon mixed with orange zest; oily on the palate with a clean malt backbone and a long, bitter finish.

BEAR REPUBLIC

✉ 345 Healdsburg Avenue,
Healdsburg, CA 95448
🖰 www.bearrepublic.com

This family-run brewpub opened in 1996, with a production brewery recently built 15 miles (24km) north in Cloverdale. Brewer Richard Norgrove (his father, also Richard, is the owner) is best known for masterful blends of hop aromas and flavors, but also works as a volunteer firefighter and drives a stock car competitively. The brewpub is decorated to reflect his varied interests.

🍺 **RACER 5** 7.0% ABV • India pale ale • This award-winning IPA exhibits delightfully fresh grapefruit and thick piney aromas, which are nicely supported by a resinous and malty-sweet middle.

▐▶ HOP ROD RYE 8.0% ABV •
Imperial India pale ale • Bright citrussy nose with spicy alcohol; a subtle blend of biscuit, clean rye notes, and incessant hops.

BJ'S

✉ Various locations
𝔊 www.bjsbrewhouse.com

Since opening its first brewery-restaurant in 1996, BJ's has expanded into nine states beyond California. Its restaurants are known as BJ's Restaurant and Brewery, BJ's Restaurant and Brewhouse, and BJ's Pizza & Grill. Each location (not all have breweries) serves seven regular beers plus seasonals and specials. Some choices are brewed across the chain, others in selected regions. BJ's recently opened a larger brewery-restaurant in Reno, Nevada, that will supply beer to many of its restaurants.

▐▶ JEREMIAH RED ALE 7.3% ABV •
Pale ale • Malt-accented, with rich caramel and toffee.

FIRESTONE WALKER

✉ 1400 Ramada Drive, Paso Robles, CA 93446
𝔊 www.firestonebeer.com

The brewery started in a corner of the Firestone Vineyard estate, first selling beer in 1996 after initial attempts to age beer in used Chardonnay wine barrels failed. Firestone Walker now employs new oak in its patented Firestone Union, which is based on the historic Burton Union that was developed in England in the 1840s (*see p.163*).

Firestone blends different percentages of beer fermented in wood and stainless steel to create its products, each blend based on batch variations and determined by sensory evaluation. Beer fermented 100 percent in oak is offered only in the brewery's tasting room, where it is the best-seller, and in a taproom restaurant in Buellton.

▐▶ PALE ALE 4.6% ABV • Pale ale •
Offers bright citrussy aromas; layers of fruit and malt on the palate, an ongoing hop character, and a hint of wood.

▐▶ DOUBLE BARREL ALE 5.0% ABV •
Pale ale • Spicier and less citrussy than the Pale Ale; more vanilla, fermention-based fruit, and a woody, rich-but-not-sweet texture.

▐▶ WALKER'S RESERVE 5.9% ABV •
Porter • Burned, bittersweet chocolate nose with a luscious molasses middle balanced by oak and spice; wood tannins.

GORDON BIERSCH

✉ Multiple locations
𝔊 www.gordonbiersch.com

Restauranteur Dean Biersch and brewer Dan Gordon opened their first brewery-restaurant in Palo Alto in 1988, focusing on German-style beer and a beer-friendly menu. They built, and eventually sold, a chain that now operates in more than a dozen states. Gordon oversees the operations of a stand-alone brewery built in 1997, which brews beers distributed beyond the west. He trained for five years at Weihenstephan Technical University in Bavaria (*see p.15*), after enrolling

Finely crafted ales, such as Firestone's Double Barrel, are becoming popular in California.

in their revered brewing engineering course, becoming the first American to graduate from the program in 50 years.

MÄRZEN 5.7% ABV • Oktoberfest märzen • Rich and malty, with a bit of spice for complexity and a clean, dry finish.

HEFEWEIZEN 5.4% ABV • Hefeweizen • Banana and subdued bubblegum to start; a hint of spicy cloves; refreshing, tart wheat flavors.

KONA

✉ 75-5629 Kuakini Highway, Kailua Kona, HI 96740

🖐 www.konabrewingco.co

Kona Brewing produces beer on Hawaii's Big Island that is distributed throughout the islands. It also sells beer brewed under contract on the mainland in a growing number of states.

PIPELINE PORTER 5.4% ABV • Porter • Brewed with local Kona coffee; well-integrated, with malt and chocolate flavors.

LAGUNITAS

✉ 1280 North McDowell Boulevard, Petaluma, CA 94954

🖐 www.lagunitas.com

Founder Tony Magee, known for cramming creative rants onto his beer's labels, founded Lagunitas Brewing in 1993 in West Marin, but soon moved to Petaluma because the brewery outgrew the town's sewage system. Although India pale ale accounts for 60 percent of sales, the brewery constantly provides new seasonals—such as a beer called Freak Out! that features cover art from a Frank Zappa album.

IPA 5.7% ABV • India pale ale Not really made "with 43 different hops and 65 various malts," but has lots of hop character—orange, grapefruit, peaches.

LOST COAST

✉ 123 West Third Street, Eureka, CA 95501

🖐 www.lostcoast.com

A black-and-white photo of the Fraternal Order of the Knights of Pythias hangs in the Lost Coast restaurant, home of its first brewhouse. The Order erected the building in 1892 and was its sole owner until Lost Coast Brewery founders Barbara Groom and Wendy Pound opened their brewery pub in 1990. The brewery quickly outgrew that facility, moving a few blocks away, and Lost Coast nows sells its beer on both coasts of the continent.

8 BALL STOUT 5.9% ABV • Stout Creamy, full-bodied, with a complex combination of bitter chocolate and coffee; possesses a brief sweetness that is soon swept away by a bitter-dry finish.

KONA PIPELINE PORTER

MARIN

✉ 1809 Larkspur Landing Circle, Larkspur, CA 94939

🖐 www.marinbrewing.com

Always a pioneer, Marin Brewing once billed itself as "The first brewery on the Internet." The brewpub opened in 1989 and is located a ferry ride away from San Francisco. In 1995, co-founder Brendan Moylan opened Moylan's Brewery & Restaurant in Novato (www.moylans.com). Both Marin and Moylan's beers, packaged in 22-ounce bottles, are easily found in the Bay Area.

SAN QUENTIN'S BREAKOUT STOUT 7.1% ABV • Stout Bittersweet chocolate and coffee at the start and end, balanced by a sweet molasses middle; roasty and dry. Named after the famous local prison.

MENDOCINO RED TAIL ALE

MENDOCINO

✉ South Highway 101, Hopland, CA 13351

🖐 www.mendobrew.com

A direct descendant of New Albion Brewing, the Hopland Brewery (now Mendocino Brewing) was California's first brewpub, opening in 1983 with equipment, employees, and yeast from New Albion. Selling mostly draft beer, it also offered 1.5-liter magnums—a six-pack weighed 42 lbs (19 kg)—that would sell out every week. In 1997, Mendocino built a new brewery in nearby Ukiah, pushing distribution into 35 states. Relics from New Albion are on display at the brewpub in Hopland. The company also owns Saratoga Springs Brewing in New York.

RED TAIL ALE 6.1% ABV • Amber ale • Earthy nose with hints of orchard fruits; layers of creamy malt and a touch of liquorice.

BLUE HERON PALE ALE 6.1% ABV • Pale ale • Orange zest and lemon rind give way to traditional biscuit malt and balanced, medium bitterness.

NORTH COAST

✉ 455 North Main Street, Fort Bragg, CA 95437

🖐 www.northcoastbrewing.com

Located in a coastal community once known for lumber milling and fishing, North Coast Brewing conjures up images of beer sturdy enough for long voyages. Brewer Mark Ruederich makes strapping beers, such as Old Rasputin and Stock Ale (vintages ranging up to 13% ABV), but he has also earned a reputation for comparatively delicate beer styles.

North Coast's products have moved into markets less common for beer. The brewery produces two organic beers as house brands for the Whole Foods chain, and brewed the grocer's 25th anniversary beer. More recently, its strong, dark, Belgianesque Brother Thelonious (part of the profits go to the Thelonious Monk Institute of Jazz) has been served in jazz clubs around the world.

North Coast operates a restaurant near its brewery. It has also resurrected Acme Brewing beers, one of California's historic brands.

OLD RASPUTIN 9.0% ABV • **Imperial stout** • Powerful, but subtle enough to allow a wide array of flavors: chocolate, burned barley, toffee, rum, dried fruits, and espresso.

RED SEAL ALE 5.5% ABV • **Pale ale** • Fresh and fruity (mostly citrus); its dry malt/caramel character perfectly balances its bracing hop bitterness.

PRANQSTER 7.6% ABV • **Strong golden ale** Complex, fruity, honeyish aromas with a medium body that offers more fruit, banana candy, and a sweet-smooth finish.

NORTH COAST
OLD RASPUTIN

as those sold under the Port name. The brewery started with a built-in pedigree earned by three Pizza Port brewery-restaurants in southern California, particularly Tomme Arthur's Solana Beach venue.

Arthur brews a variety of Belgian-inspired beers, many using unique ingredients, but most of the beers matured in 100 wood barrels in a special ageing room are uniquely American. The barrels once held various wines and whiskeys, but now nurture wild yeasts. Arthur blends a portion of beer from these barrels for limited edition bottlings sold at the brewery or via the Internet, but not otherwise distributed.

PORT/LOST ABBEY
RED BARN

RED BARN 6.7% ABV • **Saison** Floral, peppery, fruity; spices moving from front to back, then front again. Tart, dry, and refreshing.

JUDGMENT DAY 10.5% ABV • **Belgian strong dark ale** Powerful, designed for the cellar; the profoundly fruity palate (bananas, currants, raisins) has chocolate/whiskey-malt undertones.

CUVEE DE TOMME 11.5% ABV • **Belgian strong ale** • Offers cherries, smoky chocolate, dark fruits, dried fruit, woody vanilla—with flavors that grow in the mouth—balanced by restrained sourness and an acidic finish.

River Brewing became known for beers with wine-like qualities. Brewer Vinnie Cilurzo and his wife, Natalie, bought the brand from Korbel Champagne Cellars in 2002 to open a brewery-restaurant. Cilurzo has extended the "...tion" line (now numbering more than a dozen beers) that he started at Korbel with Damnation and Temptation. Supplication, for example, is a brown ale aged for 15 months with sour cherries and wild yeast in oak Pinot Noir barrels.

Cilurzo brewed the first commercial double IPA in 1994 when he started Blind Pig Brewing in southern California. His version, now called Pliny the Elder, has become a benchmark for the double/Imperial style.

TEMPTATION 7.2% ABV • **Belgian strong blond ale** • Varies from batch to batch, but always complex and vinous, with a tart pineapple nose, lean middle, Chardonnay and oak in the background, and a clean, tart finish.

DAMNATION 7.0% ABV • **Strong golden ale** • Hop spiciness and delicate fruits (pears and tangerines) brighten the nose, lingering into the well-rounded middle, with a spicy-earthy finish.

BLIND PIG IPA 6.0% ABV • **India pale ale** • Explosive floral aromas, citrus, and pine, with sturdy malt complementing and accenting its fruit character (melon, peaches); a clean, tangy finish.

PORT/LOST ABBEY

✉ 155 Mata Way, San Marcos, CA 92069
🖑 www.lostabbey.com

Port Brewing opened in the former Stone Brewing building (*see p.249*) in 2006, quickly earning accolades for the Lost Abbey brand as well

RUSSIAN RIVER

✉ 725 4th Street, Santa Rosa, CA 95404
🖑 www.russianriverbrewing.com

Founded by a winery, located in the heart of wine country, and with a brewer reared in a winemaking family, it is little wonder that Russian

SIERRA NEVADA

✉ 1075 East 20th Street, Chico, CA 95928
🖑 www.sierranevada.com

When homebrewers Ken Grossman and Paul Camusi founded Sierra Nevada

BACK TO THE WOOD

For centuries, brewers fermented and conditioned their beer in wood because they had no alternative. Today, many American brewers choose to age beer in wood because barrels unleash new flavors, some of them not previously associated with beer.

Craft brewers first turned to Bourbon barrels to impart flavor into their beers, after Goose Island Beer Co. made a splash with its Bourbon Country Stout at the 1995 Great American Beer Festival. Brewers did not stop there, however, and now use barrels that have held everything from strong brandy to a variety of delicate grapes. Some want to extract flavors already in the wood, while others treasure the barrels as a breeding ground for wild yeasts.

La Roja beer from Jolly Pumpkin Artisan Ales derives its flavour from wild yeasts cultivated in oak barrels.

Examples of ongoing innovation in the use of barrels are easy to find. Massachusetts brewpub Cambridge Brewing created a beer called Cerise Cassée by starting with an anaerobic sour mash. Brewer Will Meyers later added sour cherries and an abbey yeast during a second fermentation, and let

Barrels once used in distilleries and vineyards find a second lease of life in craft breweries, where they are used to create unique beers.

the beer finish for nine months, during a third fermentation, with wild yeast in French oak Pinot Noir barrels.

Tiny Jolly Pumpkin Artisan Ales in Michigan ages all its beer in oak. Brewer-owner Ron Jeffries nurtures wild yeast in the wood so that his beers develop into a complex fog of wood, rich malt, fruit, and spice.

To celebrate its 10th anniversary, Firestone Walker (*see p.245*) created Firestone 10, a blend of special brews aged in a variety of barrels. The final mix was chosen after input from a panel of brewers and Santa Barbara County winemakers.

Brewing in 1979, their business plan was to produce a maximum of 3,000 barrels per year. Today the growing brewery sells more than 200 times that amount. It has focused on quality from the outset and is an industry leader in good environmental practices. As well as excelling at a wide range of styles, Sierra Nevada still rolls out experimental beers.

PALE ALE 5.6% ABV ● Pale ale ● Perfectly balanced; the piney, grapefruity Cascade hops play against a malt fruitiness on the nose and in the flavor.

CELEBRATION ALE 6.8% ABV ● India pale ale Released only at Thanksgiving and Christmas, this ale brims with juicy hops and has a rich malty sweetness. It is spicy and bitter with a long, dry finish.

BIG FOOT 9.6% ABV ● Barley wine ● Intense from the start, with prominent citric hops, whiskeylike rich malts, and unmistakeable alcohol.

Now housed in an impressive facility, Sierra Nevada started life as a homebrewing project.

STONE

✉ 1999 Citracado Parkway, Escondido, CA 92029
🖥 www.stonebrew.com

The attitude displayed by Stone Brewing's trademark gargoyle on the label of its Arrogant Bastard Ale perfectly represents that beer and the brewery. Stone has grown 30 percent and more annually since Greg Koch and Steve Wagner founded it in 1996. After 10 years they built a larger brewery, then a restaurant area and gardens. Stone sets itself apart not only with entertaining labels, but also by making markedly hoppy beers without using the Cascade hop, now a symbol of

STONE IPA

America's beer revolution. Beyond an array of popular seasonals, the brewery has created an annual Epic Vertical series of what will be 11 bottle-conditioned beers when the last is released in 2012.

ARROGANT BASTARD 7.2% ABV ● Strong ale ● Full-on hops are matched by rich malts and flavors of dark fruits, caramel, and cherries, leading on to a lingering bitter finish.

IPA 6.9% ABV ● India pale ale Fruity hop aromas meet firm malt character at the start, before developing in complexity and finishing bitter but bright.

IMPERIAL RUSSIAN STOUT 9.4% ABV ● Imperial stout ● An intensely flavored beer, full of chocolate, roasted coffee, and dark fruits, which are kept in balance by a brooding bitterness.

OTHER COUNTRIES OF THE AMERICAS

Beer culture in Canada, Latin America, and the Caribbean is surprisingly diverse. From international brewers to craft producers making brews for a local market, beer increasingly plays an essential part in the economic and social wellbeing of millions of people.

People who have never visited Canada might be of the view that there are only two brewers in the country—Labatt and Molson—both drawing upon images of mountains, forests, wildlife, and lakes to promote their beers. But there is much more to the brewing scene in Canada. The country is in the grip of a micro-brewery revolution. From the Atlantic in the east to the Pacific in the west there is a growing band of beer heroes who are brewing fabulous beers for local communities. Many of these beers are sold only on draft in local bars.

Some of these brewers are drawing upon Europe's beer traditions, and producing British-, French-, German-, and Belgian-style beers; others look to the US for inspiration. But some are intent on establishing a distinct style for the province in which they live, and are developing imaginative beers using, where they can, local ingredients. In this geographically vast and ethnically diverse country, there are cultural variations from province to province and region to region, and in each, the best beers are made by micros and brewpubs.

Beers wait for shipment on the docks of the Amazon at Manaus in Brazil. High temperatures mean that they do not always travel well.

From Mexico in the north to the Patagonian southern tip of Argentina, Latin Americans like to drink beer. Most produced here draws upon German influences, and the beers are in the main light lagers, although darker beers can be found, notably in Mexico and Peru. After all, the peoples of this region can draw upon the brewing traditions of many countries—Spanish, Portuguese, and Italian influence can all be found. But American Indians, Asians, and even Africans have all given something of their cultures to the mix. In 2004, the region's largest brewer, the Brazilian Companhia de Bebidas das Américas (AmBev), combined with the Belgian-owned Interbrew to create InBev, the world's largest brewer.

The people of the Caribbean have a reputation for enjoying a laid-back, relaxed lifestyle, inspired by the tropical and subtropical climates and idyllic island life. As with many warm regions of the world, beer is drunk here for refreshment, meaning that light pilsner styles dominate the local markets. Some of these beers have now become brands that are known all over the world, as people from this region emigrated to Europe—particularly the UK—and North America. However, there is also a strong local tradition of drinking dark, sweet stouts.

Canada

Ontario • Alberta • Quebec • British Colombia • Nova Scotia • New Brunswick

There has never been a better time to enjoy beer from Canada's craft brewers. In recent years, a real revolution has taken place, and a country that once seemed to produce only two brands, Labatt and Molson, now plays host to many wonderful microbreweries.

Although Canada's big three brewers, Labatt, Molson, and Sleeman, are now all under foreign ownership, Canadians have recently been discovering the varied and exciting beers produced by the nation's growing number of craft brewers. By combining time-honored brewing methods, natural ingredients, and sheer brilliance and innovation, these beer artisans produce ales, lagers, and stouts that are truly world-class. Most remain locally minded, employ environmentally responsible brewing methods, and sell their beers only in bars close to their breweries. Most are eager to share their passion for beer, opening their doors gladly not just to connoisseurs, but also to curious visitors looking for a new drinking experience. Brewpubs worth visiting include Dieu du Ciel in Montreal (*see facing page*); Toronto's C'est What (67 Front Street), and Fogg 'n' Suds in Vancouver (450 Swift Street, Victoria), although many more await discovery.

Beer festivals are becoming very popular across the country. The Great Canadian Beer Festival is held in Victoria, British Columbia, in September. It is Canada's largest festival of micro-brewers, and showcases 40 breweries from Canada and the Pacific Northwest. The Montreal Beer Festival attracts 50,000 beer enthusiasts to the city every June and serves about 300 different types of beer. Toronto's Festival of Beer, held in August, features more than 200 beers and offers workshops presented by some of the country's best craft brewers.

Gleaming coppers at the Steamworks Brewery in Vancouver create a traditional feel, but subtle innovations are everywhere in Canadian brewing.

AMSTERDAM BREWING CO.

✉ 21 Bathurst Street, Toronto, Ontario M5V 2NG
🌐 www.amsterdambeer.com

Toronto's first brewpub was founded in 1986; Amsterdam was the name of the company's original premises. The business moved to King Street in 1988 as the Rotterdam Brew Pub. As the market for craft beers grew, the brewery expanded to occupy the site's restaurant facilities, and in 2005 the company moved again, to Bathurst Street. There is now a retail shop on the site, and tours of the brewery, with a chance to sample the beer, are available.

🍺 **KLB NUT BROWN ALE** 5.0% ABV • Brown ale • Dark brown in color, this beer has the unmistakeable tang of East Kent Goldings hops. Sweet in taste, it has hints of honey and chocolate.

🍺 **WHEAT BEER** 4.0% ABV • Wheat beer • Light in color, this beer has a malt sweetness and a hint of fresh bread. It is often served chilled with a slice of lemon.

BIG ROCK

✉ 5555–76th Avenue, Calgary, Alberta T2C 4L8
🌐 www.bigrockbeer.com

Big Rock was founded in 1985 by the fiercely independent barley farmer and lawyer Ed McNally, who had tired of national brews and wanted something that used locally sourced Alberta ingredients. All of its beers are brewed to German purity law standards.

The brewery is named after the Big Rock: a huge "glacial erratic" (a stone formation carried far from its place of origin by a glacier) in the foothills east

AMSTERDAM BREWING CO. KLB NUT BROWN ALE

of Okotoks. Brewery tours are available.

🍺 **McNALLY'S EXTRA ALE** 4.0% ABV • Irish ale
A strong, full-bodied Irish ale. It has a flowery aroma and a rich, fruity maltiness.

BRICK BREWING

✉ 181 King Street South, Waterloo, Ontario N2J 1P7
🌐 www.brickbrewery.com

Jim Brickman, founder of Brick Brewing, set up the brewery back in 1984 simply because he loved beer. At the time his decision to open a micro-brewery, the first of its kind in eastern Canada in 37 years, was a bold move.

He was inspired by his travels: in 1979, he began a worldwide journey of research and discovery that took him to 68 breweries in 29 countries. His dream was to create a small brewery that would produce unique, high-quality beers that were different from those already available in the province of Ontario.

The town of Waterloo hosts a Bavarian beer festival every October.

🍺 **BRICK BOCK** 7.0% ABV • Dark bock • A seasonal brew, with ingredients that change annually. Dark and malty with licorice overtones.

LE CHEVAL BLANC

✉ 809 Rue Ontario Est, Montreal, Quebec H2L 1P1
🌐 www.lechevalblanc.ca

Back in 1986, Le Cheval Blanc became the first brewpub in Montreal. It is located in what used to be called the Molasses District, and is decorated with marbled Formica walls and terrazzo floors, which recall its roots as a working-class, old-time tavern. Art exhibitions and music

BIG ROCK McNALLY'S EXTRA ALE

evenings are held on the brewery's premises.

🍺 **AMBER** 5.0% ABV • Red ale
A classic caramelized red ale, with a clean, refreshing bitterness.

🍺 **INDIA RED** 6.0% ABV • India pale ale •
A reddish American-style IPA. Dry-hopped with Centennial hops, this has masses of bitterness.

CREEMORE SPRINGS

✉ 139 Mill Street, Creemore, Ontario L0M 1G0
🌐 www.creemoresprings.com

Creemore, the home of Creemore Springs Brewery Limited, is a charming village nestled in a valley between the Mad and Noisy rivers. The 100-year-old brewery can be found in the center of town and holds regular brewery tours. In August, it hosts an annual street party called the Copper Kettle Festival.

Owned by Molsons since 2005, Creemore still retains its own distinct identity.

🍺 **PREMIUM LAGER** 5.0% ABV • Dry lager • Amber in color; soft malt and fruit flavors give way to nutty overtones and a dry, hoppy finish.

🍺 **URBOCK** 6.0% ABV • Dark bock
Dark brown, with a sweet, nutty texture; fruit aromas are released as the beer warms in the glass.

DIEU DU CIEL

✉ 29 West Laurier Avenue, Montreal, Quebec H2T 2N2
🌐 www.dieuduciel.com

Jean-François Gravel is a wonderful brewer who is pushing at the boundaries of creativity as he continues to learn more about the art and science of brewing. He started brewing in 1991 aged 19, and for many years delighted his friends with the quality of his creations. Over time, he realized that his passion for beer could be much more than a hobby and in 1998 opened a brewpub of his own.

Like an artist with a near-infinite palette of colors, he loves to create new beers, because for him, beer is a wonderful adventure.

■ SOLSTICE D'ÉTÉ

5.0% ABV • Berliner weisse A cloudy blond beer, lightly tinted by the fruits that are steeped in it: strawberry, raspberry, or blueberry, depending on the season. Initial acidity gives way to fruit sweetness.

■ CORNEMUSE (BAGPIPES)

7.5% ABV • Dark ale • A ruby- and copper-colored ale with a lovely caramel aroma touched by a light cherry fragrance. Lightly effervescent, the first sip offers a wonderful taste of caramel.

FAT CAT BREWERY

✉ 940 Old Victoria Road, Nanaimo, British Columbia V9R 6Z8

🖰 www.fatcatbrewery.com

Victoria is British Columbia's capital of craft brewing. The Fat Cat is one of the new wave of Canadian microbrewers, and opened in 2000. Quirky and adventurous, its beers have acquired a reputation for being well-made. The Crow & Gate Pub (2313 Yellow Point, Manama) is a great place to sample a wide range of Fat Cat's craft beers.

■ FAT HEAD IPA

6.0% ABV • India pale ale • A very well-balanced beer; amber in color, it has a lot of hops.

■ POMPOUS POMPADOUR

4.0% ABV • Porter • A ruby-black porter, very dark with lots of chocolate and cream.

■ HONEY BEER

5.0% ABV • Ale Made with special organic Honeydew honey from New

Zealand, which is produced from beech-tree sap by the bees. Malty in flavor.

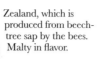

FAT CAT BREWERY
FAT HEAD IPA

FERME BRASSERIE SCHOUNE

✉ 2075 Ste-Catherine, Saint-Polycarpe, Quebec J0P 1X0

🖰 www.schoune.com

Located southwest of Montreal in the village of Saint-Polycarpe, this craft brewery was founded by Marcel and Cécile Schoune, farmers of Belgian extraction who came to settle in Canada in 1980.

All beers are Belgian in style and they can be heavily spiced. The yeast is of Belgian origin and remains in the bottle. All beers are pure barley malt, except for the White, which includes local wheat.

■ LA REB'ALE

7.5% ABV • Strong ale • The rock-and-roll product of the Schoune beer range. Copper-red in color, La Reb'Ale has a deep maltiness and a powerful caramel mouthfeel.

GRANITE

✉ 1662 Barrington Street, Halifax, Nova Scotia B3J 2A2

🖰 www.granitebrewery.ca

One of a chain of brewpubs; other locations are in Windsor, Nova Scotia, and Toronto. Granite began life in the 1980s when Kevin Keefe decided to join the craft brewing revolution,

Traditional ales, such as Granite's Peculiar, are becoming more popular in Canada.

which was then still in its infancy in North America. Undaunted by his lack of brewing experience, he took a course at Peter Austin's renowned Ringwood Brewery in England. Granite also holds brewery banquets with a legendary reputation.

PECULIAR 5.6% ABV • Ale
A dark red ale with a slightly sweet but dry palate.

McAUSLAN

✉ 5080 St-Ambroise, Montréal, Quebec H4C 2G1

🖑 www.mcauslan.com

Now one of Quebec's best-known craft breweries, McAuslan was established in 1989. Founder Peter McAuslan was a homebrewer for many years before finally jumping into commercial brewing.

McAUSLAN ST-AMBROISE RASPBERRY ALE

In 1997, the brewery launched a range of seasonal beers. Brewed exclusively in season, they include: Apricot Wheat Ale, brewed in the spring; Raspberry Ale, which is available during the summer months; Spiced Pumpkin Ale for the fall; and Strong Ale during the winter.

ST-AMBROISE OATMEAL STOUT 5.0% ABV • Oatmeal stout
Brewed from 40 percent dark malts and roasted barley, this intensely black ale carries strong hints of espresso and chocolate.

ST-AMBROISE RASPBERRY ALE 5.0% ABV • Fruit beer • Ruby-red in color, this fruit ale is a summertime treat that yields a delicate aroma of fresh raspberries.

GRIFFON RED ALE 4.5% ABV • Red ale • A mahogany-colored beer, with nutty flavors that result from McAuslan's use of crystal malt and a touch of roasted barley as the basic ingredients for this brew.

MOOSEHEAD

✉ 89 Main Street West, Saint John, New Brunswick E2M 3H2

🖑 www.moosehead.ca

Moosehead is Canada's oldest independent brewery, tracing its roots back to 1867. Today, the company is still owned and operated by its founders, the Oland family. Its best-known beer is its eponymous lager, which today lacks the character of earlier years. Moosehead has a stake in the McAuslan brewery in Quebec (*see left*) and owns the Niagara Falls Brewing Company (*below*) in Ontario.

TEN-PENNY OLD STOCK ALE 5.3% ABV • Ale
A robust top-fermented ale full of malt and hop body.

NIAGARA FALLS

✉ 6863 Lundys Lane, Niagara Falls, Ontario L2G 1V7

Founded in 1989, Niagara's early brews quickly acquired a reputation for being adventurous. Niagara is credited with being the first brewer in North America to produce an eisbock, a style of beer created by freezing it and removing the ice, leaving

behind a more concentrated beer. It is brewed annually, and has a special label for each vintage. Each year's brew is slightly different but full of wonderful character and complexity.

HONEY BROWN 5.0% ABV • Brown ale • An American brown ale, with an inherent sweetness and hints of honey and caramel. Light to drink, it has a short, dry finish.

EISBOCK 8.0% ABV
Eisbock • A robust throat-warming beer. Dark red in color, it is full of chewy toffee flavors.

RUSSELL

✉ 202-13018 80 Avenue, Surrey, British Columbia V3W 3B2

🖑 www.russellbeer.com

Founded in 1995, the Russell Brewing Company was formed with a single goal in mind—to brew the best pure, natural beer. Currently, its beers are available on draft in the Vancouver area, although there are plans to put them into bottles and cans. Brewery tours are available on Friday afternoons by appointment.

PALE ALE 5.5% ABV • Scottish ale
The malts used to make this amber-colored beer come from Scotland, while its hops

The highly drinkable beers of the Russell Brewery place an emphasis on purity and quality.

derive from the Yakima Valley in Washington State. It has soft citrus overtones.

CREAM ALE 5.0% ABV • Cream ale • Made with English malts; smooth and dark golden in color; the result of Canadian barley married with American hops.

SPINNAKERS

✉ 308 Catherine Street, Victoria, British Columbia V9A 3S8
🖰 www.spinnakers.com

At the forefront of British Columbia's beer revolution, this is one of Victoria's must-visit brewpubs. It offers accommodation, and is the perfect base from which to explore the other creative craft brewers in the area. Its beers, including one made with fresh raspberries, draw on styles from all around the world. Its restaurant overlooks Victoria's inner harbor and is the perfect place to have wild Pacific salmon with a glass of beer.

IMPERIAL STOUT 7.8% ABV • Stout • A strong stout, brewed with English floor-malted grains to form a rich and aromatic brew.

STEAMWORKS

✉ 375 Water Street, Gastown, Vancouver V6B 5C6
🖰 www.steamworks.com

Steamworks is a popular pub and brewery located in the historic Gastown area of Vancouver that offers great views across the harbor.

Its beers draw from some of the world's greatest styles and include an India pale ale and a pilsner. There is a Belgian cherry beer, made with whole Montmorency cherries from a local orchard in the Fraser Valley, and a Bavarian lager. There is also a seasonal Pumpkin ale: a malty, copper-colored brew spiced with cinnamon, cloves, nutmeg, and ginger. The brewer adds 100 lbs (45 kg) of pumpkin directly to the

Stylish retro design and an eclectic range of beer styles typify the Steamworks approach.

mash and the resulting beer tastes just like pumpkin pie in a glass.

HEROICA OATMEAL STOUT 8.0% ABV • Oatmeal stout A generous portion of rolled oats and black roasted barley give this beer a warm, roasted nose and a distinct dryness.

UNIBROUE

✉ 80 Des Carrieres, Chambly, Quebec J3L 2H6
🖰 www.unibroue.com

In the spring of 1992, Unibroue produced its first bottle-conditioned beer, the Blanche de Chambly. It is made from a blend of unmalted Quebec wheat and pale barley malt, to which spices and natural aromatics are added, along with a light hopping. Naturally a Champagne color, it looks white because it contains fresh yeast in suspension. Although the brewery is now owned by Sleeman, its excellent beers continue to prosper.

BLANCHE DE CHAMBLY 5.0% ABV • Wheat beer Pale golden color; effervescent foam, and hints of spice and citrus in the nose.

UNIBROUE BLANCHE DE CHAMBLY

VANCOUVER ISLAND

✉ 2330 Government Street, Victoria, British Columbia V8T 5G5
🖰 www.vanislandbrewery.com

This brewery was established in 1984 by islanders who wanted to create beers for the West Coast palate.

The brewery's Eis Bock Hermannator is brewed in August and then frozen and aged in a cellar tank for three months to be ready for consumption in mid-November. This process produces complex chestnut colors and spicy flavors, and the beer drinks like a glass of warmed brandy.

HERMANN'S DARK BAVARIAN LAGER 5.5% ABV • Dark lager A toasty malt nose with similar flavors on the palate that take on a nutty character.

WELLINGTON BREWERY

✉ 950 Woodlawn Road West, Guelph, Ontario N1K 1B8
🖰 www.wellingtonbrewery.ca

This brewery owes its name to Arthur Wellesley, the first Duke of Wellington, who commanded the British forces that defeated Napoleon's French army at Waterloo in 1815. Wellington first opened its doors in 1985, making it one of Ontario's oldest craft breweries. The brewery is known for its distinctive conical rooftop, which replicates that of an oast house—a building traditionally used for drying and packing hops.

COUNTY ALE 5.0% ABV • Ale • A full-bodied and traditional British ale, matured slowly for smoothness and balance. The cask-conditioned version is best drunk at 55°F (12.7°C); as it warms in the glass, it releases wonderful grassy and citrus aromas.

Caribbean

Cuba • Antigua • Trinidad • Jamaica

The Caribbean has a strong beer culture and emigration has spread the popularity of several beers from the region, which is best-known abroad for its light-tasting lagers. However, many Caribbean drinkers have a taste for stouts, such as Dragon or Guinness Foreign Extra.

A porridgelike beer brewed with corn was once produced in the Caribbean, but the arrival of European brewers in the 19th century saw the introduction of lighter, crisper, pilsner-style beers. The biggest regional brewery is Cervecería Bucanero, formed as a joint venture between the Cuban government and Labatt, and now owned by InBev. One Cuban beer, La Tropical, a light pilsner, was first brewed in 1888. Production ceased in the 1960s, when Castro came to power, but the beer was revived in 1988 by a group of businessmen in Florida.

Easy-drinking brews and a laid-back spirit of fun in the sun represent Caribbean beers in the popular imagination of the world's drinkers.

ANTIGUA

✉ P.O. Box 241, St. John's, Antigua
🖱 www.antiguabrewery.com

The Antigua Brewery makes a range of lagers and stouts, but is best known for its flagship beer Wadadli. Wadadli Beer is a refreshing pale lager named after the original American Indian word for the island. Since its release in 1993, Wadadli has become an Antiguan synonym for beer. The brewery was built on the Crabbs Peninsula to a German design, and its beers are enjoyed all over Antigua and Barbuda. In addition to its own products, it brews Guinness, Red Stripe, and Carib beers under license. Tours of the brewery can be arranged.

📖 **WADADLI BEER**
5.0% ABV • Lager •
A pale lager-style beer; best drunk ice-cold as a thirst-quencher.

CARIB

✉ Eastern Main Road, Champs Fleurs, Trinidad
🖱 www.caribbeer.com

The brewing industry in Trinidad and Tobago was inherited from the British, and the first commercial brewery there was founded just after World War I. The Carib Brewery was founded in 1947 and in 1957 it became the only brewery on Trinidad, when it bought out the Walters' Brewery. In September 1950, the brewery launched its own beer, the dry-tasting Carib Lager. A stronger lager, Stag, followed in 1973.

📖 **CARIB LAGER** 5.2% ABV
• Lager • A full-bodied beer, with a pale golden straw color. Dry but slightly aromatic, with a neutral balance between malt and hops, sweet and bitter.

CARIB LAGER

DESNOES AND GEDDES

✉ 214 Spanish Town, Kingston, Jamaica
🖱 www.jamaicadrinks.com

Eugene Desnoes and Thomas Geddes began brewing in 1927. The company's best-known beer, Red Stripe, was first brewed in 1934. It was an instant success, and a year later Jamaica's Governor sent a dispatch to London warning: "This local industry turns out a beer so excellent, and at so cheap a price, that the English beers are unable to compete." The answer was prompt: "Tax local beer, but not British imports." A public outcry followed and the order was quietly withdrawn. Desnoes and Geddes was acquired by Guinness in 1993.

📖 **DRAGON STOUT** 7.5% ABV •
Sweet stout • A deep, dark-colored beer, primed with sugar on bottling. The flavor is malty with a hint of molasses.

Latin America

Argentina • Brazil • Mexico • Peru

Beer is big business in Latin America, and today it is dominated by InBev. Most beer is distantly derived from the Germanic tradition of pale, light lagers, although the occasional dark, strong beer can be found, such as Noche Buena from Mexico's Moctezuma brewery.

Beers from InBev are on sale just about everywhere in Latin America. InBev was formed in 2004, when Interbrew and Companhia de Bebidas das Américas (AmBev) combined to create what is now the world's largest brewer by volume. It sells 5bn gallons (202m hectoliters) of beer each year, amounting to 14 percent of global beer consumption. InBev has operations in Peru, Venezuela, Guatemala, Ecuador, El Salvador, Nicaragua, and the Dominican Republic. Through its association with Quilmes, it also has a presence in Argentina, Uruguay, Paraguay, Bolivia, and Chile.

Fortunately, it is still possible to find beers other than Brahma, Antarctica, Polar, and similar InBev brews. Among notable brewers is Argentina's Cervecería Blest, in the Patagonian ski resort of Barilcohe. This brewpub produces a refreshing pilsner and a Scotch ale. Also in Argentinian Patagonia is Cervecería El Bolsón, which has brewed beer since 1984, at first for sale in the bar of a campsite, but now with a much wider distribution. The Gibraltar bar in Buenos Aires is a good place to try beers, including the locally produced Antares Scotch ale.

The city of Blumenau in Santa Catarina state, southern Brazil, was founded by German immigrants in 1850. Home to Eisenbahn and several other craft breweries, Blumenau is said to be the Brazilian beer capital. It holds its own annual "Oktoberfest"—a traditional Bavarian-style beer festival.

Blumenau's Oktoberfest, set up to celebrate the region's survival of major flooding in 1984, now attracts thousands of visitors each year.

ANTARES

✉ 12 de Octubre 7749, Mar del Plata, Buenos Aires, Argentina

🖳 www.cervezaantares.com.ar

This brewpub is part of a chain of six stylish, upmarket bars that share the same name. Antares's excellent, largely British- and American-influenced beers include a Scotch ale, a porter, a honey beer, a cream stout, a barley wine, a kölsch, and an Imperial stout. Some are truer to style than others.

▥ **IMPERIAL STOUT** 8.5% ABV • Stout • Dark and handsome, with a strong licorice and toasted palate that gives way to even more intense roasted coffee and caramelized orange flavors.

▥ **KÖLSCH** 5.0% ABV • Kölsch Well-hopped and highly drinkable; good fruity overtones make it an ideal partner to food.

▥ BARBAROJA

✉ Ruta 25 2567, Escobar, Buenos Aires, Argentina

🖳 www.cerveceriabarbaroja.com.ar

This stunning Escobar brewpub opened in 1998 in a 5-acre (2-hectare) leisure complex with a pirate theme. BarbaRoja brews a range of 11 beers, and the heritage of most can be traced back to Germany. September is a good time to visit, as it coincides with Escobar's celebrated festival of flowers.

▥ **NEGRA** 4.5% ABV • Munich dark lager • A crowning white head contrasts with the black body; fresh-tasting, smooth.

BULLER BREWING COMPANY

✉ Presidente Roberto M. Ortiz 1827, Buenos Aires, Argentina

🖳 www.bullerpub.com

This Buenos Aires brewpub is near the Recoleta cemetery, where Eva Perón is buried. It has six beers on tap, including a strong honey beer and an IPA, which lacks a deep hoppy bitterness. Locals and tourists mingle here over pints, peanuts, and pop music. Most locals prefer the refreshing Buller Light Lager (4.5% ABV), which has a low bitterness.

▥ **HONEY BEER** 8.5% ABV • Strong ale • Malts and Argentinian honey give this beer a highly assertive character.

▥ **OKTOBERFEST** 5.5% ABV • Oktoberfest beer • Vienna and Munich malts are used, imparting a strong flavor; the low level of hop-bitterness allows the malt to dominate.

CERVESUR

✉ Variante de Uchumayo 1801, Sachaca, Arequipa, Peru

🖳 www.cusquena.com

Based in southern Peru in the Andes, Cervesur has been brewing since 1898. Its main brand is Cusqueña ("cus-ken-ya"), Peru's top-selling lager. Traditional Peruvian custom holds that when drinking in a group, only one glass is used. The drinker pours a glassful from the bottle, knocks it back, then passes glass and bottle to the next person.

▥ **CUSQUEÑA** 5.0% ABV • Lager Brewed with water from a high Andean source; crisp and refreshing, with a lingering lemon aroma.

EISENBAHN

✉ Cervejaria Sudbrack Ltda, Rua Bahia, 5181—Salto Weissbach 89032-001 Blumenau SC, Brazil

🖳 www.eisenbahn.com.br

In 2002, unhappy with Brazilian mass-market beers, Juliano Mendes and his family decided to build this Blumenau craft brewery. The brewery was named Eisenbahn, which means railroad, after another local brewery of the same name that closed in 1909, unable to compete with bigger commercial firms. Eisenbahn's beers follow traditional European styles, ranging from the Germanic weizenbier to Belgian-style ales. Eisenbahn is now Brazil's largest craft brewery, and its beers are exported to Europe and to the US.

▥ **KOLSCH** 4.8% ABV • Fruity kölsch • A top-fermenting beer brewed with four different malts, including wheat malt. Golden; medium-bodied and malty, with a slight fruity aroma and a low bitterness.

MOCTEZUMA

✉ Monterrey/Veracruz-Llave, Mexico

🖳 www.femsa.com

Perhaps surprisingly, Mexico's smallest national brewer is the country's biggest exporter of beers. Founded in 1890, Moctezuma is today a subsidiary of the beverage giant FEMSA. Its beers tend to be smooth with a spritzy finish. Sol lager is sold in style bars around the world; Dos Equis is broadly a Vienna-style lager; and Noche Buena has rich fruit and malt overtones.

▥ **NOCHE BUENA** 6.0% ABV • Munich dark lager • Deep amber-brown Christmas beer; smooth, brown-sugar sweetness; long, dry finish.

MOCTEZUMA NOCHE BUENA

ASIA AND AUSTRALASIA

From Tokyo in Japan to Adelaide in South Australia, beer culture is blossoming throughout Asia and Australasia. Increasing numbers of drinkers in both continents are seeking out craft-produced beers that stand out from the generic offerings of industrial brewers.

Many countries across Asia and Australasia now play host to a burgeoning craft-brewing scene. Japanese brewing was dominated by two large lager producers for many years, but the country now has scores of craft brewers, producing beers that do not merely mimic European or American styles, but form part of a distinctive Japanese beer culture. The movement received a major boost in 1994, when laws making it easier to obtain a brewing license were introduced. Today, ingredients such as soybean paste, citrus fruit, and Cabernet grapes can be found in the mash tuns and kettles of small breweries across the country. One brewer is even using wild, airborne yeasts to make a distinctive Japanese-style lambic beer.

The beer scene in the southern Pacific is changing, too. Forget the myth that Australians drink only light-colored, yellow lagers: in fact, that never was the case. The nation's drinkers are increasingly looking for innovative, quality beers—a demand that is being met not only by the bigger brewing concerns, but also by a growing number of independent craft producers. Today, there are more than 100 indigenous breweries, producing an exciting array of beer styles. The change in Australia's drinking culture has been driven partly by the explosive growth of the country's wine industry, but beer is now establishing itself as a serious presence on the market.

The beermaking industry of New Zealand was controlled by two major brewers until the end of the 1980s. Since then, however, there has been a steady growth in the number of microbreweries and brewpubs. While its beers are still relatively unknown on the international market, New Zealand is becoming increasingly well-known among brewers as a source of high-quality hops.

The brewing industry is still evolving in other parts of Asia and Australasia, and it will be interesting to see how it develops among the giant populations of China and India in the future. Beijing and Shanghai already have brewpubs of distinction, and the island of Sri Lanka continues to produce Lion Stout, a beer that is known and loved by beer enthusiasts all over the world. Large, multinational brewers still dominate many other parts of both continents, but experience suggests that eventually people will want to buy locally produced craft brews that satisfy local tastes.

A billboard promotes lager from the giant Japanese brewer Asahi. While such products remain popular, innovative craft brews are gaining ground.

Japan

Honshu • Hokkaido • Kyushu • Shikoku

Liberated from restrictive brewing laws in the mid-1990s and inspired by the burgeoning US craft-brewery movement, Japan has a new generation of small-scale brewers producing beers in an impressive variety of styles, both classic and original.

As sake is made from a cereal grain (rice), it is surely not a wine, but a beer. If that is accepted, then Japan is one of the oldest beermaking nations in the world. In the years following World War II, Japan essentially produced only lagers, with the long-popular Kirin lager defining the Japanese style. By the early 1980s, Kirin controlled about two-thirds of the market, with the remainder divided between the Asahi, Orion, Sapporo, and Suntory breweries.

There has been a surprising degree of traditionalism among Japanese brewers, but the 1987 introduction of Asahi Super Dry, a light, crisp lager fermented with a highly attenuating yeast to minimize natural sweetness, marked the beginning of a change. At almost the same time,

a handful of importers, notably Konishi Shuzo—the 400-year-old brewer of Shirayuki sake—began importing Belgian brews. Starting with Hoegaarden and other brands, the company now imports a large portfolio of Belgian ales into Japan, alongside nearly 20 other importers.

Real change occurred in 1994, when the annual capacity requirement for obtaining a brewing license in Japan was reduced from 528,344 gallons (2m liters) to just 15,850 gallons (60,000 liters). This opened the door for the proliferation of small craft breweries, although their growth slowed from 1999 amid a long economic slump. In 2002, craft-beer consumption began to decline as the novelty wore off for consumers, but by 2006 it was rising again, as brewers started to produce fuller-flavored and higher-quality beers. A small craft-beer niche has been created, and it looks set to broaden. While standard lagers still dominate the market in Japan, the future looks bright for craft beer.

The Sapporo brewery on Hokkaido. Sapporo has long been a dominant force in Japanese brewing.

BAIRD BREWING

✉ 19-4 Senbonminato-cho, Numazu, Shizuoka 410-0845
🖰 www.bairdbeer.com

American Bryan Baird and his wife Sayuri founded this microbrewery in 2001, brewing almost daily on a 8-gallon (30-liter) system in a small room behind the bar. Within a year, Baird developed a reputation for brewing some of the country's finest craft ales.

In 2006, he opened a 66-gallon (2.5-hectoliter) brewery nearby, and now supplies a number of pub and retail accounts nationwide. Competition has increased in recent years, as the better craft brewers further hone their skills and diversify their approaches, but Baird still retains a top reputation. Only two hours away from Tokyo, Baird's Fishmarket Taproom draws in many city folk on weekends.

🍺 **RISING SUN PALE ALE** 5.0% ABV • US pale ale • The citrussy hop flavor, powerful malt presence, and crisp finish place this in the US West Coast tradition.

🍺 **RED ROSE AMBER ALE** 5.4% ABV • Amber ale • Lower-temperature fermentation gives this robust, fruity ale a refreshingly crisp finish.

BAIRD BREWING RISING SUN PALE ALE

ECHIGO BEER

✉ 3790 Fukui, Nishikan-ku, Niigata City 953-0076
🖰 www.echigo-beer.jp/bluepub.html

Echigo opened in February 1995 as Japan's first brewpub by Uehara Shuzo, a noted sake brewer that supplies to the Japanese royal household. A larger brewery was opened nearby in April 1999 to supply less expensive canned and bottled products. The original brewpub still makes the company's better beers, and supplies kegs to beer specialty bars elsewhere. Despite its remote location, it is definitely worth a visit if you have the time.

🍺 **STOUT** 6.0% ABV • Dry stout • Robust, with aromas of dark roast coffee. Creamy texture; appreciably different from Echigo's cheaper canned version.

🍺 **PILSENER** 5.0% ABV • Pilsner • Solid yet refreshing pilsner brewed exclusively with Saaz hops.

HAKUSEKIKAN

✉ 5251-1 Hirukawa Tahara, Nakatsugawa, Gifu 509-8310
🖰 www.hakusekikan-beer.jp

One of the most distinctive and original breweries in Japan, Hakusekikan was founded in 1997 within the grounds of a traditional stone-cutting theme park in the mountains of the largely rural prefecture of Gifu.

Brewmaster Satoshi Niwa works with unusual yeasts, including an airborne strain native to his area, to produce high-gravity ales with unique character, along with standard-type beers and even a non-alcoholic ale. Much of the brewery's output is sold online, and some is shipped directly to restaurants and retailers. In addition to Shizen Bakushu and Super Vintage (*see above right*), beers of particular note are the pale and heavy Crystal Ale (12% ABV); orange-scented Golden Ale (5% ABV); and Hurricane (16.3% ABV)—a monstrously

HAKUSEKIKAN SHIZEN BAKUSHU

delicious ale that is available only at the Beer Club Popeye in Tokyo.

🍺 **SHIZEN BAKUSHU** 5.0% ABV • Strong ale • A richly fruity, yet sharply tart, light-colored ale made with malt, honey, and natural airborne yeast; low in bitterness.

🍺 **SUPER VINTAGE** 14.3% ABV • Strong ale • Exceedingly fruity initial sensation, laced with noticeable alcohol, followed by layers of malt unfolding over a sherrylike tartness. A remarkable beer, and a festival favorite.

HITACHINO NEST

✉ 1257 Konousu, Naka City, Ibaraki
🖰 www.kodawari.cc

Produced by old-line sake brewer Kiuchi Shuzo, Hitachino Nest may be the most famous Japanese craft beer outside Japan, with roughly half of production exported—primarily to the US. Aside from US-style craft beers and a few Belgian styles, distinctive brews with Japanese touches are also produced by Hitachino Nest.

There is also an interesting brew-on-premise (BOP) facility where customers brew small batches of beer, with the company handling taxation, bottling, and shipping, because home-brewing is still illegal in Japan. This enterprising brewery also produces distilled spirits and even wine made from Hitachino's own grapes.

🍺 **WHITE ALE** 5.0% ABV • White ale • Patterned loosely after a Belgian witbier, but with more expansive spice flavors and a distinct citrus flavor in the background that brings orange juice to mind.

🍺 **EXTRA HIGH** 8.0% ABV • Strong ale • Again, this beer is loosely patterned after a Belgian double or heavy brown ale, with a reddish-brown color, vigorously complex aroma, and a nearly seamless integration of a diverse array of flavors.

ISEKADOYA

✉ 6-428 Jingu, Ise, Mie 516-0017
🖐 www.biyagura.jp

Established some 400 years ago as a tea house, this enterprise grew into a manufacturer of soy sauce and miso, and brewed beer for a short period in the late 19th century. Brewing resumed in the late 1990s, and Isekadoya now makes restrained but alluringly delicious brews. Recent seasonal releases include Weizenbock and Imperial Smoked Porter.

▶ PALE ALE 5.0% ABV • Pale ale
A superb execution that is neither British nor American, with moderate Cascade hopping and a complex but subdued malt profile.

▶ YUZU PALE ALE
5.0% ABV • Fruit beer
A slightly different pale ale recipe seems to form the base of this seasonal ale made with yuzu (a native aromatic citrus). Unlike other fruit beers, the flavor is restrained, emerging only in the aroma and in the long, soft aftertaste.

KINSHACHI

✉ 1-7-34 Sakae, Naka-ku, Nagoya City 460-0008
🖐 www.kinshachi.jp

Created in the late 1800s by sake brewer Morita Shuzo, Kinshachi Beer was revived in 1996 by a subsidiary company, Morita Land Beer. Next to Kinshachi's headquarters in downtown Nagoya is Beer Circus, the flagship taproom and restaurant, while the brewery

itself is located in the suburbs. Kinshachi is most famous for two types of lager that contain miso (fermented soybean paste)— a specialty of Nagoya. The original Red Miso Lager was created for the Aichi Expo in 2005, and Black Miso Lager was launched the following year. Kinshachi also brews pilsner, alt, stout, and pale ale styles, and seasonals, such as dunkelbock.

KINSHACHI BLACK MISO LAGER

▶ RED MISO LAGER
6.0% ABV • Specialty lager • Dark reddish-brown; rich, tangy, and full-bodied with sharp hop bitterness and a creamy texture. The taste of miso is kept far in the background, but contributes to the beer's richness.

▶ BLACK MISO LAGER
6.0% ABV • Specialty lager • Very deep reddish-brown; has a rich aroma with hints of soy sauce, and a rich tanginess that lingers in the long finish. An interesting new flavor in dark beer.

MINOH AJI BEER

✉ 3-19-11 Makiochi, Minoh, Osaka 562-0004
🖐 www.minoh-beer.jp

Minoh AJI beer was founded in 1997 in northern Osaka by resident liquor-store owner Masaji Ohshita, who

Dark beers, such as this stout from Minoh Aji, are growing steadily more popular in Japan.

put his daughters Kaori and Mayuko in charge of brewing duties. The company also operates three pubs in the Osaka area specializing in their beer.

Minoh AJI Beer's forward-thinking and diverse product portfolio includes pilsner, lager, weizen, pale ale, double IPA, and hemp styles, plus an ale made with Cabernet grape juice.

▶ DOUBLE IPA 9.0% ABV • Strong ale • Patterned after the hoppy high-gravity beers that are currently popular in the US, with a rich, tangy malt profile and a brisk, hoppy bitterness.

▶ STOUT 5.5% ABV • Stout
This is a rich, malty stout with minimal bitterness, featuring roasty flavors that are accented by just a touch of sweetness.

OTARU BEER

✉ 263-19, Zenibako 3-chome, Otaru, Hokkaido 047-0261
🖐 www.otarubeer.com

Thoroughly German in style, Otaru Beer is a true gem of a brewery located in a seaport on Hokkaido, the most northerly of Japan's major islands.

Brewmaster Johannes Braun makes absolutely superb versions of pilsner, dunkel, and weiss beers that would certainly make his counterparts in Germany jealous. The brewery ships its products only within a 60-mile (100-km) radius to ensure quality and freshness.

OTARU PILS 4.9% ABV • Pilsner
This is a Czech-style pilsner brewed with fresh aroma hops. Colder fermentation and extended lagering time create a crisp, refreshing taste on the palate.

OTARU WEISS 5.4% ABV • Weiss beer • A true weiss beer is rare in Japan, and Otaru does this one particularly well. It is filtered to be bright and golden, with light clove and banana aromas.

OTARU DUNKEL 5.2% ABV • Dunkel • Wonderfully fine; deep reddish amber with a bright off-white head. Its texture is smooth and soft, with caramel malt flavors predominating over the brisk, snappy finish.

T.Y. HARBOR

✉ 2-1-3 Higashi Shinagawa, Shinagawa-ku, Tokyo 140-0002
🖐 www.tyharborbrewing.co.jp

Founded by warehousing company Terada Sohko at their premises on the Tokyo Bay waterfront, this is the only microbrewery operation of any consequence in central Tokyo. In addition to wheat ale, organic lager, pale ale, amber ale, and porter styles, a variety of seasonals are crafted by brewmaster Kazunaga Abe. Noted American chef David Chiddo creates culinary masterpieces in the brewery's restaurant.

TENNOZU PALE ALE 5.0% ABV • Pale ale • This highly hopped beer is the company's flagship brew, and is definitely in the US West Coast style. It sports a bright bronze color, a creamy ivory head, and a lingering, floral hop finish.

YOHO BREWING

✉ 1119-1 Otai, Saku, Nagano 385-0009
🖐 www.yohobrewing.com

Yona Yona Pale Ale is one of the most widely available craft beers in Japan, and is sold on tap and in colorful cans. However, producer Yoho Brewing makes a number of different beers that are relatively unknown. Its seasonals have included a Belgian-style abbey ale, a Scottish ale, and even a French-style bière de garde. Brewmaster Toshi Ishii, who had previously worked at Stone Brewing in California (*see p.249*), recently created another high-profile product, Tokyo Black, which is aimed at the growing market for dark beer.

The brewery is located in the picturesque mountain resort region of Karuizawa, where a great deal of whiskey is also produced.

YONA YONA PALE ALE 5.0% ABV • US pale ale • The strong dose of Cascade hops tips you off immediately that this is a US West Coast-style pale ale, with a creamy malt texture strong enough to balance its hop aromas and bitterness.

TOKYO BLACK 5.0% ABV • Porter Opaque near-black, with a dark tan head; aromas of dried fruit, sweet coffee, and chocolate cake. Smooth texture, with only a little deep, roast, burned flavor.

EIKOKU BAKUSHU BARLEYWINE 8.5% ABV • Strong ale • This is a decidedly Japanese take on the classic British strong ale, with very good malt character and a lot of hop bitterness. It is wonderfully warming and rich, but not too strong.

Tennozu Isle, home of the T.Y. Harbor brewery, which is visible in the foreground.

Other countries of Asia

China • India • Indonesia • Hong Kong • Singapore • Sri Lanka • Thailand

European-style beers have been brewed in Asia since the late 1800s, but few would have predicted the growth of the beer market in recent years. Consumption in China, for example, now exceeds that in the US, spurred on by a rise in average earnings and economic reforms.

The Chinese beer market is very complex and still largely regional, with most towns having their own brewery. The leading national brand is Tsingtao, —a hoppy, light-bodied pilsner that is also well known outside China.

India, too, has a large and thriving brewing industry, dating back to the early days of the British Empire, when breweries were built to slake the throats of the troops. Kingfisher and Lal Toofan are two of India's best-known beers.

There is huge potential for growth in the region: India alone has a population of more than 1 billion, but consumes less than 1¾ pints (a liter) of beer annually per head. This has not gone unnoticed by the bigger breweries. While Asia has

its own international brewers, such as the Singapore-based Asia Pacific and San Miguel of Indonesia, it is the real behemoths of world brewing that are likely to reap the spoils, and they are already eagerly buying up blocks of shares in Asian companies as markets in the region become more open. The US giant Anheuser-Busch, for example, now has a 27-percent share in Tsingtao, while Heineken owns part of the Singapore-based Asia Pacific and Indonesia's Multi Bintang. SABMiller and InBev also have large stakes in the region.

But all is not lost, as brewpubs are springing up in cosmopolitan cities such as Beijing and Shanghai, with German brewer Paulaner leading the way.

Indonesia's largest brewer,
Multi Bintang, is one of the jewels in Heineken's Asian crown.

BINTANG
— Pilsener —

ASIA PACIFIC BREWERIES

✉ 459 Jalan Ahmad Ibrahim, Singapore 639934
🖰 www.tigerbeer.com

Asia Pacific Breweries has more than 20 breweries in 10 countries across the region. Its best-known brand, Tiger Beer, has been produced since the 1930s, when the "Time for a Tiger" slogan was first coined. Bland to taste, it is best drunk well-chilled. Asia Pacific also produces the creamy, roasty, medium-dry ABC Extra Stout. Heineken now has a share in the company.

🍺 **TIGER BEER** 5.1% ABV • Lager • Golden; refreshing but bland. It is normally served so chilled that its taste and aromas are largely masked.

ASIA PACIFIC BREWERIES TIGER BEER

BOON RAWD

✉ 999 Samsen Road, Bangkok, Thailand 10300
🖰 www.boonrawd.co.th

Boon Rawd, Thailand's first and largest brewery, was founded by Phraya Bhirom Bhakdi in 1933 with the aid of German engineering expertise. At present, the company operates three breweries, producing 211m gallons (8m hectoliters) of beer per year.

Boon Rawd's best-known beer, both home and abroad, is its hop-bitter Singha Lager, which is easily recognized by the lion that graces its label. The company also produces a draft unpasteurized version. Thai Beer, at 6.5% ABV, is also widely available.

🍺 **SINGHA** 6.0% ABV • Lager A full-bodied, clean-tasting barley malt beer with a strong hop character.

🍺 **SINGHA LIGHT** 3.5% ABV • Lager Lacks both the complexity and vitality of its much stronger stablemate.

HONG KONG S.A.R. BREWING COMPANY

✉ 29 Wong Chuk Hang Road, Vita Tower Unit A1, 1/F, Aberdeen, Hong Kong
🖰 www.wrongdesign.com/hksarb/

Opened in 1995, this was one of the first micro-breweries in Asia, and supplies many Hong Kong pubs with its exclusive brews. Its beers are sold to pubs, such as the East End Brewery in Causeway Bay (www.elgrande.com.hk). This cosy bar, which also stocks some of the world's best microbrewed beers, proudly displays its slogan "Let No Man Thirst For Want Of Real Ale" and is well worth a visit. The brewery's beers can also be enjoyed at the Hong Kong Brew House in Wyndham Street, and at similar outlets in Singapore and in Manila in the Philippines.

🍺 **TOO SOO** 4.5% ABV • Lager Full-bodied with fine hop notes; the use of Vienna malt gives it a slightly reddish hue.

MULTI BINTANG

✉ Surabaya, Central Java, Indonesia
🖰 www.multibintang.co.id

Bintang means star in Indonesian, and Indonesia's largest brewery is certainly a star in Heineken's crown. It produces and markets a range of products including Bir Bintang, Heineken, Guinness Stout, and the low-alcohol beer Green Sands.

Bintang was founded in 1929 as NV Nederlandsch Indische Bierbrouwerijen. Heineken became the largest shareholder in 1936. The company's first brand was Java Bier. The Indonesian government appropriated

the company in 1957, banning the Heineken name and replacing it with the Bir Bintang name. It remained under state control until 1965. Heineken became involved again in 1967. Today, Bintang operates breweries in Sampang Agung and Tangerang.

🍺 **BINTANG BIR PILSENER** 4.8 ABV% • Pilsner • Light gold; the fresh malty aroma gives way to a palate with a hoppy bitterness and a dry, hop-bitter finish.

LION BREWERY

✉ Nuwara Eliya & Biyagama, Sri Lanka
🖰 www.lionbeer.com

Sri Lanka's first brewery was founded in 1881 by Scottish tea planter Sir Samuel Backer. Located 3,500 ft (1,000 m) above sea level in the hill region of Nuwara Eliy, it sits beneath one of Sri Lanka's most famous waterfalls, known as Lover's Leap. In 1999, the company built a new brewery in the town of Biyagama. After the Indian Ocean tsunami of 2004, the brewery's production facility in Colombo switched to producing bottled water for survivors of the disaster.

🍺 **LION STOUT** 8.0% ABV • Stout A world-class beer with pruney, mocha aromas and flavors. It has a tarlike oiliness of body, and a peppery, bitter-chocolate finish.

LION STOUT

Australia

Victoria • Western Australia • South Australia • New South Wales • Tasmania

The spectacular growth of Australia's wine industry in recent times has dramatically changed the country's drinking landscape. The mainstream beer brands have faltered, but this has been more than offset by a rapid rise in demand for local premium and craft beers.

Ironically, Australia's best-known beer brand—Foster's Lager—is largely ignored by drinkers at home, where it commands a mere one percent of the Australian beer market. Victoria Bitter (VB) is the best-selling brand nationally, accounting for one in every five beers consumed. Both brands are made by Foster's, the country's largest brewer, which has diversified heavily into wine and other alcoholic beverages in recent years.

Foster's' nearest rival, Lion Nathan, controls a quartet of breweries in different states—Tooheys (New South Wales), XXXX (Queensland), Swan (Western Australia), and the South Australian Brewing Company. The group also recently made an unsuccessful attempt to buy out the family-owned Coopers Brewery in Adelaide. After Lion Nathan, Coopers and the Tasmanian Boags are, respectively, the country's third and fourth largest brewers.

The number of microbreweries has doubled in the past five years and there are now more than 100 operators—most concentrated in Victoria and Western Australia. Significantly, Matilda Bay, the craft-beer market leader, is now under the ownership of Foster's, while Lion Nathan controls the Malt Shovel Brewery and has increased its shareholding in Little Creatures. In addition to these three leading players, there is a whole raft of independent craft brewers of all shapes and sizes, all contributing to the vibrant diversity of beer currently available Down Under.

Cascade Brewery sits against the majestic backdrop of Mt. Wellington.

CASCADE BREWERY

1824   1927

BOOTLEG

✉ Pusey Road, Wilyabrup, Margaret River, Western Australia 6285
🖰 www.bootlegbrewery.com.au

In operation since 1994, this microbrewery is based in a sprawling homestead-style building that incorporates a tasting room, bar, restaurant, and spacious outdoor beer garden overlooking a lake. As such, it makes a popular lunchtime destination not only for beerhounds, but also for wine tourists exploring the Margaret River region. There are currently four other craft brewers in the area.

▮ **TOM'S BROWN ALE** 4.0% ABV • English brown ale • Deep garnet-brown; roasty and bitter initially, with treacle notes; dry finish.

▮ **RAGING BULL** 7.1% ABV • Strong dark ale • Dark mahogany; complex coffee, treacle, and bitter chocolate notes; late bitterness.

CASCADE

✉ 131 Cascade Road, South Hobart, Tasmania 7004
🖰 www.cascadebrewery.com.au

The founder of the Cascade Brewery Co., Peter Degraves, vowed to give his customers "beer that cannot be excelled in this colony." Australia's oldest operating brewery and, arguably, the most picturesque, Cascade is now part of the Foster's empire. In recent years there has been a series of limited-edition brands from this brewer, including the annual First Harvest Ale made with unkilned, Tasmanian-grown hop flowers. Blonde (2006 World Beer Cup gold medal winner) is the sole survivor from the short-lived Cascade Four Seasons range.

▮ **BLONDE** 4.8% ABV • Summer ale • Clean and crisp; a hint of citrus hop flavor.

▮ **STOUT** 5.8% ABV • Medium stout Coffee notes upfront, with milk chocolate; moderately bitter finish.

COOPERS
SPARKLING ALE

COOPERS

✉ 461 South Road, Regency Park, Adelaide, South Australia 5010
🖰 www.coopersbrewery.com.au

Established in 1862, Coopers is a family-run Adelaide brewery that has specialized in bottle-conditioned "cloudy" ales and stouts for much of its existence, only belatedly embracing kegs in the 1980s. Sustained for many years by a cultlike following, Coopers has now grown to be a significant national player, especially after the opening of its new, ultramodern brewery in 2001.

▮ **SPARKLING ALE** 5.8% ABV • Pale ale • Cloudy and fruity, with a hint of peaches; rounded, dry, yeasty finish.

▮ **EXTRA STOUT** 6.4% ABV • Dry stout • Espresso and bitter chocolate notes, with banana hints; robustly bitter finish.

GAGE ROADS

✉ 14 Absolon Street, Palmyra, Western Australia 6957
🖰 www.gageroads.com.au

This ambitious Palmyra outfit began in mid-2005, and was soon calling itself "Australia's largest independent craft brewer." Started by Peter Nolin and Bill Hoedemaker, who honed their brewing

skills at Fremantle's Sail & Anchor brewpub, Gage Roads was soon distributing its flavorsome beers across the whole country.

▮ **PURE MALT LAGER** 4.7% ABV • German lager • Full-bodied; rich malt balanced by a bold bitterness (like a northern German lager).

▮ **IPA** 5.1% ABV • India pale ale Big malty palate; robust bitterness emerges late and lingers on and on.

HOLGATE

✉ 79 High Street, Woodend, Victoria 3442
🖰 www.holgatebrewhouse.com

Paul Holgate started his microbrewery during the late 1990s in a shed adjacent to his home in Woodend. In 2002, he and his wife Tanya leased the sprawling, 100-year-old Keatings Hotel and put their beers on tap. They subsequently relocated the brewery to the pub. Both of the beers below are served by traditional handpump and are also available bottled.

▮ **ESB** 5.0% ABV • English bitter Softly carbonated; hints of toffee and apricots; well-bittered.

▮ **MAHOGANY & MALT** 6.0% ABV • Porter • Chewy caramel and dark chocolate notes; rounded, warming finish. Released seasonally in bottles with the name Winter Ale.

HOLGATE
ESB

KNAPPSTEIN

✉ 2 Pioneer Avenue, Clare, South Australia 5453
🖰 www.lion-nathan.com.au

In the 1970s, the Knappstein winery set up home at the Enterprise Brewery in the Clare Valley. Beer had not been produced in this gorgeous stone building since 1916, but history turned full circle in 2006 when a micro-brewery was installed and beer flowed once more as a sideline to the regular winemaking activities. Knappstein is owned by Lion Nathan.

RESERVE LAGER 5.6% ABV • Bavarian lager • Complex, with ripe fruit notes (passionfruit, melons) and rich malt; fulsome bitterness.

LITTLE CREATURES

✉ 40 Mews Road, Fremantle, Western Australia 6160
🖰 www.littlecreatures.com.au

Started in 2000 by a group of Matilda Bay executives, Little Creatures introduced the hoppy US pale-ale style to the Australian market with its flagship bottle-conditioned beer. The microbrewery, housed inside a large warehouse on the waterfront at Fremantle, has a pizzeria and bar inside the working brewery, with tap beer poured directly from serving tanks.

Yeast is added to every bottle of Little Creatures pale ale, allowing fermentation to continue right up until the point of drinking.

PALE ALE 5.2% ABV • US pale ale • Citrus (grapefruit) hop aromatics, chewy malt; robust bitterness.

Amber ale • Biscuity malt notes; caramel-laced mid-palate; spicy-citrus hoppiness.

LORD NELSON

✉ 19 Kent Street, The Rocks, Sydney, New South Wales 2000
🖰 www.lordnelson.com.au

The longest-running modern brewpub in Sydney, the Lord Nelson has been pumping out English-style ales for two decades. Housed in a striking historic sandstone building, the Lord Nelson is a must-visit for serious beerophiles. The flavorsome Three Sheets pale ale, their biggest seller, and Old Admiral are now available in bottles.

OLD ADMIRAL 6.7% ABV • Strong ale • Hints of toffee and dark fruit; substantial bitterness; warming afterglow.

MALT SHOVEL IPA

MALT SHOVEL

✉ 99 Pyrmont Bridge Road, Camperdown, Sydney, New South Wales 2050
🖰 www.maltshovel.com.au

Relaunched in 1998 under the guidance of brewmaster Dr. Charles Hahn, Malt Shovel has blossomed as the successful craft-beer division of the Lion Nathan group. Its regular brands are named after James Squire, a reformed highwayman and convict who became Australia's first successful brewer and hop-grower.

IPA 5.6% ABV • India pale ale Chewy, caramel-tinged maltiness balanced by robust (dry-hopped) hop flavor and lingering bitterness.

ORIGINAL PILSENER 5.0% ABV • Czech pilsner • Rich, malty palate, with honey notes and a substantial bitterness.

PORTER 5.0% ABV • Porter Hints of espresso, dark chocolate, and dark fruit (plums); smooth finish.

MATILDA BAY

✉ 130 Stirling Highway, North Fremantle, Western Australia 6159
🖰 www.matildabay.com.au

Matilda Bay, Australia's pioneering craft brewer, was set up in Fremantle in 1984 and soon established a niche with exotic beer styles such as hefeweizen (Redback) and dark lager (Dogbolter). Bought out by Foster's in 1990, it has been revamped and revitalized in recent years. Matilda Bay brands are now produced at various breweries within the Foster's group, including the so-called "garage" brewery outside Melbourne, which produces a range of "out-there" styles, such as saison (Barking Duck) and Crema (a coffee-infused pale ale).

ALPHA ALE 5.2% ABV • US pale ale • Rich, caramel-toffee

AUSTRALIAN ALES

In the colonial era, Australia's early brewers struggled to produce English-style ales in often hostile temperatures. Consequently, when refrigerated lager-brewing arrived in the late 1800s, it was embraced with relish. Foster's Lager was one of the first brands produced by this "new" form of brewing, which soon superseded the "old." A handful of ales survived, mainly in Adelaide (made by Coopers) and New South Wales, where they are still called "old" (as in Tooheys Old Ale and Kent Old Brown). Many ale brands simply became lagers, so that today many "ales" are in reality all rather bland lagers.

TOOHEYS OLD ALE

malt character; resinous hop flavor; bold, bitter finish.

▥ BOHEMIAN PILSNER 5.0% ABV • Czech pilsner • Solid maltiness, well balanced by a generous hop bitterness.

▥ DOGBOLTER 5.2% ABV • Dark lager • Roasty, dark chocolate notes; complex mid-palate; smooth finish.

MOO BREW

✉ 655 Main Road, Berriedale, Hobart, Tasmania 7011
🖰 www.moobrew.com.au

This microbrewery, an off-shoot of the Moorilla Estate on the outskirts of Hobart, is one of the best-appointed in the land. There are sweeping views up the Derwent River from the second-story, glass-fronted brewhouse, and Mt. Wellington looms behind.

▥ WHEAT BEER 4.9% ABV • Hefeweizen • Flavorsome and yeasty; prominent banana notes and a hint of cloves.

▥ DARK ALE 5.0% ABV • US brown ale • Subtle roasted notes entwine with citrus hop flavors in this beer.

MOUNTAIN GOAT

✉ Corner North and Clarke Streets, Richmond, Melbourne, Victoria 3121
🖰 www.goatbeer.com.au

Good mates Cam Hines and Dave Bonighton helped to make craft beer hip when they started their Mountain Goat brewing venture in the late 1990s, and they have since been an inspiration for dozens of aspiring Victorian brewers. Mountain Goat hosts "open nights" every Friday at its new Melbourne brewery, so that "goat army" regulars can trot in for their ale fix.

▥ HIGHTAIL ALE 5.0% ABV • English pale ale • Cloudy amber; chewy malt, with bristling hop flavor and bitterness.

REDOAK

✉ 201 Clarence Street, Sydney, New South Wales 2000
🖰 www.redoak.com.au

Since launching in mid-2004, brewer David Hollyoak has won numerous awards and raised eyebrows with his staggering array of beer styles, all of which can be sampled at the Redoak Boutique Beer Café (the brewery is located in western Sydney). His love affair with esoteric beer styles and matching foods borders on the obsessive.

▥ FRAMBOISE FROMENT 5.2% ABV • Fruit-based ale • Hazy, crimson; tart raspberry notes; super-dry finish.

REDOAK FRAMBOISE FROMENT

▥ BLACKBERRY HEFEWEIZEN 5.2% ABV • Hefeweizen • Pinkish-purple (brewed with real blackberries); banana notes; tart, fruity finish.

SCHARER'S

✉ 180 Argyle Street, Picton, New South Wales 2571
🖰 www.scharers.com.au

Country publican Geoffrey Scharer was one of the craft-beer movement's pioneers. In 1987 he installed a second-hand microbrewery into the George IV Inn, Picton, to brew and serve unfiltered German lager and bock (no other beers were available in his pub). In 2006 he sold the enterprise, but the new owners are committed to continuing Scharer's vision.

▥ SCHARER'S LAGER 5.0% ABV • Bavarian lager • Hazy, floral hops, with caramel notes and a generous bitterness.

▥ BURRAGORANG BOCK 6.4% ABV • Bock • Dark brown; chocolate and Horlicks notes; smooth, warming finish.

WIG AND PEN

✉ Canberra House Arcade, Civic, Canberra, Australian Capital Territory 2601
🖰 www.wigandpen.com.au

This busy brewpub has been going strong since 1993. Brewer Richard Watkins recently clocked up 10 years' service and reckons he's brewed just about every beer style imaginable in that time. Wig and Pen's seasonal brews complement ten regular beers, including three hand-pumped real ales.

▥ PALE ALE 5.3% ABV • US pale ale • Cask-conditioned; floral hops, toffee notes; dry finish.

▥ CREAMY VELVET STOUT 6.0% ABV • Dry stout • Creamy body; chocolate and caramel notes; smooth finish.

New Zealand

Auckland • Wellington • Christchurch • Dunedin

Famous for fine white wines, New Zealand is also a top beer nation. Its brewing history dates from 1773, when Captain Cook made a famous brew using molasses spiced with sprigs from the native trees manuka and rimu to fend off scurvy among his crew (*see* The Mussel Inn, *p.274*).

With its rugged terrain, long distances between cities, and comparatively small population—even today only four million people live in a land mass roughly the size of the UK—New Zealand is ideally suited to having small regional breweries serving local communities. In fact, a hundred years after Cook's first beer, the country boasted one brewery for every 6,000 people.

Sadly, a century later the situation had changed dramatically. As a result of mergers within the industry and some of the world's most repressive licensing laws—including the early closing of pubs, which led to the infamous "six o'clock swill"—New Zealand was reduced to just two major brewing groups, New Zealand Breweries (now Lion Nathan) and Dominion Breweries (DB).

The breakthrough came in 1981, when former All Black rugby player Terry McCashin opened Mac's Brewery. Its success led to a steady stream of new breweries, breaking the stranglehold of the "big two." While the major players still dominate New Zealand's beer market, there are now about 50 microbreweries and brewpubs dotted around the country. New Zealand is also a significant hop-producer, and around 80 percent of its annual crop is exported. One of only three regions in the southern hemisphere where these aromatic plants flourish, New Zealand is respected by brewers worldwide for the quality of its hops.

The Avon River flows placidly past Oxford Terrace in Christchurch. European influences abound here, including in the region's beers.

DUX DE LUX

✉ Corner Hereford and Montreal Streets, Christchurch, and 14–16 Church Street, Queenstown

🖥 www.thedux.co.nz

With a brewpub in the arts center in Christchurch and another in Queenstown, close to the shores of Lake Wakatipu, Dux de Lux is one of South Island's most revered craft brewers. Brewer, winemaker, and chef Richard Fife oversees the brewing of a broad range of lagers and ales, plus limited-release seasonal specialties—anything from a blueberry brown ale to a porter aged in pinot-noir barrels.

🍺 **NOR'WESTER ALE** 6.5% ABV • **Strong English-style pale ale** Copper-colored; has a grainy sweetness, with hints of nuts and smoke, fruity esters, and a deep, lingering hop dryness in the finish.

🍺 **BLACK SHAG STOUT** 5.5% ABV • **Irish-style dry stout** • Dense; a creamy head and silky-smooth body; dry hops and a roasted-grain tartness.

EMERSON'S BREWERY

✉ 14 Wickliffe Street, Dunedin
🖥 www.emersons.co.nz

Richard Emerson's first brew —a dry, roasty porter—was launched in 1993 into a Kiwi beer market dominated by sweet, bland lagers. Thirteen years later, in 2006, Emerson celebrated brewing his millionth liter and a second relocation to larger premises in Dunedin.

Emerson's, New Zealand's most awarded microbrewery, offers an enviable portfolio of year-round beers, as well as seasonal specialties such as Taieri George, a spiced dark ale, and APA, an American strong ale featuring American hops.

Aside from Bookbinder Bitter, which is sold only on tap, Emerson's beers are available both on draft and in 500 ml bottles. When

EMERSON'S 1812 IPA

visiting Dunedin, be sure to find time for a pint or two at the remarkable Inch Bar, opposite the city's Botanic Gardens.

🍺 **1812 IPA** 5.0% ABV • **Pale ale** Amber; a delightful orange marmaladelike fruitiness, and an earthy, hoppy finish.

🍺 **OLD 95** 7.0% ABV • **Barley wine** Deep amber; a rich, toffeelike maltiness, with a dry, resiny, hoppy finish.

🍺 **PILSNER** 4.9% ABV • **Pilsner (organic)** • Golden; bursting with passionfruit and citrus notes (Saaz hops), with a lingering dry finish.

🍺 **OATMEAL STOUT** 4.8% ABV • **Oatmeal stout (organic)** • Dark brown to black; sweetish, with chocolate, caramel, and coffee flavors, and a soft, oily palate.

GALBRAITH'S ALEHOUSE

✉ 2 Mount Eden Road, Mount Eden, Auckland
🖥 www.alehouse.co.nz

Based in the former Grafton library in Mount Eden, Auckland, the North Island's only "real ale" brewpub first fired its kettles in June 1995. Despite a background in the wine industry, owner-brewer Keith Galbraith developed a love of traditional cask-conditioned English ales when he was traveling in the UK. He was subsequently taught how to brew them by Bob Hudson, formerly the brewer at Larkins of Kent.

These days the brewery's range also includes fine Bohemian- and Munich-style

lagers, but the hand-pulled ales, which are notably hoppy and full-flavored, remain the pub's main attraction. Galbraith's also offers a fine selection of imported and New Zealand craft beers.

🍺 **BOB HUDSON'S BITTER** 4.0% ABV • **English-style bitter** A full-flavored "session" bitter that bears more than a passing similarity to Timothy Taylor's Landlord (*see p.166*).

🍺 **BELLRINGERS BITTER** 4.5% ABV • **English-style best bitter** Coppery, with a flowery hop character and dry finish.

🍺 **GRAFTON PORTER** 5.0% ABV • **Porter** • Dark brown to black; full-bodied, with chocolate flavors, and a bitter-sweet finish.

🍺 **RESURRECTION** 8.0% ABV • **Belgian-style abbey ale** • Dark amber; warming ale with plenty of bubblegum, plus spicy and medicinal notes.

GALBRAITH'S ALEHOUSE RESURRECTION

MAC'S

✉ 660 Main Road, Stoke, Nelson
🖥 www.macs.co.nz

Eighteen years after opening his pioneering microbrewery in an old cider factory in Nelson, former All Black Terry McCashin sold the brand to Lion Breweries (part of Lion Nathan) in 1999. Since then, the Mac's range has been extended and production is now split between Nelson and Lion's Shed 22 brewery on the Wellington waterfront.

Mac's has employed several British-born head-brewers. The current brewer,

BEER—KIWI STYLE

New Zealand's traditional styles are very mild, sweet lagers. The term "draft" indicates an amber brew in New Zealand, while "lager" refers to a paler, golden beer. The designation "dark," often appended to the word "ale," is indiscriminately used to describe fuller-colored variants. Beers are invariably served very cold in New Zealand and are usually highly carbonated, although thankfully the Australian tendency to also keep glassware in the fridge is relatively uncommon.

In the last decade, there has been a steady decline in the market for traditional Kiwi draft beers, with global golden lager brands, imported ales, and craft beers coming to the fore.

STEAM BREWING CO. FUGGLES BEST BITTER

Belfast-born Colin Paige, learned his craft at Scotland's Heriot-Watt University and at the Fuller's and Hopback breweries in southern England. The Mac's range has continued to evolve and improve. There have been several innovative limited releases, including Brewjolais —a fresh-tasting amber ale made with the first green hops of the 2006 harvest.

BLACK MAC 4.8% ABV • Dry stout • Dark brown to black; full-bodied and stout-like, with roasted malt, dark chocolate, and caramel notes.

SASSY RED 4.5% ABV • New World best bitter • Amber; hopsack nose; toffee, nut, chocolate, and toast flavors.

GREAT WHITE 5.0% ABV • Belgian-style witbier • Pale straw coloration; gently spiced, soft, creamy, and fruity.

MONTEITH'S

✉ Corner Turamaha and Herbert Streets, Greymouth
🖰 www.monteiths.co.nz

With roots dating back to 1868, this revered West Coast brewery is now one of four belonging to the DB group, which itself is overseen by Heineken. With coal-fired boilers and open fermenters, the Greymouth site is well worth a visit, although much of the beer is now made at DB's breweries in Auckland and Timaru.

DB beers (including Monteith's) often have an estery (banana, pineapple) character, which is produced during fermentation by the lager yeast strains working at comparatively warm, alelike temperatures.

PILSNER 5.0% ABV • Pilsner Golden; mild and firm-bodied, with distinctively grassy hop notes and a lingering, sweetish finish.

BLACK 5.2% ABV • Schwarzbier Dark brown to black; soft and malty; notes of nuts, chocolate, and coffee— and a hint of ripe banana.

THE MUSSEL INN

✉ Onekaka, Nr Takaka, Golden Bay
🖰 www.musselinn.co.nz

Opened in 1995, this quirky brewpub and café is located in one of the country's most remote and unspoiled regions. As well as beer, the Mussel Inn makes its own ciders, wines, and soft drinks.

The beer portfolio includes interesting brews such as Red Herring, a smoked ale, and Heat Rash, a chili lager. The famous Captain Cooker

THE MUSSEL INN
CAPTAIN COOKER
MANUKA BEER

Manuka Beer (seasoned with manuka leaves) commemorates Cook's first brew in New Zealand. Among locals it is fondly known as "The Pig," because it was Cook who brought the first pigs to the islands.

MONKEY PUZZLE 10.0% ABV • Belgian-style abbey ale Coppery; big, spicy, and warming, yet delicately balanced—highly suppable!

CAPTAIN COOKER MANUKA BEER 4.0% ABV • Wood-flavored lager Amber; perfumey nose; sweetish palate, with a pine-like spiciness that varies in intensity according to the season. This iconic Kiwi beer is now replicated by Belgium's Proef brewery (see p.128).

SHAKESPEARE BREWERY AND HOTEL

✉ 61 Albert Street (corner Wyndham and Albert Streets), Auckland
🖰 www.shakespearehotel.co.nz

Nowadays owned by former All Black Ron Urlich, the country's first new-generation brewpub started producing beer in 1986. Shoehorned behind the bar of this well-known Victorian city-center pub, the cramped brewhouse is overseen by brewer Barry Newman. Many of his limited-release creations have been so successful that they have become year-round beers. There are now nine regular beers in many styles.

SUMMER'S DAY BOHEMIAN LAGER 5.5% ABV • Bohemian pilsner • Fragrant; firm and malty sweetness, balanced by grassy, spicy hops.

KING LEAR OLD ALE 8.0% ABV • English-style old ale • Deep red; creamy head and full body; nose of orange, toffee, and chocolate; palate is similar, but more savory; long, floral, hop-driven finish.

PUCK'S PIXIL(L)ATION 11.1% ABV •
• Belgian-style grand cru ale
Coppery gold; spicy aroma;
a rich, heady brew, with
clovelike phenolics; sweet
malt and floral hops in the
palate, and a long finish.

STEAM BREWING COMPANY

✉ 186 James Fletcher Drive,
Otahuhu, Auckland
🖰 http://steam.brewing.co.nz

Established in 1995 in
Pakuranga, Auckland, the
Steam Brewing Company
began with a 317-gallon
(1,200-liter) brewery
behind the bar of what
later became the Cock &
Bull English-style pub.
Nine years later, with
five more Cock
& Bull pubs in the
chain, the company
acquired the old
Auckland Breweries
site, along with
its high-tech
packaging line.
  Along with its Cock
& Bull range of beers,
Steam Brewing has
recently launched the
Epic Brewing Co.
brand. The company
also brews beers under
contract, including the
Limburg Beer
Company range (previously
brewed in Hawkes Bay) and
Taa Kawa, an ale seasoned
with kawakawa leaves.

STEAM
BREWING
COMPANY EPIC
PALE ALE

MONK'S HABIT 7.0% ABV •
US-style strong red ale • Rich
copper; the floral and
resiny hop flavors are
balanced by a malty
sweetness.

FUGGLES BEST BITTER
4.8% ABV • English-style best bitter
Tawny; creamy head;
toffeeish and nutty malt
flavors gradually give way
to tangy (English) hops; has
a long, satisfying, dry finish.

EPIC PALE ALE 5.4% ABV •
American pale ale • Rich gold;
honeyed sweet malt flavors
with citrus and pine notes
supplied by American
Cascade hops.

EPIC MAYHEM 6.2% ABV •
US-style strong pale ale • Amber;
an explosion of American
hops (Simcoe, Amarillo,
Cascade, and Centennial)
grabs you and never lets go.

LIMBURG HOPSMACKER
5.0% ABV • New World-style pale
ale • Orangey-amber;
passionfruit (New Zealand
Saaz D hops) tempered by
sweet, biscuity malt.

LIMBURG CZECHMATE 5.0% ABV •
Bohemian-style pilsner • Golden;
palate has a spicy bitterness,
a soft maltiness, and great
complexity.

TUATARA BREWING COMPANY

✉ 183 Akatarawa Rd.,
Waikanae

Named after an
endangered native
reptile, the Tuatara
brewery is located
in hill country, an
hour north of
Wellington.
  With the backing
of The Malthouse
bar in Wellington,
brewer Carl Vasta
crafts beers in a
range of European
styles using a
selection of yeasts.
Tuatara's success
prompted the
installation of a new,
German-designed
brewhouse in 2007.

PILSENER 5.0% ABV • New
World-style (late-hopped) pilsner
Golden; generous late-
hopping (New Zealand Saaz
B hops) gives this aromatic
beer a fresh, jutelike, hopsack character.

HEFE 5.0% ABV •
Bavarian-style hefeweizen
Cloudy amber; the
palate is sweetish,
with notes of banana
and bubble gum.

INDIAN PALE 5.0% ABV
• English-style IPA
Earthy and citrussy
English hops dominate
the aroma and palate,
although there is also
a hint of nutty malt.

TWISTED HOP

✉ 6 Poplar Street (corner Poplar
and Ash Streets), Christchurch
🖰 http://thetwistedhop.co.nz

In 2003, disappointed by
mainstream Kiwi beers,
Martin Bennett and Stephen
Hardman, two ex-pat
Londoners, decided to set up
a brewery and bar and to
produce English-style cask-
conditioned ales.
  Set in a quiet backstreet
and with a pleasant curbside
drinking area, The Twisted
Hop is bright, airy, and
modern. As well as its own
ales, four of which are hand-
pulled, "The Hop" offers a
selection of tap beers from
other Kiwi craft breweries
and a range of imported and
locally brewed bottled beers.

GOLDING BITTER 3.7% ABV •
English-style bitter • Golden;
light and crisp, with a fresh
and leafy hop character.

CHALLENGER 5.0% ABV •
English-style best bitter
Coppery; full-bodied;
fragrant, fresh hop aroma;
toffeeish middle; long, earthy,
hop-driven finish.

THREE BOYS WHEAT 5.0% ABV •
Belgian-style witbier • Brewed
by the Three Boys Brewery
(in Christchurch's Heathcote
Valley) and available on tap
only at The Hop, this spritzy
wheat beer is flavored with
lemon zest instead of dried
orange peel.

TWISTED HOP GOLDING BITTER

AFRICA

Legend has it that the Ancient Egyptian god Osiris taught people to brew, and the Egyptians used beer in religious ceremonies and as a source of nutrients. Today, the African brewing industry is strong, with both local and international companies vying for market share.

A frica can lay claim to having produced some of the world's first brewers. Ancient Egyptian communities produced beer at least 3,000 years ago, using malted barley and an early form of wheat, called emmer. In most parts of the continent, however, the climate is too hot and dry for growing barley. The high plains of Kenya are one exception, and research into growing more malting barley in South Africa is underway.

The ancient Egyptian method of brewing was probably similar to methods still in use in some parts of Africa, such as Sudan. Wheat, barley, or millet was coarsely ground and one quarter of the grain soaked and left in the sun. The rest was formed into loaves of bread and lightly baked so as not to destroy important enzymes. The loaves were crumbled and mixed with the soaked grain. Then water and some beer were added and the mixture was left to ferment. Fermentation complete, the liquid was strained.

Except for the most fundamentalist Muslim nations, all African countries have their own breweries, many of which carry African names such as Tusker, Safari, Kilimanjaro, or Lion. The majority were set up by European brewers, often in partnership with state governments. Most of their beers are standard golden lagers, intended to be drunk very cold, and such products can be found from Morocco to Zimbabwe and South Africa. The continent has strong Dutch influences and Heineken has breweries in Burundi, Cameroon, Congo, Egypt, Ghana, Morocco, Namibia, Nigeria, Réunion, Rwanda, and Sierra Leone. German influences are found in many countries: for example, an urbock brewed with Munich barley is produced by Namibian Breweries.

Nonetheless, it is still possible to find beers like Chibuku (see p.279) from Botswana, Malawi, and Zimbabwe, which is made from sorghum and corn. These traditional brews, versions of which can be found in other continents, do not resemble modern beers at all.

Many African brewers produce stouts, and Guinness is made in several different strengths. South African Breweries produces Castle Milk Stout and the country's first microbrewery, Mitchell's, which opened in 1983, brews the luscious Raven Stout using a blend of British and German techniques. Such beers reflect a growing interest in microbrewing.

A chilled lager provides welcome relief from the parching heat prevalent in many African nations, and beers are brewed to be climate-tolerant.

EAST AFRICAN BREWERIES

✉ Port Bell, Kampala, Uganda
🖰 www.eabrew.com

Founded in 1922, East African Breweries is a large and highly successful company, which also owns Kenya Breweries and Uganda Breweries. One of its best-known beers is Tusker, which is sold under the patriotic slogan "My Beer—My Country." The Tusker bottle has the profile of an elephant head on the label and the brand is named in memory of one of the brewery's founders, George Hurst, who was killed by an elephant in 1923.

🍺 **TUSKER LAGER** 4.2% ABV •
Lager • A soft malty nose, crisp palate, and even a hint of malty biscuits before a light, hoppy finish.

🍺 **BELL LAGER** 4.8% ABV • Lager
Golden-red in color; brewed using German hops, it has

Crisp, refreshing lagers are the mainstay of African brewing, and make great thirst-quenchers.

a light taste. Named in honor of the brewery's site near Lake Bell.

🍺 **ALLSOPPS** 5.8% ABV • Lager
Orange in color, and brewed with extra-roasted equatorial barley.

🍺 **GUINNESS** 5.0% ABV • Stout
The basis for this local version of the classic Irish stout is an unfermented but hopped wort extract that is shipped from Dublin.

MAROC

✉ Boulevard Ahl Loghlam, B.P.
2660, Aïn Sebaâ, Casablanca

In the classic 1942 film *Casablanca*, starring Humphrey Bogart and Ingrid Bergman, the hottest spot in town was Rick Blaine's bar. If that celluloid gin-joint had served beer, it would surely have been made by Maroc. Although based in Marocco, Maroc has links with the Heineken brewing group.

🍺 **CASABLANCA LAGER** 5.0% ABV
• Lager • A pale-golden European-style beer, with a hoppy nose. Sweet to taste.

ANCIENT BREWS

Brewing was practiced in Egypt and Mesopotamia at least 5,000 years ago, and formed an important part of Ancient Egyptian culture. The hieroglyphic symbol for food depicted a pitcher of beer and a cake of bread, and the phrase "bread and beer" was sometimes used as a greeting. Beer was the staple drink of the poor, but was also consumed by wealthy families, and was placed in tombs as part of sacred funerary rites. Osiris, the Egyptian god of agriculture, was also the patron deity of brewing.

MITCHELL'S

✉ Arend Street, Knysna Industrial Area, Knysna, South Africa 6570
🖰 www.mitchellsknysnabrewery.com

Lex Mitchell established Mitchell's Brewery in 1983, in a small building in the tourist town of Knysna in South Africa's Western Cape region. In 1985, his small operation moved to the Knysna Industrial Area, creating the extra space necessary to add Bosun's Bitter to their Forester's Draught beer—previously their only product. Since then, the company have added various other beers to their repertoire, including a hoppy, pilsner-style brew and a light lager intended for everyday drinking.
Mitchell's ales are unpasteurized and produced using a mix of British mashing and German lagering techniques to create beers uniquely suited to South African conditions.

🍺 **RAVEN STOUT** 6.0% ABV •
Stout • Black, full-bodied, and full of chocolate and roasted coffee flavors, Raven has a distinctive citrus hop aroma.

OLD 90/- ALE (NINETY SHILLING)
5.0% ABV • Traditional ale
A heavy, spicy Scottish-style ale, which has a gloriously round, full palate and a complex aroma.

NAMIBIAN BREWERIES

✉ 9000 Wiundhoek, Namibia
🖥 www.nambrew.com

Commercial brewing in Namibia began when the first German immigrants arrived in the country at the end of the 19th century. Two such immigrants, Carl List and Hermann Ohlthaver, amalgamated several smaller breweries into the South West Breweries company in 1920.

When Namibia gained its independence in March 1990, the company changed its name to Namibia Breweries Limited, and in April 2003, the brewery announced a new joint venture with Heineken and Diageo, who took a 29.8 percent stake in the company, assuring its future.

TAFEL LAGER 4.0% ABV • Lager
Brewed to German purity law standards, light to drink and low hopped. It has a soft malt aroma.

URBOCK 7.0% ABV • Bock
Brewed with Munich barley malt, giving it a rich malty flavor. Produced once a year for sale in May.

NIGERIAN BREWERIES

✉ Iganmu House, Abebe Village Road, Iganmu, Lagos, Nigeria
🖥 www.nbplc.com

Established in 1946, this growing company has plans to become a regional rival to South African Breweries (*see right*); an agenda that was given fresh impetus when Heineken bought a stake in 2003. The first bottle of the company's flagship Star Lager rolled off the bottling lines in its Lagos brewery in June 1949. This was followed by the commissioning of the Aba brewery in 1957; the Kaduna brewery in 1963; and the Ibadan brewery in 1982. In September 1993, the expanding company acquired its fifth brewery in Enugu, while in October 2003, a sixth brewery, located in Ama in Enugu state, was commissioned.

STAR 4.8% ABV • Lager
Golden-yellow in the glass, with a hint of popcorn on the nose. Best served well-chilled on a hot day.

GULDER 5.0% ABV • Lager
A pale lager with a citrus hop nose, malt body, and sweetish taste.

SOUTH AFRICAN BREWERIES (SAB)

✉ 65 Park Lane, Sandown, Sandton, South Africa 2146
🖥 www.sabreweries.com

South African Breweries (SAB) was founded in 1895 by a Swedish entrepreneur called Jacob Letterstedt to provide beer for the thousands of miners and prospectors in and around Johannesburg. In 2002, the company merged with the Miller Brewing Company, forming one of the world's largest brewery groups, and the combined enterprise is now known as SABMiller.

SAB CASTLE LAGER

CASTLE LAGER 5.0% ABV • Lager • A thirst-quenching beer that should be drunk cold. Little hop aroma; some honey on the palate.

CASTLE MILK STOUT 6.0% ABV • Milk stout
Dark roasted malt provides this beer's distinctive dark coloration. As a true milk stout, lactose sugars are added to the mix during the brewing process.

HANSA PILSENER 4.5% ABV • Pilsner • First brewed in 1975, Hansa has a gentle aroma of Saaz hops. Light in color, it has a crisp, low-bitter taste.

SORGHUM BEERS

Traditional, milky-white homebrewed beers, fermented from sorghum and other grains, have a long tradition in many parts of Africa. They are considered as much a food as a drink, as they are a valuable source of carbohydrates, vitamins, and minerals. In Botswana, Malawi, and Zimbabwe, sorghum beer is produced commercially and sold under the brand name Chibuku. It is known locally as Shake Shake, because it separates and must be shaken inside the wax-paper containers it is sold in, to restore its grainy, bad-yogurt consistency.

Sorghum beers are made from a porridgelike mixture of sorghum, other grains such as corn, and water, to which yeast is added.

GLOSSARY

ABBEY ALE, ABBEY BEER
Belgian family of strong, fruity beers either produced or inspired by Trappist monastery brewers.

ABV Alcohol by volume, expressed as a percentage. A measure of the beer's strength.

ABW Alcohol by weight, expressed as a percentage. Outdated system, producing misleadingly low figures.

ALE A beer made with *ale yeasts*. Styles include golden ale, brown ale, *mild*, and *bitter*.

ALE YEASTS Yeasts used in traditional *top-fermenting* ales, originating from recycled yeast skimmed from the surface of the last batch. They ferment at room temperature.

ALT, ALTBIER German style of beer similar to British *bitter* or *pale ale*, especially associated with Düsseldorf.

BARLEY WINE An extra-strong style of *ale*, originally English, but now produced by many US brewers.

° BALLING A measure of fermentable sugars in *wort* and therefore of potential final alcohol content. Scale devised by Czech brewing scientist Carl Joseph Napoleon Balling. Later refined as ° Plato.

BITTER, BEST BITTER English beer style, usually designating a well-hopped *ale*. Best bitter usually refers to stronger variants.

BITTERING HOPS Hop varieties that are rich in chemical compounds that result in the bitter taste-sensation in beer. Other hop varieties are grown primarily for their aromatic qualities.

BLOND, BLONDE A mainly French and Belgian term for a golden beer.

BOCK A German term for a strong seasonal beer. Several variations.

BOTTLE-CONDITIONING The process by which beers are bottled with fermentable sugars and live *yeast* still in solution, extending storage life and allowing flavor to develop over time.

BOTTOM-FERMENTING
Term describing *yeasts* of the *Saccharomyces carlsbergensis* strain that are used to make *lager*. During lagering (storage) the yeast sinks to the bottom of the brew, producing a clean-tasting beer.

BRETTANOMYCES A semi-wild genus of *yeast* used in *lambic* beers and some *porters* and *stouts*. Provides a distinctive aroma and flavor.

BREWKETTLE The vessel in which the *wort* is boiled with hops to combine their flavors, usually for about 90 minutes.

BREWPUB A bar or restaurant with its own small brewery on the premises.

BURTON UNION A system of *fermentation* in galleries of linked casks, in which a stable *yeast* culture develops over time. Introduced in the 19th century in the brewing town of Burton upon Trent in England.

CARBONATION Refers to the amount of carbon dioxide dissolved in a liquid. Carbonation is the cause of effervescence in beer, and is generated by the metabolic action of *yeast* or by artificial introduction of pressurized gas.

CASK-CONDITIONING The practice of bringing draft beer to maturity in the cask in the cellar of a pub.

CONTRACT-BREWING
Commercial arrangement in which the creator of a beer contracts to have it produced at a brewery with spare capacity.

COPPER Alternative name for *brewkettle*. Many copper kettles survive, but today a greater number are made from stainless steel.

CRAFT BREWER Term referring to breweries opened since the late 1970s that produce specialist beers.

CURAÇAO A small, bitter orange grown in the former Dutch colony of Curaçao in the Carribean. A tasting note associated with some wheat beers.

DRAFT Beer on tap. The classic form is *cask-conditioned ale*, a predominantly British product. Draft beers tend to be fresher than beer in bottles or cans.

DRY-HOPPING The addition of hops to the finished brew to enhance its aroma and flavor.

ESTER A natural chemical compound that imparts fruity and spicy flavors (strawberry, banana, clove).

FERMENTATION The conversion of malt sugars to alcohol and CO_2 by *yeast*.

FESTBIER German term for any beer that is traditionally brewed for a festival. Sometimes it refers to *märzen* and *oktoberfest* styles, both strong variants of *Vienna lager*.

GOSE Distinctively salty style of wheat beer native to Leipzig.

GRIST Ground malt (or other grains) which, along with warm water, forms the basis of *wort*.

GUEUZE, GEUZE A blend of young and old *lambic* beers, blended to produce a sparkling, refreshing beer.

HEAD The foam that forms on top of a beer when it is poured.

HEAVY A traditional style of Scottish *ale* characterized by its relatively high alcoholic content and malt-accented flavor.

HEFEWEIZEN German term for wheat beer with *yeast* sediment.

HELL, HELLES German term designating a pale-colored beer.

HOGSHEAD A large vessel for storing wine or beer, and also a standard unit of volumetric measurement, equivalent (for beer) to 54 gallons (245 liters).

HOP BACK A sievelike vessel through which a brew is filtered. Its purpose is either to remove hop petals, or, when pre-filled with fresh hops, to add flavor to the brew.

IBU Acronym for International Bitterness Units, a standard scale of measurement for determining the bitterness of beers.

IMPERIAL STOUT Extra-strong *stout* made for export; named for its popularity with the Russian court.

IPA India pale ale; a robust, heavily-hopped beer originally made to withstand export by sea to India from Britain. Now also produced in the US.

KELLERBIER "Cellar beer" in German: usually an unfiltered *lager*, hoppy and only lightly carbonated.

KÖLSCH Light style of *top-fermenting* golden ale made in and around the city of Cologne (Köln).

LACE Pattern of foam left clinging to the sides of the glass.

LACTIC, LACTIC ACID An acid that imparts a sour flavor to beer, produced when *lactobacilli* metabolize sugars.

LACTOBACILLUS A family of bacteria, usually benign, that convert sugars to *lactic acid*. The resultant sourness defines certain styles, such as Berliner weissebier.

LAGER Family of *bottom-fermented* beer styles. Examples range from black beers (such as *schwarzbier*) to the more familiar golden *pilsner*.

LAMBIC Designates beers fermented by wild, airborne *yeasts* in small, rural breweries in the Payottenland region of Belgium.

LATE-HOPPING The technique of adding hops to the *brewkettle* in the final minutes of the boiling process, imparting pronounced hop flavors to the resulting beer.

MALT Barley or other grains that have undergone a process of controlled germination, which is arrested at a point when the seed contains high concentrations of starches. After drying, kilning, or roasting, the malt may be made into *grist* for brewing.

MALTINGS A facility in which grain is steeped in water, allowed partially to germinate, and dried.

MÄRZEN Originally German style of medium-strong beer brewed in March (März in German) and matured until September or October.

MASH The mixture created when the *grist* is steeped in hot water. The mashing process breaks down grain starches into fermentable sugars.

MICROBREWERY Generic term for small breweries founded from the 1970s onward. The US Brewers Association defines the term as a brewery that produces less than 15,000 barrels of beer per year.

MILD A lightly-hopped and thus mild-tasting style of *ale*, usually

of modest alcoholic strength. Traditionally associated with industrial regions of Wales.

MILK STOUT A sweet *stout* made with unfermentable lactose sugars (derived from milk) that sweeten its final taste.

NONIC GLASS A classic style of smooth-sided beer glass, typically made in half-pint and pint sizes. It is characterized by a bulge in its profile that aids grip.

OKTOBERFEST A two-week beer festival held in the Bavarian city of Munich in Germany.

ORIGINAL GRAVITY A measure of the density of *wort*. High density indicates abundant fermentable sugars. The more sugar is present, the stronger the resulting beer will be.

PALE ALE A style of beer that originated in Britain, characterized by the use of pale malts. Mostly applies to bottled beers.

PASTEURIZATION Heat treatment process applied to beer to maintain its stability during storage. Arguably, pasteurization deadens flavor slightly.

PILSNER, PILS A popular style of golden *lager* pioneered in the Czech town of Plzeň, or Pilsen.

PORTER A family of very dark beers characterized by dark-chocolate malt flavors and assertive hop bitterness.

PRIMING The addition of sugar to a beer before it is bottled to encourage *carbonation*.

RAUCHBIER A German style of *lager* made from malt that has been smoked over beechwood fires. A Franconian specialty.

REINHEITSGEBOT German beer purity laws enacted in the 16th century; now superseded by updated legislation, but still a guiding principle in German beermaking.

SAISON Originally a Belgian beer style; a dry, strongish *ale* for summer, often bottle-conditioned.

SCHWARZBIER "Black beer" in German. A dark, opaque style of *lager* beer.

SEASONAL BEERS Beers made for limited periods of

sale, usually to suit climatic conditions at a given point in the year, or to celebrate a holiday or commemorate a historical event.

SESSION BEER Term describing an easy-drinking beer that is relatively low in alcohol and thus suitable for drinking in quantity.

SOUR ALES, SOUR BEER Ales originating in Flanders that typically undergo ageing of 18 months to two years in oak *tuns*, during which they gain a sharply thirst-quenching acetic character.

STEIN A traditional German beer tankard, made either of glass or ceramic (*stein* translates as "stone.")

STOUT A dark style of beer, usually *top-fermenting*, that is made with highly roasted grain.

TAP, TAPROOM On-site bar serving a brewery's products direct to visiting drinkers.

TOP-FERMENTING Descriptive of *ale yeasts* of the *Saccharomyces cerevisiae* strain, which produce a thick foam at the top of the *fermentation* tank.

TUN A vessel in which *mash* is steeped.

URTYP "Original type" in German: term used to emphasize that a beer is an authentic example of an established style.

VIENNA LAGER Bronze-to-red lager with a sweetish malt aroma and flavor. Pioneered by Austrian brewer Anton Dreher.

WEISS, WEISSE "White" in German, denoting a wheat beer.

WEIZENBIER Wheat beer.

WIT, WITBIER "White"/"white beer" in Belgian: wheat beer.

WORT An infusion containing fermentable sugars that is produced by the *mashing* process. The wort is filtered, boiled, and cooled before *yeast* is added to initiate the process of *fermentation*.

YEAST A large family of unicellular fungal organisms, certain species of which are active agents in brewing and baking.

YORKSHIRE SQUARES Square fermenting vessels associated with traditional brewing in the English county of Yorkshire.

ACKNOWLEDGMENTS

Author's acknowledgments

In my earliest travels, I was often puzzled by the unfamiliar tastes of local beers. At the time, speciality beers simply didn't cross national borders. By tasting everything I could, asking questions, and publishing my conclusions, I became beer's first foreign correspondent. My views have been appearing for 30 years, from Finland to Japan, from Seattle, Washington, to Sydney, Australia.

Today's astonishing diversity of beers deserves a broader range of eyewitnesses. With the help of my research assistant Cathy Turner, I assembled a team to divide the world into regions. As the beer revolution spread, I found myself adding correspondents, but never as many as I would have liked. There will soon be no corner of the world without brewpubs, micros and speciality imports.

Stan Hieronymus and his wife Daria Labinsky travel the US tasting beers. They are quiet Americans, and write in a measured, understated style about the world's most exciting brewing nation. In my hands alone, this book's world view might have frightened the dray-horses. Tim Hampson's style is far from being institutional, despite long experience with a trade body, but his caution tempered my revolutionary fervour.

My earliest writings attracted endless challenges and questions from Derek Walsh, a Canadian who lives in The Netherlands and frequently pops over the border to Belgium. Given the opportunity he deserves, Walsh has mellowed. His writing takes us by the hand, and leads us with care and judgment. Alastair Gilmour loves British beer and pubs, and writes about both in gossipy style for the *Newcastle Evening Chronicle*, where I worked in my youth.

The best-known writer on beer in the German language is Conrad Seidl, a distinguished political journalist in his native Austria. Here, he reports in crisply informative English but insists on wearing his lederhosen. While most of the brewing countries are drinking more wine, grapey Italy is the new star of the beer world. Lorenzo Dabove writes about his homeland with a passion that even such a densely packed book could not restrain.

Bryan Harrell is an opinionated and diligent writer with whom I have enjoyed countless pints in Japan over two decades. I first met Geoff Griggs over pints of Fuller's, in our neighborhood local in West London. Now he is a tireless and fastidious reporter of the New Zealand scene. Willie Simpson was a New Zealander and is now an Australian. Whether his jersey is All-Black or Green-and-Gold, he still knows that real rugby is played 13-a-side. I trust his judgment on all matters.

Publisher's acknowledgments

Dorling Kindersley would like to thank the Editor-in-Chief and all of the contributors to the book for their tireless commitment and hard work. Also, thank you to the team at cobalt id for managing the book so efficiently. Cobalt id would like to thank Judy Barratt and Carolyn Walton for editorial assistance; Hilary Bird for the index; Charles Wills and Jenny Siklos for Americanization; and Ian O'Leary for commissioned photography. Thank you, too, to all of the breweries and brewing companies who kindly supplied photographs, information, and samples of their beers. We are very grateful to Derek Clarke at Beers of Europe for his help with obtaining some of the more obscure brews and for the passion that has driven him to have assembled such an extensive array of beers.

BEERS OF EUROPE—the UK's leading online beer stockist, with more than 1,000 different beers from over 50 countries. Visit them at www.beersofeurope.co.uk

Picture credits

The publisher would like to thank the following for their kind permission to reproduce their photographs:

(Key: a-above; b-below/bottom; c-centre; f-far; l-left; r-right; t-top; rh-running header)

1 jupiterimages: Foodpix / John Campos (t). 4 Corbis: Envision (c). 5 Cephas Picture Library: Ian Shaw (t). 6–7 Sapporo Brewery: (c). 8–9 Sierra Nevada Brewing Co.: (tc). 9 Hakusekikan Brewery: (bc). 10 Black Sheep Brewery: (c). 10–20 iStockphoto.com: Mario Hornik (rh). 12 Alaskan Brewery Co: (c). iStockphoto.com: Mark Kuipers (tl). 13 Corbis: Thomas A. Kelly (br). 15 Alamy Images: vario images GmbH & Co.KG (br). 16 Schneider Weisse: (tc). 16–17 Alamy Images: nagelestock.com (bl). 17 Alamy Images: isifa Image Service s.r.o. (tr). 18 Alamy Images: Mary Evans Picture Library (cb). Corbis: Owen Franken (tc). 19 Shepherd Neame Brewery: (br). 20 Alamy Images: Mark Sunderland (tl). 21 Corbis: Roulier/Turiot/photocuisine (bc). 22–23 Fremantle Brewery: (bc). Marek Walisiewicz: (tc). 24 iStockphoto.com: Alexander Hafemann (ca); Tobias Ott (rh). 24–35 iStockphoto.com: Ulrike Hammerich (rh). 26 Alamy Images: Cephas Picture Library (tc). 27 Alamy Images: Jack Sullivan (tr); Kathy Wright (br). 28 Alamy Images: Holt Studios International Ltd (tc). Duncan Baird Publishers: (b). 29 Murphy Brewery Ireland: (ftl). Ridleys: (tl2). Anthony Blake Photo Library: Mark Turner (br). 30 Corbis: Skyscan (b). 31 Alamy Images: Robert Estall photo agency (tr). iStockphoto.com: (bl). 32 Victory Brewing Co.: (tr). 33 Timothy Taylor & Co.Ltd: (bc). 35 Boulevard Brewing Co.: (tl). Fuller, Smith & Turner P.L.C.: (c). 36–37 Alamy Images: Caro (c). 38 Stoudts Brewery: (tc). 39 Alamy Images: CW Images (c). 40 Corbis: Archivo Iconografico, S.A. (tr). 41 Corbis: Ludovic Maisant (b). Brouwerij Boon (tc). 43 Alamy Images: f1 online (bl); Maximilian Weinzierl (tr). 44 Alamy Images: WoodyStock (b). 45 Alamy Images: Cephas Picture Library (br). 47 Alamy Images: Cephas Picture Library (tc). Derek Walsh: (br). 48 Alamy Images: Tricia de Courcy Ling (bl) Samuel Smith Brewery: (c). 49 Alamy Images: Michael Juno (br); Mary Evans Picture Library (tc). 50 Fuller, Smith & Turner P.L.C.: (b). 51 Hall & Woodhouse: (tr). Marek Walisiewicz: (bc). 52 Marek Walisiewicz: (tc). 53 Alamy Images: Werner Dieterich. 54 Alamy Images: SPP Images (b). Burgerbrau Brewery: (tc). 55 Alamy Images: Robert Harding Picture Library Ltd (tr). Radeberger Gruppe KG: (bc). 56 Alamy Images: Pat Behnke (tl). Köstritzer Schwarzbierbrauerei GmbH & Co: (bc). 58–59 Photolibrary: Johner Bildbyra. 60 Inveralmond Brewery: (ca). 60–69 iStockphoto.com: Eva Serrabassa (rh). 61 Corbis: Frank Leonhardt (c). 63 Alamy Images: Iain Masterton (tl). 64 Piccolo Birrificio: (ca). 65 Great Lakes Brewing Co: (tc). Schloss Eggenberg: (tr). 66 Redoak: (b). 67 Corbis: Owen Franken (tl). 69 Garrett Oliver: (tr). 70–71 Alamy Images: nagelestock.com. 72 Jennings Brewery: (c). 72–279 iStockphoto.com: Alexander Hafemann (rh). 73 Getty Images: Carlos Casariego (c). 74 Alamy Images: Frank Chmura (c). 75 iStockphoto.com: perets (t). 76 Budejovický Budvar, n.p. (Budweiser Budvar n.c.): (tr) (bl). 77 Marek Walisiewicz: (bl). 78 Plzensky Prazdroj, a.s. / SAB Miller plc: (tl). Marek Walisiewicz: (br). 79 Alamy Images: Chris Fredriksson (br). Marek Walisiewicz: (t). 80 Alamy Images: Jon Arnold Images (c). 81 iStockphoto.com: perets (t). 82 Alamy Images: David Crossland (b). 83 Radeberger Gruppe KG: (cl). 84 Bürgerbräu Bad Reichenhall: (tr) Brauerei Aying: (bl). 85 Alamy Images: Yadid Levy (b).

86 Fürst Wallerstein: (br). Marek Walisiewicz: (tl). 87 Staatliches Hofbräuhaus in München: (tl). Marek Walisiewicz: (br). 90 Marek Walisiewicz: (tr). 91 Schlossbrauerei Herrngiersdorf: (tl). Marek Walisiewicz: (br). 92 Alamy Images: Christoph Weiser (t). Spaten-Franziskaner-Bräu GmbH: (bc). 93 Marek Walisiewicz: (tl) (br). 94 Alamy Images: ImageState (b). 95 Bergbrauerei Ulrich Zimmermann: (tl). Radeberger Gruppe KG: (br). 96 Bitburger: (t) (br). 97 Marek Walisiewicz: (cl). 98 Hoepfner: (bl) (tl). Privatbrauerei Hoepfner GmbH: (bc). 99 Alamy Images: David Crossland (b). 100 Alamy Images: FAN travelstock (tr). Marek Walisiewicz: (bl). 101 Radeberger Gruppe KG: (br). Marek Walisiewicz: (cl). 102 Obergärige Hausbrauerei GmbH: (br). 103 Veltins: (b). 104 Alamy Images: imagebroker (tr). Marek Walisiewicz: (bl). 105 Radeberger Gruppe KG: (b). 106 Privatbrauerei Iserlohn: (tc). Veltins: (b). 107 Alamy Images: Maximilian Weinzierl (b). 109 Radeberger Gruppe KG: (tl). Feldschlößchen Dresden: (tr). 110 Alamy Images: Michael Klinec (b). Radeberger Gruppe KG: (tc). 111 Hallesches Brauhaus: (t). 112 Radeberger Gruppe KG: (cr). 113 Papiermuhle: (bl). 114 Wernesgruner: (b). 115 Alamy Images: Bildarchiv Monheim GmbH (br). 116 Drei Kronen Memmelsdorf: (cr); Modern Media Production (br). 117 Marek Walisiewicz: (cr) (bl). 119 Marek Walisiewicz: (tl) (br). 120 Alamy Images: Yadid Levy (c). 122 Alamy Images: Brian Harris (b). 123 Derek Walsh: (tl) (br). 124 Brouwerij Bosteels: (tl). Alamy Images: Andrew Cowin (b). 125 Marek Walisiewicz: (tr) (bl). 126 Brouwerij Duvel Moortgat NV: (tl). Brouwerij Liefmans: (br). 127 Anthony Blake Photo Library: Graham Kirk (b). 128 Marek Walisiewicz: (tl). Derek Walsh: (br). 129 Marek Walisiewicz: (br). Derek Walsh: (tc). 130 Marek Walisiewicz: (tl) (br). 131 Derek Walsh: (tr) (b). 134 Alamy Images: Peter Horree (b). 135 Marek Walisiewicz: (br). 136 Domus Pub and Brewery: (c). Derek Walsh: (br). 137 Corbis: Jean-Pierre Lescourret (br). 138 Brouwerij De Keersmaeker: (c). 139 Alamy Images: Stephen Roberts Photography (b). 140 Marek Walisiewicz: (tl). Derek Walsh: (br). 141 Marek Walisiewicz: (br) (tc) (tr). 142 Marek Walisiewicz: (cl). Brasserie Dubuisson: (br). 143 Marek Walisiewicz: (cl) (br). 144 Alamy Images: Cephas Picture Library (tr). Trappistes de Rochefort: (bl). 145 Derek Walsh: (tc). La Brasserie à Vapeur: (br). 146 John Warburton-Lee: Julian Love (c). 147 iStockphoto.com: perets (t). 148 Alamy Images: Eric Nathan (b). 149 Hall & Woodhouse Ltd: (br). Marek Walisiewicz: (tl). 150 Marek Walisiewicz: (br). George Bateman & Son Ltd.: (bl). 151 Alamy Images: Images Etc Ltd (tr). Brakspear Beers: (bl). 152 Camerons: (tl). The Durham Brewery: (br). 153 Alamy Images: Paul Felix Photography (b). Crouch Vale: (tc). 154 . Fuller, Smith & Turner P.L.C.: (b). Marek Walisiewicz: (cl). 155 Hambleton Ales: (br). Marek Walisiewicz: (tl). 156 Highgate Brewery: (bl). Wadworth: (tr). 157 Hook Norton Brewery: (tl). Marek Walisiewicz: (br). 160 Kelham Island Brewery: (tl). McMullen: (tr). 161 Alamy Images: Leslie Garland Picture Library (b). 162 Marek Walisiewicz: (tr). 163 Ringwood Brewery: Ringwood. 164 Shepherd Neame Ltd.: (tr). Marek Walisiewicz: (cl). 165 Alamy Images: Panacea Pictures (t). Marek Walisiewicz: (br). 166 Timothy Taylor & Co.Ltd: (tl). Marek Walisiewicz: (br). 167 Wells and Young: (tl). Woodfordes: (b). 168 Alamy Images: AA World Travel Library (b). 169 Cairngorm Brewery Company: (bc). Marek Walisiewicz: (tl). 170 Inveralmond Brewery: (tl). Williams Bros Brewing Co.: (br). 171 Alamy Images: Lee Pengelly (tr). SA Brain & Co Ltd: (bl). 172 Alamy Images: James Osmond (b). 173 Marek Walisiewicz: (tl). Murphy Brewery Ireland: (br). 174 Alamy Images: Frank Chmura (c). 175 iStockphoto.com: perets (t). 176 Alamy Images: Barry Lewis (b). 177 Derek Walsh: (tr); (bl). 178 Alamy Images: Petr Svarc (br). Derek Walsh: (tr). 179 Derek Walsh (tl); (fbr). 180 Photolibrary: Jtb Photo Communications Inc (b). 181 Marek Walisiewicz: (tl). 182 Alamy Images: David Kilpatrick (br). 183 A. Le Coq: (br). Alamy Images: JadroFoto (t). 184 Alamy Images: Chris Fredriksson (b). Okocim: (bl). 185 Alamy Images: JadroFoto (br). Marek Walisiewicz: (tl). 186 Alamy Images: imagebroker (b). 187 Brauunion: (bl) (tr). 188 Brauunion: (tr). Schloss Eggenberg: (fbl). 189 Alamy Images: Marina Spironetti (t). Brauunion: (br). 190 Alamy Images: BL Images Ltd (b). 191 Marek Walisiewicz: (tr). 192 Photolibrary: Yvan Travert (b). 193 Brøckhouse: (tl). Finlandia Sahti: (br). 194 Hansa: (tc).

Marek Walisiewicz: (bl). 196 Alamy Images: mediacolor's (b). 197 Brasserie Castelain à Bénifontaine: (tl). Brasserie La Choulette: (br). 198 Marek Walisiewicz: (br). 199 Alamy Images: Cephas Picture Library (bl). Marek Walisiewicz: (tr). 200 Corbis: Franz-Marc Frei (cr). 201 Alamy Images: CuboImages srl (b). 202 Beba: (br). Lorenzo Dabove: (tl). 203 Lorenzo Dabove: (tl) (br). 204 Lambrate: (tl). Lorenzo Dabove: (tr). 205 Le Baladin: (tl). Birrificio Montegioco: (br). 206 Piccolo Birrificio: (cl). Turbacci: (tr). 207 Alamy Images: Kevin Foy (tr). Simonds Farsons Cisk plc: (bc). 208 Brooklyn Brewery: (c). 209 iStockphoto.com: (tc). 210 Brewery Ommegang: (b). 211 Allagash Brewing Company: (tl). Brooklyn Brewery: (br). 212 Clipper City Brewing Company: (bl). Flying Fish Brewing Company: (tl). 213 Corbis: JP Laffont / Sygma (tr). Harpoon Brewery: (bl). 214 d.b.a: (ca). Stoudts Brewing Co.: (cl). 215 Magic Hat Brewing Company: (tl). Brewery Ommegang: (b). 218 Pennsylvania Brewing Company: (tl). 219 Matt Brewing: (b). Smuttynose Brewing Company: (tl). 220 Stoudts Brewing Company: (bl). Victory Brewing Co.: (tr). 221 Abita Brewing Company: (b). 222 Abita Brewing Company: (cl). Atlanta Brewing Company: (b). 223 Carolina Beer & Beverage: (tl). Real Ale Brewing Company: (br). 224 Shiner: (bl). Sweetwater Brewing: (cr). 225 Boulevard Brewing Co.: (tl). 226 Marek Walisiewicz: (tl). Boulevard Brewing Co.: (br). 227 Marek Walisiewicz: (cr). 228 Great Lakes Brewing Co: (bl). Leinenkugel's: (cr). 229 Advertising Archives: Image courtesy of The Advertising Archives (br). Stan Hieronymus: (tc). 230 New Glarus Brewing Co.: (bc). 231 Schlafly Beer: (b). Summit Brewing Company: (tl). 232 New Belgium Brewing Company: (b). 233 Avery Brewing: (bl). Big Sky Brewing Co.: (tc). 234 Alamy Images: David L. Moore (tl). Great Divide Brewing Co.: (br). 235 Corbis: Dave Bartruff (b). Oskar Blues Grill & Brewery: (tc). 236 Jason E. Kaplan: (br). Left Hand Brewing: (tc). 237 Alamy Images: Richard Wareham Fotografie (tl). Utah Brewers: (br). 238 Alamy Images: David L. Moore (b). 239 Alaskan Brewery Co: (bl). Deschutes brewery: (tr). 240 Fish Brewing: (tl). Full Sail Brewing: (bc). 241 Hale's Ale Brewery & Pub: (tl). David Parker: (br). 242 Rogue: (bl). Widmer: (tr). 243 StudioSchulz.com: (b). 244 Anchor Brewing: (tc). 245 Firestone Walker Fine Ales: (bl). 246 Kona Brewing: (cl). Mendocino Brewery: (tr). 247 North Coast Brewing: (bl). StudioSchulz.com: (tr). 248 Cambridge Brewing Company: (b). La Roja: (tr). 249 Sierra Nevada Brewing Co.: (br). StudioSchulz.com: (c). 250 Alamy Images: David R. Frazier Photolibrary, Inc. (c). 251 iStockphoto.com: perets (t). 252 Steamwork brewery: (b). 253 Amsterdam Brewing Co.: (bl). Big Rock: (tl). 254 Fat Cat Brewery: (bl). Granite Brewery: (br). 255 McAuslan (tl). Russell Brewing Company: (br). 256 Steamworks: (tc). Unibroue: (cr). 257 Alamy Images: geogphotos (tr). Marek Walisiewicz: (br). 258 Alamy Images: Cro Magnon (b). 259 Cervecería Cuauhtémoc Moctezuma, S.A. de C.V.: (br). 260 Alamy Images: Neil Setchfield (c). 261 iStockphoto.com: perets (t). 262 Alamy Images: Iain Masterton (b). 263 Baird brewing: (tl). Hakusekikan: (br). 264 Kinshachi: (cl). Minoh AJI Beer Brewery: (tr). 265 Corbis: Ken Straiton (b). 266 Alamy Images: John Eccles. 267 Marek Walisiewicz: (tl). Ceylon / Lion Brewery Ltd.: (tr). 268 Alamy Images: TinCup (b). 269 Coopers Brewery: (tc). Holgate Brewhouse: (br). 270 Malt Shovel: (tr). 271 Tooheys (Lion Nathan Co.): (tc). Redoak: (br). 272 Alamy Images: David Wall (b). 273 Emersons Brewing Co.: (tc). Galbraith's Alehouse: (cr). 274 Steam Brewery Company: (tl). The Mussel Inn: (cl). 275 Steam Brewery Company: (cl). The Twisted Hop Brewery: (br). 276 Photolibrary: Johan Wingborg (c). 277 iStockphoto.com: perets (t). 278 Alamy Images: Jack Sullivan (b). 279 Corbis: Roger De La Harpe. Marek Walisiewicz: (cr). 280–288 iStockphoto.com: Mario Hornik (rh).

Every effort has been made to trace the copyright holders. The publisher apologizes for any unintentional omission and would be pleased, in such cases, to place an acknowledgment in future editions of this book.

All other images © Dorling Kindersley
For further information see: www.dkimages.com